Y0-BCR-761

WOODROW WILSON: *The Early Years*

WOODROW WILSON

The Early Years

by GEORGE C. OSBORN

LOUISIANA STATE UNIVERSITY PRESS • BATON ROUGE

LIBRARY OF CONGRESS CARD CATALOG NUMBER: 68–13451
MANUFACTURED IN THE UNITED STATES OF AMERICA BY
THOS. J. MORAN'S SONS, INC., BATON ROUGE, LA.
DESIGNED BY JULES B. MCKEE

For

four women

who have meant much

in my life

BETTIE HENDRICK OSBORN, *my mother*
EVA RIGGIN OSBORN, *my stepmother*
MARGARET OSBORN MAHONY, *my sister*
MARGARET MCMILLEN OSBORN, *my wife*

Preface

With the centennial of Woodrow Wilson's birth in 1956, there came a national renewal of interest in Wilson. In making a careful study of the manuscript collections of the Wilson era and of the books written about the World War I President, I discovered that there was much new material which was not accessible to biographers two decades or more ago. Ray Stannard Baker, Wilson's official biographer, dealt with him in sufficient detail, but was completely eulogistic in his approach. Professor Arthur S. Link, editor of *The Papers of Woodrow Wilson* and the current scholarly biographer, has given us the excellent *Wilson: The Road to the White House*. But the space devoted to his subject's life until 1902—that is, up to the time that Wilson became president of Princeton University—is necessarily limited. It is this early period, the years of training and teaching, with which this volume deals.

None of his biographers, save perhaps Baker, and he over a third of a century ago, has made any attempt to treat adequately Wilson as an author. Yet some knowledge of Wilson's early statements of principle is necessary if the reader is to understand properly later Wilsonian idealism and political policy. I have therefore included brief discussions of a number of Wilson's writings during the years in which he was a student and a teacher. Until now, many readers have been unable to familiarize themselves with these writings because of inaccessibility of the sources. Only in the rare book room of the Library of Congress can one find a copy of *The State, An Old Master and Other Political Essays,* and *Mere Literature*—all of which are rich in Wilsonian idealism and philosophy.

This is not a psychoanalytical study of Wilson. Anyone interested in the psychological makeup of the twenty-eighth President of the United States can read the recently published volume which William Bullitt persuaded Sigmund Freud to write with him. Yet the Bullitt-Freud book is neither good history nor good biography. Written out of bitterness and spite, it is not even good psychoanalysis.

My study is an attempt to submit the facts and to permit the reader to draw his own conclusions. I have deliberately tried to avoid injecting into the narrative any interpretations to support a preconceived theory. It is my hope that the personality of Wilson will emerge from the presentation of the facts.

For aid in the preparation of this book, I am indebted to many persons. In the manuscript division of the Library of Congress, Mr. David C. Mearns and his associates, Dr. C. Percy Powell, Mr. Robert H. Land, Miss Katherine E. Brand, and Dr. Joseph Vance showed me every courtesy. At the University of Virginia, Charlottesville, Alderman Library, which contains the Heath Dabney Papers, both Mr. Francis L. Berkeley, custodian, and Mr. William H. Runge, curator of the rare book room, were most hospitable. I am indebted to the late Mr. Sidney Painter of the History Department at the Johns Hopkins University, formerly in charge of the History and Political Seminary Records, for courtesies shown me there. Mr. Robert H. Haynes and others in the Widener Library and in the Houghton Library at Harvard University extended every favor when I worked in the Albert Bushnell Hart Papers and in the Frederick Jackson Turner Correspondence. I wish to express my appreciation for the courtesies shown me by Mr. Alexander P. Clark and his assistant, Mrs. J. D. Dinardo, in the Manuscript Room of the Princeton University Library. Nor would I omit favors shown me by the attendants in charge of manuscript collections in the Boston Public Library and in the Wisconsin State Historical Society Library at Madison.

To Professor Wendell Holmes Stephenson of the University of Oregon History Department, who read the manuscript, I owe a debt of gratitude for his timely suggestions. To Mr. Charles East and Mrs. Marilyn Smallwood Paul, I am obligated for editing the final draft of my manuscript. To my wife, Margaret McMillen Osborn, I am indebted most of all. Not only has she read the entire manuscript critically, but we have discussed together many phases of the book. Her counsel, encouragement, and inspiration are the very best that any writer could have.

Even with the help that these people have generously given to me, this book could not have been written without the research grants that I have received from the American Philosophical Society and from the University of Florida. Funds from these two sources combined have made possible the research and writing of *Woodrow Wilson: The Early Years.*

Gainesville, Florida
May 15, 1967

GEORGE C. OSBORN

Contents

Preface vii

CHAPTER I *Family and Youth 3*

CHAPTER II *Early Education 20*

CHAPTER III *Student of Law 47*

CHAPTER IV *First Romance 70*

CHAPTER V *Failure at Law 84*

CHAPTER VI *Graduate Student 102*

CHAPTER VII *Second Romance: Marriage 127*

CHAPTER VIII *At Bryn Mawr 145*

CHAPTER IX *At Wesleyan 177*

CHAPTER X *Return to Princeton 202*

CHAPTER XI *Teacher and Lecturer 223*

CHAPTER XII *The Educator 242*

CHAPTER XIII *The Historian 260*

CHAPTER XIV *The Author 281*

CHAPTER XV *At Home and Abroad 300*

Bibliography 329

Index 339

List of Illustrations

FOLLOWING PAGE 146

Wilson as a senior at Princeton

Joseph Ruggles Wilson and Janet Woodrow Wilson

Wilson with members of the Jefferson Society

Ellen Axson Wilson

Harriet Woodrow

Wilson with the Johns Hopkins Glee Club

Wilson with members of the Wesleyan faculty

Page from Wilson's class lecture notes

WOODROW WILSON: *The Early Years*

CHAPTER I *Family and Youth*

Woodrow Wilson often spoke of his Scotch-Irish background. He recognized the fact that he was not only the physical descendant of the stern Scotch Covenanters but in the truest sense their spiritual heir. His grandfather, James Wilson, had migrated to the United States from northern Ireland in 1807. James Wilson settled in Philadelphia and there married Anne Adams, a girl with a Scotch-Irish background like his own. He became a printer and helped William Duane publish the strongly Jeffersonian *Aurora.* By 1815 he was living in Steubenville, Ohio, where he became editor of the *Western Herald and Gazette.*[1]

Elected to the Ohio legislature in 1816, James Wilson immediately became a states' rightist in the long fight against the second United States Bank. On the political stump, in the legislative

[1]Francis P. Weisenburger, "The Middle Western Antecedents of Woodrow Wilson," *Mississippi Valley Historical Review,* XXIII (June, 1936–March, 1937), 375–90.

halls, and through the columns of his paper he urged internal improvements, opposed slavery, favored the right of petition, and sought reforms in the penitentiary system. As an Adams–Clay man, Wilson opposed the rising Jacksonian democracy and denounced the anti-Masonic movement. Not only did he fight for the National Republican cause in Ohio, but in 1832, in Pittsburgh, he founded the *Pennsylvania Advocate* which subsequently championed Whiggism.[2] When the Harrison ticket—"Tippecanoe and Tyler too"—was elected in 1840, he was delighted.

James and Anne Wilson had ten children, of whom Joseph Ruggles Wilson, born February 28, 1822, was the seventh and last son. In a young frontier community, in an atmosphere of restless energy, Joseph grew into manhood. After his graduation from Jefferson College at Cannonville, Pennsylvania, in 1844, he taught school at Mercer for several years before he entered the ministry.[3] Having decided to become a preacher, he returned to his formal education and studied at Western Theological Seminary at Allegheny, and subsequently at Princeton College, which awarded him a B.D. degree in 1846. Although licensed to preach the following year, Joseph Wilson failed to locate a church and returned to teaching, this time in the Steubenville Male Academy. While an instructor there he met Janet ("Jessie") Woodrow, a student of the Steubenville Seminary. Barely twenty-one years of age, Jessie had lovely gray eyes, a broad mouth, a somewhat large nose, and light brown hair, which she wore in curls that hung almost to her shoulders. She soon fell in love with the promising young teacher-minister five years her senior, and they were married June 7, 1847, at Chillicothe, Ohio, by the bride's father, the Reverend Dr. Thomas Woodrow.[4]

Thomas Woodrow, the grandfather after whom Woodrow Wilson was named, was born March 15, 1793, the third son in a family of seven children. He spent his youth in Parsley, Scotland, was educated at the Theological Academy of the University of Glas-

[2] *Ibid.*

[3] *Ibid.*, 387.

[4] Ray Stannard Baker, *Woodrow Wilson, Life and Letters* (New York, 1927–39), I, 13–14.

gow, and, after a stint as a missionary in the nearby Orkney Islands, in 1820 accepted a call to the Annetwell Street Congregational Church in Carlisle, England. During the fifteen years that Thomas Woodrow served as minister in Carlisle, his wife Marion Williamson bore him eight children. The fifth child, Janet, born December 20, 1826, was destined to become Woodrow Wilson's mother.[5]

The minister resigned his pastorate in June, 1835, after having doubled the church's membership. The following November the Woodrow family sailed from Liverpool in a packet ship. They arrived in New York sixty-two days later. The voyage was a perilous one, especially the dreadful night when, as Thomas Woodrow later recalled, "a mighty sea broke over us, carried off our hatch, and poured down upon us in torrents." [6] During most of the trip Marion Woodrow was sick in bed, but she seemed to recuperate in clearer weather. She never really recovered from the illness of the long voyage across the North Atlantic, and died shortly after the family arrived in New York, while her husband was at Poughkeepsie conducting a series of religious meetings. "Little did I anticipate," wrote the sorrowful minister, "that my removal to this country would be effected at so great a sacrifice." [7]

Isabella Williamson mothered the children of her deceased sister when the family moved to Brockville, Canada. The Reverend Dr. Woodrow was unsuccessful in his efforts to "raise a congregation" in that community, and two years later he became stated supply of the First Presbyterian Church of Chillicothe, Ohio. Since he was from a foreign communion, he was received on probation. In September, 1838, however, Thomas Woodrow was made an active member and formally inducted as the regular pastor.[8]

During these years of heated discussions on doctrinal standards

[5]*Ibid.,* 17–18.

[6]Thomas Woodrow to Robert Williamson, February 23, 1836, in Ray Stannard Baker Papers, Library of Congress.

[7]*Ibid.*

[8]Robert C. Galbraith, Jr., *History of the Chillicothe Presbytery* (Chillicothe, 1889), 137, 142.

and slavery, Dr. Woodrow remained a staunch conservative. The Presbyterians of southern Ohio split into two presbyteries on the slavery issue, but Dr. Woodrow and his congregation remained with the conservatives in the original Chillicothe Presbytery. Even in this group, resolutions were adopted in 1839 condemning the institution of slavery as a "heinous sin against God and man" and denouncing slaveholding as "blasphemy of Almighty God, and a shocking prostitution of his word." Dr. Woodrow and eight others formed a minority against the resolution.[9]

Wilson biographer Ray Stannard Baker wrote that "Dr. Woodrow made so notable a success as a pulpit orator, and his reputation for learning was so great, that he was called to the pastorate of the Hogg Presbyterian Church of Columbus, Ohio, where he remained until his death." [10] Actually, when Dr. Woodrow resigned at Chillicothe, April, 1848, he gave ill health as the reason. Moreover, there was no "Hogg Church" in Columbus. The First Presbyterian Church of Columbus, was, out of respect for its pastor emeritus James Hoge, sometimes referred to as "Dr. Hoge's Church." Indeed, Thomas Woodrow's next pastorate was north of Columbus at Worthington, where he served a small church of only forty-seven members from 1849 until 1857. Wilson's grandfather was never regular pastor of the First Presbyterian Church at Columbus, although he may have filled the pulpit a few times. After leaving Chillicothe he served small churches, none of which had as many as a hundred members.[11]

Baker also spoke of the "strong family feeling" that bound the Woodrows together.[12] One looks in vain in Baker's *Life and Letters of Woodrow Wilson* for any mention of Dr. Woodrow's marrying again soon after his first wife's death, and of his loss of interest in the children of his first wife, including Wilson's mother, as they grew into adulthood and as his children by his second wife continued to arrive. The old minister's will, made less than a year before his death on April 25, 1877, mentioned

[9]Lewis G. Vander Velde, *Presbyterian Churches and the Federal Union,* Harvard Historical Studies (Cambridge, 1932), 13–15.

[10]Baker, *Wilson Life and Letters,* I, 18–19.

[11]See Weisenburger, "Middle Western Antecedents," 388–89.

[12]Baker, *Wilson Life and Letters,* I, 19.

six children by his second wife, Harriet Renick, but none of the eight children by his first wife.[13]

Within a fortnight after the marriage of Joseph Ruggles Wilson and Jessie Woodrow, the young teacher was ordained by the Chillicothe Presbytery. He became pastor of the Hill Presbyterian Church, one of the oldest churches of the Calvinistic faith west of the Allegheny Mountains. Located one mile east of Chartiers, Pennsylvania, this small congregation was "pastored" for several years by the young preacher, who in 1851 also taught rhetoric in nearby Jefferson College. It was in Chartiers that Joseph and Jessie Wilson's first child, Marion, was born. In 1853 the Wilsons crossed the Mason-Dixon Line into Virginia, where Wilson taught chemistry and natural sciences at Hampden–Sidney College. Soon after he joined its faculty, a second daughter, Anne, was born.

In June, 1855, Dr. Wilson became pastor of the First Presbyterian Church at Staunton, Virginia, seat of the large and wealthy county of Augusta. The town was situated in a highly productive and picturesque region, and in the 1850's was a thriving business community.

The substantial white brick manse into which the Wilsons moved in 1856 was situated on a hill opposite the First Presbyterian Church. When the weather permitted, Dr. Wilson sat at a small table on a little porch at the back of the house to work on his sermons. From there the minister could look across a valley to his church on an opposite hill. Built of brick in typically southern colonial architecture, the church was adequate for its membership of almost two hundred. When the church built a new sanctuary after the War Between the States, the building in which Dr. Wilson preached was used as the main building of the Mary Baldwin Academy.[14]

Near midnight on December 28, 1856, in the large lower room on the left of the Manse, the third child and first son of Joseph and Jessie Wilson was born. He was named Thomas Woodrow for his maternal grandfather. The neighbors came to see the firstborn

[13]Will recorded in Probate Court, Franklin County, Ohio, Book G, 1875-77, p. 220.

[14]Baker, *Wilson Life and Letters,* I, 24.

son of the new Presbyterian minister and pronounced him "a beautiful boy." The baby's mother testified that "he is a fine healthy fellow . . . just as fat . . . and just as good as he can be . . . as little trouble as it is possible for a baby to be." [15]

In the summer of 1857, Joseph Wilson went to Augusta, Georgia, to perform the marriage ceremony for his brother-in-law James Woodrow and Miss Felies Baker. While there, he preached to the congregation of the First Presbyterian Church. Then without a pastor and delighted with Dr. Wilson's sermon, members of the church extended him a call to become their minister.[16] As he and his wife pondered the call to a new charge, the newly-married couple visited them. The "new aunt" remembered being introduced to "a lovely, fair baby, about seven months old, in a white dress and blue ribbons" and being told "this is Tommy." [17] By autumn the decision was reached, and the trek to Augusta was made. Although born in Virginia, Thomas Woodrow Wilson "became" a Georgian before his first birthday.

The town to which young Wilson, his two older sisters, and their parents came to live had been founded by early Georgia settlers at the head of navigation on the Savannah River. Augusta was a thriving community of approximately sixteen thousand people, of whom about half were Negroes. Surrounded by fertile cotton plantations, it was a center of trade. In a spacious grove in the heart of the town stood the First Presbyterian Church. Constructed of brick, with a square tower and white spire, the building had a recessed central doorway with a rose window above.[18] Joseph Wilson preached his first sermon as pastor in this church in January, 1858.

In February, 1860, the trustees and congregation of the church, "wishing to provide a more commodious home for their clergyman," purchased a new manse. Located on the corner diagonally

[15]Jessie W. Wilson to Thomas Woodrow, April 27, 1857, in Woodrow Wilson Papers, Library of Congress.

[16]Memo in Baker Papers, Library of Congress.

[17]Mrs. James Woodrow to Woodrow Wilson, July 20, 1902, in Wilson Papers, Library of Congress.

[18]Federal Writers Project, *Augusta* (Augusta, Ga., 1938), 32, 70, 101.

across from the church, the home was a substantial brick building with a brick chimney at each end. Well shaded by tall trees, it hid a tiny garden in the rear. There was also a small stable which sheltered a black horse. In this comfortable home Tommy Wilson and his family lived for a decade.

The Reverend Dr. Wilson was the hero of Tommy's youth, the companion of his young manhood, and the intimate friend of his adulthood until the father died in the son's home many years later. Throughout his long life, the minister was a student and a scholar; he read widely, not only the Bible and biographies, but novels and poetry. Since the preacher was a habitual and prodigious smoker, the smell of tobacco usually enshrouded him. He especially relished a long-stemmed pipe with a clay bowl which he considered a symbol of democracy. Nor was Dr. Wilson immune to an occasional toddy. He frequently indulged in teasing, and was a superb story-teller. Joseph Wilson was a large man, broad-shouldered, full-bodied, slightly under six feet in height. He had a heavy crop of brown hair which he combed back from a high forehead. In early manhood he had side whiskers which met under his chin; fine lines about his face emphasized the bright brownness of his eyes and a long, straight nose, which seemed to have a flexible tip during animated conversation. At times, Tommy envied his father's face and figure for Joseph Ruggles Wilson possessed a commanding presence.[19]

Tommy's mother was more sedate than his father. Underneath an enforced reserve, she was a woman of strong religious feeling. She was refined in taste, dignified in manner, independent in her convictions, and, when any of her people were involved, capable of becoming strongly indignant. Possessed of a firm Scottish character, she loved her husband, adored her children, and delighted in her home. "I remember how I clung to her (a laughed-at 'mama's boy')," Wilson wrote to another, "till I was a great big fellow; but love of the best womanhood came to me and entered my heart through those apron-strings." [20] Although in memory during

[19]Baker, *Wilson Life and Letters,* I, 30–31.

[20]Woodrow Wilson to Ellen Axson Wilson, April 19, 1888, in Ellen Axson–Woodrow Wilson Letters, Firestone Library, Princeton University, hereinafter cited as Axson–Wilson Letters, Princeton.

his adult years Wilson held his mother in tender affection, it was his father with whom he was most intimate.

Together the father and son played games of tag about their spacious home, or in the shaded yard. When short of breath or fatigued by physical exertion, they returned to the Manse, where a game of chess or a contest at billiards was begun. Never a match for his father at chess, Tommy occasionally bested him at billiards.

During Tommy's early impressionable years, his father often found time to retire to his study to read aloud to members of his family. Dr. Wilson, as he read, would often recline on the floor with his head on the back of an upturned chair. In the room on such occasions sat Jessie Wilson, characteristically erect, with some darning, knitting, or sewing in her lap. The two sisters—Marion, six years older than Tommy, and Anne, two years his senior—sat side by side on the sofa or in separate chairs. Tommy, stretched out on the floor near the reader, was not only informed by what he heard but he was taught a lesson in vocal interpretations. "The sound of words, the flow of language, his father's oratory, were stamped indelibly upon Tommy's youthful memory." [21]

A day in the Wilson home was not completed until the family devotions were held. The minister or, in his absence, the mother read a passage from the Holy Bible. Then, as all members of the family knelt, the father prayed. Frequently, the family sang together some of the great old hymns of the Presbyterian Church or some of the popular tunes of the period, including the new song "Dixie," heard in Augusta's theatre for the first time in the late 1850's. There was no musical instrument in the Wilson home to accompany the singers, though the two Wilson girls, especially Anne, would later become accomplished pianists. Tommy would develop a fine tenor voice and sing in glee clubs at Princeton, the University of Virginia, and Johns Hopkins University.

From the time Tommy could toddle he frequently accompanied his father as the latter visited his parishioners at their stores and

[21] George C. Osborn, "Influence of Joseph Ruggles Wilson on His Son, Woodrow Wilson," *North Carolina Historical Review,* XXXII (1955), 519–43.

shops, at the cotton gins and corn mills, and, after the war began in the iron foundries and the ammunition plants. The minister was delighted to explain the business and manufacturing processes to his son. When the visiting was over and the two returned to the Manse, Tommy was invited to relate to other members of the family his experiences while his father listened attentively. If Tommy expressed himself in incorrect English, his father would call his attention to the error and have him correct it. If the boy uttered a vague or an indefinite statement, he was asked what he meant by the sentence. When he had explained precisely what he meant, his father would express approval. The elder Wilson made the same searching inquiries to learn if his son really understood the books which were read aloud to the family. The minister was convinced that clear thinking must precede clear expression.

Years later Wilson recalled these experiences. "When I was a boy," he said, "my father would not permit me to blurt things out or stammer a half-way job of telling whatever I had to tell. If I became excited in explaining some boying activity, he always said, 'steady now, Thomas; wait a minute. Think! Think what it is you wish to say, and then choose your words to say it.' As a young boy, therefore, even at the age of four or five, I was taught to think about what I was going to say, and then I was required to say it correctly. Before I was grown, it became a habit." [22]

As Tommy approached adolescence, his father frequently chose some passage from a favorite writer, such as an essay from Charles Lamb or an oration from Daniel Webster, for reading aloud. The father and son would endeavor to improve the passage or to reduce the selection to fewer words without robbing it either of ideas or of eloquence.[23] In this way Tommy learned coherence of thought and succinctness of expression.

Another lesson Dr. Wilson taught his son was that man's mental facilities constituted a receptacle not to contain but to transmute. The processes of mental digestion were essential; as Dr. Wilson phrased it, "the mind is not a prolix gut to be stuffed." Woodrow

[22]David Lawrence, *The True Story of Woodrow Wilson* (New York, 1924), 18.

[23]Baker, *Wilson Life and Letters,* I, 38–39.

Wilson, as an educator of renown, would later repeat his father's meaningful expression as he lectured across the nation.[24]

The activities of the Wilson family centered around the institution that the father so loyally served. According to the Augusta newspapers—the *Chronicle and Sentinel* and the *Daily Constitutionalist*—Dr. Wilson's sermons were orthodox fundamental theology. The reality of God, a veneration for the Holy Writ, the existence of sin, the stern Calvinistic doctrine of election and of predestination, a profound sense of the final judgment of God—all of these were to become part of Tommy's thoughts and of his unyielding faith early in his life. His father's church was literally and figuratively before the son's eyes constantly. The entire family attended the services every Sabbath and sat in the fourth pew directly in front of the elevated pulpit from which the minister preached. Of his father's eloquence in the pulpit Tommy in early manhood wrote: "I wish that I could believe that I inherited that rarest gift of making great truths attractive in the telling and of inspiring with great purposes by sheer force of eloquence or by gentle stress of persuasion." [25] The acceptance by Tommy of his father's faith was complete, and the striving for his father's eloquence was never relinquished.

Tommy attended Sunday School in his father's church regularly, and eventually learned the shorter catechism. More important, perhaps, he gained a wider acquaintance with, and developed a lasting interest in, the contents of the Bible. Wilson's entire life was enclosed by the horizon of the Presbyterian Church. Indeed, he moved "always in the antiseptic atmosphere of the Presbyterian public life—i.e. lecturing, education, writing and preaching—and Presbyterian domesticity." [26] Certainly this Calvinistic atmosphere in which Wilson lived early became a part of his very nature. Anyone who would understand Woodrow Wilson must know well

[24]See Wilson's address "The Young People and the Church," given at Pittsburgh, October 13, 1904, in Ray Stannard Baker and William E. Dodd (eds.), *Public Papers of Woodrow Wilson* (New York, 1925–27), I, 474–86.

[25]Woodrow Wilson to Ellen Axson, October 23, 1883, in Axson–Wilson Letters, Princeton.

[26]Edmund Wilson, *Shores of Light: A Literary Chronicle of the 1920's and 1930's* (New York, 1952), 301.

the cardinal virtues, as well as the grave deficiencies, of the Presbyterian society that nourished him.

Wilson was only four years old when an event occurred which would forever change the world into which he was born. His earliest recollection was of standing at his father's gateway in Augusta "and hearing someone say that Mr. Lincoln was elected and there was to be war." Catching the intense tones of the passer-by's excited voice, the lad remembered running in to ask his father what it meant.[27]

The election of Lincoln in November, 1860, had indeed precipitated a crisis. On every occasion in the local theater when someone sang or as an orchestra played "Dixie," the audience cheered wildly. According to the Augusta *Daily Chronicle and Sentinel,* the most famous song in America was "Dixie": "The forests of Aroostock and the gulches of California are equally familiar with its jingle; by the shores of the Chesapeake and by the pictured rocks of Lake Superior it soundeth." Dr. Wilson, taking note of the impending turmoil, preached to a large and appreciative audience on "the dangers which beset our country and the duties of the Christian citizen in this emergency." [28]

In May, 1861, the National General Assembly of the Presbyterian Church met in Philadelphia. At this convention the "Spring Resolution" was adopted which declared secession to be an act of treason. Whereupon the Presbyterians from the southern states departed, assembled in August in Atlanta, and called for a new General Assembly, which met in December in the First Presbyterian Church of Augusta and organized the Presbyterian Church of the Confederate States of America.[29] Dr. Wilson preached the opening sermon, and a Dr. Thornwell gave the chief address, which explained why southerners were forming a new organization. The church was thronged.[30] Dr. Wilson was made permanent clerk of the Assembly and so served until 1865.

[27]See Wilson's speech "Abraham Lincoln: A Man of the People," given in Chicago, February 12, 1909, in Baker and Dodd (eds.), *Public Papers of Woodrow Wilson,* II, 83.

[28]Augusta *Chronicle and Sentinel,* November 4, 6, 1860.

[29]John N. Waddell, *Memorials of Academic Life* (Richmond, 1891), 377.

[30]G. B. Strickler, *Memorial of the Centennial Anniversary of the First Presbyterian Church of Augusta, Georgia* (Augusta, 1904), 40–42.

During the war years the First Presbyterian Church, through its energetic minister, participated in every way in the crisis. Prayer meetings were held in the lecture room of the church across the street from the Manse. Repeatedly, the pastor urged Christians of all faiths to meet "together in so good a cause." [31] The Augusta Bible Society, of which Dr. Wilson was a leader, met in his church to take the initial steps in forming a state organization.[32] This group was soon expanded into the Bible Society for the Confederate States, which raised funds to supply Bibles in the South.[33] Another wartime agency in which Tommy's father was active was the Georgia Relief and Hospital Association. At its organizational meeting, held in the Augusta Masonic Hall, Dr. Wilson was named a member of the Board of Superintendents, placed on the Executive Committee, and subsequently chosen its chairman.[34]

Tommy was too young to know about all of these things, but was not too young to miss his father when the latter went into the Confederate Army as a chaplain in the spring of 1863. Apparently Dr. Wilson was acting under the Board of Home Missions, then established in Columbia, South Carolina.[35] The little boy, so accustomed to being at his father's heels, anxiously awaited his return in the fall of that year.

Fortunately for Augusta, the city was not in Sherman's line of march. Certainly Augusta was worth a march, for it boasted the largest gunpowder factory in the Confederacy and the only large arsenal in the South, east of the Mississippi River,[36] as well as productive machine shops and gun factories.[37] The community also made notable war contributions as an inland center of trade and as a hospital base. A hospital crisis came after Mayor Robert H. May issued a public letter: "There is now in the First Presby-

[31]Augusta *Daily Chronicle and Sentinel,* April 24, July 30, 1861.

[32]*Ibid.,* October 16, 1861.

[33]*Ibid.,* October 24, 1861.

[34]*Ibid.,* October 11, 1861.

[35]Strickler, *First Presbyterian Church Centennial,* 43.

[36]Mary G. Smith Cummings, *Two Centuries of Augusta: A Sketch* (Augusta, 1926), 33–34; Federal Writers Project, *Augusta,* 80.

[37]Charles C. Jones and Salem Dutcher, *Memorial History of Augusta, Georgia* (Syracuse, 1890), 185.

terian Church in this City a large number of sick and wounded soldiers, whose pressing claims on our assistance are not to be neglected." [38] It was impossible to relieve them at the overcrowded government hospitals. While the interior of the church served the sick and wounded, the churchyard was turned into a detention camp for northern prisoners, who were marched there from the railroad and held until it was convenient to transport them elsewhere.[39]

Tommy Wilson, approaching his seventh birthday, saw much of the inconveniences, the tragedies, the sufferings, and the ravages of war. For months across the street from the Manse were prisoners under guard and men ill clad, hungry, sick, wounded, and dying. Perhaps he did not know many of the details, but he was conscious that his mother spent much time caring for the sick and wounded in the church-hospital, that she made many bandages for these war casualties, and that the Wilson household was constantly readjusted to the changing conditions of war. The necessity of temporarily dispensing with Sunday School and worship services, he was told, was caused by the war. The *Daily Chronicle and Sentinel* reported that the Greene Street Baptist Church offered the congregation of the Presbyterian Church its auditorium "entirely free to them, both at morning and night services every Sabbath and at all other meetings during the period of their exclusion from their own House of Worship." [40] Within a few Sundays, Tommy began accompanying the other members of his family to the Greene Street church, where his father preached to his Presbyterian flock. This practice continued until January, 1864, when the Presbyterian Church was thoroughly renovated.[41]

Although the footsteps of enemy forces never sounded in the streets of the city, there were times when many feared the invaders would come. Especially was this true in 1864 when General Sherman cut his swath through Georgia and sent a detachment toward Augusta. The city was placed under the rule of a pro-

[38]Augusta *Daily Chronicle and Sentinel,* October 2, 1863.
[39]Strickler, *First Presbyterian Church Centennial,* 44.
[40]Augusta *Chronicle and Sentinel,* October 18, 1863.
[41]*Ibid.,* January 7, 1864.

vost marshal. No one was permitted on the streets at night without a pass. While no conquering army entered Augusta, tens of thousands of Confederate soldiers marched through going to battle.[42] In the chaplain's manse, as in many other homes, there was fear of a shortage of food. At times the Wilsons made substitutes or did without some commonly used commodities, but they were never hungry.

In 1864 Augusta was infested with marauders, robbers, and thieves. Nightly one or more churches, homes, or places of business were robbed. Some sacrilegious thieves broke into the First Presbyterian Church, stole the Communion table, chairs from the pulpit and rooms, carpets from the aisles, pulpit, and pews, and pew cushions. Other churches fared little better at the hands of the rascals.[43] A year later, thieves again plundered Dr. Wilson's church. This time they not only stole the furniture that had been placed there within the year, but made off with portions of the fence which surrounded the church.[44]

Another phase of the war was brought home to Dr. Wilson within his own church, namely, the position of the Negro in the community. There were slaves and free Negroes in the First Presbyterian Church long before the Wilsons became citizens of Augusta. As members, Negroes continued to attend services and to participate in the activities of the church during the Civil War and until Dr. Wilson resigned in 1870. The pastor showed a sustained interest in the spiritual welfare of the colored members of his congregation. In the fall of 1860, before the war began, Dr. Wilson created a Sunday School for Negroes and supported its continuance as long as he was pastor of the church.[45] However, the Negro members had their balcony pews and their special Sunday School; they were not integrated with the other members. In 1865 it was necessary for the Wilsons, as for other southerners, to make adjustments to a new mode of life. As the war ended, Negroes flocked to the community where patient members of the

[42]Jones and Dutcher, *Memorial History of Augusta,* 187.

[43]Augusta *Daily Chronicle and Sentinel,* October 20 and December 15, 1864.

[44]*Ibid.,* December 2, 3, 1865.

[45]Baker, *Wilson Life and Letters,* I, 53.

Freedmen's Bureau explained freedom, encouraged work, and doled out government supplies.

The Wilsons, like many other American families, were separated and divided during the "Brothers' War." Not having seen her father nor her brothers and sisters for years, Mrs. Wilson took her three children with her on a trip to Ohio at the conflict's end, in the summer of 1865. For weeks she visited among her people. For the first time Tommy saw many of his cousins and was introduced to aunts and uncles whom he had never known. Thomas Woodrow, Tommy's grandfather, promised to bring Tommy's step-grandmother and pay them a visit the following year.

As the time approached for the Woodrows to come South, Dr. Wilson wrote his wife's father of the enthusiastic welcome that awaited him. He wanted the Scottish clergyman to come prepared to preach. He and his people would be "greatly pleased to have you occupy my pulpit, even if you (Ohioans) have voted the radical ticket!"

Eventually the old minister and his wife came to Augusta. The friendship between the stern Scotch Covenanter and his alert grandson begun the year before developed into one of intimacy and mutual affection. The grandfather entertained young Wilson with the stories and folklore of Scotland, while Tommy, in turn, told of scenes that he had recently witnessed in connection with the war. How, for example, he and his family had silently watched the Yankees bring Jefferson Davis under heavy guard as a prisoner through the streets of Augusta.[46] Or, how he and other youngsters a short while later had been eager to get a glimpse of General Robert E. Lee, the South's greatest hero of the Civil War, as he paid a short visit to Augusta. Tommy had stood momentarily beside the great military leader and looked up into his sad, silent face.[47]

Also during his visit, the old Scotsman saw for the first time his newest grandson, who had arrived shortly before he did.

[46]*Ibid.,* I, 52.

[47]See Wilson's speech "Robert E. Lee: An Interpretation," given at Chapel Hill, North Carolina, January 19, 1909.

Tommy's baby brother, Joseph Ruggles Wilson, Jr., was almost ten years younger than he.[48]

Among the Wilsons' closest friends in Augusta was the James W. Bones family. Mrs. Bones was the former Marion Woodrow, Tommy's aunt; her husband served as a deacon and as superintendent of the Sunday School in Dr. Wilson's church. Jessie Woodrow Bones, the Bones' oldest daughter, was six or seven years Tommy's junior, but they played together much during the Wilsons' last few years in Augusta. Jessie recalled how young Wilson read James Fenimore Cooper's *Leatherstocking Tales* and then acted them out. Donning the "most abbreviated garments that decency would permit, on bodies stained with poke berry juice, a headdress of feathers . . . and armed with bow and arrows, we would sally forth." Not far away in the pine thicket there were several Negro cabins. Jessie and Tommy would lie in ambush along the trail through the pine thicket until some unsuspecting Negro children happened along. With wild war whoops, the cousins would spring out flashing tomahawks, bows, and arrows, and chase the small Negroes to their cabins. Rather cruel sport but "it was certainly lots of fun to us at least," remembered Jessie. If no youthful Negro came along, Tommy's cousin would be the victim. Once when she hid in a tree, Tommy found her and, in his enthusiasm, "shot" her with an arrow. She tumbled out of the tree and fell at his feet. Terrified, he picked up his cousin's limp body, carried her to the house, and laid her on the bed beside her ill mother, saying in tragic tones: "I have killed her, Aunt Marion. I am a murderer." The accident, recalled the victim, stopped the Indian games.[49]

A shy, frail lad, Tommy was sometimes considered a sissy. Though not usually sociable with children his age, Wilson did join a group of boys—"The Lightfoot Club"—shortly before his family left Augusta. The youths met occasionally in the loft of Dr. Wilson's barn to argue inconsequential questions. Tommy had

[48]Joseph R. Wilson to Thomas Woodrow, October 22, 1866, in Wilson Papers, Library of Congress; Zoe H. Beckley, "At the Old Home," *World Magazine,* January 19, 1913.

[49]Jessie B. Brower to Ray Stannard Baker, May 9, 1926, in Baker Papers, Library of Congress.

watched his father preside at many meetings and he soon led the boys in drawing up bylaws and a constitution for their club, and usually presided over the gatherings. The group organized a baseball team on which Tommy played, although he was not very enthusiastic about it. He was handicapped by his glasses which he had been compelled to wear since the age of nine. He sometimes lost control of his temper, and had been known to throw down the bat and walk off the playing field when he thought a decision had gone against him unjustly.

And so went Tommy's boyhood. Although he grew up in his native Southland after Appomattox, he never acquired the bitterness that the Reconstruction period aroused in many of his compatriots, but, on the contrary, seemed to have been in sympathy with the sectional reconciliation that was part of the New South as portrayed by Henry C. Grady.

CHAPTER II *Early Education*

All phases of southern culture were disrupted by the war, though some cultural dimensions recovered more rapidly than others. Certainly the schools suffered for several generations. Few schools were available during Reconstruction, and Tommy was very slow in starting his education. At nine years of age, he began to learn his alphabet; not until his eleventh year did he begin reading. Wilson's poor eyesight contributed to his slowness, as did the family custom of having the father or sisters read to the young boy. Tommy's family, especially his mother, shared the responsibility of endeavoring to interest the boy in learning to read. The young Wilson was not dull intellectually; he just was not interested, and unusually slow to mature.

After the war Joseph T. Derry, former Confederate officer, established "a select school for boys" and respectfully solicited patronage of the public.[1] The following year Derry was chosen prin-

[1]Augusta *Daily Chronicle and Sentinel,* November 4, 1865.

cipal of the Boys' Department of Houghton Institute. "To the principal's chair," said the local press, "Mr. Derry brings a well balanced and highly cultivated intellect and will, no doubt, give satisfaction." [2] It was to Houghton that Tommy Wilson came for his first formal schooling.

The Houghton Institute was located at the corner of Bay and McIntosh streets, on the bank of the Savannah River near the Episcopal church. The daily opening exercises of the school consisted of reading a psalm and reciting the Lord's Prayer. Principal Derry taught Latin, history, spelling, and grammar. His assistant, Henry Pelot, held classes in arithmetic, geography, penmanship, and bookkeeping. The pupils studied Webster's old 'blue-back' speller, Smith's grammar, Davies' arithmetic and algebra, Bingham's Latin grammar, Andrews' Latin reader, Mitchell's geography, and Stephens' *History of the United States.*[3] Tommy Wilson found his place near the foot of his class and remained there. His teachers were sure that he had average mental ability, but his progress was indeed slow.

One incident, remembered by both teacher and students, was the day certain boys, including Wilson, played hookey from school to see a circus parade. Anticipating a thrashing when they reported to the principal, the boys stopped at a nearby cotton warehouse, padded the seats of their trousers with cotton, then went straight to the principal and received their whipping. Seemingly, this was the only whipping Tommy received in school.

Among young Wilson's schoolmates at Houghton were a few destined for unusual attainments. Thomas R. Gibson later served as United States consul at Beirut, Syria; William Kenner became dean of Columbia University Law School; Joseph R. Lamar was appointed a member of the United States Supreme Court; and Pleasant Stovall became editor and owner of the Savannah *Press* and was named minister to Switzerland during Wilson's presidency.[4]

If Tommy showed no promise in his school work and received

[2] *Ibid.,* May 5, September 8, 27, 1866.

[3] "When He Was Just Tommy," *Ladies Home Journal* (November, 1918), 138.

[4] Baker, *Wilson Life and Letters,* I, 42.

little formal schooling before 1870, there were those who were determined to help him. His father, although discouraged, was not defeated by his son's lack of interest in his studies. His mother continued to work with him. Marion, the oldest child, began attending the Mary Baldwin Academy in Staunton in 1868,[5] but Anne replaced her as one of Tommy's educational aides. Mrs. Bones spent many hours trying to interest her nephew in the study of the English language. Besides reading aloud to Tommy, she had endless discussions with him "as to the pronunciation and use of the purest English." [6] These individuals who gave so much time and attention to the lad's early education must have agreed that Tommy was not responding, that he was completely disinterested. It was not until years later that the boy came to himself educationally and built upon that to which he had been exposed by loved ones and teachers. His progress then was much more rapid than it could have been if his family had not spent so many laborious and seemingly fruitless hours with him in his early years.

A deep interest in the education of young people prompted Dr. Wilson to accept a call to teach in the Columbia Theological Seminary in South Carolina. In the summer of 1870, he resigned from his church in Augusta to become a professor of pastoral theology at the Presbyterian seminary, and the family prepared to move.

The Columbia to which the Wilsons moved that fall was an old city, noted for its beauty, with wide avenues shaded by ancient trees. Columbia at that time had a population of about nine thousand, some five thousand of whom were Negroes. It had many homes whose aristocratic owners rightly prided themselves on their genial manners, their generous hospitality, and their gracious living. Five years earlier, in February of 1865, Columbia had suffered one of the greatest holocausts of the Civil War. Apparently drunken soldiers of General William T. Sherman's army, which occupied the city for two days, set fire to some of the houses, and high winds turned the town into a raging inferno.[7] The fire consumed three-fifths of the city, including many beauti-

[5] Joseph R. Wilson, testimonial for Mary Baldwin Academy, January 2, 1868, in Baker Papers, Library of Congress.

[6] Jessie B. Brower to Ray Stannard Baker, November 5, 1925, in *ibid.*

[7] John G. Barrett, *Sherman's March Through the Carolinas* (Chapel Hill, 1956), 70–91.

ful homes with their choice works of art, their libraries, costly furniture, delicate glassware, hand-painted china, and exquisite tapestries.[8] When the Wilsons became citizens of Columbia, however, changes were in evidence, and many parts had been freshly rebuilt. The physical wounds were healing but the emotional scars were deep. The political institutions were utterly demoralized.

The Wilson family at this time consisted of the two middle-aged parents and three teen-age children—Thomas Woodrow, fourteen years of age; Anne, sixteen; Marion, nineteen—and baby Joseph, only three. In resigning from the pastorate of the First Presbyterian Church at Augusta, Dr. Wilson left one of the wealthiest churches in the General Assembly of the Southern Presbyterian Church, but he felt called to the seminary chair. His salary as a professor in the seminary was considerably lower than his salary as a minister had been, nor did he have a house furnished him in Columbia. The family moved into the Pryor house, nearly opposite the theological seminary at the corner of Pickens and Blanding streets.[9] Nearby lived the Reverend Dr. George Howe, a leader in the theological seminary, and his family. His son, George Howe, Jr., would later marry Anne Wilson.

The first Sunday the Wilsons were in their new home, Dr. Wilson shared the pulpit with the pastor, Reverend W. E. Boggs, at the First Presbyterian Church. Three weeks later the Columbia *Phoenix* announced that Dr. Wilson would preach both services, morning and evening.[10] In December, 1870, the Charleston Presbytery dissolved the pastoral relations between the Reverend Mr. Boggs and his church.[11] Dr. James Woodrow, Tommy's uncle, who was a teacher in the seminary, was influential in having Dr. Wilson chosen as stated supply to the congregation with a stipulated salary of $1,500, per annum.[12] This position Tommy's father

[8]John T. Trowbridge, *The Desolate South 1865–1866: A Picture of the Battlefields and of the Devastated Confederacy,* ed. Gordon Carroll (New York, 1956), 295.

[9]Columbia *Phoenix,* September 25, 1870.

[10]*Ibid.,* October 16, 1870.

[11]*Southern Presbyterian and Presbyterian Index,* February 2, 1871.

[12]See Minutes of the First Presbyterian Church, Columbia, South Carolina, February 2, 1871, in South Carolina Department of Archives and History, Columbia.

held until shortly before he left Columbia. Dr. Wilson's compensation as pulpit supply, added to his salary as professor in the theological seminary, made his income almost equal to what he had been receiving as pastor in Augusta.

Dr. Wilson's church in Columbia had among its members many Negroes. In 1869, shortly before Tommy's father became stated supply, there were 50 Negroes in the congregation; of the 435 children on the First Presbyterian Church's Sunday School rolls, 325 were colored.[13] Relations between the two races within the church were apparently ideal. Dr. Wilson infrequently administered the sacrament of communion at Ladson Chapel to the Negro congregation, and he preached especially to the Negroes.[14] During much of the Reconstruction period in Columbia, most of the Board of Aldermen and nearly all of the police force were Negroes.[15] Some of these conditions which Tommy observed seemed detrimental to the best interests of both races. Quite naturally his views on the race issue were influenced by his early contacts with the problem during his youthful years in Augusta and in Columbia.

Soon after the Wilsons moved to Columbia, William Woodrow, a bachelor brother of Tommy's mother, died in Nebraska and left most of his property and money to his sister. When the money came to Mrs. Wilson she turned it over to her husband for the purchase of a lot on Hampton Street at the corner of Henderson, only a block or so from the seminary. Tommy's mother made the plans for a new house, going out almost daily during the months of construction to watch, to make suggestions, and to supervise the building of a new home for her family. Into the white, two-story house the Wilsons moved in 1872, but they remained there scarcely longer than a year.[16]

There were a few struggling private schools in Columbia in the 1870's, one of which was owned by Charles H. Barnwell, who

[13]Helen Kahn Henning (ed.), *Columbia, Capital City of South Carolina, 1786–1936* (Columbia, 1936), 197.

[14]Minutes of the First Presbyterian Church, Columbia, South Carolina, October 8, 1871.

[15]James F. Williams, *Old and New Columbia* (Columbia, 1929), 137, 140.

[16]Columbia *Daily Phoenix,* July 27, 1872. This was the *Phoenix* that added the word *Daily* when it became a daily in 1872.

held classes in a crude building at the rear of his home. The school was directly across the street from the Pryor house where the Wilsons were living. A former student at the universities of Virginia and South Carolina, Barnwell did all of the teaching, charging his boys seven or eight dollars per month for instruction in Latin, Greek, and a few other subjects. According to the Columbia *Phoenix,* he opened his school in the fall of 1870 with only three pupils—"Thomas W. Wilson, James H. Baldwin, and one of the McMaster boys." [17] Tommy continued as a pupil in the Barnwell school for approximately three years, until he was ready to enter Davidson College.

The education that young Wilson received from the classical courses taught by Barnwell was supplemented elsewhere. For a child who did not learn to read until after his eleventh birthday, Tommy was beginning to read avidly and widely. His vivid imagination was engrossed by sagas of the sea, and he delighted in stories of pirates, their treasures and secret meeting places on lonely islands. Narratives of discoveries and explorations deeply interested the young Wilson and he was intrigued by descriptions of ships and their voyages to distant lands. The youth's play world, "although romantic in conception, was constructed with striking realism and meticulous attention to detail." [18]

Tommy's education was also promoted in his Sunday-to-Sunday attendance at worship services in the church which his father served. The church had been incorporated in 1853. In 1869, shortly before Dr. Wilson was elected pulpit supply, there were 140 members. No other church in Columbia had a cultural influence comparable to that of the First Presbyterian Church.[19] Dr. Wilson's sermons, declared the Columbia *Daily Union,* were "uniformly able and interesting—full of fresh and vigorous thought. They show profound erudition and careful and elaborate preparation." [20] There were times, said the paper, when Dr. Wilson rose above the plane of his ordinary preaching and spoke with an authority and a power above and beyond himself. These

[17]*Ibid.,* December 20, 1870.

[18]Arthur S. Link (ed.), *The Papers of Woodrow Wilson* (Princeton, N.J., 1966), I, 21.

[19]Henning (ed.), *Columbia, 1786–1936,* 197.

[20]Columbia *Daily Union,* May 13, 1872.

inspired efforts were conditioned on the speaker's belief that he had discovered some divine truth which had eluded the grasp of others, but the knowledge and utilization of which were essential to the harmonious existence and to the supreme happiness of mankind. On one Sabbath Dr. Wilson concluded his sermon by saying, "I command you to a life of religious principle, a life of religious courage, a life of religious trust." [21] What more accurate summary could be made of Woodrow Wilson's approach to the problems and issues which he would confront, as president of Princeton, as governor of New Jersey, and as President of the United States? Dr. Wilson, the most influential teacher Tommy ever had, was more successful in molding his son's mind than he realized.

A third way in which the young Wilson advanced his education was by accompanying his father to his classroom. The Columbia Theological Seminary had moved from Lexington, Georgia, in 1829, and during the intervening years had strongly influenced the intellectual climate of that town. From the time the seminary was first located in Columbia, the faculty, always few in numbers, consisted of "vigorous characters, fluent in written and oral argument, who rapidly became leaders of the large Scotish-Irish element in the piedmont upcountry of South Carolina." [22] Devoted to Calvinistic theology and rich in talent, the seminary was poverty-stricken in its physical plant. In 1870 there was only one building, called the chapel, which was really a reconstructed stable. Faculty salaries were meager. In the classroom, sitting among older students, Tommy gave attention to lectures on theology and literature. His father, the son recalled years later, occasionally paused in a lecture to seek the exact word with which to express an idea. "Sometimes I would try swiftly," remembered Tommy, "in my own mind, to supply it; but rarely found the inevitable word as he did." [23]

In addition to attending his father's classes, Tommy frequently listened as the faculty members discussed their theological prob-

[21] *Ibid.,* October 28, 1872.
[22] Henning (ed.), *Columbia, 1786–1936,* 94, 196.
[23] Baker, *Wilson Life and Letters,* I, 64.

lems. Certainly, the impact of Darwin and Huxley and science on theology must have been discussed. Apparently, there were only three members of the seminary faculty at that time. In addition to Dr. Wilson, there were Dr. George Howe, neighbor and friend of the Wilsons, and Tommy's uncle, James Woodrow, professor of natural sciences and editor of the *Southern Presbyterian and Presbyterian Index*. Although born in England, Professor Woodrow grew up in the Midwest, taught science in Alabama, attended Harvard, and received his Ph.D. degree from the University of Heidelberg, *summa cum laude*. He had been teaching at the Columbia Theological Seminary since 1861, except for a stint in the Confederate Medical Corps during the Civil War.[24] On many occasions Tommy heard the three professors arguing some of the fine points of theology or denouncing the confusion, the waste, and the political corruption around them.

In Columbia, the boy attended the Sunday School and worship services of the church where his father preached. However, it seems that the person who exerted most influence on Tommy's religious experience at this period was Francis Brooke, a pupil at the seminary. Some years older than Wilson, Brooke was a ministerial student and a crusading evangelist. He began by inviting a few boys, including Tommy, to his room where he conducted a worship service. Presently, the room overflowed and they moved to the seminary chapel. There, from a low rostrum which faced the crude wooden benches, Brooke conducted his revival services. These meetings continued regularly for some time. In the summer of 1873 Tommy was converted and prepared to ask for membership in the church.[25]

According to the minutes of the First Presbyterian Church, a meeting of the Session was called by the moderator on July 5, 1873, to receive applications for church membership. "Douglas McKay, Thomas W. Wilson and Samuel H. Simonton presented themselves (three young men out of the Sunday School and well known to us all) and after a free confession during which they severally exhibited evidence of a work of grace begun in their

[24]*Ibid.*, 20–21.
[25]*Ibid.*, 66.

hearts—[they] were unanimously admitted into the membership of this church." [26]

Certainly Tommy always thought of this event as an important one in his life. His religious faith was not based on an emotional upheaval; it was an intellectual conviction and a spiritual conversion. For Wilson, the Holy Writ was God's message to man and constituted the Magna Carta of the human soul. Years later he said that the Bible "reveals every man to himself as a distinct moral agent, responsible not to men, not even to those men whom he has just over him in authority, but responsible through his own conscience to his Lord and Master. Whenever a man sees this vision he stands up a free man, whatever may be the government under which he lives, if he sees beyond the circumstances of his own life." [27] On another occasion, Wilson spoke of the central theme of the Scriptures as a "gospel of love." It was all a "question of personal relationship between man and his Maker, and a personal relationship founded upon love. For love is the only thing that I know that ever led to self-abnegation." [28] Wilson accepted completely the Calvinistic doctrine that unless God lifted one up, he would remain unlifted or lost to eternal life. During the years ahead he was to reveal this sense of selection in an obvious feeling of superiority.

During the summer of Tommy's spiritual awakening, Jessie Bones, his cousin from Augusta, came and remained for weeks as a visitor in the Wilson home. She recalled standing by Tommy's desk one day that summer as he was teaching himself Graham shorthand through a correspondence course. Glancing upward, she saw a large portrait of an important looking person and asked, "Who is that old man you have hanging over your desk?" The youth stopped his shorthand practice as he replied, "That is the greatest statesman who ever lived—Gladstone—and when I grow up to be a man, I mean to be a great statesman, too." [29]

[26]Minutes of the First Presbyterian Church, Columbia, South Carolina, July 5, 1873.

[27]Woodrow Wilson, "The Bible and Progress," in Denver, Colorado, May 7, 1911. See *Congressional Record,* 62nd Cong., 2nd Sess., Appendix 499–502 for the address.

[28]See Wilson's address, "The Young People and the Church."

[29]Jessie B. Brower to Ray Stannard Baker, October 5, 1925, in Baker Papers, Library of Congress.

Apparently, Dr. Wilson was never completely accepted by the membership of the First Presbyterian Church. Although the Wilson family joined the church on January 5, 1871,[30] the record gives evidence of a lack of co-operation between the minister and the governing bodies of the church. In September, 1871, as he prepared to leave on his annual vacation, Wilson was requested by the Session to invite the Reverend George R. Brackett to fill the pulpit, "with a view of allowing the congregation an opportunity to judge his fitness as a pastor to whom a call might be extended." This official request Dr. Wilson ignored, and the Session made other arrangements for inviting Dr. Brackett.[31] In May, 1872, the church passed a resolution which urged that a suitable pastor to minister to their needs be sought and asked the Session to invite "such Divines who shall be recommended to them as suitable for trust, that we may hear and know them, with the view of securing the services of a permanent pastor." Significantly, at the same meeting of the Session, a letter from Dr. Wilson was read which said: "Some time since you were pleased to invite me to act as stated supply in the church over which you preside. Fearing that I am in the way of your securing a regular Pastor, I hereby ask your permission to retire from the position I now occupy and in which I have endeavored to serve you to the best of my ability." [32] His explanation to the congregation, published in the *Daily Union,* stated his position. Because of the press of other public duties, he could not be pastor of the church. Although he was willing to continue as stated pulpit supply for a limited period, he urged all who had been thinking of him, "either as pastor, as a fixture, in his present relations, to drop him from their thoughts, as he could not take any position which might possibly lead to dissension in the church." [33]

Attempts of the local press to create favorable public opinion toward Dr. Wilson were unsuccessful.[34] With a resolution of appreciation for his services as stated pulpit supply, the church in

[30]Minutes of the First Presbyterian Church, Columbia, South Carolina, January 5, 1871.

[31]*Ibid.,* September 30, 1871.

[32]*Ibid.,* October 11, 1872.

[33]Columbia *Daily Union,* November 11, 1872.

[34]*Ibid.,* December 23, 1872, March 10, 27, 28, April 7, 14, 21, 1873.

the spring of 1873 accepted his resignation. In July, 1873, the very month in which Tommy was received into the church, the Session took steps to secure a pastor and to relieve Dr. Wilson of his services.[35]

Although Dr. Wilson saw fit to resign from his pulpit because of dissension in the church, he was exercising his persuasive powers upon his son to choose the ministry as his vocation. Apparently the boy said little or nothing in reply, but he soon determined not to become a clergyman. The father thought Tommy had accepted his promptings to become a preacher, and, within weeks after the younger Wilson joined the church, he decided that the boy should enter Davidson College. Founded in 1837 by the Presbyterians and located some twenty miles north of Charlotte, North Carolina, the school prepared young men for the ministry. Davidson sent many of its graduates to the Columbia Theological Seminary; moreover, Dr. Wilson was soon to be on the Board of Trustees.[36]

In the fall of 1873, when Tommy enrolled in Davidson, the little town of the same name in which the school was located was a one-street village that subsisted almost entirely on student trade. The whole area was slowly recuperating from the exhaustion of the Civil War. A station on the Atlantic, Tennessee, and Ohio Railroad, Davidson saw only an occasional slowly moving train. There was neither an express office nor a telegraph station.[37]

The college had very few buildings. Most of the campus activities were conducted in Chambers Hall, a large, imposing building with huge stone pillars across the front. Tommy roomed in the north wing of this central building on the first floor, where he shared Room 13 with John W. Leckie. They and 105 other boys composed the student body. Students at Davidson were expected to clean their own rooms, cut wood, keep the fires going in the fireplaces, and to supply their own water. The responsibility of performing such chores in the primitive life on the campus was excellent training for any young man. Expenses were relatively

[35]Minutes of the First Presbyterian Church, Columbia, South Carolina, July 5, 1873. The Reverend J. H. Bryson was chosen pastor. See *ibid.,* November 9, 1873.

[36]Memo in Baker Papers, Library of Congress.

[37]*Ibid.*

low, and some of the students worked their way through the institution.

Soon after enrolling at Davidson, Tommy joined the Eumenean Literary Society, whose object, as stated in the constitution, was "the acquirement of literary knowledge, the promotion of virtue, and the cultivation of social harmony and friendship." [38] Significantly, Tommy soon began to tinker with the society's constitution. His first appearance on the program was on December 5, soon after he joined the society, when he debated the negative side of the question: "Resolved, That Republicanism is a better form of government than limited monarchy." On February 20, 1874, he argued affirmatively for compulsory education.

The Reverend Dr. A. M. Fraser, a leader on the campus, remembered young Wilson as "witty, genial, superior, but languid." [39] The boy did not display the restless energy nor the determination that marked his later life. He was not prepared for college work, and entered Greek and mathematics classes on probation. Despite these handicaps and a frail constitution, his grades show that he did quite well. Wilson did not even approach his best in any campus activity, though he did show an interest in athletics. He played second base on the Davidson freshman baseball team, and, according to Robert Glenn, a senior on the varsity nine, would have been a good player "if he weren't so damned lazy." [40]

In the spring young Wilson was the victim of chest colds accompanied by spells of coughing. When his mother learned of his ill health, she anxiously wrote that, if the cough continued, the boy would have to come home.[41] By May, ill health forced his absence from literary society meetings.[42] In June, 1874, Tommy came back to Columbia on the verge of a physical breakdown. He would not return to Davidson. For the first time he had

[38]For Wilson's activities in the Eumenean Society, see Records of the Eumenean Literary Society in Library of Davidson College.

[39]Interview with Ray Stannard Baker, n.d., in Baker, *Wilson Life and Letters,* I, 74.

[40]*Ibid.*

[41]Janet Wilson to Woodrow Wilson, April 26, 1874, in Wilson Papers, Library of Congress.

[42]Records of the Eumenean Literary Society in Davidson College Library.

remained for several months away from home, and he was quite depressed. From his early years Wilson's lack of popularity and favorable acceptance had an adverse effect on his emotional health and made him physically ill. Shortly before he went home the boy was admonished not to imagine himself so generally disliked. "*Everybody* here in Columbia likes and admires you," his mother wrote. "I could not begin to tell you the kind and flattering things that are said about you by everybody that knows you. Why, my darling, nobody could help loving you, if they were to try." [43]

He prevailed upon his father to permit him to remain under the family roof for the next fifteen months. During this interval, the son again attended his father's concluding lecture in the theological seminary chapel and worshipped regularly at the First Presbyterian Church. In the home he read what books interested him from his father's study and listened to Dr. Wilson as he read aloud to the family. Much of the boy's time was employed in mastering the Graham shorthand which he had begun studying two years earlier.[44] Wilson's fascination with his shorthand was attested to by a youthful friend who wrote that it was only necessary to say "shorthand" and Tommy would prick up his ears "like the war horse at the sound of the trumpet." [45]

The Wilsons lived in Columbia approximately four years—from the autumn of 1870 to the summer of 1874. Tommy was at home slightly more than three of these years, and they constituted a significant period in which he began to read for the love of reading, for the adventure of learning. During this time he left home for a boarding school for the first time. More important, he came to himself spiritually. These days were the ones that he remembered best, his happy boyhood in Columbia.

In 1874 Dr. Wilson resigned as professor of pastoral theology at the seminary to accept a call to the First Presbyterian Church of Wilmington, North Carolina. A town of more than 15,000

[43]Janet Wilson to Woodrow Wilson, May 20, 1874, in Wilson Papers, Library of Congress.

[44]For an excellent summary of Wilson's study and use of shorthand see Link (ed.), *Papers of Wilson,* I, 8–19.

[45]John Danby to Wilson, July 22, 1875, in Wilson Papers, Library of Congress.

people in 1875, Wilmington boasted thirty-eight churches with an estimated Sunday School and preaching attendance of over 9,000. There were approximately 300 members of the First Presbyterian Church of which about 175 were enrolled in the Sunday School.[46] Dr. Wilson's church, located at the corner of Third and Orange streets, was perhaps the wealthiest and most aristocratic in Wilmington. With a salary of $4,000 per annum, the pastor was one of the highest paid ministers in the Southeast.

Wilmington was a seaport town, and in company with John D. Bellamy, his best friend, the young Wilson spent much time at the docks boarding and exploring moored vessels.[47] The ocean held for Tommy an increasing fascination, and he decided to run away to sea. He talked with the captain of a commercial vessel and was quite ready to go on a cruise. He confided his plan to his mother, but she prevailed upon him not to go.[48] The decision to leave the parental roof may have been influenced in part by the pressure which his father was beginning to exert on the boy. The energetic, strongly authoritative Dr. Wilson desired that his son become a minister, that the boy spend hours daily reading books suggested by the father, and that the lad not assume the "responsibility" for selecting his playmates nor for living the ordinary life of a normal youth. Indeed, young Wilson, so his father thought, seemed entirely too independent about continuing his formal education.

Tommy was not completely negligent in preparing to resume his formal education, however. An Episcopal minister tutored him in Greek and a few other subjects which would be necessary for his admission to Princeton College, where his father had received his B.D. degree.[49] In company with Bellamy he strolled about the city visiting historic spots. Sometimes one boy would listen as the other read parts of books or related what he had previously read. On occasion they would debate the greatness of some nineteenth-century military leaders or political statesmen.

[46]J. S. Reilly, *Wilmington, Past, Present and Future* (Wilmington, 1885), 33.

[47]Jessie B. Brower to Ray Stannard Baker, October 5, 1925, in Baker Papers, Library of Congress.

[48]Baker, *Wilson Life and Letters,* I, 60–61.

[49]James Sprunt, *Chronicles of the Cape Fear River 1660–1916* (2nd ed.; Raleigh, N.C., 1916), 542–43; Memo in Baker Papers, Library of Congress.

And at times they argued about the charms or talents of some of the girls with whom they were acquainted.[50]

In September, 1875, Tommy Wilson, a slender, angular youth almost nineteen years of age, arrived on the Princeton College campus with his clothes packed in a badly worn black valise which for years had served his father. The young man was awkward of movement and shy with strangers. After searching a bit, the young Wilson accepted a room in Mrs. Josiah Wright's boardinghouse on Nassau Street, along with sixteen other boarders, most of whom were freshmen. From a front room on the second floor he could look out over the campus.[51] Very popular among southern Presbyterian boys as an educational institution from colonial days until the Civil War, Princeton College by 1875 had not regained its former favor among southern Calvinists. Although Tommy was not the only southerner on the campus, he was in a small minority. In fact, the few boys from the South had formed an eating club. Learning of Wilson's arrival, a junior Alabaman—Frank P. Glass—took the new arrival to eat for two weeks with the upper-class southern group.

Dr. James McCosh, president of Princeton, had made a tour of the South in 1873, stopping in the Wilson home in Columbia. Both Dr. Wilson and Professor James Woodrow were extremely fond of him. Although Tommy had met the picturesque Scot and chatted with him, he yet timidly entered President McCosh's office holding firmly a letter of introduction. After a few pleasantries, the boy felt more at home. On that September day, 1875, as young Wilson left the Princeton president's office, he could have had no idea that not only would he spend four years there as a student, but would subsequently return as a teacher and one day sit in Dr. McCosh's place as president of Princeton.

Wilson made the emotional and intellectual adjustments necessary for a beginning freshman entering a college in a different section of the country. He had come poorly prepared in some fields of study; yet, if his knowledge of Greek was below par and his skill in mathematics lacking, he was more widely read and, as a result of his father's and his Aunt Marion's training, more

[50]Baker, *Wilson Life and Letters,* I, 78–79.
[51]Memo in Baker Papers, Library of Congress.

proficient in English than most of his classmates. Moreover, his knowledge of shorthand aided him appreciably in taking notes at lectures.

Wilson employed his shorthand not only in the recording of class notes, but also in a diary of his student days at Princeton, one which he kept regularly for twenty-five weeks until November 23, 1876, with only scattered entries after that date. Wilson's diary is significant in that it reveals some of his early opinions and sheds much light on student activities in the late 1870's. A few excerpts from this book will reveal its intimate nature and give interesting glimpses into the personality of its young author.

A representative entry is one made after a discussion with classmate Alanson Enos, in which Wilson wrote that they were "both agreed very well on this point: that the limited monarchy is more preferable and is the only form of government which gives true liberty to the people. The English form of government is best by far after all." [52]

While reading Thomas B. Macaulay's *History of England,* the diarist frequently recorded his enthusiasm. For example, Macaulay's twelfth chapter fascinated him: "What a master of the English language Macaulay proved himself to be. . . . This eloquence and eminent ability to describe these events is chiefly due to Macaulay's vivid imagination, which made him imagine himself acting and working in the midst of the events which he described and which enabled him to impart some of his enthusiasm to his readers." [53] Furthermore, "the interest of these events is greatly enhanced to modern readers by the clear and splendid diction of Macaulay who makes the most stupid things alive with interest of romance." [54] Wilson confessed that he "read very slowly" but enjoyed immensely what he read. He sometimes wished that he could read a little faster but did "not know that it would be an advantage."

The Princeton sophomore's religious life is repeatedly revealed in his diary. On Sunday, June 11, 1876, after worshipping at the Episcopal Church, Wilson wrote: "I think the Episcopal service

[52]Link (ed.), *Papers of Wilson,* I, 132–33.
[53]*Ibid.,* 135.
[54]*Ibid.,* 134.

very stupid—it is in my opinion a ridiculous way of worshipping God, and one which must give very little pleasure to God". In another entry Wilson wrote: "Before going to bed, I prayed out loud and found that I enjoyed my prayer much more than usual. . . . One feels more as if he was praying to God and talking with Him when his tones are audible. I prayed last night as I have seldom done in the past few months. Oh that God would give me more of His Holy Spirit and make me something more than the cold Christian I have been of late!" [55]

Tommy's courses during his entire four years as an undergraduate were essentially those of all of his classmates. He took the regular Bachelor of Arts degree and his subjects were those required of the students working toward that degree—English, Greek, Latin, French, geology, history, philosophy, and psychology. In grades, Wilson's four-year undergraduate average was 90.3 per cent, which ranked him barely in the upper third of his class.[56] His highest grades were made in his sophomore year when he averaged for the two semesters 92.8 and 92.9 per cent, but even in his second year he ranked thirty-first and thirtieth in his class.

Wilson's sophomore year was a turning point in his life. In addition to making his highest undergraduate grades in that year, Tommy checked out more books from the library than ever before. He read *The Federalist,*[57] John R. Green's *History of the English People,*[58] the essays of Walter Bagehot, and the speeches of Edmund Burke and John Bright. Moreover, he found the *Gentleman's Magazine* on the library shelves, read an article by Henry W. Lucy on "The Orator," and forthwith resolved to become one. He was at last beginning to mature emotionally, and was trying to utilize his time and talents more completely towards achieving the objectives of his higher education. Significantly, Wil-

[55]*Ibid.,* 197–98.

[56]The lists of honor men during the eight semesters, 1875–79, that Wilson attended Princeton are in Princeton Library, Princeton University; also in Baker Papers and Wilson Papers, Library of Congress.

[57]For paragraphs of *The Federalist* that interested Wilson and his marginal comments on them, see Link (ed.), *Wilson Papers,* I, 598–601.

[58]For paragraphs of Green's *History of the English People* that impressed Wilson and his marginal comments on them, see *ibid.,* 300–302, 387–93, 542–44.

son wrote his father that he had discovered that he had a mind. His mother replied: "I am so glad that you love to study now... for now I know your future will be all right." [59]

In November of 1876 the Hayes–Tilden election contest occurred. Upon learning of Governor Hayes's nomination, Wilson expressed the hope that the Republican ticket would be defeated and the Democratic ticket would be elected. He most sincerely hoped "that the Democrats would nominate a good and prominent man like Tilden" and added that the Democrats would "be very likely to abuse power if they got it, however." [60] In the weeks that followed, many young students viewed with concern the breakdown of the election machinery and some of them, including young Wilson, wondered if alterations were not necessary. Thereafter Tommy's interest in politics increased by leaps and bounds.[61] He developed more self-confidence and began to find himself intellectually.

Princeton had three chief societies during the period Tommy was a student.[62] The Cliosophic and the Whig were the rival literary societies, and Tommy joined the second within a few weeks after he arrived on the college campus. This organization dated from colonial days, and James Madison was one of its early leaders. According to the Whig record Wilson "performed" for the first time on October 29, 1875, on the subject "Rome was not built in a day." [63] Not until Tommy was a sophomore did he share in the Whig society's program again. In January, 1877, he was among several youths who sought the sophomore oratorical medal, his subject being "The Ideal Statesman." [64] In this contest, as in other literary society contests, he failed to win first place and had to be content with second prize. But Wilson's parents were elated over his success. Indeed, his father was "intensely grati-

[59]Janet Wilson to Woodrow Wilson, September 25, 1876, in Wilson Papers, Library of Congress.

[60]Link (ed.), *Papers of Wilson,* I, 245–49, 255–57.

[61]Baker, *Wilson Life and Letters,* I, 85 ff; also Memo in Baker Papers, Library of Congress; T. W. Wilson *Diary,* June, 1876, in Wilson Papers, Library of Congress.

[62]The third society was the Philadelphian, the religious society.

[63]See Minutes of the Whig Literary Society in Firestone Library, Princeton University.

[64]For a copy of this oration, see *ibid.,* 241–45.

fied," and his mother prodded her son to "lay aside all timidity and make the most of all your powers." [65]

Defeat in his initial efforts at oratory did not dampen Tommy's spirits, nor dull his ambition to learn how to speak. During the spring of 1877, he was seen occasionally leaving the campus alone, going along a path that led to the woods. Once a classmate found him alone there practicing one of Burke's orations. Near the close of his sophomore year, he penned an editorial—"On Oratory"—which appeared in the campus paper, the *Princetonian*, in June, 1877. In this short article, Wilson noted that Princeton students were placing oratory in a false light in that they were viewing it as an end in itself rather than as a means toward an end. He said that the object of oratory was "persuasion and conviction—the control of other minds by a strange personal influence and power." If, in pursuing the proper method of study and application of oratory, any should fail to win college prizes for oratory, he need not be discouraged as training in oratory was the object, Wilson wrote. He added that the best means of training the young orator was "the imitation of classic models." Only by constantly associating with Demosthenes (the "greatest and truest model of all orators"), Cicero, Edmund Burke, Charles Fox, Edward Canning, and Daniel Webster, he concluded, could the students hope to become orators.[66]

In Tommy's junior year there were four oratorical medals offered in literary society contests. On December 6, 1877, he spoke before his fellow Whigs on "Bismarck" as a preliminary to the contest later in the scholastic year. His name was not among the medal winners.[67] When Wilson informed his parents of his keen disappointment, his father replied that the loss must have been a "sore grief and the sorer because unexpected." The son should remember that the blow was "not killing; only stunning." The interested father pleaded: "My darling, make *more* of your class studies. Dismiss *ambition* and replace it with hard industry, which shall have little or no regard to *present* triumphs but

[65] Janet Wilson to Woodrow Wilson, February 6, 1877, in Wilson Papers, Library of Congress.

[66] *Princetonian*, June 7, 1877.

[67] Minutes of the Whig Literary Society, 1877–78.

which will be all the time laying foundations for future work and wage." [68]

Another phase of the young Wilson's activities as a Whig was debating. Apparently, his first participation was on October 17, 1877, when he upheld the affirmative side of the subject: "That a liberal education is to be preferred to an exclusively practical one." [69] On May 24, 1878, he supported the affirmative of the question, "That a protective tariff is no longer necessary for the protection of our home industries." [70]

Perhaps Wilson was not having as many opportunities to participate in debate in the Whig Literary Society as he wished. Whatever his reasons, he created the Liberal Debating Club with ten of his classmates. Naturally, he claimed for himself the authorship of the selective club's constitution and bylaws. That constitution clearly revealed Wilson's conviction that the British parliamentary system was the best type for creating excellent leadership in a democracy. It also showed the Princeton student's belief in debate as the proper way for political battles to be waged in the clash and survival of ideas. Like some other things that Wilson enthusiastically created, the Liberal Debating Club was of short duration, lasting only as long as he was present to direct it—in this case, until his graduation in 1879.

The young Wilson held both appointive and elective offices in the Whig Literary Society. In the spring of his sophomore year, he was appointed to a committee of three to examine "the present conditions of the Society and to recommend what seems to them means for perfecting its workings." [71] On September 28, 1877, he was chosen to the Bank Committee; on December 6 the Whigs elected him first comptroller; and on February 1 of the following year they advanced him to the speakership, the most important office. To be speaker of the Whig Society was quite an honor for a junior. Apparently, Wilson's best contributions to Whig Hall were in administrative positions, and not as a debater nor an orator.

[68] Joseph R. Wilson to Woodrow Wilson, December 22, 1877, in Wilson Papers.

[69] Minutes of the Whig Literary Society, October 17, 1877.

[70] *Ibid.,* May 24, 1878.

[71] *Ibid.,* May 25, November 9, 1877.

If Wilson participated to any appreciable degree in Princeton campus politics, there is no record of it. Certainly, he was not a candidate for any elective office during the four-year period he was a student. He never served on any significant class committees nor, with one exception, on any student body commissions. He made no varsity athletic team, but in his senior year was named president of the Princeton College Baseball Association.[72]

Although there was a Philadelphian Society, devoted to the promotion of religious life on the Princeton campus, Tommy was not a member.[73] Probably Dr. Wilson's emotional pleadings with his son to enter the ministry caused some resentment in him, and as a result he kept aloof from the Philadelphian Society. Wilson did regularly attend prayer meetings on Sunday evenings in Dickinson Hall. Apparently these evening meetings were quite popular, as about half of the class frequently attended. Tommy also sang tenor in the college choir.[74]

In the literary realm, Wilson won recognition. In February, 1878, he received 96 votes, the highest number of votes, in the election of members to conduct the campus periodicals and became managing editor of the biweekly *Princetonian*.[75] As managing editor, he wrote editorials, contributed a column "Here and There," and at times tried to compose verse:

> "I will work out a rhyme,
> If I only have time."
> Said the man of "Here and There."
> So he tried for awhile—
> Result—a loose pile—
> Of his golden hair—[76]

More significantly, in his senior year he won a prize offered by

[72]Within a few weeks, Wilson's mother wrote urging him to resign from the presidency, adding that he would make a great mistake to permit anything to come in the way of his doing his utmost in the direction of his "future interest." See Janet Wilson to Woodrow Wilson, November 20, 1878, in Wilson Papers, Library of Congress.

[73]Memo in Baker Papers, Library of Congress. See also Woodrow Wilson Collection, Princeton University Library.

[74]*Ibid.*

[75]H. Godwin, *A History of the Class of '79: Princeton College* (Spring 1879, privately printed), 46, in Wilson Collection, Princeton.

[76]Trenton *Evening Times,* July 2, 1912.

the *Nassau Literary Magazine* for an essay entitled "William Earl Chatham."

Tommy's oration on Bismarck, delivered during his sophomore year, was published in *Nassau Literary Magazine* and signed "Atticus." The embryonic writer apparently was not yet courageous enough to publish under his real identity. A few quotations from the article, Wilson's first in a literary magazine, will show something of the twenty-one-year-old author's interest and his mode of expression.

In contrasting the Prussian statesman with English and American statesmen, the author noted: "All the energies of the English or American statesman must be spent in governing great popular assemblies, in manipulating parties, in directing and controlling popular opinion. The Prussian statesman's power does not depend upon popular assemblies whose favor he must win and whose support he must command, but rests entirely with his royal master." While the German chancellor ranked with few of his many eminent contemporaries in literary power, he stood "among them all without a peer in those powers of cool judgment, quick determination, and masterly execution which made up the statesman's character." [77]

Wilson's prize essay on William Pitt, first Earl of Chatham, appeared in the same campus magazine almost a year later—October of his senior year. For an undergraduate he gave evidence of unusual talent as a phrasemaker. A few examples will illustrate: "In the elder Pitt consummate powers kept company with small weaknesses, strong wisdom stood side by side with weak folly, truthfulness and earnestness were contrasted with affection and pedantry." In comparing William Earl Chatham to the age in which he lived, Wilson wrote:

> He was in everything enthusiastically earnest, and his age laughed at earnestness; he was vehement, and his age affected coldness and indifference; he was sternly virtuous, scorning corruption, and his age was skeptical of virtue, nursing corruption; he had eager, burning beliefs and was actuated by a warm love for principle, and his age delighted in doubtings and questionings, was guided by no principle

[77] "Atticus" [Woodrow Wilson], "Prince Bismark," *Nassau Literary Magazine,* XXXIII (1878), 99–105.

save that of expediency; he was used constantly and confidently to appeal to the higher, brighter, purer instincts of human nature, and his age doubted the existence of any such instincts, nay, even argued from its own experience that all human nature was low and pulseless.

According to Wilson, passion was the groundwork of Pitt's character. "And certainly, if we conceive of statesmanship as being that resolute and vigorous advance towards the realization of high, definite, and consistent aims which issues from the unresolved devotion of a strong intellect to the service of the state and to the solution of all the multi-form problems of public policy, Pitts' statesmanship was of the highest order."

Wilson then expressed his views on the proper relationship between a statesman and public opinion in a democracy. "In a free government, founded upon public opinion, the governmental machinery is so nicely balanced, opposite parties, opposing forces of thought, generally exercise powers so nearly equal, that great principles must be worked out cautiously, step by step, seldom attaining triumphant ascendancy by a course of uninterrupted success—by only a few bold and rapid strokes. Public opinion must not be outstripped, but kept pace with." [78]

In this prize essay, Tommy revealed himself as a phrasemaker, a painter of vivid word portraits, as a writer of long but perhaps not too involved sentences, and as a young man with opinions which he was not afraid to state.

Following Wilson's move into Witherspoon Hall his sophomore year, he and some of the others who roomed there began the custom of going early in the evening to one of the student's rooms for a social visit. The assembled group argued any topic—educational, economic, political, religious, or social—of current interest. There was always some teasing among these roomers, and at times they sang current popular songs or occasionally blended their voices in Presbyterian hymns. Soon the boys were referred to as the "Witherspoon gang"—the only "gang" that Tommy ever helped to organize. The Witherspoon crowd was composed of Wilson, Robert Bridges, Robert R. Henderson, William B. Lee, Charles W. Mitchell, Charles A. Talcott, J. Edwin

[78] Thomas W. Wilson, "William Earl Chatham," *Nassau Literary Magazine,* XXXIV (1878), 99–105.

Webster, and Hiram Woods.[79] In some instances, these young Princetonians became fast friends and remained that to the end of their lives. In their junior year several of them began eating at a friendly club of the Princeton men who called themselves The Alligators.

As one of those who knew Tommy at the Alligator Club recalled, Wilson was by no means a recluse. He realized that he could get much from those with whom he associated in college. Wilson did not, however, "hobnob with everybody" and by no means was he the most popular boy on the Princeton campus during his student days. Among some of his classmates he cultivated enduring friendships, but when he did not like a member of the student body he was sharp in his criticism. For example, C. L. Williams, a Princeton schoolmate and friend, remembered Wilson's saying of another student: "We read in *Julius Caesar* that Gaul was divided into three parts, but it seems that this young man's gall has never been divided nor diminished in the least." [80] Wilson evidenced an unusual degree of independence.

One grave mistake that the young Wilson made while an undergraduate was the neglect of his physical well-being. He gave little if any attention to building a robust healthy body. Frequently Tommy suffered from dyspepsia with abdominal pain—a symptom rather than a disease. Although some of young Wilson's troubles with ill health were probably psychosomatic, had he been subjected to a thorough physical examination and had his diet, exercise, and mode of life been properly regulated, he might have been spared much future ill health.[81]

He spent the summers between the academic sessions both at Princeton and with his family in Wilmington. When an occasional afternoon picnic or a nocturnal hayride was held for the Presbyterian young people, Wilson was one of the group. For the first time in his life, he paid attention to several girls. Although he

[79]Robert Bridges, *Woodrow Wilson: A Personal Tribute* (n.d., n.p.), I, in Wilson Collection, Princeton.

[80]C. L. Williams, "Woodrow Wilson as an Undergraduate," *Current History,* XXXI (January, 1930), 698–702.

[81]Edward P. Davis, "Woodrow Wilson's Early Years," *Saturday Review of Literature,* IV (November 19, 1927), 319–20.

carried on a stilted correspondence with one of them for a short time, there was no love affair.

In the Manse Dr. Wilson and his son discussed books and authors, orators and their orations, and the impact of science on theology. These father-son conferences were now give-and-take affairs as the son began to measure intellectual lances with his opinionated father. The youth listened, for example, as Dr. Wilson told him of the Confederate Memorial Day exercises held in Wilmington several weeks earlier. The son learned of the parade, of the speeches, of the decoration of the graves of those who sacrificed their lives for the "Lost Cause," and of his father's appropriate prayer. All of the narrative appealed strongly to the son's emotions, but, upon questioning his father in detail, he concluded that because the exercises perhaps tended to keep alive hatred and prejudice he opposed them. He won his father to his opinion, and thereafter on May 10, when the exercises were held in Wilmington, Dr. Wilson did not participate in them.[82]

Tommy's quiet summer life furnished few interesting topics for the correspondence he kept with Bobby Bridges. Apparently the only trip that Wilson took during these months was a June visit to the home of his older sister Anne and her husband, George Howe, in Columbia, where his chief delight seemed to come from romping with his young nephew. The rest of Wilson's vacation was spent in Wilmington. As he wrote: "There are plenty of excursions on the river by moonlight, etc., yacht regattas on the sound, amateur concerts, etc., and plenty of pretty girls," but he preferred reading quietly at home. One of the reasons he did not go out into society more, he confessed, was that coming there but a few months before leaving for Princeton, he had never become well acquainted with people and was almost a stranger in his own home. During the summer all whose acquaintance he cared to cultivate were vacationing in the country or at some watering place. He was contented to keep quiet and aloof from "society." Wilson let his "inclination dictate each day's occupation, sometimes reading, sometimes writing, sometimes reading some great

[82]See Wilmington (N.C.) *Morning Star,* May 10, 11, 1876, for accounts of Memorial Day exercises.

orator's productions aloud in the large church [of] which father is pastor and which adjoins our premises."

Sometime during Tommy's upper-class period at Princeton, he and Charles Talcott, a fellow roomer in Witherspoon Hall, entered into an agreement—a Calvinistic "solemn covenant," as Wilson recalled, "that we would school our powers and passions for the work of establishing the principles we held in common; that we would acquire knowledge that we might have power; and that we would drill ourselves in all the arts of persuasion, and especially in oratory . . . that we might have facility in leading others into our ways of thinking and enlisting them in our purposes." Years later Wilson could still feel the glow and the pulsations of the hopes and the purposes of the moment and he still retained some of the faith that then prompted them.[83]

Moreover, Charlie and Tommy began saying to each other as they departed "see you in the Senate," or, of their future, "When I meet you in the Senate." Wilson even wrote out on some small cards that he distributed to members of the Princeton gang:

THOMAS WOODROW WILSON
SENATOR FROM VIRGINIA[84]

In the spring of 1879, Wilson's senior year at Princeton, he was handed an autograph book by a fellow southerner and classmate, Francis C. Garmany. In it he wrote:

Although our friendship has not been as close as our common sympathies would have warranted, I have always looked upon you, as I hope you have always looked upon me, as one on whose friendship sure reliance may be safely put. I, perhaps, am colder and more reserved than most of those who are fortunate enough to have been born in our beloved South; but my affection is not less real because less demonstrative. It shall always be my aim to claim and retain and, if possible, deserve love and intimate communion of all who yet cultivate the courage, chivalry, and high purpose which have hitherto been birthrights and most cherished virtues of Southern gentlemen: and among the number of these may I ever remember Frank Garmany.[85]

[83]Wilson to Ellen Axson, October 30, 1883, in Axson–Wilson Letters, Princeton.

[84]See Baker, *Wilson Life and Letters,* I, 104.

[85]See Francis C. Garmany's autograph book in Wilson Collection, Princeton. This was signed "Thomas W. Wilson."

In June, 1879, Tommy graduated from Princeton *sans honoris.* His family was not represented at the exercises. Dr. Wilson, who most certainly would have attended if he could have, was winning laurels as moderator of the Southern Presbyterian General Assembly in Louisville, Kentucky. Upon arriving in Wilmington, Tommy read with pleasure that his father's "rulings were prompt . . . the sting was taken from them by that inexhaustible fund of rich humor which was cropping out on all occasions." [86]

Almost a third of a century later, when delivering a baccalaureate address to the senior class at Princeton, Wilson referred with nostalgia to his four years as an undergraduate there. While admitting that many changes had occurred at the college in the intervening years, changes which he had done much to bring about, he stated that his work there had become part of the "very warp and woof" of his life. With obvious feeling Wilson, then president of Princeton, declared to the 1910 graduating class that in all the intervening years Princeton for him had never held what it did "in those magical years that ran their cheerful course from the exciting autumn year of 1875 to the gracious June, 1879. The four years of college life can never be repeated or reconstructed. They stand unique in every man's experience." [87]

[86] Louisville *Courier Journal,* n.d., quoted in Wilmington (N.C.) *Morning Star,* May 30, 1879.

[87] Woodrow Wilson, "Baccalaureate Address" at Princeton University, June 12, 1910, in Wilson Collection, Princeton.

CHAPTER III *Student of Law*

Upon graduating from Princeton in June, 1879, Tommy Wilson rushed home to the Presbyterian manse in Wilmington, where he sought relaxation. He felt keenly the effects of the strain of his last months at college, and informed Charles Talcott a few weeks later that he was feeling far from well. The parting with his few intimate friends after commencement had gone harder than he had anticipated. The separation, Wilson confessed, had "most emphatically and literally struck in." [1]

Talcott had completed his courses for graduation at the end of the first semester and had returned in June to be with his classmates. Both he and Wilson had chosen law as their profession, and naturally expected to discuss this subject when they met at commencement. But apparently their future was not then mentioned. "I expect you thought it a little queer," Tommy wrote,

[1]Wilson to Charles A. Talcott, July 7, 1879, photographed copy in Baker Papers, Library of Congress.

"that I did not some time during commencement speak to you *definitely* upon the subject which had principally engrossed our thought in correspondence which followed upon your early graduation. I had promised myself an opportunity of doing so when you should return and yet I didn't." The explanation was embarrassment. When Wilson was with anyone in whom he was especially and sincerely interested, the hardest subject to discuss was that which was nearest his heart; he could, however, speak plainly in writing.[2] Wilson had no definite plans for the work which they promised themselves, but he thought they should continue to improve their speaking styles and to increase their knowledge. Then, when the time came for them to work and to write for a cause, they would be able to command a hearing and raise themselves above the pettinesses of many in their profession. In Wilson's almost daily efforts at composition and voice training he tried to keep these things uppermost in his mind. "I speak freely to *you*," he confided to Talcott, "because you know me well enough to credit me with sincerity and acquit me of affectation—or mere talk." [3]

Tommy would soon cease these routine exercises for the Wilsons were about to embark on a trek to the mountains. Shortly, in company with his mother, his younger brother, his sister Anne and her three small children, he made a terrible journey by car and stage over rough, ill-kept mountain roads to Horse Cave. Located in North Carolina's westernmost corner, where the town seemed to intrude upon Tennessee and Georgia, Horse Cave was new territory for Wilson. There, perched high in the Blue Ridge, he found enjoyment in riding horses and exploring picturesque mountain roads.[4]

Occasionally, dark clouds crowded down close, hiding completely the green mountainsides and soaking the guests who ventured too far from shelter. By keeping the young Wilson in his room, the wet weather forced work on an article on France and the

[2]*Ibid.*

[3]*Ibid.*

[4]Wilson to Robert Bridges, July 30, 1879, in Dr. Karl A. Meyer Collection of the Correspondence of Woodrow Wilson and Robert Bridges in the Library of Congress, hereinafter cited as Meyer Collection, Library of Congress.

reading of some books which he had lugged to the retreat. Whether indoors or not, he longingly waited for letters from members of his Princeton gang.[5] When Bobby Bridges accused him of having already forgotten his classmates, Wilson retorted: "I wrote to you, you dear old rascal, a week or more ago," and urged Bridges to "apologize immediately for your unwarranted abuse of me." [6]

Bridges' letter reminded Wilson of the old confidential conversations they had at college which he valued as an aid and encouragement to their friendship—"for friends cannot be such in truth unless they *know* each other, every inch both of body and soul, unless their love is one of knowledge." Although the youths had left the "generous rivalries of college for the cold porch of the world," Wilson urged that they remain college boys and classmates. "We can keep our hearts open to each other," he wrote; "thank God, *our* interests need never clash!" [7] The intimate friendship with Bridges was to continue until Wilson's death nearly forty-five years later.

Wilson was at this time striving for authorship, and was producing some evidence of success. Henry Cabot Lodge, editor of the *International Review,* had recently published an essay "Cabinet Government in the United States," which Wilson had written during his senior year at Princeton. Now that Wilson's first article in an off-campus periodical was "just out" Bobby sent his and his father's congratulations. "I appreciate and value your father's judgment of my *International* article very highly indeed," replied the young author. "Please thank him for me. You are a partial witness—though I must confess to harboring a *little* satisfaction that my work is admired by my dear friend." [8]

Wilson's article was an admission of increasing uneasiness, if not outright fear, that the United States was experiencing a marked decline in statesmanship. There was a general distrust of Congress as the legislating body. Many thought the cause of widespread discontent with the national legislative body lay in

[5]*Ibid.*

[6]Wilson to Bridges, August 8, 1879, in Meyer Collection, Library of Congress.

[7]*Ibid.*

[8]*Ibid.* For Wilson's article, consult *International Review,* VI, 146–63.

the principle of universal suffrage, but Wilson declared that "the right of every man to a voice in the Government under which he lives" was America's greatest claim to political honor. The real difficulty lay in the absorption of power by irresponsible legislature. The government, said Wilson, was practically run by the forty-seven standing congressional committees, a policy "vacillating, uncertain, [and] devoid of plan or consistency."

The young author felt that the remedy for such a situation lay in giving to the heads of the executive departments—the members of the President's cabinet—seats in Congress, "with the privilege of the initiative in legislation and some part of the unbounded privileges now commanded by the Standing Committees." Indeed, the cardinal feature of cabinet government was responsible leadership—the leadership and authority of a small body of men who had won the foremost places in their party by a display of administrative talents, as well as by evidence of high ability upon the floor of Congress in the stormy play of debate. The highest order of responsible government, argued Wilson, could be established only by forcing upon the President the necessity of selecting his cabinet from among the representatives already chosen by the people or by the state legislatures. Moreover, when responsible ministers, chosen by the Chief Executive, formed the policies of their parties, the strength of those parties would be at their command, and the course of legislation would turn upon the acceptance or rejection by the two houses of the policies which they had determined. A responsible ministry, Wilson believed, would constitute a link between the executive and the legislative branches of the government which was "absolutely necessary in a well-regulated, well-proportioned body politic."

Would responsible cabinet government revitalize the development of American statesmanship? That was the crux of the problem. While admitting that to supply the conditions of statesmanship was beyond his power, Wilson declared that he could take cold consolation from the hope that times of peril would provide strong leaders worthy of the most implicit confidence.[9]

[9]This provocative essay is in Baker and Dodd (eds.), *The Public Papers of Woodrow Wilson: College and State* (New York, 1925), I, 1942.

Obviously, this young intellectual was more convinced that statesmanship had been steadily dying out in the United States than he was assured that he had found the method of creating an environment in which a vigorous statesmanship would be restored.

Having experienced the recent pleasure of seeing his essay in print, Wilson was busy preparing another. In the main, its thesis was that the French Revolution was really yet in progress, "the 'revolutions' of this century being only natural convulsions making the turning points, or crises, of a social and political change which was as inevitable as it has been powerful." [10] In time, after careful revision, the article went to editor Lodge for publication in the *International Review*. The author was not greatly surprised when his essay was rejected, confessing to Bobby Bridges that "the article was far from good; it had no *glow* about it." [11]

The Wilsons went back to Wilmington in late September, in time for Tommy to pack his belongings for a journey to Charlottesville and the University of Virginia, where he would enter the law school. In choosing to become a lawyer he was opposing the wishes of his father who had repeatedly urged him to enter the ministry. As he confided to his fiancée: "The profession I chose was politics; the profession I entered was the law. I entered the one because I thought it would lead to the other. It was once the sure road; and Congress is still full of lawyers." [12]

The University of Virginia in the late 1870's was nourished by the spirit of its founder, Thomas Jefferson. Wilson differed from most post-Civil War southerners of his generation in that he actually opposed many of the Jeffersonian principles; in his youth he was more a disciple of Alexander Hamilton. Only after years of reading, study, and writing would he tear himself away from this Hamiltonianism.

On October 2, 1879, Wilson signed the bursar's record book and

[10]Wilson to Bridges, August 8, 1879, in Meyer Collection, Library of Congress.

[11]Wilson to Bridges, September 4, 1879, in *ibid.*

[12]Wilson to Ellen Axson, October 30, 1883, in Axson–Wilson Letters, Princeton.

thereby formally entered the university of his native state.[13] The total enrollment at Charlottesville in the session of 1879–80 was 328 students of whom 79 were in the law school. The law faculty consisted of two men, John Barbee Minor and Stephen O. Southall. Professor Minor, then head of the law school, was "a *perfect* teacher," according to Wilson—"I can say with perfect sincerity that I cannot conceive of a better." [14] Professor Minor was "a remarkable Shakespearian and Biblical scholar," [15] one of the most learned men Wilson had ever come in contact with. Indeed, his association with this gentlemanly scholar and superb teacher was possibly the most lasting influence that he encountered at the University of Virginia.[16]

The most important course that Professor Minor taught and the one in which young Wilson enrolled was Common and Statute Law. The textbooks he was required to read were Minor's *Institutes of Common and Statute Law,* Blackstone's *Commentaries,* and Stephen's *On Pleading.* Wilson's other courses included Southall's classes in Equity, in Mercantile and International Law, and in Government.

Although Wilson was fortunate in having intellectual giants as teachers, he apparently did not approach the study of law with enthusiasm. From the beginning he regarded his law courses as "unutterable bores." [17] He went through the drudgery of these classes only because they were required for admission to the bar, and law was the gateway into the American political arena.

To his friend Charles Talcott, the legal neophyte revealed himself: "Law is indeed a hard task-master. I am struggling hopefully but with not *over* much courage, through its intricacies and am swallowing the vast mass of its technicalities with as good a

[13]See Bursar's record book, 214, in the Rare Book Room, Alderman Library, University of Virginia. Although Wilson signed his name Thomas W. Wilson on October 2, 1879, the next year he altered it to T. Woodrow Wilson. *Ibid.,* 231.

[14]Wilson to Bridges, November 7, 1879, in Meyer Collection, Library of Congress.

[15]David Culbreth, *University of Virginia* (New York, 1908), 431.

[16]"Woodrow Wilson's Student Days at the University of Virginia," *University Magazine,* XLIII (March, 1913), 295.

[17]Baker, *Wilson Life and Letters,* I, 116.

grace and as straight a face as an offended palate will allow." He had no idea of abandoning the study of law merely because of its unpleasant features. Anyone would prove himself a fool who expected to find any work that was worth doing easily done. Assuming this to be true, still one may be permitted an occasional complaint, if for no other purpose than to relieve his feelings. Therefore, wrote Wilson, "I wish now to record the confession that I am most terribly bored by the noble study of Law sometimes, though in the main I am thoroughly satisfied with my choice of profession." It was the want of variety that disgusted him. If only law could be served with some of the lighter and spicy sauces of literature, it would no doubt be an exceedingly palatable dish. As Wilson himself expressed it, "this excellent thing, the Law, get as monotonous as that other immortal article of food, *Hash,* when served with such endless frequency." [18]

In the fall of 1879, the student body of the University of Virginia included several young men of promise. There were, for example, William Cabell Bruce, later to represent Maryland in the United States Senate; LeRoy Percy, afterwards to win a Mississippi seat in the Senate; Robert Heath Dabney, soon to be Wilson's intimate friend and later dean of the Graduate School at the University of Virginia; William Echols, Jr., destined to serve a long tenure as a professor at the same institution; Richard E. Byrd, a native Virginian, who would be eclipsed in fame by his two sons in the twentieth century; and John Bassett Moore, destined for distinction in international law. As Wilson stated, "there are men here from all parts of the South and East—some from the West." Despite the cosmopolitanism of the place, one felt that the intellectual forces of the South were forming there. Indeed, the university was looked upon in this area "much as Oxford or Cambridge is regarded in England or Harvard in New England." [19] Nor was Wilson himself a complete nonentity when the doors of the law school opened to him. As author of the recently published "Cabinet Government in the United States," Wilson

[18]Wilson to Talcott, December 31, 1879, in Baker Papers, Library of Congress.

[19]Wilson to Bridges, November 7, 1879, in Meyer Collection, Library of Congress.

was soon sought after on the campus. When he entered the university library, he noticed a copy of the periodical containing his article on the main table.[20]

During Wilson's first few weeks on the Charlottesville campus, he was repeatedly contrasting and comparing the University of Virginia with Princeton. They were totally different in almost every respect. Virginia fellows were divided into innumerable groups of friends, but there were no *class* bonds to bind them together. The tendency, in such a community as the University of Virginia, was toward disintegration. Tommy wrote that "living within common limits and pursuing like ends, students are necessarily thrown together and have many sympathies in common." But, he said, there was nothing to replace class unity—and no college feeling existed except in a vague sort of way. If this was the unattractive side of the institution, there were many attractive features for the men attending the professional schools. As Wilson saw it, there was a great deal of freedom. "You are free to do just as you please," he wrote. Moreover, "the place was extensive, both materially, having long and picturesque ranges of buildings, and intellectually, there being every variety of mental activity." Study was a serious business and the loafer was the exception. Everyone had the highest regard for culture and scholarship. There was on all sides an "intelligent interest in matters of learning and a keen appetite for literary pursuits." While admitting that he did not altogether understand the university, Wilson was convinced that there was no pretense about it. It was in reality a university, with every branch a specialty. And there was definitely more thorough work done than the law student ever expected to see done by young men.[21]

These conclusions were not Wilson's final evaluation of the University of Virginia as an educational institution. Some weeks later on New Year's Eve, as he reflected over the recent months, he concluded that "the university was a splendid place for the education of the *mind* but not the sort of place for the educa-

[20]Baker, *Wilson Life and Letters,* I, 114.

[21]Wilson to Bridges, November 7, 1879, in Meyer Collection, Library of Congress.

tion of the *man.*" In other words, if students were regarded "as mere studying machines, with ambition or pride or necessity for motive power," it was a fine machine shop; but if one suspected that "man was not intended to live by the accumulation of knowledge alone, but by the satisfaction of his *heart* needs as well," then this institution was more or less a failure. A person had every opportunity of learning as much in numerous fields of knowledge as he could well cram into his head during an ordinary college course but, according to Wilson, opportunities for "moral growth and intellectual invigoration" such as those experienced by the men who met after prayer meeting in room number 9, East Witherspoon Hall at Princeton were "fewer and further between than the proverbial angel's visits." [22] The university was better suited to one who had completed his collegiate training than to a beginning freshman from preparatory school. The intellectual environment was conducive to mental effort and growth; it was the disregard for spiritual stimulation that shocked the newcomer from Wilmington.

Upon arrival at Charlottesville, Wilson found himself settled in room 158, House F, Dawson's Row, on the periphery of the university campus. For the first few days he knew practically no one, but shortly he was visited by members of the Phi Kappa Psi social fraternity to whom he had been recommended by Hiram Woods, a recent member of the same group at Johns Hopkins University. Because of the cost of becoming a fraternity man, young Wilson requested his father's permission to join the Phi Psi's.[23] "Of course we approve of your having joined the Greek society you spoke of," his mother replied for both parents.[24] The chapter had only eight members, but these were to the new member's liking. Previously, Wilson had written of his loneliness but now he made several friends. Indeed, he wrote Bobby Bridges, "I'm beginning to believe that it don't [*sic*] take me long to make

[22]Wilson to Talcott, December 31, 1879, in Baker Papers, Library of Congress.

[23]See Osborn, "The Influence of Joseph Ruggles Wilson on His Son," 519–43.

[24]Janet Wilson to Woodrow Wilson, October 28, 1879, in Wilson Papers.

friends, although I used to think myself so reserved as to be hard to become acquainted with." [25]

Phi Kappa Psi chose Tommy in the fall of 1879 to represent the chapter at the fraternity's national convention which met in February, 1880, in Washington, D.C. During the convention he met "a great many fine fellows from all parts of the country." His chief delight, however, was in seeing again Hiram Woods, now studying medicine at Johns Hopkins. After the convention was over Tommy went over to Baltimore with Woods to spend a weekend. "Some of the old Princeton spirit came over me," he confessed to Bridges, "and it was a rude breaking of the spell to have to come back here to the grind-stone once more." Even so, Wilson noted: "I really had no business to neglect my studies here and run off on a pleasure trip as I did but the temptation was too great to be regretted." [26] Subsequently, Wilson was chosen General President of Virginia's Alpha chapter of Phi Psi in the fall of 1880.[27]

The young law student joined the University Glee Club and found a place in the chapel choir. According to a contemporary critic, Wilson sang first tenor "with a harmonious sweetness peculiarly pleasing." [28] The glee club gave few public concerts during the period of Wilson's membership, but the chapel choir performed with far more regularity.

By no means was all of Tommy's time consumed in the concentrated study of his law courses, in the regular practices of his choral groups, and in the weekly meetings of the Phi Psi's. He found time to read quite a few books. There are some records which indicate his taste in literature. For example, soon after Wilson arrived at the university he received from his uncle, James Bones, several books, including Mill's *Political Economy,* Chitty's *Blackstone,* an edition of *The Federalist,* and Jebb's *Attic Ora-*

[25] Wilson to Bridges, November 7, 1879, in Meyer Collection, Library of Congress.

[26] Wilson to Bridges, February 25, 1880, in *ibid.*

[27] Charles W. Kent, "Woodrow Wilson's Undergraduate Days at the Virginia Alpha," in Harry S. Gorgas and James D. Campbell (eds.), *Centennial History of the Phi Kappa Psi,* 1852–1952 (Binghamton, N.Y., 1952), II, 168–74.

[28] Memo in Baker Papers, Library of Congress.

tors.[29] During 1880 he drew from the university library four books—Newman's *Chats,* Lecky's *Eighteenth Century,* Goodrich's *British Eloquence,* and Parson's *Contracts,* and several volumes of the *Congressional Globe* for the middle 1850's.[30]

Wilson had been active in literary society work in the Eumenian Literary Society at Davidson and in the Whig Literary Society at Princeton. At the University of Virginia he was among the students elected members of the Jefferson Literary Society on October 18, 1879.[31] Although the minutes of the society reveal that occasionally absurd or even silly questions were selected for debate, Wilson repeatedly "insisted upon fresh and practical themes about which people were thinking at that time," [32] such as "Have weak nations a right to combine and make war upon a powerful neighbor in consequence of her great accumulation of power?" and "Is Communism a natural result of democracy?" [33] According to the record, the first debate in which he took part was on February 18, 1880. He upheld the affirmative side of the question "Would a restriction of the suffrage ameliorate our political conditions?" [34] On this occasion, he had no political convictions which prohibited his arguing for a restricted suffrage.

Tommy had already acquired some reputation on the campus as an orator dating from December 20, when he was chosen to present medals to the winners of the various events in the university fall games—a campus-wide field day. The youthful orator began by reciting two love limericks that enjoyed great popularity in their day but which contained no reference to athletic prowess. After reciting these verses in a melodramatic manner, he "made a perfect little medal delivery speech" before he calmly handed the medals over to the victors. Without any further ado, he sat down. The athletes and the crowd of students who had gathered

[29] Baker, *Wilson Life and Letters,* I, 116.

[30] *Ibid.,* 117.

[31] See Minutes of the Jefferson Literary Society in the Rare Book Room, Alderman Library, University of Virginia.

[32] A. W. Patterson, *Personal Recollections of Woodrow Wilson* (Richmond, 1929), 8. Patterson was a classmate of Wilson's in the law school of the University of Virginia.

[33] See Minutes of the Jefferson Literary Society in the Rare Book Room, Alderman Library, University of Virginia.

[34] *Ibid.*

to witness the event "realized at once the incongruity of the speech and nearly mobbed the wag in their enthusiasm." [35]

With this example of Wilson's speech-making ability a topic of recent campus conversation, many expressed a desire to hear him deliver his oration. Consequently, the society decided to invite all who were interested to his oration on March 6. Ladies, seemingly for the first time, sat in the solemn precincts of the society's hall. "They began to come in shortly before seven o'clock and soon so many of the seats were occupied by the 'calico' and their escorts that those students who had not been prudent enough to come early were obliged either to stand up or to squat tailor fashion in the aisle." [36]

The orator of the evening chose the career of John Bright as his subject. "His opening sentences captivated his audience and he had spoken only a few minutes when his reputation as an orator was established. Inspired by the bright eyes and approving smiles of many fair visitors, he delivered his oration with an earnestness and vigor that drew down much well-deserved applause" at its conclusion.[37] The oration took about fifty-five minutes in delivery,[38] and was subsequently published in the *University of Virginia Magazine.*

Although Wilson confessed that he was "thoroughly scared," his fright was not evident.[39] He began by pointing out the dangers of following broad scopes of events and neglecting the achievements of individual persons. It was misleading, he said, to focus one's attention upon some one event or to sympathize with one man and ignore the circumstances out of which he sprang or the environment in which he moved. Then the young orator's speech turned to an evaluation of Bright, an English reform

[35]"Collegiana," *University of Virginia Magazine,* XIX (December, 1879), 193; "Woodrow Wilson's Student Days at the University of Virginia," *ibid.,* XLIII (March, 1913), 298.

[36]*University of Virginia Magazine,* XIX (March, 1880), 382.

[37]Patterson, *Recollections of Wilson,* 7; Minutes of the Jefferson Literary Society, March 6, 1880, Rare Book Room, Alderman Library, University of Virginia.

[38]Wilson to Talcott, May 20, 1880, in Baker Papers, Library of Congress.

[39]Wilson to Bridges, February 25, 1880, in Meyer Collection, Library of Congress.

leader, and his forensic ability. "His words were tapers, which, lit at the fire of his convictions, first made visible and then dispelled the darkness of political selfishness and social tyranny." Wilson found Bright's supreme self-restraint to be the chief charm of his delivery. The reformer's diction, as self-restrained as the orator himself, was characterized by "simple dignity and supple strength. . . . It is scholarly, but never pedantic. His refined taste and natural good sense put him above the silly affectation of mere rhetorical glitter." [40]

Wilson's oration is significant not only for his critical evaluations of Bright as an orator and as a proponent of English liberalism, but because it contains a number of the young orator's opinions. Note Wilson's tribute to eloquence: "Eloquence is never begotten by empty pates. Groveling minds are never winged with high and worthy thoughts. Eloquence consists not in sonorous sound or brilliant phrases. *Thought* is the fibre, thought is the pith of eloquence. Eloquence lies in the thought, not in the throat." Or his comment on tolerance: "Tolerance is an admirable intellectual gift; but it is of little worth in politics. Politics is a war of causes; a joust of principles." The first prerequisite of successful leadership, said Wilson, was "absolute identity with one's cause." His opinion of a complete party loyalty was concise: "I would not . . . lend any color or justification to that most humiliating and degrading precept, 'Party, right or wrong.' This is the maxim of knaves, or of fools."

Unknown to the orator, on this occasion he gave a glimpse into the house of his own future. The lesson to be learned, concluded Wilson, was

> that duty lies wheresoever truth directs us; that statesmanship consists, not in the cultivation and practice of the atrs of intrigue, nor in the pursuit of all the crooked intricacies of the paths of party management, but in the life-long endeavor to lead first the attention and then the will of the people to the acceptance of truth in its applications to the problems of government; that not the adornments of rhetoric, but an absorbing love for justice and truth and a consuming, passionate devotion to principle are the body and soul of

[40]Wilson's oration on John Bright is found in Baker and Dodd (eds.), *Wilson Public Papers: College and State, I*, 43–59.

eloquence; that complete identification with some worthy cause is the first and great prerequisite of abiding success.[41]

While Wilson was gathering information and preparing material for his oration, he developed an admiration for William E. Gladstone, a contemporary of John Bright in English politics. The result was an essay on Gladstone in the April issue of the *University of Virginia Magazine.*[42] According to essayist Wilson, the most vital characteristic of Gladstone's nature was "his keen poetical sensibility," a "breadth of sympathy such as enables its possessor to take in the broader as well as the prettier concerns of life, with unconscious ease of apprehension and unfailing precision of judgment; to identify himself with interests far removed from the walks of his own life, to throw himself, as if by instinct, on that side of every public question which, in the face of present doubts, is in the long run to prove the side of wisdom and of clear-sighted policy; such a sympathy as makes a knowledge of men in him an *intuition* instead of an experience."

Soon after Wilson's character sketch of Gladstone appeared in print, the Jefferson Society held an important debate. Because of campus-wide interest the meeting was moved from the regular meeting place to a larger hall. William Cabell Bruce and Benjamin L. Abney upheld the affirmative and J. M. Harver and Wilson argued the negative of the question: "Is the Roman Catholic element in the United States a menace to American Institutions?" After Bruce's opening speech, Wilson began his argument. He declared that in this debate he had nothing to do with Roman Catholicism as a religion: "we deal with it as a *policy.*" He entered into a brief history of the expansion of the ancient Roman Empire and of modern Catholicism and noted that "where Roman generals had found abiding victory impossible, Romish priests found enduring success scarcely less impracticable." After discussing his side of the question and citing several legal cases to support his contentions, Wilson concluded by saying that Catholicism was not a menace to American institutions,

[41]*Ibid.*

[42]See the *University of Virginia Magazine,* XIX (April, 1880), 401–26. Although this article was signed *Atticus,* in the table of contents, located on the preceding page, *By Woodrow Wilson* is found opposite the title.

because the danger was proclaimed and we forearmed; because of the historical prejudices against Roman Catholic authority which were peculiar to our race; because of our spreading and enlarging and strengthening common-school system which is throwing about us the safe-guards of enlightenment; because of the unassailable defenses of *self-government.* Our liberties are safe until the memories and experiences of the past are blotted out and the *Mayflower* with its pilgrims forgotten; until our public-school system has fallen into decay and the nation into ignorance, until legislators have resigned their functions to ecclesiastical powers and their prerogatives to priests.[43]

J. W. Mallett, chairman of the Faculty Committee on Awards, stated that "two of the contestants had shown remarkable excellence," but that the medal for the best debater should go to Bruce. For the committee, Professor Mallett expressed enthusiastic approval of Wilson's merits as a speaker of high oratorical ability for which honor a second medal was awarded.[44] Whereupon the young Wilson revealed one of the ugly traits of his personality, a trait which was to remain a part of his makeup throughout his life. He showed "keen disappointment and indicated his purpose to decline the orator's medal, saying that he made no pretensions to oratory." He declared that he was a debater, the best debater or nothing, and that his "acceptance of such a trophy was absurd." His friends in the society urged him to acquiesce, and he finally agreed to accept second place.[45]

These medals were presented by the president of the university to the victors during the commencement exercises. According to the New York *Herald,* the young Wilson in his acceptance speech made "an earnest and able protest against the style in which all of the literary societies were conducted, and pleaded for the discussion of living questions and the making of the societies training schools of statesmen as well as orators." [46] "College societies," said Wilson, "if not vain and useless affairs, must prepare for life. Life and its demands are different from what they once

[43]*University of Virginia Magazine,* XIX (April, 1880), 448–50. This summary of Wilson's debate is in Baker and Dodd (eds.), *Wilson Public Papers: College and State,* I, 60–62.

[44]"Collegiana," (May, 1880), 524–25.

[45]Patterson, *Recollections of Wilson,* 15.

[46]New York *Herald,* July 1, 1880.

were; the societies must be different." [47] He called his audience's attention to the practice at Oxford University of having a political debating society organized and conducted like a great national assembly—a House of Commons—in which its members learned to express themselves fluently and readily on any great question of public policy. "Habitual discussion of political measures," declared Wilson convincingly, "are as necessary as any scholastic course." He satirized the ignorance of many leading politicians and urged the importance of teaching young men the principles of government. "Free discussion," he argued, "must liberate us from political bondage." Wilson's speech was "the best oration which had been delivered by a student at the university for many a year," concluded the Richmond *Daily Dispatch*.[48]

Such recognition of young Wilson's efforts were proof of his capacities for leadership and of his renown as a leader on the campus. However, one must not conclude, as some of Wilson's biographers have, that he was the *foremost* leader of the campus. Mention has been made of the second place medal in the most important campus debate of the scholastic year. In the 1880 Joint Societies Celebration, held during the June finals, Professor Francis H. Smith, chairman of the faculty committee to award a gold medal to the writer of the best article published in the *University of Virginia Magazine* during the year, declared the decision of the committee as follows: "John Randolph of Roanoke: A Sketch" by William Cabell Bruce. Unstinted praise, however, was given by the faculty committee to the articles "John Bright" and "Mr. Gladstone: A Character Sketch" by Thomas Woodrow Wilson.[49] In both fields of oral and written discourse Wilson was forced to accept second place. Obviously, Bruce not Wilson, held first place in literary leadership on the campus.

As busy as Wilson was during the spring months of 1880 debating, preparing orations, writing articles for publication, driving himself to the boresome study of his law courses, he occasionally penned long letters to his former Princeton friends.

[47]Richmond *Daily Dispatch,* July 1, 1880.

[48]*Ibid.;* Wilson to Bridges, August 22, 1880, in Meyer Collection, Library of Congress.

[49]*University of Virginia Magazine,* XX (October, 1880), 50–52.

He was provokingly busy; not that the work was too difficult, but it seemed to be spread over the entire twenty-four hours of every day. In such an environment the Princeton days seemed far away. "But the memory of that dear old crowd," he hastily added, "can never die." Its influence was permanent. Indeed, his love for every one of those chums was "as real and as intense as ever one brother felt for another." [50] To Bobby Bridges, Wilson confessed his friendship and his dreams. "It is my sincerest hope that our friendship may be life long and it's my brightest dream that you and I will some day be co-laborers in a great work of disseminating political truth and purifying the politics of our own country." Bridges was far ahead in his readings on political science, but Wilson promised that when he got out of his treadmill of law he would devote "every scrap of leisure time to the study of that great and delightful subject."

Not only did Wilson have this vision for the future, but he proposed an immediate plan which he thought would aid in achieving his dream. "Let's correspond often and at length upon any topics of history or political science that may suggest themselves to us as susceptible of discussion." In this way they would clear and settle their beliefs, and would keep their acquaintance with each other. Wilson admitted that he was dependent on intellectual sympathy and believed that if they diligently followed the course he proposed, they would build a friendship more valuable to them in the future "than all the knowledge of books." "Let's keep our minds and hearts open to one another," he pleaded, "and the college friendship which we look back upon with happy recollection will ripen into a fellowship even more blessed and profitable." This was no sudden idea. To the young law student it was not a mere visionary hope, but a real definite desire and purpose.[51] Perhaps to no other man, with one possible exception, did Wilson keep his mind so completely open and his heart so unreservedly exposed as he did to Bobby Bridges.[52]

[50]Wilson to Bridges, February 25, 1880, in Meyer Collection, Library of Congress.

[51]*Ibid.*

[52]Years later, 1912–19, Wilson was to maintain such a friendship with Colonel Edward M. House, but only for a relatively brief period of less than seven years.

The exception was R. Heath Dabney. As fraternity brothers at Charlottesville, Dabney and Wilson could be seen frequently leaving the campus for long walks in the nearby valleys or along ascending paths that led into the Blue Ridge Mountains. There they revived the Wilsons' custom of reading aloud some of the best orations or books of mutual interest. The two young Virginians eagerly engaged in a friendly contest to determine which could call the other by the more opprobrious name. After repeated efforts they mutually agreed that Tommy's title would be "illimitable idiot," and for Heath Tommy could think of nothing worse than "thou very ass!" Occasionally these absurd and boyish titles were found in their intimate letters, as was the case when twenty-five years later Wilson was unanimously chosen by the Board of Trustees to be president of Princeton University. "Who would have 'thunk' it?" wrote Dabney jestingly. "Who could have guessed that an illimitable idiot would ever be selected as the President of a great university?!" [53] The friendship with Heath was the only enduring attachment that Wilson made during the fifteen months at the University of Virginia. In complete loyalty, Wilson near the end of his life penned a note of affection to his old friend: "The faith of an old friend like yourself affords me the sort of refreshment and support which I need in these days of slow recuperation." [54]

If Tommy Wilson could love a few people intimately, he could also heartily hate or utterly despise. There was little lukewarmness about his nature. The young Tommy, as the older Wilson, could never show anything but an icy politeness for a rival, especially if the rival revealed talents of leadership equal to, if not better than, those which he himself possessed. Between Wilson and William Cabell Bruce, his chief competitor in the university, there never was anything but the most strained and formal relationship.[55] Apparently, Tommy never realized that he might gain something in intellectual development or in personality growth by cultivating a friendship for one upon whom nature

[53] R. Heath Dabney to Wilson, July 20, 1902, in Robert Heath Dabney Papers, Alderman Library, University of Virginia.

[54] Wilson to Dabney, December 22, 1922, in Dabney Papers, Virginia.

[55] Baker, *Wilson Life and Letters,* I, 129.

had smiled as benevolently as upon himself when that person was pitted against him in any kind of rivalry.

This sense of preparation for something great in the future continued to possess Wilson. Moreover, he delighted in it: "Those indistinct plans of which we used to talk," he confided to Charles Talcott, "grow on me daily, until a sort of calm confidence of great things to be accomplished has come over me which I am puzzled to analyze the nature of. I can't tell whether it is a mere figment of my own inordinate vanity, or a deep-rooted determination which will be within my power to act up to." [56] For the present he was contented with the consciousness that he had such a vision; its exact nature and just what it portended for the future he was willing to leave alone.

The year 1880 was a presidential election year. Charles Talcott witnessed the New York Republican convention and in a letter denounced the affair to Wilson, who shared his viewpoint. "One can never enjoy reading of anything which is his country's curse," Wilson replied tersely. He went on to explain that "this convention system is not so old as one would be led to suppose from the amount of mischief it has worked." The country was, he hopefully believed, "gradually waking to a full knowledge—and hence an unutterable disgust of its methods." Wilson's youthful enthusiasm was wrong when he stated that "things are rapidly ripening for a radical change which will soon be imperatively demanded." He believed that change would mean improvement. "Let us hope," he said, "that the change will be for the better. I believe it will, if our English blood be not altogether corrupted by the infusion of foreign elements. The more open and notorious these corrupt methods of party management, the sooner the deliverance, and the more tremendous the indictment against them," was his concluding indictment.[57]

This was not Wilson's last condemnation of party conventions for the nomination of candidates for the Presidency and the Vice-Presidency. As President-Elect in February, 1913, he was just as determined against them as he had been as a young law student. "There ought never to be," he stated in 1913, "another

[56]Wilson to Talcott, May 20, 1880, in Baker Papers, Library of Congress.
[57]*Ibid.*

presidential nominating convention; and there need never be another. Several of the states," he continued,"have successfully solved that difficulty with regard to the choice of their governors, and Federal law can solve it in the same way with regard to the choice of Presidents." It was his mature judgment that nominations should be made directly by the people at the polls. Political conventions need not be eliminated completely, but Wilson contended that they "should determine nothing but party platforms and should be made up of men who would be expected, if elected, to carry those platforms into effect." [58]

During the 1880 campaign, the young Wilson did not take the political stump to proclaim the virtues of the candidates of his party. Despite his public silence his interest in politics and political issues was keener than ever, as he explained it, "because my rustication has for many weeks shut me off from all accurate knowledge of the course political events were taking." As for Wilson's ideas on the American political scene shortly before the Garfield–Hancock contest, he was "inclined to think that nothing but the power of prophecy would enable one to throw any *light* on this subject just at present." The country, according to the law student, was "nearing the close of a period of *transition*; . . . I firmly believe that the Republican party, is doomed to speedy death." That political organization had been going through not only a process of transformation "which has proved a process of degradation," but also through "a process of disintegration." Moreover, Wilson contended that the Democratic party stood in 1880 "just where the Republicans stood before the war" in that it advocated the same principles and possessed representatives of very similar purposes. As he viewed the political conditions on the eve of the election, he noted that the country had "the strange and ominous spectacle of, on the one side, a party departed utterly from the principles of its one-time greatest leaders, at war with itself, its only creed one of hatred for a section of their own country and their own people, and about to have torn from it its last title to regard—the possession of power: on the other side, a party turned from its early beliefs, allying itself, in its

[58]Wilson to A. Mitchell Palmer, February 5, 1913, in Wilson Papers, Library of Congress.

pursuit of power, with every damnable heresy—with Greenbackers as with protectionists—whose only claim to respect is that it is less impure than its opponent." [59] If Wilson painted an accurate portrait, was not such a state of political affairs only the confusion of the elements which preceded a great change of the political weather? The change that he foresaw came sixteen years later, in 1896, when the Democrats nominated William Jennings Bryan for President on a liberal, reform platform.

When vacation time arrived, young Wilson joined his family at Fort Lewis, Green Valley, in Bath County, Virginia. It was a delightful country of pure mountain air, splendid rural fare, very comfortable accommodations, and every facility for free, healthful, invigorating exercise. Young Wilson spent the summer in the way which just suited his tastes and rested him most—rambling through the woods, climbing, rowing.[60] He took few books with him, only Webster's *Great Speeches,* two volumes of *Bright's Speeches,* a Bible, and Bacon's *Essays.*[61] In fact, he wanted to keep away from books.

On his return to the university, Wilson found a room at 31 West Range, nearer his work. He was the first member to sign the Jefferson Society roll book in October, 1880, and at the first meeting of the society was nominated and unanimously elected president for the ensuing year. Seated in the chair, Wilson gave notice that he would at some future time introduce a resolution to appoint a committee for revising the constitution. The first known reference to Woodrow Wilson as "President Wilson" was in the society's minutes, October 16: "The House was called to order at 7 o'clock, President Wilson in the chair." [62] Although president of the society and therefore responsible for the resolution which created the constitutional revision committee, Wilson had no hesitancy in naming himself committee chair-

[59]Wilson to Talcott, October 11, 1880, in Baker Papers, Library of Congress.

[60]Wilson to Bridges, August 22, 1880, in Meyer Collection, Library of Congress.

[61]Wilson to Bridges, September 18, 1880, in *ibid.*

[62]See Minutes of the Jefferson Literary Society for the Session of 1880–81, in the Rare Book Room of the Alderman Library, University of Virginia. See also the Jefferson Literary Society Roll Book, 1856–86, Rare Book Room, Alderman Library.

man. This constitution, as others which Wilson influenced, emphasized order, conciseness, diffusion of executive power, and debate.[63] Drafting constitutions for debating societies was becoming one of Wilson's hobbies. He had been instrumental in making or remaking charters for literary societies at Davidson and at Princeton, and now at the University of Virginia.

These additional responsibilities in the Jefferson Society did not prevent Wilson from accepting the presidency—Grand Page, it was called—of the Phi Kappa Psi fraternity. This honor made further demands upon his time. Early in November, 1880, he also joined the Robert Fulton class in elocution and actively participated in its exercises.[64]

Later that term, Wilson contracted a severe cold which kept him in "stench and horrors" for almost a month and finally left him in the midst of the examination season "unfit for study and unable to afford any loss of time." When he consulted his family both parents replied. "Well, my Darling," his mother stated, "your father desires me to say to you that taking your state of health into consideration and the amount of work pressing upon you, . . . we both think that it is your *duty to come home.*" It was absolutely necessary that Tommy's health be attended to at once. The decisive father wrote curtly at the end of the letter: "pack up and leave." [65] Late in December, the ill student suddenly withdrew from the university and went home to recuperate. Wilson was not planning to return to school but would pursue his studies at home for the rest of the winter.[66] He felt that leaving the school was the most prudent step he could have taken. From his father's household in Wilmington, young Wilson wrote: "My doctor found my digestive organs seriously out of gear and has confirmed me in the belief that, had I remained at the University and there continued to neglect the systematic medical treatment of myself, I might have confirmed myself in

[63]Minutes of the Jefferson Literary Society for the Session of 1880–81, Rare Book Room, Alderman Library, University of Virginia.

[64]Memo in Baker Papers, Library of Congress.

[65]Janet Wilson to Woodrow Wilson, December 19, 1880, in Wilson Papers, Library of Congress.

[66]Wilson to Bridges, January 1, 1881, in Meyer Collection, Library of Congress.

dyspepsia and have fixed on myself a very uncomfortable future." [67]

It was not easy for Tommy with his weak physical constitution to leave the university. Although it lacked the charm of Princeton, it was a fine place. The absence of class bonds was compensated, he had decided, by the fraternities which bound the boys together "in very intimate and very delightful companionship." In leaving the university, the young Wilson lamented, "I am turning my back on college life which . . . is the very happiest a man can hope to lead. . . . I shall miss the exercises of the literary societies about as much as anything else. I've fallen fairly in love with speech making which is a real luxury after one struggles to the leadership . . . of a body of men and begins to realize that he can gain a hearing when others might find difficulty in doing so, and can, by an effort, change a vote while others fail to command their hearers' sympathies." He had spoken a great deal while at the university and had shown marked improvement over his "stilted Whig style." He was convinced, he wrote Bobby Bridges, that "an orator *is* made, . . . and if there be in me any stuff worth the making, I intend to make as much of an orator out of myself as indefatigable labor can bring out of the materials at hand." [68]

[67] Wilson to Dabney, February 1, 1881, in Dabney Papers, Virginia.

[68] Wilson to Bridges, January 1, 1881, in Meyer Collection, Library of Congress.

CHAPTER IV *First Romance*

Not all of the young Wilson's interests and activities while he was enrolled in the law school were political in nature. For the first time in his life he began to have serious thoughts socially. Across the Blue Ridge Mountains, nestled in the Shenandoah Valley, was Staunton, his birthplace. There in the fall of 1879, when Wilson first entered the University of Virginia, several of his cousins were attending the Augusta Female Seminary, which was housed in the old church where his father had once occupied the pulpit and where he himself had been baptized.[1] Tommy knew many people in Staunton; the town was full of old friends and family acquaintances. Moreover, he confided to Bobby Bridges, "I'm made much of because I'm my father's son; and I'm made much of with all the cordial warmth of Virginia hospitality."[2] One of the sources of warm hospitality was James Bones,

[1]Baker, *Wilson Life and Letters,* I, 129.

[2]Wilson to Bridges, February 25, 1880, in Meyer Collection, Library of Congress.

husband of Marion Woodrow, Tommy's aunt. Bones had recently purchased a house in Staunton, moved in his family, and established a home there. Transportation for the more than forty miles from Charlottesville across the Blue Ridge was no problem for Tommy, especially when he knew that he would always be welcomed at his Aunt Marion's.

Among the cousins attending the Augusta Female Seminary was the talented Harriet Augusta Woodrow, to whom he was soon attracted. Born on August 31, 1860, in Chillicothe, Ohio, Harriet was the eldest child of Thomas Woodrow, the favorite brother of Tommy's mother. From early childhood she made excellent grades in all of her studies and showed exceptional talent in music and in voice. During the fleeting years of youth and adolescence Wilson had seen Harriet several times on occasions of family visits, but it was not until his senior year at Princeton, when he was twenty-two, that he began to correspond with her. She spent the Christmas vacation in 1878 with the Wilsons in Wilmington.[3] Tommy, down from Princeton, warmly welcomed his cousin, who was now a beautiful young lady eighteen years of age. Under his father's roof, Tommy's cousinly regard was gradually becoming something more serious. Regular letters passed between them from the time they returned to their respective schools after the holiday. Unfortunately, few of the two hundred or more letters that they wrote to each other now remain.

By the time the young Wilson began his law courses at the University of Virginia, Harriet had already achieved success in the seminary across the mountains. Very soon after Tommy entered the university, he began spending weekends in Staunton. How delighted he was to be able to see more frequently his "darling cousin," as he often addressed her. It was soon after Wilson's first visit to the Female Seminary that Harriet's mother wrote her daughter: "You never have anything that is disagreeable in your life." [4] Apparently Hattie and Tommy's friendship had the approval of the family.

[3]Helen S. Woodrow to Harriet A. Woodrow, December 27, 1878, in Wilson Collection, Princeton. In thanking her daughter for the nice gifts which Harriet had made, the mother expressed amazement that her daughter found time to do so much.

[4]Helen S. Woodrow to Harriet A. Woodrow, October 16, 1879, in Wilson Collection, Princeton.

The Christmas vacation, 1879, found Tommy in the home of his Uncle James Bones, where Hattie was also a guest. The students at the university were given only Christmas Day off, but Wilson remained in Staunton for a week. As he wrote Charlie Talcott: "I was absent about a week—*taking* that much holiday. We were given only Christmas Day, but are not questioned severely if we take numerous vacations—only persistent neglect of College duties exposes one to the danger of being requested to withdraw." [5]

A vivid summary of this holiday vacation was found in a letter from James Bones to Wilson's mother: "We had a quiet but very pleasant Christmas and our chief enjoyment was in having dear Tommie with us for a week. He captivated all our hearts most completely, being such a manly, sensible, affectionate fellow. You certainly have great reason to be proud of your big boy. He can easily run over Saturday afternoon and return by the early Monday train in time for his lecture and has promised to come often. Hattie spent the week with us and she and Jessie [Bones] and Tommy had nice times together." [6]

In the spring of 1880, Tommy was busy meeting the demands of his law courses, participating in debates, giving orations in the Jefferson Literary Society, and writing two articles for the *University of Virginia Magazine,* but he confided to a Princeton chum that he was keeping his "resolve about visiting Staunton frequently." [7] In a letter to another friend he said that several times since Christmas he had broken the "monotony of constant study" by a trip of a day or two, generally Saturday and the Sabbath, up to Staunton. He enjoyed these trips immensely, especially as his cousins were "very sweet girls and their surroundings peculiarly interesting." [8] With the increasing frequency of Wilson's weekend visits and the flow of his letters in the late spring of 1880, Harriet was finding it increasingly difficult to have the long hours of diligent practice needed to prepare prop-

[5]Wilson to Talcott, December 31, 1879, in Baker Papers, Library of Congress.

[6]James Bones to Jessie W. Wilson, January 13, 1880, in *ibid.*

[7]Wilson to Bridges, February 25, 1880, in Meyer Collection, Library of Congress.

[8]Wilson to Talcott, May 20, 1880, in Baker Papers, Library of Congress.

erly for her part in the seminary's musical early in June. She was to appear on the program several times and was determined to perform well. When the appointed day arrived, Harriet did perform well and the musical was a grand success. Several of Tommy's cousins, students at the seminary, appeared on the program, but he made a fool of himself, he said, and "scandalized his other cousins" by applauding vociferously at the conclusion of Hattie's part.[9]

Not only did the romantic Wilson's repetitious visits to Staunton interfere with Hattie's academic demands, but *he* was almost expelled from the university for excessive absences. Early in June, 1880, the university warned that although he was "a very intelligent, appreciative student," he had been absent nine times in the last month, with the maximum of six allowed.[10] The young man's father had feared all along that Tommy's frequent absences "would end in grief." The son had acted "most imprudently and . . . the faculty would be deserving of censure if they should overlook so gross a breach of discipline." The young man, however, was assured that he had his parents' confidence and love because they knew his character. His father added: "You were foolish, not criminal. You were too independent, forgetting authority, and the necessity for it. Your head went agog." [11] After the official report the university did not disturb Wilson further.

The gods of fate for a time seemed to be conspiring to promote Tommy's first love. His mother decided that she would accompany her husband to Saratoga Springs the summer of 1880 and wrote Hattie's father of her dilemma. She did not know what to do with Tommy and young Joseph, since she was reluctant to leave things in Wilmington and there was not room for them at Fort Lewis. Thomas Woodrow replied by inviting the two boys to be their guests for the summer, and suggesting that they join

[9]Memo in Baker Papers, Library of Congress.

[10]University of Virginia to Wilson's parents, June, 1880, in Wilson Papers, Library of Congress.

[11]Joseph Ruggles Wilson to Woodrow Wilson, June 5, 7, 1880, in *ibid.* "Dismissal or suspension would be a punishment out of proportion with the offense," the father wrote, "but that some angry notice was taken of it was only proper and all the more your case, because (1) you are worth saving and (2) because your absences have been so frequent heretofore."

Hattie for the trip home. Apparently, however, the Wilson boys did not visit in the Woodrow family country house, nor did Hattie accompany her mother on a visit to Fort Lewis late in the summer where the youths eventually spent their vacation. Hattie knew the depth of Tommy's feeling for her. Realizing that she did not feel the same way about him, she chose not to encourage his affections by vacationing with him. When Jessie Bones visited the Wilsons at Fort Lewis during the summer, she upset Tommy with the news that his visits to Staunton during the preceding months had created idle gossip. Wilson wrote Hattie: "Why didn't you tell me of the annoyances to which you were subjected last winter in consequence of my too frequent visits to Staunton?" If he had for one moment so much as dreamed such a situation existed he would have foregone the great pleasure which those weekend trips gave him rather than have her embarrassed "by the reports of idle gossip." But, of course, he added "you could not have told me of such a thing!" [12]

In two letters to Robert Bridges penned during his vacation, the young Wilson spoke of his "summering off in the country, fifteen miles from a railroad, with only two mails a week" to acquaint him with goings-on in the world outside. With a family party he was spending the time in a quiet way which best suited his tastes and rested him most after a session at the university. Part of the day he spent reading, the rest of it passed as he rambled over the hilly terrain or rowed a canoe "on the pretty little stream" which ran almost at the foot of the hill on which the house stood.[13]

It was with a pang of sadness that Wilson returned to law school in September, 1880. His mother and his younger brother went from Fort Lewis to Charlottesville with him and remained for several days in a hotel in town while Tommy found lodgings in a new location—at 31 West Range. The new quarters, he wrote Hattie, were some distance from the ones he had occupied the session before, "and on the whole, much more pleasantly sit-

[12]Wilson to Hattie Woodrow, October 5, 1880, in Wilson Papers, Library of Congress.

[13]Wilson to Bridges, August 22, 1880, in Meyer Collection, Library of Congress.

uated." [14] He vowed to his cousin that he could spend his first evening in his new room in no better way than by writing to her. He was feeling lonely and disconsolate at having to plod through another long session in the law school and needed quite badly a long letter from her to brighten him up. Anticipating the future somewhat, he declared there was nothing that he dreaded more intensely than the possibility that they should drift apart now that they were separated without any immediate prospect of seeing each other again soon.

As for himself, Tommy stated that he was a great believer in absolutely free correspondence. He suspected that one might find out "almost, if not quite," as much about him from his letters as by associating with him, for he was very apt to let any thoughts or feelings slip more readily from the end of his pen than from the end of his tongue. The only difference, he informed his cousin, was that by associating with him one might discover his "unamiable traits much more clearly" than from what he had deliberately written. At any rate, since they could not possibly see each other frequently that winter, he could ask for no greater favor than that she would write him frequent letters full of herself—"I hope you won't think that I'm asking too much," he concluded.[15]

Most of Wilson's friends at the university whom he knew the preceding year had returned. In spite of the many new faces that he saw daily, everyone seemed "painfully natural here," he wrote. His fraternity had a much larger membership than previously, and Tommy tried desperately to forget his loneliness by entering into the Phi Psis' activities with renewed vigor. He did not plan to take as active a part in the Jefferson Literary Society's work as he had the preceding year. His law studies would, he feared, compel him to be a silent member of Old Jeff most of the session; but, he wrote, he felt that soon he would be "tempted into making a speech." [16]

Hattie probably informed her romantic cousin about the many dates that she had during the late summer after she returned to

[14]Wilson to Hattie Woodrow, October 5, 1880, in Wilson Collection, Princeton.

[15]*Ibid.*

[16]*Ibid.*

her home in Chillicothe. Perhaps Hattie's mother, during her visit to Fort Lewis, dropped hints or told Tommy frankly how many friends her talented daughter had. Whatever the case, it was in a somewhat retaliatory mood that he informed Hattie he was "going to be a systematic visitor of the young ladies" the ensuing winter. That would be his last college year, so he thought, and the next year he would be obliged to go into society—for which he must put himself in training. "I'm afraid," he admitted, "that I am sadly deficient in social accomplishments. I can't talk without anything to say. In fact, I'm always inclined to be mum just when I am most anxious to appear to an advantage by making myself interesting." There were, in fact, very few girls around Charlottesville that he cared to visit. Indeed, "not a single one" had any special attraction for him, he assured his cousin.[17]

Whether Tommy devoted too much time to visiting the young ladies, or whether he spent too many of his hours outside the classroom in work for his fraternity and literary society, or whether he strained his physical and mental facilities with too much study, or whether he became a victim of what physicians in the twentieth century were to call virus infection, cannot be well established. Whatever the cause or causes, his health was impaired and in December he left the university a sick young man. Although forced to drop out of school because of illness, Wilson did not lose sight of his exalted ambition for one moment: "My path is a very plain one," he wrote; "the only question is whether I will have the strength to breast the hill and reach the heights to which it leads. My end is a commanding influence in the councils (and counsels) of my country—and the means to be employed are writing and speaking. Hence my desire to perfect myself in both." [18]

Near the end of the young Wilson's third week at home, he informed Hattie that his health was improving, but slowly. Any rapid improvement was hindered by the miserable weather which was composed of a "succession of rains and damp mists." Indeed, during the almost three weeks since his return to Wilmington, he

[17]*Ibid.*

[18]Wilson to Bridges, January 1, 1881, in Meyer Collection, Library of Congress.

had seen only three days of sunshine. If the terrible weather prolonged delicate health, it also furnished Tommy "with a capital and a very acceptable excuse for not visiting" among his father's parishioners. Ill health and wet weather were enough to satisfy anybody that his stay at home was "compelled by the commonest prudence," he wrote. He had made only one social call and that was forced on him. At a service in his father's church a young lady's mother rushed up to speak to him and told him that he must call on Susie before she returned to her boarding school. "So on Susie I was forced to call," he confided to Hattie.[19]

With the advent of better weather Tommy planned to make more social calls. He had found Wilmington "full of new-fledged young ladies," most of whom had emerged from girlhood since the winter he spent there five years earlier, before he entered Princeton. Those older girls, whom he had known and called on the winter of 1874–75, were now nearly all married. He was just seventeen when the family moved to Wilmington, but because of his height and sedateness almost everyone thought him several years older; so he was invited out with fellows older than he. Now, a half decade later, he was all but without acquaintances of his own age. His mother, however, urged him to visit, and he looked forward to meeting again the girls whom he remembered only as children in his father's church. The prospect of much visiting was not an altogether pleasing one. However, the more he visited, the more he enjoyed visiting—at least when he had "interesting and intelligent people to associate with." [20]

A large box of books from the University of Virginia soon arrived, and Wilson reported to Hattie that he was arranging a study on the second floor of the Manse. Leaving the university without completing his law course, he assured her, would not cause him to suffer very much inconvenience professionally. His chief regret was that he was compelled to end his college days abruptly. He hated to say goodbye to campus life, which, after all, was about the happiest, "because the freest from care, that one can lead." But, then, he was anxious to get to work to hang

[19]Wilson to Hattie Woodrow, January 15, 1881, in Wilson Collection, Princeton.
[20]*Ibid.*

out his professional shingle, and to earn a good salary before his thirtieth year came. Consequently, his hopes for a bright future prevented his regretting more that "the past was the past." For the rest of Tommy's family, especially his father who was paying the bills for his son's education, the time would seem long before his ambitions could be realized.[21]

To Heath Dabney, Wilson reported that, although he was still far from well, he was steadily at work on the law and making very satisfactory progress. Having gone so far under competent university professorial guidance, he knew the landmarks of the subject well enough to enable him to explore it with an advantage. Between periods of studying law, he was "cultivating the acquaintance of some of the Wilmington girls," and occasionally figuring in some private musical entertainment "as one just risen in the firmament of vocal stars." Altogether, however, he was living a very humdrum student's life.[22]

Although Wilson was far from feeling completely well, time treated him kindly in the spring of 1881. He had nothing harder or more disagreeable to do than to read law according to his own devices. He was often in the company of young ladies who, if they were not always good conversationalists or skilled in entertaining, were at least uniformly good listeners.[23] Another task which Wilson assumed that spring was the teaching of Latin to his younger brother, Josie. "I had an idea," he wrote humbly, "that I knew a good deal about Latin until I came to teach it." [24]

Meanwhile, in Cincinnati, Hattie found new quarters and promptly informed Wilson of her new address. She was to spend the winter there, studying music at the conservatory. Such study, Tommy assured her, must be a delightful occupation. The ability to sing, he wrote, was a much rarer gift than the ability to play either upon the organ or the piano—"that is, the ability to sing *well*—and it oftener gives pleasure to a larger number of persons." The law student had never taken any lessons in singing and of late had been taking less pains than usual in cultivating his voice

[21]*Ibid.*

[22]Wilson to Dabney, February 1, 1881, in Dabney Papers, Virginia.

[23]Wilson to Dabney, March 22, 1881, in *ibid.*

[24]Wilson to Dabney, April 20, 1881, in *ibid.*

in that direction. He had been training his voice in other directions quite assiduously, however: "I practice elocution hard and systematically every day. I intend to spare no trouble in gaining complete command of my voice in reading and in speaking." Hattie must teach him something of what she was learning so they could sing together next summer, he wrote.[25]

Because of her conscience, Hattie refused to attend a concert on Sunday evening that was given by the music college faculty. "Isn't it sad," replied the Calvinistic Tommy, "to think how little respect is had for the Sabbath, not in Cincinnati only but in *most* of the cities of the country!" He assured her that a conscientious girl was shut out from a great many seemingly innocent pleasures. There was no pleasure in going to a Sabbath concert with an uneasy conscience as a companion. "So that, after all, one don't [*sic*] miss much real enjoyment by being conscientious," he affirmed. Moreover, if anyone could not "respect and honor your religion, his good opinion is scarcely worth having," he concluded.[26] Throughout the years ahead Wilson continued to hold in his thinking and to practice in his life a strict observance of the Sabbath.

The young Wilson revealed another facet of his personality in this interesting letter to Hattie. It was the occasion, in his father's church, for the regular annual Sabbath School picnic. Hitherto he had escaped these affairs as he was always away in May, but now he was "rather afraid of these *promiscuous* picnics. One is never sure of having a nice time at them, because one can never be sure of being able to pick one's company for the day." [27]

In addition to writing Hattie, Tommy studied his law books, read the papers, and practiced elocution for about an hour daily. His voice, he was sure, was fast improving under the treatment. In addition to the vocal exercises, he made frequent extemporaneous addresses to the empty benches of his father's church "in order to get a mastery of easy and correct elegant expression in

[25]Wilson to Hattie Woodrow, April 22, 1881, in Wilson Collection, Princeton.

[26]Wilson to Hattie Woodrow, May 10, 1881, in *ibid.*

[27]*Ibid.*

preparation for the future." He could sometimes almost see the church pews smile in approval at some of his opinions and deliverances.[28] During the spring there were all sorts of excursions and entertainments, in which Tommy went "pensively among the darlings" yet unmarried, and wondered how many years of comparative starvation would suffice to bring him enough law practice to think of risking his "fortunes in like ventures!" [29] He was much nearer risking his fortunes in the venture of matrimony than he thought when he penned that statement. In fact, his proposal of marriage to Hattie was only a few weeks away.

In August, Wilson left Wilmington for Columbia, South Carolina, to visit his sister Annie and her family. There he was joined by his cousin Jessie Bones, who recently had graduated from the Augusta Female Seminary.[30] Together they journeyed to Maysville, Kentucky, where they visited Tommy's older sister, Marion, and her family. Early in September, he and Jessie, "a very plump and pleasing person despite the lean suggestion of her [last] name," went to visit the Woodrows in Chillicothe. He was making a visiting tour among near relations previous to settling down to legal practice.[31]

The young Wilson who visited Hattie in September, 1881, was a tall, slender, deeply thoughtful young man who was very much in love. Within a few days after the arrival of Tommy and Jessie, a round of parties for the visitors began. He soon tired of the social whirl. At the third party, in the middle of a dance with Hattie, he suddenly asked her in whispered tones to go for a walk outside where they could talk alone. As they strolled arm in arm along the flower-bordered path that led to the gate, Wilson told Hattie how "dearly he loved her, that he could not live without her and pleaded with her to marry him right away." Although Hattie admitted that she had a deep affection for him, she said that she did not love him. Not wishing to hurt him unduly, she

[28]Wilson to Bridges, May [24], 1881, in Meyer Collection, Library of Congress.

[29]Wilson to Dabney, May 31, 1881, in Dabney Papers, Virginia.

[30]Wilson to Bridges, August 22, 1881, in Meyer Collection, Library of Congress.

[31]Wilson to Talcott, September 22, 1881, in Baker Papers, Library of Congress.

told him that "it would not be right for them to marry because they were first cousins." Before leaving home, Tommy had consulted his parents and received their approval.[32] He told Hattie that her father and mother also wished them to marry. Finally, she frankly confessed that she did not love him in the way he wished, that she could never love him in that way, and that she could not possibly marry him.[33]

Shortly after they returned to the dance, Wilson excused himself, went to his room, packed his bag, left his hostess' home abruptly, engaged a room at a hotel, and spent the night in agony.[34] There, after many sleepless hours, he wrote on a torn piece of yellow paper a last pleading note to her: "Now, Hattie, for my sake, and for your own, reconsider the dismissal you gave me tonight. I can not sleep tonight—so give me the consolation of thinking that there is still one faint hope left to save me from the terror of despair." He concluded "yours if you would." [35] But she would not!

At Wilson's urgent request, Hattie had another long talk with him the next morning. She repeated her opinions given to him the preceding night which, she stated, were final. She urged him to return to her home and continue the visit, but he was determined to leave Chillicothe on the first train. Both his Aunt Helen and Uncle Thomas expressed regrets at the sudden departure. Hattie's brother, Wilson, accompanied him to the railroad station. There they met Edward Freeman Welles, the handsome young man whom Hattie was later to marry, who was arriving from Marietta to attend one of the parties given in honor of Jessie and Tommy. The meeting of Edward and Wilson was cool and formal. Edward was amazed that the latter was leaving and

[32]Before leaving the university, Wilson wrote home about his love for Hattie and requested his parents' consent. His mother replied: "I find your father has a great admiration for her [Hattie] and my darling you need fear nothing in the way of disapprobation from him any more than from me!" Janet Wilson to Woodrow Wilson, December, 1880, in Wilson Papers, Library of Congress.

[33]Helen Welles Thackwell, "Woodrow Wilson and My Mother," *Princeton University Library Chronicle,* XII (Autumn, 1950), 13.

[34]*Ibid.,* 14.

[35]Wilson to Hattie Woodrow, September 19, 1881, in Wilson Collection, Princeton.

urged him to stay. Aside to Hattie's brother, Tommy concluded: "If the sentiment is not merely formal—as it probably was—it was not genuine. If he has any feeling at seeing me go away, it is probably a feeling of relief at getting me out of the way."[36]

A few hours later, from a hotel lobby in Ashland, Kentucky, Wilson endeavored to explain his hasty departure. "My Darling," he began, "I suppose that to many my abrupt departure . . . would seem a little hard to understand. . . . But I saw several reasons for doing so. One was that you seemed to desire it; another was that I thought . . . I owed it to you to leave matters . . . as they stand—to trust all to you; and yet I felt that, after the terrible nervous strain I had gone through, I would not be sure of having control enough over myself to leave the subject alone. So, to go away was the kindest service I could do you; and I did it *as such*, notwithstanding the tremendous effort it cost me."[37]

Eventually Wilson accepted the situation as inevitable. His revealing comments to Robert Bridges closed one of the most fascinating chapters of his early life.

> I have passed through an experience which has had a very deep effect upon me and which has made me feel all the more eager for the sympathy of my old and dearest friends. . . . I was on my way to Chillicothe, Ohio, to visit the family of my mother's brother, Thomas Woodrow, after whom I was named. . . . I was confirmed during my visit there, in a passion which had for some years been irresistably growing upon me—in love for my cousin, Hattie Woodrow. She went to school in Virginia . . . and it was there during my first winter at the University of Virginia that I was first attracted to her. I never knew a handsomer, more intelligent, noble or lovable girl than she! After that winter in Virginia we corresponded regularly until my visit last summer. I then, as in honor bound, told her of the character of my love for her—and she, with such assurances as led me to believe that she did so only because of our near blood-relationship, refused me.

"Now Bobby," Tommy confided, "I've related this experience to you in a very bungling, incoherent way, but I know that you will appreciate the embarrassment under which I write. You are the only person, outside the circle of my own nearest kin, to whom

[36]Wilson to Hattie Woodrow, September 20, 1881, in *ibid.*
[37]*Ibid.*

a word of this matter has been breathed; and I need not tell you that even at this distance of time I am unable to speak of it without such a feeling as makes clear expression next to impossible. You know me well enough to believe that," he continued, "although not quickly excited, my love is all the more vehement when once aroused; and you can, therefore, readily understand the suffering I have undergone during the last few months. My disappointment has been the keener and the less endurable because of the conviction that my cousin really loved me as much as I could have desired and rejected me only because of a prejudice which made her regard it as her duty to do so. Of course, I am not such a weakling as to allow myself to be unmanned even by a disappointment such as this; I have already in great part recovered from the shock, but, naturally, my work has been considerably broken in upon, and you will not be surprised to find that I am not yet in Atlanta. For various reasons I have postponed my departure thence until May." [38]

[38]Wilson to Bridges, March 15, 1882, in Meyer Collection, Library of Congress.

CHAPTER V *Failure at Law*

A few weeks after withdrawing from the University of Virginia in December, 1880, Wilson was giving some thought to the question of where he should locate as a lawyer. Having chosen politics as a profession, he wanted to begin practicing law where he would be advantageously situated to enter the political arena. As he himself stated, "the principal, if not the only consideration that makes me hesitate in my choice between the North and the South as a place in which to begin my professional work is that in the South I would have more immediate prospects of gaining an influence over political opinion." [1] True, the North offered more abundant opportunities for professional favor and for lucrative employment. Possibly, one other consideration was Wilson's romance with his cousin Harriet. Years later, Hattie's daughter

[1]Wilson to Bridges, February 21, 1881, in Meyer Collection, Library of Congress.

wrote that Wilson told her mother "that if she would marry him he would practice law in any Northern city which she might prefer." [2]

However, as Wilson wrote in 1881, his political ambition was the determining factor: "In political *principles,* in genuine political opinions honestly held, in political tendencies, and in the broader phases of party movements I become more and more interested day by day." As a native southerner, he was especially interested in the trend of opinion shown in the southern press. He was "gratified beyond measure," he said, "to hear of the liberal and independent tone taken by leading Southern journals." He was particularly glad that the Atlanta *Constitution* was prominent among the leading advocates of "these old principles made new and fitted to a re-forming society. I think it more than probable," the law student continued, "that I will finally settle upon Atlanta as my place of practice and, therefore, it is satisfactory to know that its leading journal is supported in such opinions—for I don't believe that the Atlanta *Constitution* ever freely consents to support any doctrines which are not acceptable to the majority of its subscribers." [3]

While admitting that Atlanta was not in every respect an attractive place, Wilson realized that it was one of the largest and most prosperous cities of the New South. Having made the decision to remain in the South, he declared that he did not think he could do better than to settle there.[4]

Wilson did not feel that he was very well equipped for the bar, and said as much, but he knew enough of law to be able to find whatever information he desired on any particular point. Moreover, he said, everyone who entered the profession of law must be content to begin on small accumulations of knowledge—"*mastery* in any department being of necessity a thing which only many years of close and ceaseless labor can achieve." He had determined to seek admittance to the bar early the following year—1882.[5]

[2]Thackwell, "Wilson and My Mother," 60.

[3]Wilson to Bridges, May 24, 1881, in Meyer Collection, Library of Congress.

[4]*Ibid.*

[5]Wilson to Bridges, August 22, 1881, in *ibid.*

During the winter of 1881 and the spring of 1882, Wilson worked hard at his law books. During this period, too, he was making the final selection of the signature that was to be official for the rest of his life—Woodrow Wilson. So many explanations have been offered by Wilson biographers for the deletion of his first given name, Thomas, that a brief analysis of the evolution of the name Woodrow Wilson might not be amiss.

As has been noted, he was christened Thomas Woodrow, but was called Tommy by his parents, his older sisters, and his youthful playmates from the first. This nickname he used until some time after he graduated from Princeton. Moreover, most of the letters that have been preserved which were written before his twenty-third year were signed "Tommy" or, infrequently, "Tommie," or, more formally, "Thomas W." or "T. W. Wilson." [6]

In the autumn of 1876, "T. W. Wilson of Wilmington, North Carolina," entered Princeton College.[7] As soon as Tommy established his school routine, he, as "T. W. Wilson," joined the Whig Literary Society; however, on every occasion that he served on the Whig program as a debater, his name as recorded in the minutes was "T. Wilson." During his student days at Princeton, he decided upon a career in politics, and wrote on cards which he distributed among his classmates "Thomas Woodrow Wilson—Senator from Virginia." [8]

In tracing the evolution of Wilson's name one cannot omit the early articles that he published. In his first appearances in print he chose to remain anonymous. Later, in articles published in the *Nassau Literary Magazine* in 1878 and the off-campus *International Review* in 1879, he used the name "Thomas W. Wilson." When he graduated from Princeton he had not begun to sign his name "Woodrow."

According to the bursar's record of the University of Virginia, where Wilson went in the fall of 1879 to study law, he matriculated as "Thomas W. Wilson." By the time he returned a year

[6]See letters in Wilson Papers, in Baker Papers and in Meyer Collection, all in Library of Congress; Wilson Collection, Princeton; Dabney Papers, Virginia.

[7]Consult records in Princeton University Library. Photostatic copies are in the Baker Papers, Library of Congress.

[8]Baker, *Wilson Life and Letters,* I, 104.

later to continue his courses in legal education, his name had become "T. Woodrow Wilson." [9] He contributed an essay to the *University of Virginia Magazine* in April, 1880. Although "Mr. Gladstone: A Character Sketch" was signed "Atticus," in the table of contents the author was listed as "Woodrow Wilson," the first time that his name appeared publicly as it was to be permanently.[10]

Several letters penned by the young Wilson from the summer of 1879 to 1881 are still in existence. In letters to Charles Talcott he invariably signed his name "T. Woodrow Wilson;" [11] a postscript to one gives the reason: "I sign myself thus at mother's special request, because this signature embodies all my family name." [12] To Hattie Woodrow, his first love, he signed himself "Woodrow" or "T. Woodrow Wilson." [13]

In a personal letter to his good friend Robert Bridges, Wilson signed his name "Woodrow Wilson" and added: "You see, I am no longer "Tommy", *except to my old friends;* but have imitated Charley [Talcott] in taking the liberty of dropping one of my names, as superfluous." [14] The evolution of "Woodrow Wilson" was practically complete by 1882. As Wilson declared to Bridges: "You see I am gradually cutting my name down to portable size. I'll soon have to have a 'shingle' painted, and the shorter the name the shorter the painter's bill." [15] Exceptions to Wilson's final signature were to occur as late as June, 1885, when he signed "Thomas Woodrow Wilson." [16]

Why did Wilson, shortly before going to Atlanta to begin practicing law, finally decide on "Woodrow Wilson" for his name?

[9]Consult Bursar's Records in Alderman Library, University of Virginia.

[10]*University of Virginia Magazine,* April, 1880, 401–26.

[11]Wilson to Talcott, July 7, December 31, 1879, May 20, October 11, 1880, all in Baker Papers, Library of Congress.

[12]Wilson to Bridges, November [?], 1879, February 25, August 18, September 19, 1880, January 1, February 24, May 24, 1881, all in Meyer Collection, Library of Congress.

[13]Wilson to Hattie Woodrow, April 22, May 10, 1881, in Wilson Collection, Princeton.

[14]Wilson to Bridges, August 22, 1881, in Meyer Collection, Library of Congress.

[15]Wilson to Bridges, April 1, 1882, in *ibid.*

[16]Wilson to Thomas Woodrow, June 8, 1885, in Wilson Collection, Princeton.

Was it because a Princeton associate deleted one of his names? Did Wilson shorten his name in the interest of economy, as he stated? Both of these are explanations but were they the *real* reasons? Ray Stannard Baker concluded: "After going through all the permutations and combinations of 'Tommy' and 'Tom', 'T. W. Wilson', 'Thos. W. Wilson', 'T. Wilson' and 'T. Woodrow Wilson', the last of 'Tommy' drops away—sacrificed on the altar of euphony." [17] William Allen White declared that "Tommy" was dropped because it lacked dignity. Wilson himself, in a letter to Robert Bridges, said: "I find I need a trademark in advertising my literary wares. Thomas W. Wilson lacks something—Woodrow Wilson sticks in the mind. So I have decided publicly to be Woodrow Wilson." [18] Yet another biographer has suggested that the longer signatures were altogether too lengthy, too commonplace, too lacking in distinction. "Woodrow Wilson" was brief, alliterative, and easy to remember.[19] There is one other possibility. Wilson's decision to drop the "Thomas" from his name was made at the time when his love for his cousin ended in rejection. Did he retain only "Woodrow" in sentimental remembrance of his first romance? If so, Hattie Woodrow, in rejecting Tommy Wilson's proposal of marriage several months before he moved to Atlanta, left a lasting mark on his career.

During the decade before Wilson decided to begin his law practice there, Atlanta, under the leadership of such men as Henry W. Grady, was setting the pattern for population growth in the New South. This city, Wilson wrote Talcott, "more than almost every other Southern city offers all the advantages of business and enterprise. Its growth has during late years been wonderful . . . and then, too, there seem to me to be many strong reasons . . . for my remaining in the South. I am familiar with the Southern life and manners, for one thing—and of course a man's mind may be expected to grow most freely in its native air. Besides, there is much gained in growing up with the section of

[17]Baker, *Wilson Life and Letters,* I, 137. Baker is wrong in saying Wilson never signed anything but "Woodrow Wilson" after 1881. There were some examples of variations, but not many. I found none after 1885.

[18]William A. White, *Woodrow Wilson: The Man, His Times, and His Task* (Boston, 1924), 89.

[19]Harold G. Black, *The True Woodrow Wilson, Crusader for Democracy* (New York, 1946), 38–39.

the country in which one's home is situated and the South has really just begun to grow industrially." [20]

In 1882 there were 37,000 people in Atlanta, of whom about one fourth were Negroes. If Wilson was attracted to this thriving city by evidences of opportunity for one ambitious in the law and politics, others were drawn by similar possibilities. Nowhere else in the South, at that time, were there so many young, ambitious lawyers as in the Georgia capital. Indeed, the city directory of 1883 carried a list of 143 lawyers, about one for every 270 people.[21] Apparently, Woodrow did not investigate what some had termed the over-supply of lawyers in Atlanta.

When Edward Renick, a recent law student at the University of Virginia who had begun his practice in Atlanta, heard of Wilson's decision to "hang out his legal shingle" there, he invited the fellow Virginian to office together and share expenses. Renick had shared his office with a talented North Carolinian, Walter Hines Page, but Page was gone and he was lonesome. Before his arrival in Atlanta, Wilson agreed to share Renick's law office. It was on the second floor of a building at 48 Marietta Street, opposite the Georgia Supreme Court, the State Capitol (containing the State Library), and the Post Office, and easily accessible to any clients searching for a lawyer.[22]

Once in Atlanta, Wilson began taking his meals at the home of Mrs. J. Reid Boylston, where Renick boarded. Located at 344 Peachtree Street, in one of the best residential areas of the city, the comfortable house was set back from the street in a grove of trees which shaded a spacious lawn.[23] Here the young Wilson was well received. Several months later, however, Renick and Wilson decided to move to Mrs. James S. Turpin's boardinghouse.[24]

After some consultation the two Virginians arrived at an agreeable understanding in regard to the division of their legal labors.

[20]Wilson to Talcott, September 22, 1881, in Baker Papers, Library of Congress.

[21]Baker, *Wilson Life and Letters,* I, 140.

[22]Edward J. Renick to Wilson, January 15, 1882, in Wilson Papers, Library of Congress; Wilson to Bridges, August 25, 1882, in Meyer Collection, Library of Congress; Renick to Wilson, April 29, 1882, in Wilson Papers, Library of Congress. There were two large windows that fronted on the street and the rent was $9 per month.

[23]Baker, *Wilson Life and Letters,* I, 142.

[24]See Link (ed.), *Papers of Wilson,* II, 342.

Renick assumed the duties of attorney and Wilson those of barrister. The former preferred the office work, which consisted largely of research and writing of the briefs. Wilson liked most the duties connected with the conduct and argument of cases in court. Their relations were congenial and their association was to continue to be entirely satisfactory to both of them. "Already," stated Wilson in a letter dated August 25, 1882, "some practice is coming to us and we are determined that hard work shall make it more and more." [25] He expected to argue a tax case, in resistance to a license tax levied by the city, at the next term of the Superior Court, which met in October. It would give him a good subject for a strong speech. Wilson concluded, optimistically, that the case would win "much capital for the firm of Renick and Wilson if they can gain it—may bring them into prominence even if they don't gain it." [26]

In the meantime, before he could argue a case in court, he was required to pass an examination given by the proper officials and receive his license to practice law. In October "a tall, dignified, bespectacled young man with blond hair" appeared in court before Judge George Hillyer to be examined for admission to the bar.[27] Customarily, four seasoned lawyers conducted the examination, which lasted two hours and was most severe. Although the questions were difficult and technical, the young barrister, in the opinion of those who conducted the examination, answered them brilliantly.[28] Wilson's certificate of admission to the Georgia bar was dated October 19, 1882; on March 12, 1883, he qualified to practice law before the federal courts.[29] However, as early as September 12, 1882, there appeared in the Atlanta *Constitution* the law card of the firm Renick and Wilson.[30]

Between the appearance of the Renick and Wilson legal an-

[25]Wilson to Bridges, August 25, 1882, in Meyer Collection, Library of Congress.

[26]*Ibid.*

[27]Baker, *Wilson Life and Letters,* I, 148.

[28]*Ibid.,* 149.

[29]See certificates to practice law before the Georgia courts and in the federal courts, in Wilson Papers, Library of Congress.

[30]Atlanta *Constitution,* September 12, 1882. The announcement of Renick and Wilson, attorneys at law, appeared regularly until March 13, 1883, after which it was not found at all.

nouncement in the local press and Wilson's bar examination, the *Constitution* noted that a Tariff Commission would "sit at the Kimball House, Atlanta, on Friday and Saturday, September 22, and 23." Although opportunity would be afforded for oral explanations, declared John L. Hayes, president of the commission, "parties desiring to give testimony should present their statements in writing." [31] Woodrow had not anticipated appearing before the congressional group until a promising young reporter for the New York *World* came into his law office and prevailed on him to testify. In this inauspicious way, Woodrow Wilson made the acquaintance of Walter Hines Page, whom he would one day name as United States Ambassador to England.

The *Constitution* discussed the hearings of September 22–23 in its columns the following days. Wilson seemed to be the only one who did not advocate a protective high tariff. His speech, said the newspaper, "was quite lengthy and was in favor of tariff for revenue only." Editorially, the paper concluded that the tariff commission "will undoubtedly accomplish all it was appointed to accomplish—nothing." [32]

Page, reporting for the New York *World,* had been traveling about the country with the commissioners "utterly destroying their reputation and overthrowing their adventitious dignity by his smart ridicule." [33] He wrote that the commission met with a more scornful reception in Atlanta than it had at any other place visited. Efforts were made to have well-informed and representative men of Georgia appear before the group, but those who made statements to the commission did not treat the subject seriously. Indeed, concluded the *World* reporter, only Woodrow Wilson presented arguments of dignity. A student of economics, Wilson revealed clearly the reasons why southern people in the future would be even more firmly united in favor of a tariff for revenue only than they had been in the past.[34]

[31]*Ibid.,* September 21, 1882.

[32]*Ibid.,* September 23–24, 1882. The editorial is on the earlier day.

[33]Wilson to Dabney, January 11, 1883, in Dabney Papers, Virginia.

[34]New York *World,* September 24, 1882. Page wrote that "some of the most persistent demagogues in the city, men who command no respect here whatever, have been the most prominent witnesses. They advocate a protective tariff and they are almost the only men who do advocate it."

In writing to Heath Dabney, who was abroad finishing his doctorate at a German university, Wilson described his appearance before the commissioners: "I hastily prepared a brief and undertook to make a few extemporaneous remarks before this much ridiculed body of incompetencies, influenced by the consideration that my speech would appear in their printed report, rather than by any hope of affecting their conclusions." Six commissioners sat around a long table in the breakfast room of the Kimball House and behind them sat a few local dignitaries and four or five young men, besides the reporters usually attendant upon the sittings. "Embarrassed by the smallness and character of the audience, but more especially by the ill-natured and sneering interruptions of the Commissioners," Wilson spoke without sufficient self-possession and certainly without much satisfaction to himself. He was compensated for all discomfort by the subsequent compliments of friends and the press.[35]

Wilson's views on this important political and economic question can be gathered from his testimony before the Tariff Commission. A few key sentences will suffice:

"Free trade . . . will soon become one of the leading questions in all political discussions, because . . . the people of the South will insist upon having the fruits of peace, and not being kept down under the burdens of war." . . . "There is a great deal of ignorance and indifference in regard to these questions in the South . . . but when the farmers and others begin to investigate these matters, they soon discover that they are, after all, paying these duties for the benefit of a few manufacturing classes." . . . "The province of direct taxation should be left to the States, and in order that the two systems may not clash and overburden the people, it is a part of wise policy that the national government shall make the most of its taxation indirect." . . . "No man with his senses about him would recommend perfect freedom of trade in the sense that there should be no duties whatever laid on imports." . . . "The danger in imposing protective duties is, that when the policy is once embarked upon, it cannot be easily receded from." . . . "I maintain that manufacturers are made better manufacturers whenever they are thrown upon their own

[35]Wilson to Dabney, January 11, 1883, in Dabney Papers, Virginia.

resources and left to the natural competition of trade rather than when they are told, 'you shall be held in the lap of the government, and you need not stand upon your feet.' Such theories discourage skill because it puts all industries upon an artificial basis." [36]

The appearance before the Tariff Commission was a significant event in Wilson's early professional life. He himself called the speech "a small beginning towards establishing a local reputation." [37] Certainly, the occasion which brought together for the first time the two aspiring young southerners Wilson and Page, the first link in their long chain of friendship, is worthy of note. But the speech, obviously influenced by the writings of such Englishmen as John Stuart Mill, Herbert Spencer, Bright, and Gladstone, was most significant as a pronouncement of sectionalism in accord with the principles of Calhoun. In addition, these tariff hearings prompted Wilson and a few of his local friends to organize a branch of the Free Trade Club of New York, which met twice each month for debate and discussions.[38]

Not all of the energetic young Wilson's time was consumed in caring for the few clients who climbed the steps of his law office. He found much time in which to read and to write, periods in which to cultivate his interest in Georgia politics, and hours in which to meet with intellectually inclined friends in discussions of topics of mutual interest.

With the first money Wilson earned, when he sold an article to the *International Review,* in August, 1879, he bought a bookcase; in Atlanta, he began to buy books to fill it. He purchased and read John Milton's *Poems,* volumes of Keats and Shelley works, T. Humphry Ward's *English Poets* in four volumes, Aphus Todd's *Parliamentary Government in the British Colonies,* and

[36]*United States House Miscellaneous Documents, 47th Cong., 2nd Sess.,* 3, pp. 1294–97. Wilson's statement is reprinted in Baker and Dodd (eds.), *Public Papers of Wilson,* I (New York, 1925), 89–94.

[37]Wilson to Bridges, October 28, 1882, in Meyer Collection, Library of Congress.

[38]Baker, *Wilson Life and Letters,* I, 148; Ruth Cranston, *Story of Woodrow Wilson, Twenty-Eighth President of the United States, Pioneer of World Democracy* (New York, 1945), 32; Edith G. Reid, *Woodrow Wilson: The Caricature, the Myth and the Man* (New York, 1934), 30.

Richard G. White's *Words and Their Uses.*[39] He was reading, naturally, in the fields of his greatest interest—literature, history, and political science. As he wrote Robert Bridges, he was "devouring" Houghton-Mifflin's American Statesman series and Macmillan's English Citizen series.[40] Both were altogether to his taste.

Although he devoted much time to reading, his heart was in his writing. "I'll *make* time and opportunity to write," he declared.[41] And make time he did. Some two months later, on January 4, 1883, he confided to Bridges that he had recently completed an extended essay on his favorite topic, cabinet government. It was so extended as to amount in volume to a small book which Wilson entitled *Government by Debate* and divided into five parts.[42] All but the last part of the essay he had sent to Harper's, only to have the reader advise against publication. He then sent the last part of the work to Bridges, and asked him to read it, to secure the rest of his manuscript from Harper's, and to pass judgment on it. If Bridges thought it publishable, would he not submit it to one of the *Saturday Evening Post*'s or the *Nation*'s staff to read? Wilson urged his designated publishing aide and literary critic to find a publisher who was "inclined to look favorably upon manuscripts from the South which indicate a revival of literary activity and embody healthy, unsectional sentiment." If the essay, concluded the young lawyer, had any value, it was because of its timeliness.[43]

As so often happens to many young writers, Wilson failed to find a publisher for his manuscript. Editors reacted negatively. "Too repetitious," they said.[44] The author realized that he had hammered a great deal on cardinal points but felt that he had done it with a "variety of *form and manner,* so as not to tire the

[39]Baker, *Wilson Life and Letters,* I, 143-44.

[40]Wilson to Bridges, October 28, 1882, in Meyer Collection, Library of Congress.

[41]*Ibid.*

[42]For this unpublished essay see Link (ed.), *Papers of Wilson,* II, 159–275.

[43]Wilson to Bridges, January 4, 1883, in Meyer Collection, Library of Congress.

[44]Bridges to Wilson, February 1, 1883, in Wilson Papers, Library of Congress.

reader." Endeavoring to answer other objections to his manuscript, Wilson wrote: "I admit you are right in calling the changes proposed [in the essay] radical, but that the changes I advocate are radical does not seem to me to be a fatal objection to my essay, unless they be also visionary and impracticable." It was the boldness of the proposals and the fearlessness of treatment, Woodrow believed, that gave his essay an air of originality.

Later Bridges was able to prevail on Putnam's Sons to publish "Cabinet Government" provided the author would assume the cost.[45] But to Wilson, like most young men beginning the practice of law, any cost was considerably beyond his means. He could only decline the offer and swallow his disappointment.[46] His object was not to make money but to secure literary recognition. He needed to become known to publishers and editors of quarterlies and reviews. In short, he wanted a *start* and was willing to attain it on any terms within his reach.

At Bridges' suggestion, Wilson began to gather information from the Georgia Statute Books and from press reports for an article on "Convict Labor in Georgia." [47] The system of convict labor in that state was in the experimental stage. An influential and growing minority of citizens was dissatisfied with it; every legislature tinkered with it, and nobody seemed to regard it as a settled thing. Wilson found that the state had 1,200 convicts leased to several lessees. For each convict the lessee paid $20 per annum. The lessee was to clothe, lodge, care for, and deal humanely with the criminals. He was responsible for escapees, and dismissed with a new suit of clothes any convict who was pardoned. The state was free from the care of all criminals, even those serving sentences for misdemeanors. Wilson criticized the lease system in that: (1) It was intended to be profitable to the

[45]Bridges to Wilson, March 13, 1883, in *ibid.*

[46]Wilson to Bridges, March 15, 21, 1883, in Meyer Collection, Library of Congress.

[47]Bridges to Wilson, February 15, 1883, in Wilson Papers, Library of Congress; Wilson to Bridges, January 10, 1883, February 24, 1883, in Meyer Collection, Library of Congress. In the first letter Wilson thanked Bridges for his suggestion, and in the second letter Wilson enclosed a copy of the article.

state but the lessees gained most. (2) With the object of private profit dominant, the system was open to many abuses. (3) The system was incompatible with modern ideas of the duty of society to its criminal classes.[48]

Another article, written in that extraordinarily legible hand, was entitled "Culture and Education at the South." [49] The New South was making vast strides in commerce and manufacturing, but her business failures were frequent and her bankruptcies were common. Atlanta, contended Wilson, was the leading manufacturing city of the New South with 46 per cent of her population engaged in gainful occupation. In spite of economic advances, there was an ominous cloud over the South. Her drive for wealth was getting ahead of her eagerness for learning. There was, Wilson observed, complete unconcern about the lack of education among the Negroes and the poor whites. Furthermore, the educational standards of those able to go to school were extremely low. In fact, few went to school long and very few read habitually after they quit going to school. Most southern children attended private schools, but the tide was slowly turning toward public schools. Southern colleges lacked many essentials but the greatest drawback was a lack of trained teachers. The numerous deficiencies of the regional educational system caused every friend and lover of the South, including Wilson, pangs of regret and chagrin. The southern press was working actively for education but the proper agitation of the question, he said, was blocked by prejudice. The true motto should be *Patience:* "The Southern people do not easily tolerate the too zealous agitation of any question such as this one of education." They were devotedly attached to the existing order of things in all social institutions and looked upon those who objected to that order and attacked it as "mere grumblers and malcontents who are worthy to be regarded only as nuisances, and heeded only to be put down." One could,

[48]See copy of Woodrow Wilson's "Convict Labor in Georgia," in Wilson Papers, Library of Congress; *Evening Post,* March 7, 1883; and Link (ed.), *Wilson Papers,* II, 306–11.

[49]Woodrow Wilson, "Culture and Education at the South," (MS in Wilson Papers, Library of Congress). See Link (ed.), *Wilson Papers,* II, 326–32.

therefore, "do no more than understand the situation and patiently work and wait." [50]

A budding lawyer, Wilson fed his growing enthusiasm for politics by listening to political speeches and reading accounts of the political scene in the press. Shortly before going to Atlanta, he wrote that "the formation of a new Southern party is a consummation devoutly to be wished, and I will do all in my power to aid in its formation as opportunity offers." He fervently prayed that the South would never be delivered into the hands of men like General William Mahone, United States senator from Virginia, or William H. Felton, a Georgia congressman. Rather than that, "give us back the carpetbaggers—the undisguised rascals." The young barrister declared that he was "not biased by love of *either* of the national parties." [51]

When Governor Alexander H. Stephens died on March 4, 1883, Wilson wrote that "Little Alex's" death was no grievous loss to the country but a great loss to Georgia, for just at that moment the state was suffering from the lack of talented leaders. Wilson's epitaph on Stephens is worthy of preservation:

"His virtue, his greatness of heart and uprightness of purpose, cannot, it seems to me, be overestimated; but I did not regard his mind as one of unusual strength or of unusually fine fibre. He was no genius. His mind was not large nor always clear; but his great sympathies and the intensity of his power made him use all his faculties in the way in which they would most surely tell, and his frail body, the strange association of bright talents with a wizened visage made him a conspicuous and interesting figure in our politics." [52]

"Georgians," said Wilson, "are much too economical in this thrifty state to think of indulging ourselves in the luxury of a lieutenant-governor." When Stephens died it was necessary "to put in motion all the ponderous machinery of a nominating convention, special election and an extra vote-counting session of the

[50] *Ibid.*

[51] Wilson to Bridges, March 15, 1882, in Meyer Collection, Library of Congress.

[52] Wilson to Bridges, March 21, 1883, in *ibid.*

Legislature which probably costs the people of the state a sum of money in comparison with which a lieutenant-governor may seem cheap enough, but, so long as we think we are economical, what matters it?"[53]

When the young barrister had no work to do in his legal office, he occasionally sauntered over to the gallery of the Georgia senate chamber. Once, he remembered, the senators were discussing a report of the state superintendent of education in which the latter urged a vast increase in appropriations for schools. The majority, Wilson wrote, "thrust the proposal to increased appropriations aside with a resolution that the Representatives and Senators of the State in Washington be requested to do all in their power to secure a grant from the federal treasury in aid of education." This newcomer to Georgia was impressed by one speech in opposition to such federal aid—"a sturdy appeal to self-respect and independence," the young lawyer called it. The whole proceeding impressed him "as a shameless declaration of the determination, on the part of a well-to-do community, to enjoy the easy position of a beneficiary of the national government to the fullest possible extent."[54]

At times, Woodrow spent the day reading volumes of court reports, statutes, or commentaries on law. Sometimes, his day slipped away as he endeavored to put his thoughts on paper in an essay. Again, he returned to his first love of studying history and political science or reading poetry. Whatever he did the day ran swiftly into night with time heavy on his hands. Especially was this true during the winter months, Atlanta's gay season. The city had a first-rate theater to which Wilson frequently went to view some of the nation's best traveling troupes.[55] Other evenings were happily spent with a small circle of friends who discussed theatrical productions, literary works, and political issues. Wilson often visited the W. D. Grant mansion at the corner of Peachtree and Pine streets, where the charming Sarah Frances Grant, another friend, lived.[56] And not infrequently he read aloud at nights with Katie Mayrant, who lived with her aunt, Mrs. J. Reid

[53]Wilson to Bridges, May 13, 1883, in *ibid.*
[54]Wilson to Bridges, February 27, 1886, in *ibid.*
[55]Wilson to Bridges, January 4, 1883, in *ibid.*
[56]Atlanta *Constitution,* February 26, 1956.

Boylston, in whose home Wilson was a boarder for several months.[57]

As a barrister, Wilson was not successful. In fact, as early as August, 1882, he wrote his mother that he was depressed and that he was increasingly dissatisfied with his legal outlook. His father answered that he read Woodrow's letters to "dear Mother" with deep concern. "You have only one thing to do—to stick to the law and its prospects be they ever so depressing or disgusting. . . . Conquer depression therefore as you would overwhelm your worst enemy." [58] All beginnings, whatever occupation, were difficult. A determined fair beginning, Dr. Wilson insisted to his son, must be made before the real character of things begun could be known. The neophyte barrister was admonished to get his "feet upon the ladder of actual practice and then should the ascent prove intolerable it will not be too late to see what other hill may be attempted." It was hardly like his brave boy, the worried father concluded, "to show a white feather" before the battle started.[59]

Wilson was strengthened by his father's encouraging letters, but he continued to follow the young lawyer's occupation of waiting. He had earned only a few small fees. As he himself stated, he had business enough of a certain kind, "the collection or the effort to collect—numberless desperate claims." [60] In short, he was a briefless lawyer who was hardly earning his salt. Fortunately, his father continued to send him fifty dollars each month. Defeated at law and repeatedly failing as an author, the ambitious Woodrow was miserable during the early spring of 1883. Courageously, he faced the truth that he was unfit for legal practice. He had just enough experience to prove that. But let the young man analyze himself:

The atmosphere of the courts have proved very depressing to me. I cannot breathe freely nor smile readily in an atmosphere of broken promises, of wrecked estates, of neglected trusts, of unperformed du-

[57]Baker, *Wilson Life and Letters,* I, 142. See Katie D. Mayrant to Wilson, May 25, 1883, in Wilson Papers, Library of Congress. "You can't imagine how happy your letter made me," she wrote. "Why I am just overjoyed at the prospect of seeing you so soon, and yet it is going to seem like an eternity to me."

[58]Joseph Ruggles Wilson to Woodrow Wilson, August 14, 1882, in Wilson Papers.

[59]Joseph Ruggles Wilson to Woodrow Wilson, August 20, 1882, in *ibid.*

[60]Wilson to Bridges, January 4, 1883, in Meyer Collection, Library of Congress.

ties, of crimes and of quarrels. I find myself hardened and made narrow and cynical by seeing only the worst side of human nature. But this is the least part of the argument; here lies the weight of it: my natural, and therefore predominant, tastes every day allure me from my law books; I throw away law reports for histories, and my mind runs after the solution of political, rather than of legal, problems, as if its keenest scent drew it after them by an unalterable instinct. My appetite is for general literature and my ambition is for writing. Small as has been my success in writing, I feel as if, after a thorough and undiscourageable discipline of my faculties, and an ample storing of my mind, I could write something that men might delight to read, and which they would not readily let die. My eager impulse, consequently, is to seek as broad a field of study as possible.[61]

Wilson believed firmly that he could eventually acquire a lucrative practice and earn an honorable support. Indeed, he told Bobby Bridges, he was not without encouragement already and his professional friends were increasing, but it was never his wish to be a mere lawyer. He had learned that, in struggling times of close population and limited capital, to succeed at the bar one must acquire a "most ignoble shrewdness at overcoming the unprofessional tricks and underhand competition of sneaking pettifoggers." [62] And this he could not do.

What did Wilson wish to become? He wanted to make himself an outside force in politics. This he might accomplish through a chair of political science and through speaking and writing on political subjects. As a professor he hoped he would have leisure and incentive to study with summer vacations for travel and observations.[63] He decided to enter the graduate school of Johns Hopkins University to study history and political science,[64] although his application for a fellowship at the university in Baltimore had been denied.[65]

Not only was Wilson wholly disgusted with the practice of law, but he was completely disappointed with Atlanta. "Here,"

[61]Wilson to Bridges, April 29, 1883, in *ibid.*

[62]*Ibid.*

[63]Wilson to Bridges, May 13, 1883, in *ibid.*

[64]Wilson to Dabney, May 11, 1883, in Dabney Papers, Virginia.

[65]*Ibid.* "I am determined," he wrote, "if I fail of that appointment . . . to go next winter anyhow to Baltimore to attend the University lectures and bury myself for a season in the grand libraries of that beautiful city."

he confided, "culture is very little enthroned . . . because there is so little of it. . . . For one who would succeed in North Georgia in a way that North Georgians could understand and applaud, anything more than a common school education is a positive disqualification. Here the chief end of man is certainly to make money and money cannot be made except by the most vulgar methods. A studious man is pronounced impractical and is separated and despised as a visionary. If one had the means and leisure to be philosophical, he could learn here in this provincial town of Atlanta enough of a certain sort of human nature to stock two or three immortal comedies and several conclusive essays on the characteristics of the middle class." [66] In brief, the restless lawyer had no intellectual companionship.

In February, 1883, Wilson and Renick dissolved their law partnership. As his father wrote him, Woodrow stood "where every young man ought to stand—alone." If the son was discouraged, the minister father expressed his abiding faith in his older boy: "With your education, and gifts, and character, and opportunity, you may kick the world before you, God helping you as He will for the honest asking." [67]

In June, almost exactly a year after Wilson, full of enthusiasm and hope, arrived in Georgia, he took his departure. As he put it, "Atlanta is behind me, the boats are burnt, and all retreat is cut off." [68] All along the practice of law had been secondary with him.[69] Though a failure as a barrister, Wilson had finally discovered *what* he wanted to become. He determined to be a professor of history and political science and drove himself toward the realization of that objective.

[66] Wilson to Bridges, May 13, 1883, in Meyer Collection, Library of Congress.

[67] Joseph Ruggles Wilson to Woodrow Wilson, February 13, 1883, in Wilson Papers, Library of Congress.

[68] Wilson to Bridges, July 26, 1883, in Meyer Collection, Library of Congress.

[69] Wilson to Talcott, July 5, 1883, in Baker Papers, Library of Congress.

CHAPTER VI *Graduate Student*

In February, 1883, Wilson had concluded that he was a failure at law and that he could not attain his political ambitions by a frontal assault as a barrister. He therefore decided upon a flanking attack via the roads of writing, public lecturing, and teaching. In order to prepare for his new career, Wilson applied for a fellowship in the graduate school of Johns Hopkins University. His efforts to receive financial aid from the university were unsuccessful, but in mid-summer he wrote President Daniel Coit Gilman that he planned to attend the coming winter session of Johns Hopkins, "for the purpose of pursuing special studies in history and political science." [1] On September 18 he made his formal application for admission to the university in which he stated that he had an A.M. degree, 1882, from Princeton.[2]

[1]Woodrow Wilson to Daniel Coit Gilman, July 26, 1883, in Daniel Coit Gilman Papers, Johns Hopkins University Library.

[2]See Link (ed.), *Wilson Papers,* II, 429–30, for the application.

At the same time he confided to Bobby Bridges that, although the authorities at Johns Hopkins had not honored him with an appointment to a fellowship, he would study there next winter. He hoped to win a fellowship for the session following, for two years would be none too much for the completion of the course he proposed pursuing, which included an introduction to both history and political science. His immediate subject of study was to be the constitutional history of the United States. He was eager to delve into the colonial period, for he felt it was undoubtedly in that era that the key or keys to all the country's legal systems, both state and federal, were found.[3] Since the Johns Hopkins period was the final, and perhaps the most important, link in Wilson's educational chain, all phases of his work there and all interests that he revealed at that time are of significance in properly evaluating his life.

A few months prior to his arrival at Johns Hopkins, Wilson had met and fallen in love with a certain Miss Ellen Axson. To this girl, who would become Woodrow's first bride, he communicated his impressions of campus life.

When he came to Johns Hopkins in September, 1883, the university was in its first flush of scholastic enthusiasm. Only seven years earlier, in 1876, the graduate school had opened its doors to a small, select group of students for postgraduate study. Johns Hopkins was the only institution of higher learning in the country at that time which was modeled upon the best German universities. It had been founded to compete with the German schools which were attracting many talented American students for the final years of their formal education. The university had a group of scholarly teachers, many of whom had gone abroad, explicitly to German universities, for their doctorates.

Professor Herbert B. Adams, then head of the Department of History and Political Science, was a pioneer in introducing into American universities the monographic method in the study of history. He realized that it was impossible for students to attain a profound knowledge of the entire field of history in the brief span of a year or two. Adams was a man of shrewd practicality

[3]Wilson to Bridges, July 26, 1883, in Meyer Collection, Library of Congress.

and high idealism. Possessing a peculiar power of inspiration, he was able to attract young men to him and to influence them to attack some specific historical problem with intensity, and to master fundamental facts as a sure foundation for their development.[4]

Wilson's courses his first semester at Johns Hopkins included International Law, or History of International Relations, under Professor Adams; Advanced Political Economy under Professor Richard T. Ely; Sources of American Colonial History with Professor Adams; English Constitutional History with Assistant Professor J. Franklin Jameson; as well as a weekly meeting of a seminary on political science and history.[5] He was a bit downcast when he learned that the graduate curriculum did not cover the fields of comparative governments and politics, the study of which had been his hobby for years. He was especially interested in the governments, administrative machinery, and political parties of the United States, England, France, and Germany. The professors, it seemed to him, were determined to have their students work in fields of institutional history, "digging, that is, into the dusty records of old settlements and colonial cities, rehabilitating in authentic form the stories, now almost mythical, of the struggles, the ups and downs, of the first colonists here, there and everywhere on this then interesting continent—and other rummaging work of a like dry kind." [6] To the young Wilson, so recently returned to his books, this seemed tiresome and in vivid contrast to the grand excursions among the governments, machinery, political parties, and policies which he had imagined himself doing.

He resolved to carry his disappointment to Dr. Adams. About three weeks after classes started, Wilson went one evening by appointment to unburden himself to his head professor. Dr. Adams listened patiently and then quietly informed the student that he could go his own way, just as he wished. Wilson was elated

[4]Charles K. Edmonds, "New Light on Woodrow Wilson's Formative Years," newspaper clipping (n.d.) in Miss Hilah Kilby's Scrapbook, in private possession, Suffolk, Va.

[5]Baker, *Wilson Life and Letters,* I, 174.

[6]Wilson to Ellen Axson, October 16, 1883, in Axson–Wilson Letters, Princeton.

as he wrote Ellen Axson about the incident: "After tea this evening I went to see Dr. Adams, my chief, and made a clean breast of it: I told him I had a hobby which I had been riding for some years with great entertainment and from which I was loath to dismount. He received my confidences with sympathy, readily freed me from his 'institutional' work, and bade me go on with my 'constitutional' studies, promising me all the aid and encouragement he could give me, and saying that the work I proposed was just such as he wanted to see done! Do you wonder that I feel elated and encouraged?" [7]

In the meantime, Wilson found a room at 146 North Charles Street. It had one great disadvantage however; no other university students lived near there. Consequently, in the middle of the winter he found new quarters at 8 McCulloh Street, in "a neighborhood of dignified old brick houses," and considerably nearer the campus. Moreover, he was housed with select university men, fellows in various fields but with equal enthusiasm for intellectual pursuits. For Wilson, it was a much more healthful atmosphere because he was so constituted emotionally that he could hardly bear to live for long periods beyond the reach of congenial companionship. He may not have fallen into morbid moods when he kept too much alone but his thoughts, under such circumstances, ran into ruts which were very tiresome and wearing. "At least," he confessed, "I get to thinking too much upon that most unprofitable of all subjects, *myself*." [8] In this room on McCulloh Street he remained until the spring of 1885.

By December, Wilson's enthusiasm for some of his teachers was waning. For the splendid opportunities for study at Johns Hopkins, for the fine libraries, and for the stimulating atmosphere he had only praise. He regretted to say, however, that the longer he stayed in the university, the more deeply disappointed he became in the instruction given in his major, history and political science. The department, he confided to Bridges, was manned by young men altogether, who had all the faults of young men and were without some of the advantages of their age. Professor Ely, Wilson explained, was a "hard, conscientious worker,"

[7]*Ibid.*

[8]Wilson to Ellen Axson, January 16, 1884, in *ibid.*

but he was simply stuffed full and wouldn't move intellectually "except by force of outside impulse." Professor Adams, his student thought, was "superficial and insincere, no worker and a selfish schemer for self-advertisement and advancement." Wilson concluded that he was assigned more work than he could possibly do, which quite possibly influenced his critical opinions of his professors. [9]

When Wilson's father learned of his son's disparaging remarks about his teachers he wrote that he did not approve. Such idle chatter could do no good and it could assuredly do the graduate student harm, said the father. "Never strike a blow that will not tell in the right direction, and much more never strike a blow which will never tell at all except to your own injury." [10] Fortunately, there is proof that the young Wilson's harsh judgment mellowed. Years later he wrote Professor Ely of Dr. Adams: "I would call him a captain in the field of systematic and organized scholarship. I think all his pupils would accord him mastery in the formulation of historical inquiry, in the suggestive stimulation of research, in the communication of methods and ideals." [11]

Although Wilson was extremely critical of his teachers, he complimented the university. There could be no question about Johns Hopkins being the best place in America to study, he wrote, because of its freedom and its almost unrivaled facilities. Thinking of his own future, he added that one could command from there, better than from anywhere else in the country, an appointment to a professorship. Indeed, the only rivalry of Johns Hopkins in locating a position as a professor was one of the better German universities. Because of Wilson's complete ignorance of German, he was practically barred from any of Germany's higher educational institutions. In a philosophical vein, he stated that it was inevitable that he should turn sooner or later to a systematic cultivation of history and political science: "I was born with this bent in me and there was no use trying to force nature into

[9] Wilson to Bridges, December 15, 1883, in Meyer Collection, Library of Congress.

[10] Joseph Ruggles Wilson to Woodrow Wilson, December 8, 1883, in Wilson Papers, Library of Congress.

[11] Wilson to Richard T. Ely, January 30, 1902, in Richard T. Ely Papers, Wisconsin State Historical Society Archives, Madison.

unnatural uses." Nature would indeed be most dutifully served, he added, if he could take his specialty, "the constitutional history of these United States and of their present actual constitutional system—as contradistinguished from the ideal constitution of books and of a lawyer's theories." [12]

Wilson's favorite class at the university was the weekly seminary in history and politics. For the social sciences, the seminary was somewhat analogous to the laboratory for the natural sciences; here professors, fellows, and students met to read scholarly papers and to promote discussions. When he first entered the class his eyes fastened on a motto from Edward A. Freeman, the English historian, which was painted in large letters at one end of the room. The motto—"History is past Politics and Politics present History"—was accepted by the young Wilson as part of his professional creed.[13] Among those students enrolled in the seminary were men who later were to attain distinction—Albert Shaw, for years editor of the *Review of Reviews;* Edward W. Bemis and Davis R. Dewey, both to be teachers of economics; E. R. L. Gould, future Chamberlain of New York City; Charles H. Levermore, who would win the Bok Peace Prize; Arthur Yager, whom Wilson one day would name governor of Puerto Rico; and John Dewey, later to become internationally famous as a writer and educator.

According to the minutes of the seminary, the first meeting at which Wilson participated in the program was held January 4, 1884, when he reviewed *The Banker's Magazine* for December, 1883.[14] In February, he was elected secretary of the seminary, and thereafter penned many pages of its record.

On April 18 Wilson reported on the March and April numbers of *The Banker's Magazine,* referring particularly to one article on "American Forests" as being ludicrously out of tune with the times in its optimistic view of the forests. When the interest that Wilson's report created began to lag, Professor Adams directed the discussion towards a federal aid to education in the South bill

[12]Wilson to Dabney, February 17, 1884, in Dabney Papers, Virginia.

[13]Baker, *Wilson Life and Letters,* I, 177.

[14]See Minutes of Seminary of History and Politics, January 4, 1884, Johns Hopkins University Library.

which had passed the United States Senate. Wilson spoke "at considerable length, and with great clearness and force," against the bill, confining himself mainly to the argument that the principle contained in the bill was both unconstitutional and politically inexpedient. The federal government should not in any way interfere with, or become responsible for, common school education, he stated. Justice, wisdom, and the Constitution all agreed in leaving this whole matter entirely with the respective states.[15]

Beginning on May 8 Wilson read several chapters of his congressional government manuscript to the seminary group. At this meeting Professor Adams expressed a desire to have at least one more paper from him that year, adding that he thought Wilson's studies on the national government would be advantageous. "Mr. Wilson's work," concluded chairman Adams, "is better than anything in that line that has been done heretofore in the Seminary. Another year it would be good to bring forward in the Johns Hopkins Historical Studies." [16] A week later, on May 16, Wilson again read a chapter from his study. He gave an able account of the inner working of the House of Representatives through its standing committees, discussed the duties and powers of the Speaker, and drew interesting comparisons among the House of Representatives, the English House of Commons, and the French Assembly.[17] J. Franklin Jameson recorded in his diary that Wilson showed "the greatest logical skill and ability" in the discussion of states' rights.[18] The professor also noted, "At the seminary we had about the ablest and maturest paper ever read there, the introduction to Wilson's series of papers on the national government." [19]

In January, 1884, Wilson's "Committee or Cabinet Government," appeared in *Overland Monthly*. The longest article that he had so far published, this was a critical essay on the standing committees of Congress, on the way the members of these committees were named, on the methods used by them in the treatment of

[15]*Ibid.*, April 18, 1884.
[16]*Ibid.*, May 8, 1884.
[17]*Ibid.*, May 16, 1884.
[18]Elizabeth Donnan and Leo F. Stock (eds.), *An Historian's World: Selections from the Correspondence of John Franklin Jameson* (Philadelphia, 1956), 38, entry of January 18, 1884.
[19]*Ibid.*, entry of May 9, 1884.

bills for which they were responsible, on the utter lack of debate in the national House of Representatives, and on the separation of the legislative and executive branches of the federal government. These conditions the graduate student viewed as grave ills. He felt that they could be remedied only by the introduction of the English cabinet system, with ministerial responsibility and with the fusion of the executive and the legislative branches of the government.[20] In this article Wilson wrote in some detail of what a visitor to the House of Representatives would view and hear:

"The House of Representatives," he began, "is a superlatively noisy assembly. It [is] not the noises of debate, but the sharp clapping of hands that strikes the ear." Wilson noted that however frequently one visited the Capitol, he would seldom find the House engaged in debate, it "being apparently content to leave that dignified and generally unexciting exercise to the Senate."

The House had standing committees to "do its digesting for it." It was this plan of entrusting itself to committees that Wilson felt distinguished the House of Representatives from the other great legislative bodies of the world. He thought these committees very selfish and exacting. The debates of the House were confined largely to the reports of the committees, upon which the House did not spend much time. The House made "its nearest approach to business debate when in Committee of the Whole," but legislation was "altogether in the hands of the standing committees."

The privilege and the duty of appointing these committees was vested in the Speaker, who was "the most powerful functionary in the government of the United States." Very few Speakers, Wilson was convinced, "forbid their own personal preferences and predilections a voice in the appointment of committees." The public knew "little or nothing about the motives or methods of the standing committees: and yet all legislation may be said to originate with them, and to pass all its stages under their direction." These committees, he wrote, were "the wheels of the American system:" but it was not in them that its motive power resided. One had not seen the whole of the machinery of government until he had visited the caucus "where all the fires of legislative action"

[20]Wilson to Ellen Axson, November 4, 1883, in Axson-Wilson Letters, Princeton.

were kindled. "By reason of the power of caucuses," Wilson said, Americans were "governed by a narrow oligarchy of party managers." As a consequence of these conditions, every day men spoke with "bitter despondency of the decadence of our institutions, of the incompetence of our legislators, of the corruption of our public officials, even of the insecurity of our liberties."

What was the remedy for such a situation? Wilson said it lay not in dispensing with political parties, but in party responsibility. American political parties, the young essayist wrote, "thrive as well on dead issues as on living principles." He contended that party platforms were "built only for conventions to sit on," and fell into decay when conventions adjourned. The remedy lay in abolishing the standing committees.

To create cabinet responsibility would require a constitutional amendment to admit members of Congress to seats in the cabinet. Cabinet government was the "simplest and most straight-forward system of party government;" it would put the necessary bit in the mouth of beast caucus, and reduce him to his proper service; it would secure open-doored government; it would not suffer legislation to skulk in committee closets and caucus conferences; the members of the cabinet would always be united in their responsibility. The climax of Wilson's arguments for cabinet government was that committee government was too clumsy and too clandestine a system to last. Other methods of government must be sought, and "Congress must be organized in conformity with what is now the prevailing legislative practice of the world. English precedent and the world's fashion must be followed in the institution of Cabinet government in the United States." [21]

Wilson's article was lauded for "both the matter and the style of the piece." The author amusedly recorded some of the comments from the fellow graduate students:

"Wilson," said one critic, "you've picked up a capital literary style somewhere" (Picked up, indeed! Hasn't my dear father been drilling me in style these ten years past?) "Upon whose style did you form

[21]Woodrow Wilson, "Committee or Cabinet Government?" *Overland Monthly*, Series 2, III, 17–33. This article is reprinted in Baker and Dodd (eds.), *Wilson Public Papers,* I, 95–129. See also Link (ed.), *Wilson Papers,* II, 614–40.

it? Did you come by it naturally, or have you consciously modelled after Macaulay?" (Poor Macaulay!) Another friend, who has to follow me in the course of "lectures" inaugurated by the reading of that remarkable essay upon Adam Smith, cooly asks whether I would be willing to take his materials and "put them into literary form!" I'm sure I have pain enough in putting my own materials into literary form without going through the like labours for other people.[22]

At times, Wilson was so obsessed with the idea of doing his work in his own way that he appeared to be hostile to all those whose responsibility it was to guide and direct his courses. He voiced agreement with a class wag who suggested that the daily lectures were for the students' recreation, as agreeable interruptions to their more difficult studies.[23] He accepted his father's principle that "the mind was not a prolix gut to be stuffed but a thing of life, to be stimulated to the exercise of its proper functions, to be strengthened, that is, to do its own thinking." Wilson protested that he could not *cram;* he "must eat slowly and assimilate, during intervals of rest and diversion." His chief ground of indictment against his teachers was that they gave the student infinitely more than he could digest. Moreover, if he did not refuse many of the things set before him, his "mental digestion would soon be utterly ruined." [24]

Wilson also realized that a conscientious thinker "must dig in books." One could not find history elsewhere; nor could one fully understand present experiences unless one knew many books and manuscripts. There was "duty in drudgery as well as in love and in laughter," he confessed. It was as necessary for the Christian to work as to be happy. The fatigued deserved sympathy but not release; if tiredness brought low spirits or despondency, it was not the fault of the work. In short, if a man did not find duty agreeable, he did not "deserve gratification." [25]

For a decade or more Wilson had sought mastery in the art of public speaking. At Johns Hopkins he continued to speak as he had at Davidson, at Princeton, and at the University of Virginia.

[22]Wilson to Ellen Axson, January 16, 1884, in the Axson–Wilson Letters, Princeton.

[23]Wilson to Ellen Axson, November 27, 1883, in *ibid.*

[24]Wilson to Ellen Axson, December 22, 1883, in *ibid.*

[25]Wilson to Ellen Axson, January 20, 1885, in *ibid.*

None of his professors practiced oratory in their lectures, but he thought they should. Oratory was not declamation, he declared, not swelling tones and an excited delivery, "but the art of persuasion, the art of putting things so as to appeal irresistibly to an audience." How could a teacher stimulate young men to study, how could he saturate them with great ideas and stimulate them to worthy purposes, how could he draw them out of themselves and make them become forces in the world without oratory? "Perfunctory lecturing," he said, "is of no service in the world. It's a nuisance." [26]

Since there was only one debating society, the Matriculate Society, Wilson soon joined it. Through his influence this organization became the Hopkins Literary Society[27] and later was transformed by him into the Hopkins House of Commons. For the fourth time during his academic career, he wrote a new constitution for a literary society. The Johns Hopkins House of Commons was divided into two parties, the various members of which upheld their political theories in debate. Those who were successful in convincing their fellows formed the government, but were forced out of power as soon as they failed to muster a vote of confidence.[28] This time Wilson even penned a set of bylaws for the society and presided over the meeting at which the members adopted all the new methods. It was characteristic of him that he took so much pleasure in the proceedings of the literary society. It reminded him of the time that he piloted a new constitution to adoption in the Jefferson Society at the University of Virginia. "I have a sense of power in dealing with men collectively," he wrote, "which I do not feel always in dealing with them singly. In the former case the pride of reserve does not stand so much in my way as it does in the latter. One feels no sacrifice of pride necessary in courting the favour of an assembly of men such as he would have to make in seeking to please one man." [29]

These self-revealing lines to Ellen Axson penetrate the inner

[26]Wilson to Ellen Axson, October 30, 1883, in *ibid.*

[27]J. Franklin Jameson to John Jameson, March 23, 1884, in Donnan and Stock (eds.), *An Historian's World,* 34.

[28]Charles K. Edmonds, "Wilson's Formative Years," *passim.*

[29]Wilson to Ellen Axson, December 18, 1884, in Axson–Wilson Letters, Princeton.

nature of Wilson's personality. How much power he frequently exemplified in dealing with masses of men and what a dearth of influence he often revealed in contacts with men individually! Woodrow had an innate shyness—coupled with a Scotch reserve, southern pride, and perhaps a tinge of the southern gentlemen's *noblesse oblige,*—which prohibited him from sacrificing pride at any time "in seeking to please one man." What power he exerted over people, and at times it was phenomenal, was exerted over them in mass.

Wilson's heavy graduate work and his writing, added to all of his extracurricular activities and interests, were endangering his frail physical constitution. Perhaps it was not the long hours so much as it was the intensity with which he labored that so completely dissipated his nervous energy and so frequently wrecked his digestive track. He realized that he was overworking when he began to have headaches and indigestion. He did not, however, take note of these danger signals, and by January, 1884, was compelled to go home for several weeks of recuperation.[30]

In noting Wilson's participation in numerous activities connected with university life, one must not conclude that he did not occasionally find time for recreation. "The older I get," he said, "the more does a boy's spirit seem to possess me and I chafe often not a little under the necessity of having to preserve the dignified demeanor of a man." [31] Wilson loved, therefore, the afternoons and evenings when he could slip away from his work and relax in the home of former Princeton classmate Hiram Woods, now a practicing physician. Woodrow had begun to acquire an audience for his stories, which he told in Irish, Scottish, or southern Negro dialect, and was gaining attention by his aptness in responding to toasts. His reputation was fast growing "for being irrepressible, in select circles, as a maker of grotesque addresses from the precarious elevation of chair seats, as a wearer of all varieties of comic grimaces, as a simulator of sundry unnatural, burlesque styles of voice and speech, as a lover of farces—even as a dancer of the can-can." [32]

[30]Wilson to Ellen Axson, April 27, 1884, in *ibid.*
[31]Wilson to Ellen Axson, January 4, 1884, in *ibid.*
[32]Wilson to Ellen Axson, April 5, 1885, in *ibid.*

Whatever the season, Wilson endeavored to find the time for an occasional walk, but he was not always successful in his efforts. At times he remained at his desk to "read, read, read when the open air so tempted [him] to aimless roving through its bright spaces." On a winter day he enjoyed seeing "the bright eyes, the elastic step, the rosy cheeks, the easy energy" of everyone he met when he strolled along the sidewalks with a long, even stride. He was filled with a joy in other people's living.[33] In the fall he would sometimes walk down near the wharves where the ships swung at anchor. In the spring he frequented country lanes to see the apple trees in bloom and to hear the woods alive with the calls of birds.

Although Wilson was never an extrovert, he did value the few friendships he made. During the Johns Hopkins years, as earlier at Princeton and at the University of Virginia, he formed few deep personal attachments. That he remained in contact with at least three of his Princeton friends while at Baltimore is evidenced by his papers. In addition to Hiram Woods, whom Wilson saw occasionally, he wrote letters to Charles Talcott and Robert Bridges. Of the last he wrote feelingly: "If I have any best friend in the world, that friend is Bob Bridges." For years Wilson had felt towards Bridges as towards a brother. If they had seemed to drift apart of late years it was only because necessity had separated them. In addition to these three Princetonians, Wilson continued to correspond with Heath Dabney of the University of Virginia law school days. At Johns Hopkins he was probably closer to Albert Shaw than to any other graduate student.

No narrative of the young Wilson in his graduate school days would be complete without mention of his religious conviction. For him there was never any doubt about his faith, nor would he ever discuss religion. He *knew* that he was among the Calvinistic elect and that his future, whatever it might be, was predestined. In this belief he was as steadfast as an Old Testament prophet. Ray Stannard Baker stated that Woodrow repeatedly intimated, if he did not say so precisely, that one could "hear the ancient and accepted doctrine [of true religion] only in the Presbyterian Church." [34]

[33]Wilson to Ellen Axson, April 12, 1885, January 21, 1885, in *ibid.*

[34]Baker, *Wilson Life and Letters,* I, 208.

At times, however, Wilson departed from the stern, theological terminology used by John Calvin: "I recently made a great 'find,' " he once wrote, "namely a Presbyterian Church where there is first-rate preaching—first rate by the Baltimore standard, which is not very high or exacting—and plenty of pretty girls." He became a regular attendant upon its services. Seldom did one find attractive orthodoxy in a Presbyterian pulpit and beauty in the pews, Woodrow stated, and added that he was "specially gratified because of this discovery." There was for the young Wilson decided advantage in having a strict training in the Calvinistic doctrine. "No amount of beauty in the damsels of an Episcopal or Methodist or Baptist Church," he continued, "could have led me off; but beauty in one's own church may be admired weekly with a conscience void of offence." Apparently, nothing could shake him from complete loyalty to his Presbyterian faith. Extended a cordial invitation to sing in the "finest choir in town," he declined because "it was a Methodist choir." The controlling motive, as he himself stated, was the question of religious doctrine.[35]

Wilson's complete loyalty to the religious faith of his parents gave him in the years of his youth and thereafter a clear conscience and made him acceptable to most of Calvin's followers. This was not true, however, of an uncle, Dr. James Woodrow. This illustrious brother of Wilson's mother was educated in German universities. One of the few members of the American Presbyterian church of that generation to be educated abroad, Dr. Woodrow accepted as part of his religious doctrine the higher criticism and the teaching of Darwin which were beginning to emanate from German scholars. As a professor of science and religion at the Columbia Presbyterian Seminary and as editor of a widely-read sectarian periodical, he, because of his teaching and writing, was soon branded as an unorthodox Modernist. In 1884, while Wilson was in graduate school, Professor Woodrow was tried for heresy by the state synods and the General Assembly of the Southern Presbyterian Church. "I held firmly to all the views on evolution," Woodrow's Uncle James stated, "which I have published in the last six and one-half years. All my studies during that

[35]Wilson to Ellen Axson, March 23, 1884, in Axson–Wilson Letters, Princeton.

time have convinced me more and more of their probable truth. I claim the right to advocate these views as I may have occasion."[36] He refused to recant and was ousted from the church of his faith, dismissed from the seminary faculty, and deprived of his editorship.[37]

Wilson expressed complete loyalty to his uncle and declared that all private members of the Presbyterian Church like himself "ought to withdraw without waiting for the expulsion which should follow belief in evolution." If the Presbyterians of the Lower Mississippi Valley, Wilson continued, had so precarious a hold upon their faith in an all-wise Providence that they were afraid to have their sons learn anything of modern science, "by all means let them drive Dr. Woodrow to the wall."[38]

It was during this period that Wilson began to write again. From the time his article "Cabinet Government in the United States" had appeared in the *International Review,* in August, 1879, Wilson thought much about expanding its central theme into a book. Perhaps he had originally conceived the idea from reading Gamaliel Bradford's article, "The Way Congress Does Business," which appeared in 1873 and in which the author urged the shift to cabinet government as Wilson began to do in 1879.[39] Other writers also were advocating the changes in the cabinet-Congress relationship that Wilson now sought.[40] In brief, Wilson

[36]Memo from letter (n.d.) in Wilson Papers.

[37]Dr. James Woodrow organized a bank in Columbia, South Carolina. Under his presidency, the bank prospered. Years later, after Dr. Woodrow amassed a fortune, and now without his request, he was voted back into full fellowship of the Presbyterian Church South. This is an excellent illustration of the Calvinistic attitude towards election and materialism.

[38]Wilson to Ellen Axson, June 24, 1884, in Axson–Wilson Letters, Princeton. The people felt that they could not support Columbia Seminary if Dr. Woodrow remained there as professor. "His neglect of the sanctuary, the peculiar teachings of his chair and other things have caused them to feel that they cannot trust their young men with us." J. B. Mack to Brother Boggs, June 4, 1884, in Wilson Papers.

[39]Gamaliel Bradford, "The Way Congress Does Business," *Nation,* XVI (February 27, 1873), 145–46; Gamaliel Bradford, "Shall the Cabinet Have Seats in Congress?", *Nation,* XVI (April 3, 1873), 233–34.

[40]Arthur S. Link, *Wilson: The Road to the White House* (Princeton, 1947), 15–19.

did not originate the idea, but was the first to expand it into book form. For five years he continued to read about constitutional history and administrative government. He hoped to write about the United States government as a living organism, using a functional approach. In Walter Bagehot's *The English Constitution* (American edition, 1873) Wilson found the example he was determined to follow in his book on American government.

"Of course, I am not vain enough to expect to produce anything so brilliant or so valuable as Bagehot's book," he wrote. His ambition was to treat the American Constitution as the Englishman had treated the English Constitution. If such an innovation in methodology could be applied, Wilson believed the result would be a revelation to those who were still reading the *Federalist* as an authoritative constitutional manual. Any close observer who sought to compare the Constitution with the living organism of government would at once realize the great contrast between the documentary description and the reality. In any event, if he were fortunate enough to publish the book, it would serve as material for college lectures, placing the old topics about the federal government "in a somewhat novel light." [41]

On New Year's Day, 1884, he began writing his book. He planned a series of four or five essays on the general subject "The Government of the Union," in which he wished to show, as well as he could, the constitutional system as it looked in operation. On that first day Wilson wrote a historical sketch of the modifications which had been wrought in the federal system, to be used as an introduction to some essays on Congress in which he planned to examine at length the relations between the congressional and executive branches of the government. He hoped to examine thoroughly the legislative machinery which contained the mainspring of federal action.

During the spring, progress on the book was discouragingly slow. Woodrow particularly hated the tedious chore of copying the essays on his Caligraph typewriter after they were written.[42]

[41]Wilson to Ellen Axson, January 1, 1884, in Axson–Wilson Letters, Princeton.

[42]Wilson to Ellen Axson, March 30, 1884, in *ibid.*

By April three of them were completed and were dispatched to Houghton-Mifflin in Boston.[43] Although Wilson did not know what chance he had of getting the essays published, he did read them to the history seminary and they won him a five hundred dollar fellowship for his second year at Hopkins.[44]

In May, 1884, Wilson was back under his father's roof and prepared "to tackle again constitutional history."[45] When he returned to Johns Hopkins in the fall, his book manuscript was nearly complete, and he submitted it to Houghton-Mifflin. He was encouraged by the publisher's comments on the earlier chapters, but, when the completed manuscript left his hands, he was seized by pangs of doubt and uncertainty.[46]

The essays were quite different from their original form. "At any rate the new ones are less crude, besides being entirely different both in form and in purpose," wrote Wilson. He omitted "all advocacy of Cabinet government—all advocacy, indeed, of *any specific* reform"—and devoted himself to a careful analysis of congressional government. He had abandoned the "evangelical for the exegetical" and the result was something "very much more thorough and more sober, as well as more valuable" and more likely to be acceptable if published.[47] After weeks of anxious waiting, Houghton-Mifflin wrote: "We shall take pleasure in publishing the book at our own risk and paying you the usual royalty of ten percent on the retail price of all copies sold."[48]

Of his happiness at publication Wilson wrote: "Success does not flush or elate me, except for the moment." He wished that it did, he told Ellen Axson, for he badly needed a large infusion of the devil-may-care spirit. The acceptance of his book, however, had given him "the deepest satisfaction and has cleared away a

[43]Wilson to Houghton Mifflin Company, April 4, 1884, in Wilson Papers, Library of Congress.

[44]Wilson to Bridges, May 31, 1884, in Meyer Collection, Library of Congress.

[45]Wilson to Bridges, May 31, 1884, in *ibid.*

[46]Wilson to Ellen Axson, November 1, 1884, in Axson–Wilson Letters, Princeton.

[47]Wilson to Bridges, November 19, 1884, in Meyer Collection, Library of Congress.

[48]Houghton-Mifflin and Company to Wilson, November 26, 1884, in Wilson Papers, Library of Congress.

whole storm of anxieties." It was an immense gain in every way and had sobered him a good deal too. The question was, "What next?" He must be prompt to follow up his advantage, continuing it in the direction in which he had been "preparing to do effectual political service."

The young author's first book was about the actual workings of the federal government, especially the legislative branch. For the several years that Wilson had been interested in just how the Congress functioned, he had lived most of the time either in Charlottesville or in Baltimore. Both were within easy travelling distance of Washington, but not once did he visit any part of the government in which he was so interested and about which he was writing illuminating essays. Only years later did he actually sit in the gallery and watch the House of Representatives in session. Although meetings of the congressional committees were frequently open to the public, Wilson did not endeavor to attend such a meeting. He was completely satisfied to read, to formulate his own conclusions, and to write critically about political institutions, especially the Congress.

On January 24, 1885, Houghton Mifflin released *Congressional Government: A Study in American Politics,* by Woodrow Wilson, Fellow in History; Johns Hopkins University.[49] Wilson began his book by stating that the Constitution was now the American form of government in name only. The form of the Constitution was one of nicely adjusted, ideal balances, while in reality the government was "a scheme of Congressional supremacy." [50] The balances written into the Constitution of the federal government against the states had proven the least effectual. The national government's supremacy over the states was established through the doctrine of implied powers, which was "both facile and irresistible," and through the "policy of internal improvements." [51] Wilson passed judgment on the House of Representatives, saying that it was "hard to see satisfactorily and appreciatively." Devoid of an effective organization, the Speaker of the House stood as near to leadership as anyone.

[49]Wilson to Dabney, February 14, 1885, in Dabney Papers, Virginia.
[50]Woodrow Wilson, *Congressional Government* (Boston, 1913), 6–7; 36; 43.
[51]*Ibid.,* 17–23, 28.

However, the real leaders of the House were the chairmen of the principal standing committees, who in their respective groups functioned in complete secrecy. As a consequence, "both the House of Representatives and the Senate conduct their business in what may figuratively, but not inaccurately, be called an odd device of *disintegration*." The House virtually deliberated and legislated in small sections. With such division of power and function, there was nowhere the concentration of authority with the responsibility essential to a government in democracy. Although the Speaker possessed the power over procedure and committee appointments, said Wilson, he lacked responsibility.[52]

In his essay on the Senate, Wilson stated that the body was just what the mode of its election and the conditions of public life in the United States had made it. Moreover, this group must be recruited from the lower branches of the representative system, and no stream was better than its sources. Early in American history, "Constitutional issues were ever the tides, questions of administrative policy seldom more than the eddies" of senatorial debate; more recently, however, the reverse was true. There was no feeling or enthusiasm to create recognized leadership. The Senate suffered from the same malady as the House, namely standing committees. Its proceedings bore "most of the characteristic features of Committee rule." Debate in the Senate, however, was usually "of a very high order of excellence." According to the author, the main contribution of the Senate was that it saved the people "from headlong popular tyranny." [53]

In the light of Wilson's later career in politics, his treatment of the Presidency is illuminating. The President, he wrote in 1884, could never deal with the Senate upon "a ground of real equality." He had no real presence in the Senate, and his power did not extend beyond the most general suggestion. The Senate always had the last word. Able administrators were men of experience; therefore, it was best to choose the President from among the ablest and most experienced state governors. Furthermore, the "ascendency or tact of the President himself" was the only influence to keep a "Cabinet in harmony and to dispose it to

[52] *Ibid.*, 58–60; 66–67; 91–93.

[53] *Ibid.*, 194–96; 203; 212; 218; 225; 227.

cooperation." If the President and his cabinet were of one political party and the House and Senate were of the opposite, the President's party would not be in power "beyond the hindering and thwarting faculty of the veto." In any sort of a clash between the President and the Congress, the latter was master. To learn of the Presidency, one should learn the "main conditions which mould it to the forms of congressional supremacy." [54]

In the country's increasingly complex industrial system, Wilson concluded, the vigilant oversight of administration was as important as legislation. Even more important was the guidance which the people might receive in political affairs through a "broad daylight of discussion." Congress was rapidly becoming the governing body of the nation, and the power of legislation was "the oil of government." The tendency was towards a centralization of the powers of government in the hands of federal authorities and towards the "supreme overlordship which Congress has been gradually arrogating to itself." Finally, "the federal government lacks strength because its powers are divided, lacks promptness, because its authorities are multiplied, lacks wieldiness because its processes are roundabout, lacks efficiency because its responsibility is indistinct and its action without competent direction." [55] Throughout the book, Wilson spoke favorably of the English system of ministerial responsibility, with its fusion of executive and legislative powers. "The British system," he concluded, "is perfected party government." [56]

The book was widely reviewed and well received. The review in the *Nation,* said Wilson, "quite takes my breath away." [57] Gamaliel Bradford, enthusiastic for congressional reforms, declared in that appraisal: "We have no hesitation in saying that this is one of the most important books, dealing with political subjects," which has ever issued from the American press.[58] The Chicago *Tribune* labeled Wilson's book "a very interesting treatise which deserves attention." [59] The Boston *Commercial Bulletin* thought

[54]*Ibid.,* 238, 256, 259, 266, 275, 293.
[55]*Ibid.,* 297, 301, 315, 318.
[56]*Ibid.,* 117.
[57]Wilson to Dabney, February 14, 1885, in Dabney Papers, Virginia.
[58]*Nation,* XL (February 12, 1885), 142–43.
[59]Chicago *Tribune,* May 30, 1885.

the book a "powerful criticism of the national government, but not done in a cynical or pessimistic spirit." [60] The Minneapolis *Tribune* said Wilson "pictures to us, not what the written Constitution says he ought to find, but what in fact he does find." [61] An editorial in the Boston *Beacon,* definitely critical, concluded by declaring: "What we need in this country is not a critique of our government . . . but a little more understanding of its machinery and methods." [62] In Wilson's native South, the reviews were enthusiastic generally. The Louisville *Courier-Journal* hailed *Congressional Government* "as the first attempt to study our Federal Government in the concrete," and predicted that "it will not be the last, nor will it be without effect." [63] "When we consider," said the Wilmington *Star,* "that it is the production of a young man who is not more than twenty-eight, and who has never sat in Congress or been a member of any legislative assembly, the work must strike the reflecting reader as most remarkable—as phenomenal." [64] Albert Shaw, in *The Dial,* wrote that *Congressional Government* "at once fixes its author's reputation as one of the foremost writers on American political institutions. He fairly deserves the credit of having inaugurated the concrete and scientific study of our political system." [65]

Soon after the publication of his book, Wilson, quite anonymously, stepped into a Baltimore bookshop and asked to purchase a copy. The first clerk he approached "did not know of the book and asked me 'if I remembered who it was by'!" The author simulated "an air of difficult recollection and told him that it was written by a man named Wilson." The clerk made an inquiry and reported that all copies were sold but that more had been ordered.[66]

With the publication of Wilson's book and its wide acceptance, his interest in politics was pushed to a new high. His old

[60] Boston *Commercial Bulletin,* n.d., clipping in Wilson Papers.

[61] Minneapolis *Tribune,* February 15, 1885.

[62] Boston *Beacon,* February 21, 1885.

[63] Louisville *Courier-Journal,* n.d., clipping in Wilson Papers.

[64] Wilmington *Star,* March 12, 1885.

[65] *The Dial,* March 1885, 291–94.

[66] Wilson to Ellen Axson, January 26, 1885, in Axson–Wilson Letters, Princeton.

and passionate desire for the political arena, never for long dormant, blossomed forth. Although he was experiencing the intellectual stimulation of graduate study under able instructors, he yearned for something more. "Yes," he confessed, "there is and has long been, in my mind a lurking sense of disappointment and *loss*," as if he had missed from his life something to which his gifts, his inclinations, and his ambition gave him a claim. "I do feel a very real regret," he lamented, "that I have been shut out from my heart's first—primary—ambition and purpose, which was, to take an active, if possible leading, part in public life and strike out for myself, if I had the ability, a *statesman's* career." That was his heart's, or rather, his "mind's deepest secret." Had the gods of fate given him independent means of support, "even of the most modest proportions," he would have sought an entrance into the political arena. Furthermore, once having entered politics, he would have fought his way to a place of influence "even amidst the hurly-burly and helter-skelter of Congress." In a glowing self-appraisal, Wilson said that he had "a strong instinct of leadership, an unmistakably oratorical temperament, and the keenest possible delight in affairs"; and it had required very constant and stringent schooling to content him "with the sober methods of the scholar and the man of letters." [67] He had no patience for the "tedious toil of research," but had an aggressive "passion for interpreting great thoughts to the word." Anticipating more than three decades into the future, Wilson wrote Ellen that he would be complete if he could inspire a great movement of opinion, if he could "read the experiences of the past into the practical life of the men of today and so communicate the thought to the minds of the great mass of the people as to impel them to great political achievements." Although he said that "of all the world's workers those which take by far the highest rank are the writers of noble books," it is extremely doubtful if he spoke sincerely. His true feeling was that such literary talents as he had were secondary to his equipment for political achievement. As he himself expressed it: "My power to write was meant to be a handmaiden to my power to speak and to organize action." As a devout Presbyterian, he was ready to

[67]Wilson to Ellen Axson, February 24, 1885, in *ibid.*

accept the providential ordering of his life as infallible on that point.[68]

To Charles Talcott, Wilson declared that since he had no "independent fortune to fall back upon for support" should politics fail him, his only proper course was to give up, for the present anyway, all ideas of an active political career and spend his best energies writing on questions of politics and statecraft. In order to realize this alternative ambition, he sought the profession which would offer him "more legitimate opportunities for such work than were to be found in a law office." [69]

During his last year at Johns Hopkins, Wilson had several problems to occupy his time in addition to the publication of his first books. Professor Richard T. Ely decided to write a history of American economic thought and pressed Wilson, along with another graduate student, into the enterprise as collaborator. Throughout the spring of 1885 Woodrow's time for other work was limited as he read the writings of Perry, Bowers, Wayland, Vethake, and the other members of the Ricardian school of economics. Though he busied himself with the reading, the research, and the writing necessary for the joint authorship of the history, he was worried about the value of the book.[70] As it turned out, the book was never published.

A difficult decision that Wilson had to make that last year at Hopkins was whether or not he should try for a doctoral degree. He was definitely against working toward the doctorate, not because he anticipated failure but because he did not want to do the reading and study that would be necessary. Fearing that his decision not to try for the degree was a mistake, he appealed to his father, in a sixteen-page letter, "on the pros and cons of cramming" for the required examinations. Dr. Wilson, having received his professional title *honoris causa*, advised against the special study necessary for the degree. As Wilson recorded the incident: "father advises me not to try for it; and, since his advice coincides with my own coolest judgment in the matter, I have concluded to make no special effort in reading for it."

[68]*Ibid.*
[69]Wilson to Talcott, July 5, 1884, in Baker Papers, Library of Congress.
[70]Wilson to Dabney, February 14, 1885, in Dabney Papers, Virginia.

He was positive that he would profit much more substantially from reading according to his own tastes and choosing than he would from the reading necessary for the Ph.D.—although his inclinations would take him through the most important topics of that course.

This decision made, Wilson began to look for a teaching position for the next year, since he could not marry Ellen until he had some hope of being able to support her. When a new Quaker College, Bryn Mawr, located in a suburb of Philadelphia, needed a young man to help organize the history and political science departments, Wilson was recommended by his professors. "Just before lecture [it was late in November, 1884], Dr. Adams came to me and asked me if I wouldn't come into his office a moment and 'meet some persons who were interested in me and in historical work.' " A few moments later, Woodrow was introduced to Miss Carey Thomas, dean of Bryn Mawr, and to Dr. James E. Rhoads, a trustee of the recently organized girls' school. According to Wilson, Dean Thomas was selecting her faculty with great care "because each teacher chosen will, of course, have to lay the foundation of his, or her, department—will have to *organize* it and give it direction and plan." [71] Other conferences between the dean and the graduate student followed. Out of these meetings came Wilson's first job.

Woodrow was anxious to begin his professional career. He had none of the objections to a girls' school that he held for a coeducational institution. He would have more leisure there for private study than elsewhere, and the salary would be comfortable. It was not his purpose to spend his life in teaching. He did prefer to teach young men, however, and if he found that Bryn Mawr stood in the way of his going to a man's college, he would resign.[72] Nevertheless, Wilson was glad to accept the Bryn Mawr offer and was soon busily formulating organization plans for the Department of History and Political Science. He wrote Heath Dabney that Miss Thomas had promised him complete freedom in teaching methodology, a comparatively limited number of subjects

[71]Wilson to Ellen Axson, November 27, 1884, in Axson–Wilson Letters, Princeton.

[72]Wilson to Ellen Axson, November 30, 1884, in *ibid.*

to teach, and a relatively small number of hours per week to teach them.[73]

Wilson's career as a graduate student at Johns Hopkins had been an exceptional one. He showed more appreciation for his teachers as he became better acquainted with them and was able to recognize and evaluate their abilities. Moreover, he had learned that education, in the truest sense of the word, was acquired directly by the student, not transmitted by another. His participation in the meeting of the history seminary had certainly been above the average of the graduate student group, and his teachers were impressed with his abilities. After several years of partial success, Wilson had won generous praise as a writer through the publication of his first book. Failing to receive a fellowship during his first year as a graduate student, he had received that recognition during his second year at the university. Although he did not try for a Ph.D. in the spring of 1885, he must have been encouraged by his graduate committee to prepare himself eventually for the required examinations. Forced by economic circumstances to give up his chief ambition to enter politics through his law practice and instead to enter the classroom, he was determined to do his best in achieving success in his second-choice career.

[73]Wilson to Dabney, February 14, 1885, in Dabney Papers, Virginia.

CHAPTER VII *Second Romance: Marriage*

In 1873 Woodrow Wilson came to himself spiritually when he joined the Presbyterian church. During his student days at Princeton and at Johns Hopkins he came to himself intellectually. In this chapter we shall see how he matured emotionally in the love for a woman who would give Wilson the man the ballast that his mother had given Wilson the child.[1]

In mid-April, 1883, Wilson was called from Atlanta to Rome, Georgia, to confer with his uncle, James W. Bones, who had until recently been in charge of Jessie Wilson's business. Upon Woodrow's admission to the Georgia bar, he had become his mother's attorney-at-law. It was now necessary to confer with Uncle James before the final settlement of an estate belonging to Mrs. Wilson was made.

Many times, while a student in the University of Virginia law

[1]Donald Day (ed.), *Woodrow Wilson's Own Story* (Boston, 1953), 20.

school, Wilson had visited in the Bones' home in Staunton. About the time he withdrew from the university, the Bones family moved from the Shenandoah Valley to North Georgia and opened a merchandise establishment in Rome.[2] Cousin Jessie Bones was now married to A. T. H. Brower and lived there also.

Although legal business for his mother brought him to Rome, Wilson was in the frame of mind for fun while visiting among his kinsmen. Several times in the late 1870's, while a student at Princeton, he had visited in Rome. In many instances, he was renewing acquaintances among the friends of his relatives. Among the friends of Wilson's cousin Jessie was Ellen Louise Axson. Ellen's father, the Reverend Edward Axson, had begun a pastorate of the First Presbyterian Church at Rome when only thirty years of age, and by 1883 had lived in Rome for sixteen years.[3] Some two years earlier, his wife Margaret had died from complications which followed the birth of her fourth child.[4] Ellen, the oldest of the four children, was mistress of her father's household in which she and her two younger brothers lived.

Ellen was now nearing her twenty-third birthday. Her golden bronze hair, which she usually wore parted in the middle, softly waved at the sides, hanging in shoulder-length curls at the back. Her large, deep-brown eyes were emphasized by wide, heavy eyebrows. Her nose was well shaped; her rather thin lips formed a somewhat wide mouth.[5] Intelligent and demure, Ellen made an attractive picture when Woodrow Wilson first took note of her in April, 1883.

On Wilson's first Sunday in Rome he had accompanied his Aunt Marion, his Uncle James, and his cousin Helen to the First Presbyterian Church in which Bones was an elder and of which the Reverend Edward Axson was pastor. It was on that morning, at some time during the service, that Wilson, as he later wrote to Ellen, saw her face to note it. "You wore a heavy crepe veil and I

[2]Baker, *Wilson Life and Letters,* I, 159–60.

[3]Memo in Baker Papers, Library of Congress.

[4]Ellen Axson was born May 15, 1860, Stockton in 1867, Edward in 1876, and Magaret in 1881. Upon the mother's death, the baby, Margaret, was taken into the family of "Aunt Louisa" Wade of Gainesville, Georgia.

[5]See picture of Ellen Axson taken 1883, reproduced in Baker, *Wilson Life and Letters,* I, 160.

remember thinking 'what a bright, pretty face; what splendid mischievous, laughing eyes! I'll lay a wager that this demure little lady has lots of life and fun in her!' " After the service as Ellen was leaving the church, she spoke to a number of people including Mr Bones. At that moment the slender Wilson took another look at the minister's daughter and concluded that he should seek an introduction. Within the next day or so he took an early opporunity of calling on the Reverend Mr. Axson at the manse. Wilson vividly recalled the meeting: "That dear gentleman," he informed Ellen, "received me with unsuspecting cordiality and sat down to entertain me under the impression that I had come to see only him. I *had* gone to see him, for I love and respect him and would have gone to see him with alacrity if he had never had a daughter; but I had not gone to see him *alone*." The truth of the matter was that ever since Wilson had seen Ellen, he could not remove her from his mind. When he asked rather pointedly about his daughter's health, the minister, in apparent surprise, summoned Ellen to the parlor. With formal introductions over, the three sat down. The young lady listened with pretended interest as the middle-aged theologian imposed upon the youthful barrister the vexing question: "Why have night congregations grown small?" [6]

Within the next few days Woodrow saw Ellen a number of times. There were buggy rides along the picturesque, meandering country roads that led to Rome. Afternoons were spent in long walks along the shaded banks of the Oostanaula River. Wilson later recalled one such stroll: "We had chosen the railroad bed because it led along the bank of the river and would lead us to where we would find a seat near the water on a big jutting rock which stood with its feet in the river commanding a view of one of the prettiest bends of the stream." He remembered every incident of the walk and was quite conscious that he was very much in love with his companion.[7] Occasional boat rides furnished a romantic setting for their conversations as they became better acquainted.

And so it was "a fast and furious courtship," as the Presbyterian

[6]Wilson to Ellen Axson, October 11, 1883, in Axson–Wilson Letters, Princeton.

[7]Wilson to Ellen Axson, October 23, 1883, in *ibid.*

clergyman's son daily sought to woo the Presbyterian preacher's daughter. If Woodrow had spent his youthful years in a manse surrounded by books and religion, so had Ellen. His education was more formal than hers, but her intellectual interests were not narrowed by specialization as were his. Consequently, Ellen acquainted him with the literary world of William Wordsworth, the exquisite imagery of Sidney Lanier's poetry, and the love sonnets of Robert and Elizabeth Browning. Gifted with an unusual artistic talent, Ellen also introduced Woodrow to the world of art.

When Wilson left Rome for Wilmington, relatives and friends were aware of his serious intentions towards Ellen. The Reverend Mr. Axson wrote a long letter to Stockton, Ellen's brother, who was away at school, and chose Woodrow as his text. "My father," remembered Stockton, "went on the theory that his [Woodrow's] example would do more for my upbringing than wordy precepts, and so the first homily he ever delivered to me was in the form of a long letter written just after Woodrow Wilson had ended a visit to his relatives in Rome. My father," continued Stockton, "made this young man ten years older than myself for his text, described him and held him up to me as a pattern of young manhood." Stockton recalled one line of the letter virtually verbatim. His father stated that he could "think of nothing that would make me so happy as to have a son like that." [8]

In the meantime, the young Wilson withdrew to Atlanta to sell or pack for shipment his belongings in the law office. By the middle of June he had taken down his professional shingle, had disposed of his share of the office equipment, had shipped his books and bookcases to Wilmington, and had said goodbye to his friends. He did not go immediately to Wilmington but spent the latter half of June in Rome with his relatives and in the company of Ellen Axson.

Naturally, Woodrow kept his parents informed of his feelings toward Ellen. At first his mother was "greatly taken by surprise" and felt distressed that her son "should be involved in any way

[8]Stockton Axson, "The Private Life of Woodrow Wilson," *New York Times Magazine*, October 8, 1916.

just yet," as she saw there "needs would be a weary waiting." On the other hand, from all Wilson's mother had heard of Ellen, she felt assured that there was no "sweeter or purer girl than she." And, if Woodrow succeeded in winning Ellen someday, no one would be more delighted than his mother.[9]

Wilson decided upon a persistent courtship. To Bobby Bridges he wrote with disarming frankness:

> You will smile to learn I forgot my loss of my cousin by falling in love with a charming brown-eyed lassie who is attractive not only because of her unusual beauty, but also because of her unusual accomplishments. She belongs to that class which has contributed so much both to the literature and to the pleasures of social life. She is a clergyman's daughter. The condition of her life and her natural inclination have led her into extensive reading of the best sort, and the dear lassie has become learned without knowing it, and without losing one particle of freshness or natural feminine charm. But I can't describe her. If future favors me, you shall know her some day and find her out for yourself; for I've made up my mind to win her if I can.[10]

When Wilson reached home on July 4, anxiety and sadness awaited him. His mother was desperately ill with typhoid fever. He helped his sister with the nursing and was soon able to report that the patient was convalescing. The family planned to go to the mountains in the western part of the state for recreation and recuperation.

As Woodrow thought over the immediate past, he had a feeling of deep relief in having escaped the imprisonment of the bar. In this feeling he was encouraged by several friends, among whom was Heath Dabney who wrote of his happiness at Wilson's decision, adding that a professorship was what "every man ought to have who wished to lead an intellectual life, and to do independent and original work." [11] By his resolution to enter the graduate school of Johns Hopkins University, Woodrow was convinced

[9]Janet Wilson to Woodrow Wilson, June 21, 1883, in Wilson Papers, Library of Congress.

[10]Wilson to Bridges, July 26, 1883, in Meyer Collection, Library of Congress.

[11]Dabney to Wilson, July 22, 1883, in Wilson Papers, Library of Congress.

that he was within reach of a literary career which before many years would produce results.[12]

In August he escorted his mother and his sister Anne to Flat Rock, North Carolina, but soon journeyed on to Arden Park.[13] Shortly thereafter, Ellen went to visit other friends vacationing in nearby Morgantown. Efforts of Woodrow to contact Ellen by mail failed and he departed for Baltimore. In the meantime, Ellen received word of her father's illness and his request for her to return home. After a brief delay she went to Asheville, where she went to the Eagle Hotel to await a train for Knoxville. An hour or so later Wilson alighted from a train in Asheville and, as he strolled up the street, noted a girl silhouetted against a window in the nearby hotel. Recognizing instantly the way Ellen's hair coiled about the back of her neck, he sprang up the steps to meet her. It was by sheer coincidence that she was at the hotel, whiling away the time between trains by reading a book. At Woodrow's persuasion she agreed to postpone her departure for Rome, until he left for Baltimore several days later.

The day before Wilson left for Baltimore he rented a horse and buggy, bundled Ellen on the seat beside him, and drove to Arden to present her to members of his family. She endeared herself to Woodrow's family as she had to him. To Wilson's mother, Ellen seemed "so sweet, so bright and intelligent—that it was impossible not to love her." [14] With Ellen as his constant companion for the long weekend, Woodrow lost not a moment in pressing his affections, and this time he was successful.

In a letter to Ellen two months later, Wilson recalled his feeling at the moment of their engagement:

> When I recall my first feeling for you; how passionate love grew rapidly upon me; how all my thoughts used to center in plans to win you; what castles my hopes used to build and how I used to sicken at the prospect of hope deferred; and then how . . . we met and you gave your heart to me, it all seems so like a sweet dream that I am afraid to credit my memory. . . . Although you had spoken

[12]Wilson to Bridges, July 26, 1883, in Meyer Collection, Library of Congress.

[13]Wilson to Bridges, August 10, September 12, 1883, in *ibid.*

[14]Janet Wilson to Woodrow Wilson, September 19, 1883, in Wilson Papers, Library of Congress.

the words which will always live in my memory, 'I will do anything to make you happy'; although I had taken that sweet sealing kiss and had been permitted to hold you in my arms, I remember calling you 'Miss Ellen' to the last and being utterly unable to speak any part of the love and joy that were in my heart.[15]

Only five months had elapsed since Woodrow asked rather pointedly of Dr. Axson about the health of his daughter.

Wilson lost no time in seeking the approval of Ellen's father. He knew that Dr. Axson would not be surprised, and he trusted that the minister would not be displeased to learn that his daughter had won Woodrow's "warmest love." Although just out of a sick bed and quite feeble, Dr. Axson replied that he entirely sanctioned Ellen's engagement. He could not think that her happiness would be "at all hazarded" in Wilson's hands.[16]

After his arrival in Baltimore, Woodrow penned a note to his mother and told her of his happiness.[17] Although "very, very glad to hear the good news," she replied, "I was not very much surprised for I thought I could discover that she cared for you when she was here . . . and now that she is my previous boy's promised wife, I shall love her very dearly." In thinking of Woodrow's entrance into the graduate school at Johns Hopkins University in the near future, his mother added: "and now [that] your heart is at rest you will be able to give yourself to the work before you with all of your heart—and I have no fear for the result." [18]

Once Woodrow was settled in a room on North Charles Street he purchased an engagement ring and dispatched it with haste to "my own darling," as he now addressed his fiancee. "I know you will think it pretty," he wrote. He had nothing engraved in it because he preferred to learn Ellen's taste and preference in the matter. He wanted her to wear it as it was until he could be

[15]Wilson to Ellen Axson, November 18, 1883, in Axson–Wilson Letters, Princeton.

[16]Stockton Axson to Wilson, September 24, 1883, in Wilson Papers, Library of Congress.

[17]Apparently this letter was lost, but the date must have been September 17, 1883.

[18]Janet Wilson to Woodrow Wilson, September 19, 1883, in Wilson Papers, Library of Congress.

with her again. Then, they could have what she wished engraved in it and he could place it on her finger "with appropriate ceremonies of our own invention." [19] To Ellen, the ring was a "*perfect beauty* in every respect," although she could not help asking, "Are you not very extravagant?" She was "really startled and amazed at the unexpected apparition of a diamond." [20]

Immediate marriage was out of the question. The plans which Woodrow had made must be carried out as pre-arranged. But now the young Wilson was a different student from the one who, four years earlier, had entered the law school at Charlottesville. There was no emotional tug now for weekend trips across mountains or elsewhere. Gone was any doubt of failure in the adventure of romantic pursuit. As Wilson's mother, with full understanding, had written him, his heart was completely at ease and he could apply himself to his work without emotional obstacles.

From the day Ellen accepted Woodrow's proposal, he resolved to relate to her the deepest feelings of his heart. "I suppose," he confessed, "that there never was a man more dependent than I on love and sympathy, more devoted to home and home life; and, my darling, my heart is overflowing with gratitude and gladness because of the assurance that it now has a new love to lean upon—a love which will some day be the center of a new home and the joy of a new home life. I shall not begin to live a complete life, my love, until you are my wife." In a different vein, Wilson continued: "Can you love me in every humour? Or would you prefer to think of me as always dignified? I am afraid it would kill me to be always thoughtful and sensible, dignified and decorous. . . . I have no fears as to what you will think of the boy that is constantly cropping out when I'm not under the constraint of 'company manners.' " [21]

Wilson did not believe that any man who was not "merely a student, simply a thinking machine, could wish to marry a woman . . . who expels sentiment from life." He wanted a wife

[19] Wilson to Ellen Axson, September 25, 1883, in Axson–Wilson Letters, Princeton.

[20] Ellen Axson to Wilson, October 2, 1883, in *ibid.*

[21] Wilson to Ellen Axson, October 2, 1883, in *ibid.*

who would be able to come into his study as his "close companion." [22]

Ellen Axson appreciably broadened his horizons in literature, in art, and in architecture. She brought to Wilson her experiences of wide reading, her taste for poetry, and her enthusiasm for fiction. The two of them began even before they were married to supplement each other's reading. As Wilson put it: "We will purvey for each other in separate literary fields." Time would not permit him to read many things which he really wanted to know about; he must labor unceasingly in one or two fields of specialization. Ellen could ascertain for him what was going on in the world of literature, what subjects were currently being discussed in the periodicals. Having gathered this information, she could recite to him the plots and read to him the "choice parts of the best novels of the day," and fill his too "prosy brain with the sweetest words of the poets"; could, in short, keep his mind from "dry rot by exposing it to an atmosphere of fact and entertainment and imaginative suggestion." [23]

Woodrow began to reveal to her something of his professional ambition: "I want to contribute to our literature," he wrote shortly after he entered the graduate school at Johns Hopkins, "studies in the philosophy of our institutions, not the abstract and occult, *but the practical and suggestive,* philosophy which is at the core of our governmental methods; their use, their meaning, 'the spirit that makes them workable.' " [24]

Such ambition as that, obviously, must go unfulfilled in the life of a lawyer. Indeed, the study of history and political science, for which Woodrow, both by nature and by acquired habit, was best fitted could not be pursued in the lawyer's office. Consequently, he was forced, in justice to himself, to find a vocation which best suited his talents and his ambition. "A professorship," he concluded, "was the only feasible place for me, the only place that would afford leisure for reading and for original work, the only strictly literary berth with an income attached." [25] As he

[22]Wilson to Ellen Axson, October 18, 1883, in *ibid.*
[23]Wilson to Ellen Axson, January 23, 1885, in *ibid.*
[24]Wilson to Ellen Axson, October 30, 1883, in *ibid.*
[25]*Ibid.*

wrote Ellen, he realized that a man without an independent fortune "must in any event content himself with becoming an *outside* force in politics." With this reality before him, he would be satisfied with the prospect of exerting whatever political influence he could "through literary and non-partisan agencies." [26]

Acquiring the ability to write with power in the political realm was one of the main reasons for Wilson's return to formal education. With utter frankness he confessed to Ellen that he came to Baltimore "to get a special training in historical research and an insight into the most modern literary and political thoughts and methods." He hoped to become "an invigorating and enlightening power in the world of political thought and a master in some of the less serious branches of literary art." [27]

It was natural that Woodrow should eventually explain to Ellen his courtship of Harriet Woodrow. Fresh from Princeton, where he had spent four years away "from all society, but the society of men," he went to Charlottesville, he told her, determined to "find a lady-love, if possible." At that time he felt that he "had a great unexpended store of affection which someone ought to appropriate," and it was with that conviction that he met Harriet. In the summer of 1881 he had gone to Ohio to visit her and during that visit he had "completed the little drama by proposing to her and being refused." Although all traces of the wound were gone, he wrote Ellen, his "pride . . . winced at the memory of the huge mistake" he had made with "such willful blindness." [28] "It had been "weak and silly" said Wilson, to do so unfortunate a thing as fall in love with his cousin. Indeed, he added, it was Ellen who had taught him "the vast, immeasurable difference between a youth's fancy and a man's overmastering love." [29]

Ellen heard a great deal about Woodrow's proposed book. He became so intensely interested in his reading and in making plans for the writing of his book that he decided against any Christmas trip home or vacation at all. "I am beginning to think," he confessed, "that I have made a mistake in working all

[26] *Ibid.*
[27] *Ibid.*
[28] *Ibid.*
[29] Wilson to Ellen Axson, October 18, 1883, in *Ibid.*

through the vacation without allowing myself any respite at all." Except for the time which he spent writing to Ellen or to his family, he had spent his days studying. He did not go near any of his Baltimore friends. Being "such an excessively proud and sensitive creature" and looking upon the Christmas season as one "specially sacred to *family* reunions and festivities," he did not choose to visit any of the families of his acquaintance, lest he might interfere in some way with their holiday plans.

The mental exertion, the nervous tension, and the physical exhaustion to which he relentlessly drove himself during the holiday vacation began to take their toll. His usual physical maladies of upset digestion, headaches, extreme nervousness, and insomnia possessed him. He was saddened by the knowledge that Ellen's father had been committed to the Georgia State Mental Hospital in Milledgeville, and left Baltimore to join her.[30] He soon found it necessary to go to Wilmington for rest and relaxation. He apparently made a visit to the family physician, who told him that he was overworking. Regularity of habits, easing up some on the work, and lessening of tension brought about improvement and he returned to his studies.

Apparently Wilson kept secret, except from his parents, a suddenly made decision to marry Ellen at the end of his first year of graduate work. His mother was much distressed when she read her son's letter which told of his plans. In reply she said she wished, as did Woodrow, for the marriage to take place *"at the earliest possible day,"* but she wondered whether a marriage under the existing circumstances would "lead to happiness"—she thought not.[31] Dr. Wilson replied at great length to his favorite son. After prayerful thought, the father advised "against the precipitancy" to which Woodrow's heart inclined—"Your *heart* rather than your *judgment,* I must believe," he added. Would it be wise, he asked, to involve Ellen in a relationship "where she would be constrained to fill her dependence upon your mother and me." His first impulse, wrote Dr. Wilson, was to say marry,

[30]Wilson to Ellen Axson, February 2, 1884, in *ibid.* The visit was the third week in January.

[31]Janet Wilson to Woodrow Wilson, May 15, 1884, in Wilson Papers, Library of Congress.

bring the bride home, and the four of them would get along together as well as possible. Better counsel was to wait still longer until Woodrow had "something of his own to lay at the feet of his bride." He was certain that his son wanted the truth, for by nothing less could he stand or in nothing less could he be happy.[32]

In the early summer Woodrow was back in Wilmington trying to work on his book. But he wrote Bobby Bridges that he was thinking of going to see a "certain charming young lady in Georgia." "Courtship," he added, "beats constitutional questions any day." [33] It was not only courtship that prompted Woodrow to think seriously of paying Ellen a visit, however. She needed him. Her father had never recovered from his illness of the preceding winter. Fatigue, worry, and physical illness all united to affect his mind. Late in May, 1884, he died. Woodrow penned a note of condolence: "Your dear father, however sad or tragic his death may have been, is happy now. His Saviour, we may be sure, did not desert his servant at the supreme moment; and it is a joy to think that he is now reunited to the sweet, noble mother who went before him." [34] Stricken with grief, Ellen needed Woodrow's comforting presence and the assurance of his words of sympathy. He arrived in Rome in time for Dr. Axson's funeral and remained with Ellen and her brothers for two weeks.

Although Woodrow obviously gave much attention to Ellen in her bereavement and to their plans for a future together, his work on the book was never far from his thoughts. In Wilmington, he found no intellectual companionship, no mental stimulation, save in his own work. At times Wilson was lonely; frequently he was just plain bored. Whatever his mood, Ellen always knew of it. He wrote after breakfast, drove in the afternoon, and usually read aloud after supper, while his mother sewed or embroidered. Between the morning of writing and the afternoon drive, he answered his father's business letters and attended to his own correspondence. Jessie Wilson declared that the buggy ride was not enough exercise for her scholarly son and ad-

[32]Joseph Ruggles Wilson to Woodrow Wilson, May 17, 1884, in *ibid.*

[33]Wilson to Bridges, May 31, 1884, in Meyer Collection, Library of Congress.

[34]Wilson to Ellen Axson, June 1, 1884, in Axson–Wilson Letters, Princeton.

monished him to take long walks and to practice calisthenics. These things Woodrow grumblingly regarded "as much too big a price to pay for the privilege of devoting my mornings to study." Yet Woodrow confessed to Ellen that he did "need some powerful antidote when [taking] original composition in large doses." There was not half as much wear and tear for Wilson in mastering the contents of a score of books as in writing one. He was certain that no amount of reading taxed him as severely as two or three hours of concentrated writing.[35]

Wilson learned in mid-summer that Ellen had inherited enough from her father's modest estate to make it possible for her to further her education in the fine arts. She planned to spend the winter of 1884–85 studying at the Art Students' League in New York. When the visit was over Woodrow accompanied her as far as Baltimore. Presently his mother and father sent him their impressions of Ellen: "She is very lovely—so intelligent and in every way attractive," wrote Wilson's mother.[36] The usually sentimental Dr. Wilson spoke of Ellen as the girl "whom we both love paternally and maternally."[37]

When Ellen began her study at the Art Students' League, Woodrow confessed his own ignorance of her field: "I have the sincerest sympathy with your present studies," he wrote, "and for various reasons. First and foremost of course, because they are yours; but scarecely less because I have always had, and been conscious of having, a great store of potential enthusiasm for just such occupations and accomplishments." Wilson visualized a kinship of creativeness between the artist and the orator: "I suppose that it would be idle for me to hope ever to be an orator if I did *not* have these artistic sympathies." In fact, one of his few grave misfortunes was that he had known least of the two things that moved him most deeply—painting and poetry. "My sensibilities in those directions," he concluded, "seem to me like a musical instrument seldom touched, like a harp disused."[38]

[35]Wilson to Ellen Axson, August 31, 1884, in *ibid.*

[36]Janet Wilson to Woodrow Wilson, October 11, 1884, in Wilson Papers, Library of Congress.

[37]Joseph Ruggles Wilson to Woodrow Wilson, October 9, 1884, in *ibid.*

[38]Wilson to Ellen Axson, November 23, 1884, in Axson–Wilson Letters, Princeton.

Woodrow and Ellen were seeing each other during these months of their engagement as frequently as the exigencies of their respective student careers would permit. After a weekend visit in New York, Woodrow returned to Baltimore to write that it wasn't "pleasant or convenient to have strong passions. . . . I have the uncomfortable feeling that I am carrying a volcano about with me." His salvation was in being loved. Furthermore, Ellen was the only person in the world—except the dear ones at home with whom he did not have to act a part—to whom he "did not have to deal out confidences cautiously." [39]

For Woodrow the Christmas season of 1884, the last before his marriage, was a memorable one. He went to New York, registered at the Metropolitan Hotel near where Ellen lived, and spent every day with her.[40] Together they visited the theaters and art galleries; they strolled in the parks; they went sight-seeing about the city; and they window-shopped along the main thoroughfares. Wilson remembered these days as the happiest he had ever spent.[41] He was more determined than ever upon an early marriage; he would not be alone any longer than he could possibly help.[42]

Soon after returning to the Hopkins campus, Wilson experienced the thrill of holding in his hands the first copies of his book. To whom should the author send the first copy? Woodrow answered the question: "I received two copies of *Congressional Government* last evening," he wrote Ellen, "and immediately reversed the wrappers about one of them and sent it off to you—in hopes that you would get it before Sunday." "I *wanted* to say," he added, "that everything in the book was yours already, having been written in the light and under the inspiration of your love; that every word of it was written to you, with thoughts of what you would think of it, and speculations as to your delight should it receive favour from the publishers and the public; that, as your love runs through this my first book, so it must be the enabling

[39]Wilson to Ellen Axson, December 7, 1884, in *ibid.*

[40]Wilson to Ellen Axson, January 2, 1885, in *ibid.*

[41]Eleanor W. McAdoo (ed.), *The Priceless Gift: The Love Letters of Woodrow Wilson and Ellen Axson Wilson* (New York, 1962), 106.

[42]Wilson to Bridges, January 28, 1885, in Meyer Collection, Library of Congress.

power in all that I may write hereafter, for without your entire love and faith and sympathy it must also be the *last* book into which I could put any of myself. . . . In sending you my first book, darling, I renew the gift of myself." [43]

Not even Ellen knew to whom Wilson dedicated *Congressional Government*. If she felt any pang of disappointment in learning that dedication was to Woodrow's father—"the patient guide of his youth, the gracious companion of his manhood, his best instructor and most lenient critic"—no one ever heard of it. When Wilson showed her the letter from his father telling how the dedication affected him, she rejoiced. "Never have I felt such a blow of love," the proud father, with uncontrolled emotions, exclaimed. "God bless you, my noble child, for such a token of your affection." [44]

In the meantime, the young people were discussing plans for their marriage in the summer. When Ellen consented to a June wedding Wilson was most happy: "Can it be true that I am to have, as my heart's most inestimable treasure, the loving wife for whom my life has so long awaited? Are you really to be my bride, my lifelong sweetheart, the joy and pride of my manhood, and if God will, the comfort and strength of my old age?" [45]

Woodrow, thinking of an early summer marriage and no place to take his bride until school opened in September, wrote his mother suggesting that they come to Wilmington.[46] How very much the mother wished they could come home to spend the summer "but, unfortunately, we will have no home." The Presbyterians, beginning the Southwestern Seminary at Clarksville, Tennessee, had enticed Dr. Joseph R. Wilson from his pulpit at Wilmington with the offer of a chair in theology. Woodrow's mother, with apparent regret, wrote that she could only comfort

[43]Wilson to Ellen Axson, January 24, 1885, in Axson–Wilson Letters, Princeton.

[44]Joseph Ruggles Wilson to Woodrow Wilson, January 30, 1885, in Wilson Papers, Library of Congress.

[45]Wilson to Ellen Axson, January 25, 1885, in Axson–Wilson Letters, Princeton.

[46]Apparently this letter was lost, but Wilson's mother replied to the request on January 29, 1885.

herself "with the thought that Clarksville will be . . . our place for you to come to us in future summers!" [47] Woodrow's younger brother, Joseph, broke the news to Ellen that the Wilsons were planning to leave Wilmington for Clarksville in April.[48]

For a while Woodrow and Ellen toyed with the idea of honeymooning in New England. There they would rusticate, making themselves happy "with books and pen and pencil and *each other* until it is time to come back to the work a day world!" [49] But there were a great many practical difficulties in the way, and the dream of a New England honeymoon was given up for a mountain spot in the South.

As Ellen confided, the trouble with her was "simply a want of time and money." She would not finish at the Art Students' League until the first of June and then she would be completely bankrupt. "I ought really to spend the summer mending my broken fortunes," she wrote. "And, yet, again perhaps, I ought *not*. I am afraid it wouldn't be *just* to him, after my hard winter's work to spend the summer in the same way and then go to him worn out, perhaps broken down in health. It would perhaps be wiser to sacrifice a portion of my little principle, buy my trousseau ready made and take no thought of the morrow." [50] Her heart also had its reasons and these she in complete confidence revealed: "I am anxious to do as he wishes; in fact, I wish it so *strongly* myself that my judgment is apt to be biased. This separation is becoming *unbearable,* almost, to *me* as to my *passionate lover*. Formerly I was *willing* to be his wife *some time*—now I *long to be,* as soon as possible. *I thought* I loved him at the first, but I find I had only begun to love, but then he has given me so much reason to love him. No one will ever know all he has been to me." [51]

Wilson now began to inform his former Princeton friends of his plans. To Charles Talcott he wrote that, although he had a

[47] Janet Wilson to Woodrow Wilson, January 29, 1885, in Wilson Papers, Library of Congress.

[48] Joseph R. Wilson, Jr., to Ellen Axson, January 26, 1885, in *ibid.*

[49] Ellen Axson to Anna Harris, March 8, 1885, in Ellen Axson–Anna Harris Correspondence, Princeton University Library.

[50] *Ibid.*

[51] *Ibid.*

place on the Bryn Mawr faculty, he was not going to identify himself "with the higher education of women, much as I sympathize with it, by spending my life at Bryn Mawr." In teaching the "demure friendly damsels," however, he could ground himself in history, "as I would not otherwise be grounded and can, I hope, at some time at least keep the rust off my special studies, against the day when they will need to be bright for present use." Furthermore, he wanted a period long enough for the accumulation of raw materials, "such as a chap must gather before he can venture upon the manufacture of formal lectures." [52] Obviously, before the young Wilson even gave a lecture or taught a class at his first teaching post, he had decided that he would be there only temporarily.

He wrote Bobby Bridges that he and Ellen were to be married in Savannah, on June 24—the wedding was to be a "private, family affair, with no formal invitations sent out." Woodrow wanted to write each member of his Princeton gang to come to see him set out on a new and better stage of his career.[53] To Bobby's invitation to join the Princeton gang at commencement and stay with him until June 15, Woodrow replied: "I would give the world to come, my dear fellow: the disappointment can't hurt you and the others of our dear old chums half as much as it will hurt me.... Think of me as much as you can at Princeton—get the boys to drink to my health as a token that they remember me and I'll try to get along with that." [54]

At the conclusion of his university work, Woodrow went to the home of his sister Anne in Columbia, South Carolina. Ellen reached Savannah a few days later. Their bondage to pen and paper was at last at an end.[55] In the manse of the Independent Presbyterian Church of Savannah, on June 24, 1885, Woodrow Wilson and Ellen Axson became husband and wife. Ellen's grand-

[52]Wilson to Talcott, March 25, 1885, in Baker Papers, Library of Congress.

[53]Wilson to Bridges, May 21, June 10, 1885, in Meyer Collection, Library of Congress. Wilson to Talcott, June 9, 1885, in Baker Papers, Library of Congress.

[54]Wilson to Bridges, May 22, 1885, in Wilson Collection, Princeton.

[55]Wilson to Ellen Axson, June 21, 1885, in Axson–Wilson Letters, Princeton.

father, the Reverend I. S. K. Axson, who was minister of the church, performed the ceremony. He was assisted by Wilson's father.

Years later, Stockton Axson remembered how Woodrow and he "chatted about the books in my grandfather's bookcases while we waited for the bride to come downstairs." He also recalled a "less idyllic circumstance, how bliss was jarred and the scent of orange blossoms temporarily annulled while two small boys, the bridegroom's nephew, William Howe, and the bride's brother, Edward Axson, 'mixed it up' in a gorgeous fight over some difference in boyish opinions. The bride was much shocked; but I caught a twinkle in the bridegroom's eye, which seemed to say, "let's separate them; but don't let's be in too desperate haste about it." [56] Any man who "could rejoice in a kin fight on his wedding day surely has that broad catholic taste in joy which shows the understanding heart." [57]

Wilson's marriage meant everything to him. It would be almost impossible to overemphasize its importance in his life. To Ellen he had written of their love, their marriage, their future together so many times and in such words of dedication. In one such letter he quoted Hamerton's *Intellectual Life,* noting that "the intellectual life is sometimes a fearfully solitary one. . . . Give him one friend who can understand him, who will not leave him, who will always be accessible by day and night—one friend, one kindly listener, just one, and the whole universe is changed. It is deaf and indifferent no longer, and whilst *she* listens, it seems as if all men and angels listened also, so perfectly his thought is mirrored in the light of her answering eyes. . . . There surely never lived a man," he concluded, "with whom love was a more critical matter than it is with me." [58] And with him this continued to be true.

[56]Stockton Axson, "Private Life of Woodrow Wilson."

[57]William A. White, *Wilson: The Man, His Times, and His Task,* 102.

[58]Baker, *Wilson Life and Letters,* I, 242.

CHAPTER VIII *At Bryn Mawr*

Early in September, 1885, Wilson arrived on the Bryn Mawr campus with his bride, ready for his first professional duties as a teacher. This newly chartered college for girls, beginning its first session, was located on an ancient farm among rolling hills and picturesque woodlands in a suburban area about ten miles northwest of Philadelphia. As Bryn Mawr was founded by a Quaker who was a trustee of Johns Hopkins University, it was frequently spoken of as "Jane" or "Johanna" Hopkins.

Two moderately sized buildings, Taylor Hall and Merion Hall, formed the nucleus of the campus. The former housed the administrative offices, the classrooms, and the almost bare library; the other was the dormitory for the spare student body. Constructed near the edge of the campus and facing Taylor and Merion Halls, were three small wooden houses. Dean Thomas lived in one, appropriately called the Deanery. Another of the houses, with a grand view of the countryside, was known as the Scenery. Between these two plain cottages was a third, not inappropriately designated as the Betweenery. There, in a small upstairs apartment, Woodrow and Ellen Wilson began housekeeping.[1]

Dr. James E. Rhoads, officially president of the college, made no pretense of administering the affairs of the institution, but left these things entirely in the hands of the youthful dean, Dr. M. Carey Thomas, who had recently received her Ph.D. from the University of Zurich. Dean Thomas was one of the first American women to receive the doctorate from a recognized European university. The daughter of a Johns Hopkins University trustee, she was the guiding genius, the real leader of Bryn Mawr. The young woman was completely inexperienced as an administrator but she possessed a towering intellect and a dominating personality. Assisted by President Rhoads, the dean chose the charter members of the faculty. The staff consisted of Edward W. Hopkins, who later had a successful career as a philologist at Yale; Edward H. Keiser, chemistry; Charlotte A. Scott, mathematics; Paul Shorey, who was to gain distinction in the classics at the University of Chicago; and Wilson, history and political science. All of these teachers were young and ambitious; all were educated in German universities or at Johns Hopkins. With the exception of Wilson, all were doctors of philosophy and all had the rank of professor (Wilson was an associate professor). Though few in numbers, the faculty was ample for the forty-two students.

If Wilson "hesitated long" before deciding to become a member of the Bryn Mawr faculty, there is evidence that President Rhoads and Dean Thomas were not without doubts about employing him. At that time he had neither his advanced degree nor any experience as a teacher. His promising career as a student, his published articles which had received favorable comment, and the strong recommendations of his Johns Hopkins professors had encouraged Bryn Mawr to risk appointing him.[2] As for Wilson, in the winter of 1884–85 he was passionately in love but poor. Desperately he wanted a job so that he and Ellen could be married. His southern provincialism with its chivalrous and romantic attitude towards women kept him from having any

[1]Baker, *Wilson Life and Letters,* I, 251–52.

[2]Edith Finch, *Carey Thomas of Bryn Mawr* (New York, 1947), 155.

CULVER PICTURES, INC.

Woodrow Wilson as a student at Princeton, 1878, during the period he described as one of the happiest of his life.

PHOTOGRAPH BY G. V. BUCK
UNDERWOOD & UNDERWOOD, N.Y.

Wilson's parents, the dogmatic Reverend Joseph Ruggles Wilson and the overly protective Janet Woodrow. Under their sheltering influence, the young Wilson matured very

Wilson in 1880, in his law school days, with other members of the Jefferson Society. He served as president of the University of Virginia debating group.

Ellen Axson, Wilson's first wife, was a constant source of strength and encouragement in his early career. She is pictured about the time Wilson met her, in 1883.

PRINCETON UNIVERSITY LIBRARY

Harriet Woodrow, Wilson's cousin, was his first love.

A moustached Wilson (second from left, top row) appears in this photograph of the first Johns Hopkins Glee Club, organized in 1882.

Wilson is third from left, bottom row, in this group shot of the Wesleyan faculty in 1889. He taught on the Middletown campus from 1888 to 1890.

3

Political Economy
(Elements).

II. Public and Private Economy Contrasted.

1. The production of wealth that can be calculated (i.e. which gets into exchanges) vs. that which is domestic and incalculable.

The work of women and children

Relative amounts of the seen and unseen in this connexion.

Apparent tendency of the seen, the exchanged, to increase, and of the domestic to decrease.

2. Individual as contrasted with social production: the unsteadiness and vicissitudes of of the one, steadiness and uniformity of the other. = Laws discoverable in the one, and general causes; but not in the other.

This longhand page from a political economy lecture outline dated March 13, 1891, shows Wilson's methodical carefulness in preparing his class presentations.

sympathy with the movement to extend higher education to them. He recognized, as he wrote his fiancee, that he was on the losing side of the issue. "The question of the higher education of women," he said, "is certain to be settled in the affirmative, in this country at least, whether my sympathy be enlisted or not." [3] Wilson was not particularly pleased when he learned that the person who was to be in authority on the Bryn Mawr campus was a woman who had a doctoral degree and who was actually younger than he. He talked the matter over with President Rhoads, and assured Ellen: "I would not be under a woman, so far as I can learn, but my own master, under Dr. Rhoads." [4]

Quite naturally, Wilson was deeply concerned about his salary. He was prepared to refuse anything less than $2,000 per annum. He was offered only $1,200. Could two live on any such a modest income? This amount, he wrote Ellen, would leave "absolutely no margin" on which one could collect a small library or on which the beginning teacher and his family could escape from Bryn Mawr for a brief vacation in the summers.[5] No wonder he was downcast! Encouraged by his fiancee, however, Wilson tried to be optimistic. From Professor Adams he received promises of aid in securing opportunities to lecture in Philadelphia and in arranging lectures for him at Johns Hopkins. First, however, the would-be teacher must learn *how* to teach and Bryn Mawr was an excellent place to gain experience.

When Wilson admitted loss of sleep due to mental anguish over the Bryn Mawr job, Ellen offered objections to his taking it.[6] Thrown on the defensive, he argued for acceptance, and promised to have further conferences. "And," he wrote, "if my darling, after further consideration continues to think that the position I have consented to seek is one which she should be sorry to have me accept, I will at once and without hesitation withdraw from the candidacy: I will not take, contrary to her choice and judgment, this first step that we shall take together!" [7]

[3]Wilson to Ellen Axson, November 30, 1885, in Axson–Wilson Letters, Princeton.

[4]*Ibid.*

[5]Wilson to Ellen Axson, December 5, 1884, in *ibid.*

[6]Wilson to Ellen Axson, November 28, 30, 1885, in *ibid.*

[7]Wilson to Ellen Axson, December 6, 1884, in *ibid.*

Several evenings later, Wilson dined with the dean and related the experience to Ellen. Dean Thomas wanted to know if he would become head of the department of history and political science if the salary was increased some over the original offer of $1,200. Woodrow believed that he would be offered more, with promise of advance both in academic rank and in salary upon his completion of two years' service.[8] For five weeks he waited for the final offer from President Rhoads. The resulting agreement was that Wilson would serve as associate professor of history for two years at a salary of $1,500 per annum.

Of course, Wilson had kept his parents informed of his negotiations for his first teaching job. They knew of the perplexities and uncertainties affecting his decision. When he wrote home of the terms of the contract and of his temporary interest in the position, from his father came the sage advice: "Hasten slowly. A year or so at Bryn Mawr will be nothing lost." Although the salary was small, it was sufficient. Woodrow's rank in the faculty, thought his proud father, was "absurd, but not necessarily humiliating."[9] Bobby Bridges was delighted that Wilson had accepted the Bryn Mawr position because it would keep him "in range with the Eastern colleges and the chair at Princeton, which I believe awaits you."[10]

Obviously Wilson accepted his first teaching job as a place of temporary employment. Neither he nor Ellen liked Dean Thomas, a situation of which the latter was certainly aware. Wilson and the dean made no effort to create a friendship; their natures were antipathetic. But it was the characteristics which they had in common—a strong will, a ruthless ambition, and, perhaps, a sense of superiority—that kept them apart. Wilson thought women should be sweet, gentle, pretty, accomplished in the social graces and in the household arts. Of the independent women, such as Dean Thomas, he disapproved, especially when she "meddled in

[8]James E. Rhoads to Wilson, January 10, 1885, in Wilson Papers, Library of Congress; Wilson to Ellen Axson, January 13, 1885, in Axson–Wilson Letters, Princeton.

[9]Joseph Ruggles Wilson to Woodrow Wilson, January 15, 1885, in Wilson Papers, Library of Congress.

[10]Bridges to Wilson, January 30, 1885, in *ibid.*

serious concerns of masculine life such as scholarship."[11] Wilson dispatched with haste, if not distaste, all of his routine business with the dean. As at the University of Virginia so again at Bryn Mawr, when Wilson came into contact with an intellect perhaps equal to his own, he treated the person as a potential enemy.

If Wilson's contacts with Dean Thomas lacked cordiality, what were his professional relations with the other faculty members? Ray Stannard Baker wrote of Wilson's "infectious gaiety" among his colleagues, of how he "could set the table in a roar."[12] Another writer states that Wilson's colleagues "found him a congenial, if somewhat distant table companion."[13] In her excellent biography *Carey Thomas of Bryn Mawr,* Edith Finch wrote that Wilson's fellow teachers "respected his intellect," and that those who shared a table with him "found him a pleasant, entertaining companion. He told a good story, delightfully."[14] Apparently, Woodrow had neither time nor inclination for more than casual relations with other faculty members. He spent very little time creating personal friendships.[15]

If Wilson was cool toward the administration and his colleagues, he was an inspiring teacher. In this day of narrow specialization, the scope of his courses seems incredible. History should be taught at Bryn Mawr, said President Rhoads at the college's official opening, so "as to bring into prominence the great laws which underlie historical movements and to display the moral lessons they afford."[16] As the only teacher of history and political science, Wilson's courses could encompass world history in its entirety. No wonder he drove himself relentlessly to his task.

Early records of Bryn Mawr show that his class in the History of Ancient Greece and Rome was composed of seven

[11]Finch, *Carey Thomas,* 175.

[12]Baker, *Wilson Life and Letters,* I, 262.

[13]Arthur P. Dudden, "Woodrow Wilson at Bryn Mawr College," *Bryn Mawr Alumni Bulletin,* XXVI (Fall, 1955), 6–7, 32–33.

[14]Finch, *Carey Thomas,* 330.

[15]*Ibid.,* 331.

[16]See early records of Bryn Mawr College in Bryn Mawr College Library. These records include class enrollments, where classes met, and the college catalogues.

students. He had only one student in Constitutional History, and he taught Modern European History, "from the fall of the Western Empire to the establishment of the Empire of Charles the Great," to a small number of girls. In another course dealing with current events Wilson treated "the influence of leading historical characters upon contemporary events." In his second year he attracted eleven students to his class in English History and the same number took his course in United States History. Fourteen girls signed for his lectures on the History of France, while fifteen regularly attended his discussions of the Renaissance and Reformation. By Wilson's third year at Bryn Mawr, he was doing the research for and writing a textbook, *The State,* and he offered courses more in keeping with his new interests—French and German Socialism, Government of the United States, Political Economy, and a course which he ostentatiously labeled the History of Government, of Public Law, and of Modern Constitutions.[17]

As a teacher, the young Wilson was always neat in his appearance. Never without coat or cravat, he was freshly shaven and well groomed. His coat, which usually matched his nicely pressed trousers, was buttoned firmly as high as it would go. Invariably, Wilson entered the classroom smiling. To his students he was amusing and witty, seldom revealing the slightest irritability or impatience.[18] He began his lecture by reading slowly from a memorandum four or five general statements so that they could be easily noted down by the students. He would then develop the subject at length. Frequently, he added pertinent comments on current politics.[19] The assurance with which Wilson delivered his lectures, the perfection of their form, and the idealism of their content impressed his students greatly.[20]

The beginning teacher's ideas for supplementing his lectures were excellent. For example, in his course in Modern European History, he required each student to prepare a biographical paper about a leading character of the period covered. These papers

[17]*Ibid.* Also see announcements of classes in Wilson Papers, Library of Congress.

[18]Baker, *Wilson Life and Letters,* I, 262.

[19]Woodrow Wilson Lecture Notes, in Wilson Collection, Princeton.

[20]Finch, *Carey Thomas,* 331.

were read and criticized in class. Wilson also held weekly conferences with his graduate students. Lucy Salmon, who enrolled in one of his seminars, remembered their conferences in the History and Political Science Library and Seminary: "We sat and talked as unconventionally and unacademically as we would have done in any library or study in a private house." [21] Wilson's students at Bryn Mawr were inspired by his lectures but noted the reserve with which he dealt with them. Although he challenged their intellects, he seldom warmed their hearts.

Because of Wilson's interest in the English parliamentary system, he influenced his students to organize, as had his friends at Johns Hopkins and as did his students later at Wesleyan, a parliament modeled on the English House of Commons. During the three years he taught at Bryn Mawr this parliament met fortnightly to debate bills dealing with problems of current public interest.[22] Wilson inaugurated a series of fortnightly lectures on the campus to discuss public affairs. All members of the college community were invited, and as a rule the lectures were well attended. Later, however, when Wilson began to lecture elsewhere for money and when he returned to his writing, he was forced to discontinue these lectures.

Ellen Wilson's acceptance in the community was all that her husband could have desired. Her beauty and amiability won for her immediate and general acceptance on the campus. During their three-year stay at Bryn Mawr, since Ellen was either pregnant or nursing a child, she had little enthusiasm for the usual campus social amenities. Her absorption in domestic tasks and Woodrow's increasing devotion to professional duties gave them little time for campus society.[23]

As the helpmate of an ambitious husband, Ellen became a powerful stabilizing force in her husband's hectic life. Her influence was one of moderation, one of wise counseling against unwise deeds. Admittedly, this was no easy role to play, but Ellen Wilson made in this way her greatest contribution to her husband's success. To Heath Dabney, recently returned from Europe

[21]Baker, *Wilson Life and Letters,* I, 261.
[22]Finch, *Carey Thomas,* 331.
[23]*Ibid.,* 330–31.

with a doctorate from the University of Heidelberg, Wilson confided that he was happier than he had ever dared to hope he would be. He was "desperately in need of such a companion" as Ellen to turn his thoughts away from morbid contemplation of his own frame of mind. Above everything else, Wilson confessed, he "needed to be absorbed by somebody else"—and he was.[24]

At this time, the months of her first pregnancy, Ellen became seriously ill. In January, 1886, Woodrow wrote his mother that he was trying to arrange for Ellen's proper care in the home of some member of the family when their baby was born. His mother was astonished and tried to shame her son. "If you must send our darling Ellie away from you *anyhow*," she wrote, "send her to me—But my dear boy, *can* you bear to send your little wife away from you?" [25] The professor, busy about his teaching work, did not find the time to reply to his mother's reprimand. Really, the decision to go South for the baby's birth was Ellen's, not Woodrow's. At least two factors influenced her decision to return to Georgia, namely, her husband's proneness to worry about her health and the greater cost to them if she remained at home, where she would have had to hire a nurse. When Ellen's Aunt Louisa Wade learned that the expectant mother wanted to come to her home in Gainesville to have the baby, she was quite happy. At Ellen's request her aunt engaged an experienced nurse and a local physician.

As the time drew near for the delivery of the child, Woodrow escorted Ellen as far as Washington on her way to Gainesville. There, in the state where she was born, where she met Woodrow, and where they were married, she gave birth to her firstborn the day after her arrival in the home of her aunt. A baby girl, named Margaret, arrived at 11:30 A.M. on April 16. Aunt Louisa reported to the anxious father: "I never saw any lady bear the pangs of labor so heroically as the dear child did: she did not let a groan escape her, and would smile meekly between the pains and kiss me so affectionately. The tears came into her eyes once and she said 'I am not crying for the pain but for Woodrow.' "

[24]Wilson to Dabney, October 28, 1885, in Dabney Papers, Virginia.

[25]Janet Wilson to Woodrow Wilson, January 4, 1886, in Wilson Papers, Library of Congress.

Although extremely busy with his professional chores, Woodrow wrote daily to his wife. "I love you, oh, I love you with a yearning, ever-growing love," he said on April 15. When he learned of his baby's safe arrival, he exulted: "If ever a man was blessed in having a baby—and a baby *daughter*—I am, because a baby—especially a little *girl*—completes *your* life and happiness as no gift of our heavenly Father could—besides elevating my life by a new love and a new responsibility." [26]

Before the birth of the baby, when he had accompanied his wife to Washington, Woodrow went to see his old friend and former Atlanta law partner Edward Renick, now an official in the Treasury Department. He and Renick called on several bureau heads in the hope of securing for Wilson a position in government. Although several bureau chiefs professed interest in *Congressional Government,* none proffered its author a job. Significantly, Wilson, for the first time, visited Congress and saw in actual operation that about which he had been writing.

While Ellen was regaining her strength, Wilson took advantage of the spring holiday to make a first visit to Boston. Now his mind was less anxious and he could enjoy the trip. From Boston he kept his wife informed of his daily routine as he visited the publishers of *Congressional Government,* called on the editors of the *Atlantic Monthly,* and conferred with officials of D. C. Heath and Company about publishing a textbook. From the United States Hotel, where he stayed, Wilson wrote of his visit with Heath. He found the publisher "a very pleasant, open-faced, cordial, and yet business-like gentleman of about 35 or 40 years." Their amiable chat centered on the textbook *The State,* which Wilson was contemplating writing. Turned loose in the alcoves of the Athenaeum Library, Wilson browsed among the books until dinner, after which he went directly to the Harvard Library. At the day's end, he wrote that he had not found any books that would be especially helpful in his work, but was getting "a bird's-eye view of what's being written." [27]

The following day, April 24, Wilson visited with Abbott L. Lowell, who, like Wilson, was destined to serve as a university

[26]Wilson to his wife, April 15, 1886, in Axson–Wilson Letters, Princeton.
[27]Wilson to his wife, April 23, 1886, in *ibid.*

president—Lowell of Harvard, Wilson of Princeton. Wilson and Lowell were both the same age, both were lawyers, and both were teachers of political science. The day ended with a long ride about Cambridge in Mr. Houghton's carriage "seeing the homes of all the literary celebrities." [28] On Sunday afternoon Woodrow went to tea with biographer Gamaliel Bradford and stayed until about ten in the evening, "talking on all sorts of topics." [29] After a few memorable days in Boston, Wilson returned to Bryn Mawr. As he confided to Ellen, he was again in their "cozy little rooms," but not at home because she was not there.[30]

In March, 1886, he took what he hoped would be the initial step in his leaving Bryn Mawr. Invited by Bobby Bridges to attend a meeting of the Princeton alumni in New York, he considered the matter thoroughly both in the light of his class schedule and of a purse depleted by recent large purchases of books and concluded that it just could not be done.[31] When he received a special invitation to speak at the alumni banquet, however, he accepted, hoping that by emphasizing his identity with the Princeton alumni the trip would have business bearings for him in the future; that is, "unless I make a complete fizzle in my toast speech." [32] And that was just what Wilson did! He was too eager and too serious. He spoke for nearly an hour, delivering a carefully prepared, well-written, but much too solemn speech on "The College and the Government." Chauncey Depew, who followed Wilson, poked good-humoured fun at the deadly seriousness of the young professor and it cut him to the quick.

During his first year at Bryn Mawr, Wilson became increasingly aware that for the college teacher the Ph.D. degree was a "highly valuable, almost indispensable ticket of credit." [33] With

[28]Wilson to his wife, April 24, 25, 1886, in *ibid.*

[29]Wilson to his wife, April 25, 1886, in *ibid.*

[30]Wilson to his wife, April 27, 1886, in *ibid.*

[31]Wilson to Bridges, March 14, 1886, in Karl A. Meyer Collection of Correspondence of Woodrow Wilson and Robert Bridges, Firestone Library, Princeton University.

[32]Wilson to Bridges, March 17, 1886, in *ibid.*

[33]Wilson to Dabney, October 28, 1885, in Dabney Papers, Virginia. Dabney was seeking a job and Wilson wrote: "If you find any difficulty in getting a position, it will be only because history is taught in such a ridiculously, such a shamefully small number of colleges in this country."

Ellen prodding him and with Dean Thomas insisting that all teachers on her faculty have the doctorate, he began seriously to face the situation. On April 2, 1886, he wrote to Dr. Herbert B. Adams that all along he "had courted such recognition as a Ph.D. degree from the Hopkins would give." And more recently he had found rather unexpectedly that he needed the degree, that not having it operated "as a sort of technical obstacle" to his immediate promotion. "I am consequently forced," he continued, "to ask frankly but with the sincere hope that I may be understood to ask without the least taint of presumption, for a special consideration of my case." [34]

Johns Hopkins cooperated splendidly by accepting Wilson's book, *Congressional Government,* which was not a footnoted study and which had been published almost eighteen months previously, as his doctoral dissertation, and waived all foreign language requirements. Dr. Adams conferred with Professor Ely and with President Gilman before writing the young teacher that there was no chance of a degree without examinations. There would be two written examinations of three hours each and a one-hour oral examination over his thesis before the Board of University Studies. Dr. Adams assured the worried candidate that he and Dr. Ely would conduct the examinations "in a manner at once considerate and just." Wilson was asked to submit two copies of his book, which would be taken apart and rebound to comply with a regulation that all theses be uniformly bound for presentation to the library.[35]

Immediately Wilson replied that he appreciated the kind consideration they extended to "a nervous fellow who for the life of him can't pull in ordinary harness." [36] Late in May, Wilson went to Johns Hopkins to take the exhausting written and oral examinations. To Ellen, who was still in Georgia, he exulted: "Hurray—a thousand times hurrah—I'm through, I'm THROUGH—the degree is actually secured! Oh, the relief of it!" [37] He gave Ellen all

[34]Wilson to Herbert B. Adams, April 2, 1886, in Herbert B. Adams Papers, Johns Hopkins Library.

[35]Herbert B. Adams to Wilson, April 7, 1886, in Wilson Papers, Library of Congress.

[36]Wilson to Herbert B. Adams, April 8, 1886, in Adams Papers, Johns Hopkins.

[37]Wilson to his wife, May 29, 1886, in Axson-Wilson Letters, Princeton.

the credit. "I won the degree for you . . . my spur in the struggle of preparation I have just been through was to please you, and to make you more comfortable. In so far as a degree has a commercial value, it was earned for you; in so far as it has a sentimental value, it was won for you! If there's any triumph, it is *yours.*" [38]

Such obliging generosity on the part of a well-recognized university to a doctoral candidate would be hard to duplicate. It can be explained by at least three factors: Woodrow's record as a graduate student; the wide acceptance of *Congressional Government* as an unusual literary achievement; and the young man's tactful letters to his head professor, Dr. Adams.

The month before Wilson was awarded the doctorate, an article which he wrote on "Responsible Government Under the Constitution" appeared in the *Atlantic Monthly.* Many times during these years he had compared and contrasted the American governmental system with that of England and this essay was no exception: "The difference between our own case and that of Great Britain's," he wrote, "upon which we have most reason to congratulate ourselves is that here, because of our *written Constitution,* public opinion has definite criteria for its conservatism; where in England it has only shifting, uncertain precedent."

According to Wilson, the preserving strength of the American constitutional system was the "strength of self control." This "legal conscience constitutes . . . the only guarantee of that chief arrangement of our constitutional system, the division of powers between the state and the federal governments." Finally, he wrote, "the integrity of the powers of the States has depended solely upon the conservative, legal conscience, of the federal courts. . . . State functions have certainly not decayed, but the prerogatives of the States have been preserved, not by their own forces of self-defense, but by the national government's grace of self-restraint."

Back of the federal courts stood the Congress. Indeed, Congress stood at the front of all government, because it was the "one mature, original power set up by the constitution." Moreover, Congress held the constitutional power "to overwhelm opposition of the Supreme Court upon any question by an increase in the num-

[38]Wilson to his wife, May 30, 1886, in *ibid.*

ber of justices and a refusal to confirm any appointments to the new places which do not promise to change the opinion of the court." Wilson was advocating here what journalist-humorist F. Peter Dunne's comic philosopher "Mr. Dooley" witnessed in 1901, namely, that the Supreme Court follows the election returns.

The Bryn Mawr professor admitted that the executive department was responsible for making administration "pure, business-like, and efficient"; but he maintained that the prominence of administration in reform furnished "no legitimate illustration of the singularity of executive influence in this country." Although the President had always been the "titular head of a great nation," and he had sometimes been the "real master of its destinies," he had been powerful only at such times as he had "Congress at his back." In any clash over the prerogatives of power, Wilson added, one must not forget that "government *lives* in origination, not in defeat, of measures of government."

"Whilst all real power is in the hands of Congress," the essayist contended, its exercise was brought "almost to a standstill by the competition of the committees." Congress could be "integrated so as to impart to its proceedings systematic and party responsibility . . . by entrusting the preparation and initiation of legislation to a single committee in each house, composed of the leading men of the majority in that house." To integrate the whole system, "there must be some common meeting-ground of public consultation between the executive and the houses." That could be accomplished only by the admission to Congress of "official representatives of the executive who understand and are interested and able to defend the administration." [39]

As a graduate student at Hopkins, Wilson had foreseen an increasing study of the science of government. "There is certainly a very strong educational current settling towards the study of Political Science in this country," he declared. There was every reason to expect, he thought, "an early awakening of the fiduciary consciences of the boards of trustees which will result in the establishment of a great many special chairs for instruction in its several branches." In the meantime, he and others could

[39]Woodrow Wilson, "Responsible Government Under the Constitution," *Atlantic Monthly,* LVII (April, 1886), 542–53.

pursue the study of it with the promise of rich intellectual rewards.[40]

During Wilson's first year at Bryn Mawr he spent much of his scant leisure time in writing on government topics, which he could not begin to "teach to young ladies here." Although what he was doing had not yet taken definite enough shape to be described, he was "feeling after the real conditions which make popular institutions workable and the most practicable means whereby they can be made and kept healthy and vigorous." If he had depth, he confided to Bobby Bridges, "I'll come out all right." [41]

Wilson's visit to Boston greatly whetted his ambition along this line. In fact, shortly after his return to Bryn Mawr, he outlined in a long letter to Editor Horace Scudder of the *Atlantic Monthly* a plan for a comprehensive work on government and politics. This work Wilson called "Studies in Politics," but later it became known as "Philosophy of Politics." He explained to Scudder that the work would have to go on very slowly, since he had a full teaching load, with classes in history and political economy. Consequently, all work in his special field was necessarily handicapped, and would be until he could secure a chair in which his professional and original work could go hand in hand.

Having had time to digest the young professor's unusual proposal, Scudder replied by inviting Wilson to join him at his seaside cottage where they could discuss Wilson's literary plans at length.[42] The invitation reached Woodrow very inopportunely in that he was in the midst of performing the duties of the closing days of the college year. He was exceedingly anxious to finish his teaching year so that he could join his wife and baby daughter. Little Margaret, almost two months old, had yet to see her father.

Wilson arrived in Gainesville, Georgia, to find not only his wife and daughter but his younger brother-in-law, Stockton Ax-

[40]Wilson to J. W. Moncrief, March 4, 1885, in Baker Papers, Library of Congress.

[41]Wilson to Bridges, December 20, 1885, in Meyer Collection, Princeton.

[42]Apparently this letter has been lost, but Wilson wrote of the invitation in his reply on July 10, 1886.

son. Wilson was at last reunited with his wife, and held this child tenderly in his arms for the first time. For the moment he shelved research and writing to indulge himself in rest and relaxation.

Having spent some time in North Georgia, the Wilsons began a circuit of visits among relatives. They were finally stationary for the summer in the home of his parents, who had recently moved to Clarksville, Tennessee.

After further thought about his extended *Novum Organum* of politics, Wilson again wrote at length to Horace Scudder about his plans. Scudder suggested to the professor that he exclude all deeply controversial matter from his multivolume work, a suggestion which the latter accepted in principle but from which, for personal reasons, he demurred. He persuaded himself that by advancing his own professional interests he would advance the interest of his work. In other words, he thought that by issuing the work in fuller form than he had originally planned, he might make a reputation for himself and increase his chances of securing a chair of political science. Without the advantages of such a position, Wilson continued, the work would have to be done "out of hours" and, he feared, would "suffer much in consequence." Furthermore, Woodrow admitted that he was a slow writer and, with his present college duties, he must produce "with painful slowness and perhaps with more than the inevitable amount of imperfection, because of the absence of all proper conditions for concentrated and continuous thought." Upon further reflection, he concluded that he must trust to occasional writings "to win favor with college authorities" while his book was being written.

Wilson wanted to write of the true nature of the modern democratic state by way of an accurate exposition of the history of democratic development. In realizing this objective, however, he desired to "keep safely within sober induction from concrete examples of political organization and of realized political thought." He wanted to trace the genesis and development of modern democratic institutions. According to the professor, most political writers—such as Hobbes, Locke, and Rousseau—had evolved government out of the primitive conditions of mankind "for the actual existence of which they could adduce no sort of evidence." As one could know persons, Woodrow continued, "only from what they say and do, and the manner of their acting and speaking," so one could know equally well "governments from what *they* say and do and the manner of their speech and action."

Wilson summarized his ideas in a concluding paragraph: "I would apply the now common inductive method to the study of democratic government—to the study of the genesis and the development of *our* government in particular. . . . Aristotle studied politics so, but did not get further than the outward differences of institutions—did not press on beyond logical distinctions to discover the spiritual oneness of government, the life that lives *within* it. The ideal thing to do would be to penetrate to its *essential character* by way of a thorough knowledge of all its outward manifestations of character." [43]

For years, apparently, Wilson collected notes for his *Philosophy of Politics.* In the Wilson Papers in the Library of Congress, several boxes of cards marked "P.O.P." reveal his youthful enthusiasm and his extensive reading, in anticipation of writing a *Novum Organum* of politics. It remained, however, one of Wilson's unrealized ambitions. When he died, thirty-eight years later, his *magnum opus* was unwritten.

Wilson took one step towards the realization of his dream when he learned that many of the books he wished to read were in German. Although he had received his doctorate the previous June, he did not read German. Aided constantly by a dictionary, he studied that language for months. Try though he did to learn German "well enough to be emancipated from the constant use of the dictionary in reading it," he failed. Consequently, he conceived the idea of going abroad for one or two years. He wrote to Heath Dabney, recently returned from Germany, "to estimate the cost of living in Berlin for a man, wife and child who would not care a peppercorn for style, but who would require for a while, perhaps, a nurse, and always *comfort.*" Woodrow hoped to spend most of the time in Berlin,

[43]Wilson to Horace E. Scudder, July 10, 1886, in Wilson Collection, Princeton.

because that was the "centre of German affairs." He would not attach himself to any university, but would give his time to "digging at German," to observing people, to extensive reading, and to writing.[44]

Of course, such a trip, Wilson wrote Dabney, would necessitate resigning from the Bryn Mawr faculty, but he was prepared to take the risk of getting employment upon returning. In fact, he said, he had already received repeated invitations to accept a place in the faculty at the University of Indiana, but had refused. He wanted a chair of politics, not of history; and he didn't want to go west.[45]

While Wilson waited for an affirmation of his plans from Dabney, he unfolded his ambition to Bobby Bridges. All of his plans for professional and literary work rested upon the intimate acquaintance of the actual constitutions of European States, "not only as they live in books but also as they live and move in practice." He must know not only "comparative constitutional *law* but comparative constitutional *life*." And this last he could not know "without seeing foreign systems and foreign people . . . without coming into contacts with living organisms of their governments." Moreover, he could not learn even what books told him "without coming into contact with the living organisms of German and French *languages*."

In order to remain with his family in Europe as long as possible, he was casting about in his mind for ways and means of adding to his small financial reserves while over there and so spinning out his resources that they might cover as long a period

[44]Wilson to Dabney, November 7, 1886, in Dabney Papers, Virginia.

[45]*Ibid.* With the aid of Indiana's new president, David Starr Jordan, Wilson had secured the job for Heath Dabney. In November, 1886, when Wilson was at Cornell to read a paper, he talked with a fraternity brother who was a student at Indiana the preceding year. Wilson informed Dabney that the student reported Dabney's predecessor "had been turned out because he too often spoke before he thought and thus speaking let drop 'Calhoun views' on the Constitution. . . . You have gotten into a chair where the incumbent is expected, not the scientific truth with reference to our Constitutional history, whether that truth be on the side of Webster or of Calhoun, in great historical argument, but *'Yankee sentiments'*—sentiments agreeable to that eminent body of scholars, the Grand Army of the Republic. It's a shame!"

as possible. "Do you think a fellow of my kind and calibre," he asked Bridges, "could make a few hundred dollars writing foreign letters to newspapers?" Newsletters were prohibited, Bridges thought, but perhaps "descriptions of legislative bodies and their practices, discussions, given in as light a touch as possible, of foreign governmental methods; letters about current foreign politics" could be published. Would Bobby see, asked Wilson, if he could find two or three New York journals willing to take such merchandise and ascertain what they would be willing to pay for such articles? Woodrow wrote that he felt that he had reached a critical point in his career. He was so anxious to make the trip "count for as much as possible" that he was bold in asking aid.[46]

The work he hoped to do abroad was just the kind to secure for him the professional place he desired when he returned. "Though out of sight, I don't intend to be out of mind of college trustees and presidents." [47] When his father learned of Woodrow's serious thoughts of going to Europe to live and study, the minister replied that his son's wish was the measure of his wisdom and added: "You are my *alter* ego: what pleases you equally pleases me." [48]

Wilson wrote Bridges: "I am going [to Europe], God willing, next summer." [49] By June, 1887, however, Ellen Wilson was again pregnant. For her a trip to Europe was out of the question, and Wilson needed his meager savings for his increasing family. In fact, the professor's trip abroad was postponed for nearly a decade.

Wilson's family life during these years was for him one of increasing responsibilities, but certainly one of happiness. In everything that he did, Ellen was his complete confidante. She widened his intellectual vision, encouraged his ambition, and frequently dulled the sharpness of his criticism of others. In addition to doing the housework, with which Woodrow assisted,

[46]Wilson to Bridges, April 6, 1886, in Wilson Collection, Princeton.

[47]Wilson to Bridges, November 28, 1886, in *ibid.*

[48]Joseph Ruggles Wilson to Woodrow Wilson, November 15, 1886, in Wilson Papers, Library of Congress.

[49]Wilson to Bridges, November 28, 1886, in Wilson Collection, Princeton.

Ellen made her own clothes and sewed for her infant. With all of these demanding chores, she still found time to help her husband. In the evenings she sat near Woodrow with a German-English dictionary in her lap, assisting her husband in his unsuccessful efforts to master the difficult German language. Regardless of what Wilson was writing, whether perfunctorily doing a book review, penning an article for some periodical, or preparing a book manuscript for publication, his wife was his best critic.[50] Apparently, she found time to read almost all that he wrote.

Two people as busy as Ellen and Woodrow found little time for visiting with others of the campus community. In writing to his friend Bobby Bridges, Wilson summarized his routine and revealed his tendency to criticize harshly those with whom he labored at Bryn Mawr: "My class duties are driving me at an uncommonly rapid pace; but I am well, and as content as one can be who is in a boarding house and has at every meal to hear nonsense rattle down from the empty pate to the clattering tongue of a fool or two." [51]

If the demands of Wilson's classes drove him at a rapid pace during the session, the requirements of his writing kept him busy during his vacations. Invited to join his Princeton friends at the Thanksgiving Day football game, he regretfully declined to take leave of his work. "I just must use every holiday—every half-holiday even," he said, "to advance my work on the text-book." [52]

Largely as an additional source of income needed to meet the increasing obligations of his family, Wilson wrote several stories under a *nom de plume* and sent them to Bridges, who at this time was a member of the editorial staff of *Scribner's*. But, as a fiction writer, Wilson had no talent. In spite of Bridges' influence, all of the professor's fiction came back to him with rejection slips. In analyzing his failure as a creative writer, Wilson declared: "I believe that every man who essays to write stories—

[50]Apparently, Wilson's first published book review was of Charles C. F. Grenville's *A Journal of the Reign of Queen Victoria, From 1837 to 1852,* in *Dial* (February, 1886), 269–71.

[51]Wilson to Bridges, November 18, 1886, in Meyer Collection, Princeton.

[52]*Ibid.*

i.e., to portray life—ought to have the *detective* somewhere in him, the ability to read the mysteries of motive which go to make up life." [53] This detective trait was missing in Wilson's mental makeup.

Shortly thereafter, Ellen became quite sick with her second pregnancy. Her husband was in daily and constant attention. Confronted with his wife's poor health and recent developments in his work, Wilson signed a three-year contract with Johns Hopkins to deliver two lectures per week for thirteen weeks for $500 on the general topic "Administration, or the Comparative Public Law—the functions and organs of government." Since this was his favorite field of study, and since he contemplated giving the same course at Bryn Mawr to senior students, he was really doing little extra work. He wondered whether Princeton might not like the same series the second half of the semester for the same price, but Princeton was not interested.[54]

With the developing of Wilson's plans for his initial lectures at Johns Hopkins, he seemed to evaluate more sympathetically his position at Bryn Mawr. His conditions of work there were certainly pleasant, he told Bobby Bridges, and the Philadelphia libraries were adequate.[55] Then, too, being in the East was, from the literary man's point of view, an advantage. He could lecture regularly to his classes and still have some time left for his own private enterprises of study. Altogether, he informed Heath Dabney, now on the faculty of Indiana University, he had come to the conclusion that he could hardly find a better place for work—until the chair in comparative politics for which he was waiting turned up. "Since one must struggle with classes," Wilson wrote, "he ought to be thankful for so comfortable a berth—where classes are docile, intelligent and willing—where the Administration is honest, straightforward, and liberal and where

[53] *Ibid.*

[54] Wilson to Herbert B. Adams, January 21, 1887, in Adams Papers, Johns Hopkins.

[55] Wilson to Bridges, January 23, 1887, in Meyer Collection, Princeton. The lectures were given at Hopkins in the winters of 1886–87; 1887–88, 1888–89. The contract was renewed and the lectures continued for ten years.

there is sympathy to be found in one's work for the searching." [56]

Near the close of the first semester at Bryn Mawr, Wilson began his weekly trips to lecture at Hopkins. He enjoyed being on the campus again, renewing friendships among the faculty, and making acquaintances with the students. Certainly, not least among his pleasant experiences while on the Hopkins campus was attending on February 11 the weekly meeting of History and Political Science Seminary. Professor J. Franklin Jameson noted in his diary that he spoke to Wilson about contributing an article to a volume that he was contemplating editing.[57] Out of the Hopkins lectures, given three successive years, would come for Wilson two enduring friendships: one with Frederick Jackson Turner, a graduate student with whom he later began to correspond; and the other with Mrs. Edith G. Reid, the attractive and talented wife of a Hopkins faculty member, with whom Wilson exchanged letters for years.

In March, 1887, Wilson published an article—"Of the Study of Politics"—in the *New Princeton Review.* "Government is as old as man," he wrote; "men have always been politicians." In writing on politics one could not "lift truth so high that men cannot reach it"; one could not "ask them to climb where they cannot go without leaving terra firma." "Politics," continued the author, "is the life of the State, and nothing which illustrates that life, nothing which reveals any habit contracted by men as a political animal comes amiss in the study of politics." Furthermore, politics could be effectually expounded "only by means of the highest literary methods." The professor advised his readers that, if they wished to know anything about government, they must "see it alive." [58]

Woodrow's father lauded the latest essay from his son's pen as having a "rich racy style which was its own decoration, needing no help from rhetorical millinery." The essayist had "struck a vein of inquiry into the philosophy of politics," which, the

[56]Wilson to Dabney, January 25, 1887, in Dabney Papers, Virginia.

[57]Donnan and Stock (eds.), *An Historian's World,* 42.

[58]Woodrow Wilson, "Of the Study of Politics," *New Princeton Review,* III (January–May, 1887), 188–99.

father felt, "must attract the attention" of many who in "their field of study care to arrive at the truth." [59]

Early in his second year as a teacher, Wilson prepared a treatment of the history of the science of administration for the *Political Science Quarterly*.[60] It was the object of administrative study, he began, "to discover, first, what government can do properly and successfully, and, secondly, how it can do these proper things with the utmost possible efficiency and at the least possible cost either of money or of energy." Though administration was the most obvious part of government, the science of administration was the "latest fruit of the study of the science of politics." Wilson was among the first to realize the increasing need for trained personnel in administration. The functions of government, he said, were becoming more complex and difficult; they were also vastly multiplying in number. Writing within a few months of the passage of the Interstate Commerce Commission Act of 1887, Wilson expressed the concern of many: "Even if our government is not to follow the lead of the governments of Europe in buying or building both telegraph and railroad lines, no one can doubt that in some way it must make itself master of masterful corporations."

American government had expanded in nature and grown great in stature, according to the author, but had also become "awkward in movement." Thus, one of the great needs was for a science of administration which would seek to straighten the paths of government, to make its business less unbusinesslike; to strengthen and purify its organization. Wilson recognized the problems involved in achieving reform. It was more difficult for democracy to organize administration than for monarchy because a sovereign people "have no single ear which one can approach." Consequently, wrote Wilson, wherever public opinion was the first principle of government, practical reform must be slow and

[59]Joseph R. Wilson to Woodrow Wilson, March 12, 1887, in Wilson Papers, Library of Congress.

[60]Wilson to Edwin R. A. Seligman, November 11, 1886, in Edwin R. A. Seligman Papers, Library of Congress. Mr. Seligman, professor of political science at Columbia University, was editor of the *Political Science Quarterly*.

all reform must be full of compromises. Whoever would effect a change in a modern constitutional government must first educate his fellow-citizens to want *some* change. That done, the author continued, he must persuade them to want the particular change he wants. "He must first make public opinion willing to listen and then see to it that it listens to the right things. . . . The reformer must not forget that a truth must become not only plain but also commonplace before it will be seen by the people." The ideal for America, Wilson concluded, was a "civil service cultured and self-sufficient enough to act with sense and vigor and yet so intimately connected with the popular thought, by means of elections and constant public counsel, as to find arbitrariness or class spirit quite out of the question." [61]

When a reader, who was interested in the evolving science of public administration, wrote enthusiastically about the article, Wilson replied at great length. He feared that his article was too broad, too general. "To have the assurance therefore, that it has arrested the attention of one so specially and adequately fitted to judge whether there was anything of point in it is indeed an encouragement. Your letter was the help I needed." [62]

The Wilsons were becoming increasingly conscious of their crowded upstairs rooms in the Betweenery. Margaret was almost a year old and was beginning to walk. Since Ellen was expecting another baby, there was increasing need for room. In a deep ravine a quarter of a mile back of the college was a house which had been used as a Baptist parsonage. For a moderate sum, the Wilsons rented the Baptist manse, and very shortly were comfortably settled.[63] Once established in the roomy house, Ellen invited a cousin, Mary W. Hoyt, to live with them and to attend Bryn Mawr the next year. When the college session began in September, 1887, not only was Mary Hoyt a member of the Wilson household, but Ellen's younger brother, Edward, also lived in

[61]Woodrow Wilson, "The Study of Administration," *Political Science Quarterly,* II (June, 1887), 197–222.

[62]Wilson to Almond Barnes, June 28, 1887. This letter and a copy of the article are in the Rare Book Room, Library of Congress.

[63]Memorandum of conversation, Ray Stannard Baker with Stockton Axson, February 8, 10, 1925, in Baker Papers, Library of Congress.

the parsonage on Gulph Road.[64] The custom of having cousins and in-laws live in one's household was a southern tradition, and the Wilsons continued the practice for almost a quarter of a century. Most of those who at one time or another became members of the Wilson household came as youngsters to remain until a college or university career was completed. By inviting the young people into their home for the duration of their higher education, the Wilsons helped to remedy a situation in the homes of relatives that was caused by too few dollars or too many children or a combination of the two.

Wilson was never a domestic man in the sense that he was gifted with tools. Although he liked flowers, he had no green thumb. There were some chores about the house that seemed more masculine than feminine, such as firing the furnace and drawing or pumping the water; these Woodrow habitually performed. If circumstances necessitated, he would run errands in town or buy groceries for his wife. As a matter of practice, however, he gave Ellen the money and left all household management affairs to her. She took her responsibilities seriously—she took lessons in cooking, attended lectures on diets, sewed for the family, and kept accurate records of all household expenditures. Ellen's ability to economize with the household budget was widely known. In fact, it was largely her shrewd management that enabled the Wilsons to live as well as they did on Woodrow's salary.

The teacher's Calvinistic conscience did not permit him to work on the Sabbath. The Wilsons always attended religious services, in which Woodrow sometimes participated. Then on Sunday afternoons the family, including the young kin living under the Wilson roof, would assemble to listen as Woodrow read aloud from one of Shakespeare's plays, or passages from speeches of Gladstone, or excerpts from the works of Bagehot or Burke. After these reading sessions, Ellen and her husband often went for a walk. If Wilson were too tired to work on his lectures or his

[64]Baker, *Wilson Life and Letters,* I, 287. When the Wilsons left Bryn Mawr, Mary Hoyt remained. She graduated in 1893. See Dudden, "Wilson at Bryn Mawr," 6–7.

writing when Friday night arrived, the evening was sometimes spent in singing.

In June, 1887, Wilson's name was proposed by Thomas Dixon, Jr., to the Wake Forest College trustees for the LL.D. degree. A copy of *Congressional Government* was in the college library, and the professor's name was magical when suggested to the faculty for approval. With the approval of the trustees, Wilson was awarded his first degree *honoris causa.*[65] Wake Forest College, rejoiced Woodrow's father, was the "very best in North Carolina, apart from the University." The son was admonished to "wear the degree long, my Darling, and wear it shiningly." [66] In time there would be other honorary degrees from a number of institutions of higher education, but the one from the Baptist college in North Carolina was his first.

The Wilsons remained at home in the Baptist parsonage back of the college until July, when Ellen and little Margaret went to Georgia. The professor, working on materials for his textbook, remained temporarily at Bryn Mawr. In Gainesville on August 28, Ellen gave birth to a second daughter, Jessie Woodrow. Ellen did not recover as rapidly this time as she had in the spring of 1886. Her husband realized that she was not regaining her strength and suggested that she and the children remain in Gainesville for the time being. Lizzie Adams Ervin, one of the Wilsons' North Carolina friends, visited Ellen and returned to her home to urge Woodrow not to let his wife overtax her strength. "Watch her closely," wrote Mrs. Ervin, "I am afraid that she will manage to deceive you with her energy and bright ways." [67] Wilson's father expressed delight at the arrival of the new granddaughter and concluded that he "wished for the advent of a boy but maybe next time you will do better than this!" [68]

When Bryn Mawr students began attending classes in Sep-

[65]Thomas Dixon, Jr., to Wilson, June 7, 1887, and W. H. Pace to Wilson, June 20, 1887, in Wilson Papers, Library of Congress.

[66]Joseph R. Wilson to Woodrow Wilson, June 11, 1887, in *ibid.*

[67]Lizzie Adams Erwin to Wilson, September 1, 1887, in *ibid.*

[68]Joseph R. Wilson to Woodrow Wilson, September 6, 1887, in *ibid.*

tember, 1887, Ellen Wilson and her two children were still in Georgia. Only Woodrow, Edward Axson, and Mary Hoyt occupied the rented manse. Wilson began his third year of teaching with a misunderstanding with the college administration over the promise of an assistant for his department. The professor's new Fellow in history was certainly not to his liking. In describing her to Ellen, Wilson wrote: "She seems to talk largely out of her memory; her travels overshadow her reasoning powers; her knowledge of the world makes her ignorant of conclusions which interpret the world. . . . I'm *tired* carrying female Fellows on my shoulders! When I think of you, my little wife, I love this 'College for Women' because *you* are a woman; but when I think only of myself, I hate the place very cordially." [69]

Weary after a day of lecturing to classes of unresponsive, or, at least, unenthusiastic students, Wilson confided to a journal that he kept irregularly: "Lecturing on the history and precepts of politics to young ladies is no more appropriate or profitable than lecturing to stone masons on evolution of fashion in clothing." There seemed to be "a painful *absenteeism* of mind" amongst his listeners. His lecture, he wrote, "generates no heat, because it passes through a vacuum." He concluded with a more generous judgment, that "this may be result of their undergraduatism rather than their femininity." [70]

When Ellen and the children returned home, Wilson was quieted by the sage counsel of his wife. Together, they began to plan a way out of the depressing environment. Three avenues of escape appeared as possibilities. Woodrow frequently confided his dreams to Bridges and this was no exception: "Somehow there has come over me of late," he said, "a deep desire to do writing of a distinctly literary sort. I have more than one story longing to be told and no less than a dozen essays on literary subjects struggling towards utterance—some of them partly uttered in *mss.*" The struggle was, he continued, with his surroundings and they demanded "every scrap of connected thought or speech that I can produce with days of ordinary length." With tongue in cheek,

[69]Wilson to his wife, October 4, 1887, in Axson–Wilson Letters, Princeton.

[70]Woodrow Wilson, "Journal," October 20, 1887. This diary is in the Wilson Papers, Library of Congress.

perhaps, he declared that he was "discontented, not a bit. But I am tantalized." [71] Although in his dreams Wilson returned repeatedly to the idea of becoming a literary figure, he never embarked upon such a career.

In the same letter Wilson confessed that the last day or two had brought him a curious temptation. He was generally and favorably known in Washington, and a friend there had written to urge that he take steps to have his name "put forward for the vacant [first] Assistant Secretaryship of State!" Wilson's former law partner, Renick, believed he had a good chance of appointment since the job was not sought after by politicians and Secretary of State James A. Bayard, who liked "gentlemanly, scholarly associates," was finding it difficult to fill the place. "Absurd as the idea of my candidacy seems," Woodrow wrote, "I should hate to miss it." [72]

To James B. Angell, president of the University of Michigan, the professor also wrote, seeking aid. He wanted a seat inside government, "a seat high enough to commend views of the system. . . . I dread becoming a doctrinaire. I dread writing what will be of no practical usefulness—a mere closeted student's view of affairs." Another reason for desiring the office at this time was that his teaching that year lay "altogether in the field of political economy and in my own special field of public law and I already feel that teaching such topics to women threatens to relax not a little of my mental muscle." Before he taught elsewhere, he wanted to mix with rough practical things again in order to recover what he termed the proper atmosphere for his studies.[73]

The Michigan educator replied that probably the office in the Department of State should be filled from within the department by someone with experience in diplomatic service.[74] Lacking any political influence whatsoever, Wilson watched his hopes fade away but not without one final protest. He wanted the office *"in*

[71]Wilson to Bridges, November 5, 1887, in Meyer Collection, Princeton.

[72]*Ibid.*

[73]Wilson to James B. Angell, November 7, 1887, in James B. Angell Papers, Library of Congress.

[74]Angell to Wilson, November 13, 1887, in *ibid.*

order to learn," he said. "Experience in affairs, is what I most imperatively need to vivify my chosen studies. . . . I love the stir of the world; that stir is what I chiefly desire to study and explain," concluded Wilson.[75] But his efforts were not successful. "My race for the Washington place did not even reach the stages of actual candidacy," the professor lamented.[76]

Bobby Bridges supplied Woodrow with a third avenue of possible escape from Bryn Mawr by mentioning that Professor William Sloane might become president of Princeton. Wilson was enthusiastically interested in trying to replace Sloane as teacher, and discussed his possibilities at length with Bridges. As usual, there were problems. Woodrow was under contract to deliver twenty-five lectures a year at Johns Hopkins that session and the next, but the Baltimore men were disposed to make any arrangements for the lectures that would best fit into his other work. In the preceding March he had signed a contract to teach 10 hours weekly at Bryn Mawr for $2,000 per year,[77] but that contract, Wilson insisted, was no longer binding, for in it the Trustees had agreed to give him an assistant—"that was the condition upon which I signed—; but they failed to appoint anyone and I consider myself quite free to enter into any other engagement."

The chief difficulty, as stated by Woodrow, was that he knew Professor Sloane only casually. In case Sloane became president, Wilson would be at a loss in "instituting a candidacy." Moreover, "somehow I have got it into my head that he don't [*sic*] think me 'any great shakes.' " Woodrow thought he would eventually secure a "chair of some sort at Baltimore—and Bryn Mawr would be a good place to wait meantime." [78]

Throughout the fall the professor was "head over ears in work," and several times expressed the fear of a breakdown in his health.[79] The reason was not his actual classes, but the far too many hours of intense outside work. He scarcely stopped at all during the holidays and, consequently, at the beginning of the

[75]Wilson to Angell, November 15, 1887, in *ibid.*
[76]Wilson to Bridges, November 30, 1887, in Meyer Collection, Princeton.
[77]See contract in Wilson Papers, Library of Congress.
[78]Wilson to Bridges, November 30, 1887, in Meyer Collection, Princeton.
[79]*Ibid.*

New Year he fell ill. For nearly three weeks he was in bed, but recuperated enough to resume his professional tasks at the end of January.

In February, Wilson began the second series of lectures at Baltimore. He was driving himself again. This time he was putting the finishing touches on a paper—"Taxation and Appropriations"—that appeared in a book, *The National Revenues: A Collection of Papers by American Economists,* edited by Albert Shaw. The tariff laws, wrote Wilson, were "full of complexities and absurdities of the most irritating and unnecessary sort; and the yield of revenue was greatly in excess of the needs of the government and at some points altogether unnecessary for the purposes of protection. . . . The people ought to be made to feel their fiscal policy all the time," continued the author. He contended that "an ideal financial policy for the United States would not hasten payment of the national debt since haste would involve more inconveniences, both financial and political, than advantages. An ideal policy, he concluded, "would join hand to hand appropriations and taxation." [80]

On April 15, Wilson's mother died suddenly.[81] The first news he had of her illness was the news of her death. He quickly left the campus and rushed to Clarksville to be with other members of the bereaved family. Interment was in the cemetery of the First Presbyterian Church, Columbia, South Carolina. After the funeral, Woodrow returned with his grief-stricken father to Tennessee and stayed as long as professional duties at Bryn Mawr would permit. His oldest sister, Marion, wrote to her brother: "You were *always,* from your first appearance in this world until this *present time,* the delight and pride of that mother's heart." [82] Woodrow told his friend, Heath Dabney: "My mother was a mother to me in the fullest, sweetest sense of the word, and her loss has left me with a sad, oppressive sense of having somehow

[80]See copy of article, "Taxation and Appropriation," in Wilson Papers, Library of Congress.

[81]Joseph R. Wilson, Jr., to Wilson, April 15, 1888, in *ibid.* (Telegram)

[82]Marion Wilson Kennedy to Wilson, April 21, 1888, in *ibid.* In November, 1887, Wilson's mother fell down the stairs at her home. Josie heard her fall and ran to find her at the bottom of the stairs. See Joseph Wilson, Jr., to Wilson, November 21, 1886, in *ibid.*

suddenly *lost my youth.* I feel old and responsibility-ridden. I suppose that feeling will in time wear off, however, that I shall ultimately get my balance again. In the meantime, I crave your sympathy, old fellow—I need all you can give." [83] The worst of the situation was not Woodrow's bereavement but his father's dilemma. With his two daughters married and living elsewhere with their families, Dr. Wilson and his younger son, Joseph, were left practically without a home. Woodrow's happy home and the stupendous amount of work which he found to do dulled the pain of his own loss.

As Wilson's third wedding anniversary approached, he revealed his deep convictions on the institution of marriage, especially his own:

> No one is so sensitive, as a rule, as the student—and there's no cure for sensitiveness like a wife's sympathy,—no strength like that to be gotten from her love and trust. Marriage has been the *making* of me both intellectually and morally. Of course, a fellow's ecstatically happy at first, and all that is genuine and to be cherished—that first feeling of conjugal union; but, *afterwards,* as years add to months, the first ecstacy [*sic*] is succeeded by something even better,—a settled, permeating, sustaining, invigorating sense of strength and completeness and satisfaction which a man, if he be a man, would not exchange for all the wealth and success and fame that the world contains.[84]

Accounts vary greatly over the details of Wilson's leaving Bryn Mawr. The clause promising him an assistant in his department read: "He should have an assistant as soon as practicable." [85] President Rhoads and Dean Thomas merely stated that it was "not practicable" to add an assistant for 1887–88. Certainly, Wilson *thought* the clause signified intent to add a member to his department at that time. In the spring of 1888, a second member for Wilson's department *was* appointed to begin work that next September, but Wilson thought that too late. The professor had written that he deemed the three-year contract nullified because an assistant was not given him by September, 1887, and in April, 1888, he informed President Rhoads that he considered

[83]Wilson to Dabney, May 16, 1888, in Dabney Papers, Virginia.
[84]Wilson to Dabney, May 31, 1888, in *ibid.*
[85]See copy of contract in Bryn Mawr library.

his contract no longer binding since he was not given departmental help earlier.[86]

In June, Wilson was offered the Hedding Professorship of History and Political Economy at Wesleyan University, Middletown, Connecticut. Wesleyan offered him $2,500 per year in salary with an eight-hour weekly teaching load.[87] President Rhoads expressed astonishment and declared that he expected Wilson to continue to teach at Bryn Mawr in accordance with his contract, which the Board of Trustees insisted was valid.[88] Woodrow consulted a lawyer and was supported with legal advice that such contracts were not binding. When President Rhoads learned of the advice, he urged the trustees to accept the professor's resignation, since he would be "dissatisfied and exacting if retained." [89] In a called session the trustees approved their unanimous judgment that the contract was binding upon both parties, but, inasmuch as the teacher entertained a doubt as to the validity of the agreement, the trustees acquiesced in his withdrawal from the college.[90] Wilson maintained that he acted with the best of professional ethics and with a clear conscience. By no means would all agree with him.

Wilson admitted: "I have for a long time been hungry for a class of *men*." [91] At the time, it was thought that Dean Thomas played a significant role is his resignation, but this was exaggerated. The ambitious young professor and the young woman administrator were anathema to each other, but they had been that from the beginning. Woodrow was on the way up; the move to Wesleyan University was in every way a promotion. Moreover, he had earned the advancement, and he was ready for it. Bryn Mawr could not have expected to keep such an ambitious young

[86]Finch, *Carey Thomas,* 176–78.

[87]Wilson to James E. Rhoads, June 7, 1888, in Wilson Papers. The professor stated that his duty to his family made it even "more imperative" that he should seek rapid advancement in his profession. "You will," concluded Wilson, "I am confident, believe that in taking this course I am simply following what I feel to be my plain duty."

[88]Rhoads to Wilson, June 27, 1888, in *ibid.*

[89]Finch, *Carey Thomas,* 176–78.

[90]Rhoads to Wilson, July 6, 1888, in Wilson Papers, Library of Congress.

[91]Wilson to Bridges, August 26, 1888, in Meyer Collection, Princeton.

man for many years. As Renick stated: "Princeton, Harvard and The 'Johns' [Hopkins] will be soon seeking you." [92] Before Woodrow went to Wesleyan, he wrote of his going there exactly as he had written of his joining the faculty at Bryn Mawr: "My going to Middletown," he informed Bobby Bridges, "will not interfere at all with my future acceptance of a call elsewhere." [93]

[92]E. I. Renick to Wilson, August 17, 1888, in Wilson Papers, Library of Congress.

[93]Wilson to Bridges, August 26, 1888, in Meyer Collection, Princeton.

CHAPTER IX *At Wesleyan*

Once Wilson succeeded in cutting his professional ties with Bryn Mawr, he seemed busier than ever. The summer of 1888 was for him a hectic one, filled with visitors, work, and preparations for moving. The Wilsons had a house full of relatives, and the teacher was forced to work on his textbook to the accompaniment of family gossip and noisy children. Work he did though, because he knew that he would have no time later.

Just as the Wilsons were in the final stages of packing, word came of the death of Bobby Bridges' father. Because so many have thought Wilson devoid of genuine sympathy, perhaps a few sentences from his letter to Bridges should be given:

Sure as I am that you do not need to have me *say* that you have my heartfelt sympathy in your great, great loss in order to be sure of it, I am equally certain that necessity rests upon me to speak out of deep, the heart-deep feelings for you that has [*sic*] sprung up within me since the reading of your letter. Oh, I am so glad that you feel that you can speak of such grief to me, that I am the proper person by reason of friendship to whom to detail particulars of those last days of your father's lifetime: and my dear Bobby you may rest assured that such a narrative is as sacred in my eyes as you could wish it to be. I tried to read your letter aloud to Mrs. Wilson, and could scarcely get through with some passages of it articulately. . . . My dear father is still spared to me, God be thanked; but the death of my mother last Spring went near to break my heart, and has left me with a permanent sense of loneliness, of maimedness, such as I could never before have imagined. Think of having a father or a mother whom we could *not* honor and revere! and what measure that affords of the blessing of being upheld by the memory and example of such a father as yours! [1]

The Wilsons left Bryn Mawr late in August, stopped for a few days along the New England coast, and arrived at Middletown early in September. The old colonial house on High Street in which they were to live during their stay at Wesleyan was not yet ready for occupancy, so for days after their arrival in Middletown they were literally taken in by members of the faculty. The acting president of the university, Dr. John M. Van Vleck, and his wife received the new professor and his family into their home for several days. Then Woodrow, Ellen, and their two small children were guests for some time in the home of Professor and Mrs. Morris B. Crawford. The hospitality shown them at Wesleyan was so much warmer than the reception they had received at Bryn Mawr that they were very favorably impressed.

Before the Wilsons arrived, several teachers had organized a "Conversational Club" which met fortnightly in the homes of the respective members. Included in the group were Dr. Caleb T. Winchester, professor of rhetoric and English literature; Dr. William W. Hedding, professor of history and political economy; Dr. William N. Rice, professor of geology and secretary to the faculty; and Dr. Andrew C. Armstrong, professor of philosophy.[2] Wilson accepted an invitation to become a member of the club, and he greatly enjoyed the nights of free discussion.[3] This small group of teachers seemed to Wilson to resemble an intellectual family.

[1]Wilson to Bridges, August 29, 1888, in Meyer Collection, Princeton.
[2]*Wesleyan University Annual Catalogue, 1888–1889.*
[3]Baker, *Wilson Life and Letters,* I, 300.

The Wilsons also found a congenial church home in Middletown. Until his father left the First Presbyterian Church of Wilmington in the spring of 1885, Woodrow retained his membership there. Since then the professor's church letter had been in his trunk. Soon after her marriage in June, 1885, Ellen had withdrawn from the First Presbyterian Church in Savannah. During the three years at Bryn Mawr, the Wilsons had formed no church connection. In Middletown, their church letters were accepted on November 4, 1888, by the First Congregational Church. One of several enduring friendships that Wilson formed at this time was with the Reverend Dr. A. W. Hazen, minister of that church.[4]

According to the university catalogue, Wilson offered a full schedule of courses during his first year at Wesleyan, including the History of England and France, a History of Institutions, the Constitution of the United States, and Political Economy and Statistics.[5] Apparently no record was kept of the number of students who attended his lectures. Since there were only 218 students enrolled in the university, however, his classes must have been relatively small. As a teacher Woodrow had an earnestness and an enthusiasm that were contagious. Carl F. Price, one of his students, remembered him as he stood before a table, bending slightly towards his class, "with his hands forward, the tips of his fingers just touching the table, his face earnest and animated." [6] But it was not Wilson's posture, nor his earnest facial expression, that inspired his students; it was his unusual ability to illuminate an otherwise dry and tedious subject by an eloquent flow of language, by clear and concise exposition, by an apt phrase. What the student perhaps did not realize was that Wilson spent many hours preparing his lectures.

The faculty newcomer soon endeavored to impress his students with his enthusiasm for the English cabinet system. He had begun a House of Commons at Johns Hopkins and at Bryn Mawr, and on January 5, 1889, he called a meeting of the Wesleyan

[4] *Ibid.*

[5] *Wesleyan Catalogue, 1888–1889,* 31–32.

[6] *Wesleyan University Alumnus,* March, 1924. See also Baker, *Wilson Life and Letters,* I, 300–301.

students to propose the institution of a similar body. The function of the House of Commons, said its sponsor, was debate, which was the basis for the special art of oratory. He added: "We shall imitate the British House of Commons, thereby introducing a dramatic element in that a body of ministers resigns when defeated." Since the ministers would support questions they believed in, natural party lines would arise without any arbitrary decisions. It was the establishment of interest in debate which was being sought, Wilson concluded.

The students evidenced more interest in the new organization than they had in their old literary societies. Meetings were held regularly; bills and resolutions were debated. Because the ministers were careful to sponsor only popular issues, a ministry was infrequently defeated. Soon, however, attendance lapsed, interest lagged, and the students showed a desire to return to their literary societies. The enthusiasm was short-lived because the two antagonistic political factions which already existed among the students looked upon Wilson's plan as an opportunity to appear in open conflict and to create divisions, which had no reference whatever to the work of the parliament.[7] Like many things in Wilson's professional and public careers, when his personal enthusiasm vanished, interest in what he advocated disappeared. The excitement lay in Wilson's magnetic mass appeal, not in the subject itself.

The new professor was quite interested in sports, and was soon elected to the Faculty Athletic Advisory Board. During the two football seasons that he served at Wesleyan, Wilson made three important contributions to the football team. First of all, he battled for democracy among the players, challenging the privilege various fraternities enjoyed of naming their brothers for positions on the team. Dean Frank W. Nicholson felt that the professor's greatest service to athletics was his insistence upon minimizing this fraternity influence in choice of players.[8] Wilson also assisted the Wesleyan football coach in working out a series of successful offensive plays which contrasted sharply with pre-

[7]Charles E. North to Wilson, January 21, 1911, in Woodrow Wilson Collection, New Jersey State Library, Trenton.

[8]*Wesleyan Argus,* January, 1889, to June, 1890.

vious formations. But by no means the least of his contributions was that which he made to team morale, introducing into the student body a new sense of support for the team, an eager enthusiasm that had previously been lacking. His efforts were quite evident on Thanksgiving Day, 1889, at the game against Lehigh. The fans were shivering in the cold rain as the players on the field fought back and forth in a sea of mud. Twice Lehigh scored touchdowns. The Wesleyan boys seemed to be defeated, the game appeared to be lost, when suddenly from the Wesleyan bleachers a tall, lanky man wearing heavy rubber boots and raincoat rushed out front near the side lines. Closing his umbrella and using it as a baton, he shouted to the Wesleyan contingent, "reproaching them for not cheering for their team; and at once began to lead in the Wesleyan yell, beating time for them with his umbrella. This he continued violently until . . . the tide of the game turned." [9] The Wesleyan boys scored two touchdowns; the game ended in a tie. The Lehigh players credited the zealous cheerleader, Dr. Woodrow Wilson, with the change of morale among the Wesleyan players which saved the team from defeat.[10]

These extracurricular activities in which the professor so enthusiastically engaged won for him a warm spot in the hearts of the students. The atmosphere at Wesleyan was one in which Wilson felt at ease, one in which he enjoyed his work. The degree to which he and his family were received into the university community is evidenced by the arrangements for Thanksgiving dinner. As Wilson wrote Bridges: "We have been taken possession of by these good New England folks and are instead of making, to be given our 'Thanksgiving.' " [11]

As the Christmas season approached, the professor's thoughts turned to his father and younger brother who, for the first time, would spend the Yuletide alone. The younger brother informed Woodrow that when he did not write to his father the latter was hurt, saying that "*Mother* was the one we cared most for." [12]

[9]Carl F. Price, *Wesleyan University Alumnus,* March, 1924.

[10]*Ibid.*

[11]Wilson to Bridges, November 27, 1888, in Meyer Collection, Princeton.

[12]Joseph R. Wilson to Woodrow Wilson, December 16, 1888, in Wilson Papers, Library of Congress.

With Josie's prodding, Wilson wrote a long letter to "My Precious Father":

My thoughts are full of you and dear "Dode" all the time. Tennessee seems so far away for a chap as hungry as I am for a sight of two men whom I love. As the Christmas recess approaches, I realize, as I have so often before, the *pain* there is in a season of holiday and rejoicing away from you. As you know, one of the chief things about which I feel most warranted in rejoicing is that I am your son. I realize the benefit of being your son more and more as my talents and experiences grow: I recognize the strength growing in me as of the nature of your strength; I become more and more conscious of the hereditary wealth I possess, that capital of principle, of literary force and skill of capacity for first-hand thought; and I feel daily more and more bent toward creating in my own children that combined respect and tender devotion for their father that you gave your children for you. Oh, how happy I should be if I could make them think of me as I think of you! You have given me a love that grows, that is stronger in me when I am an old man than it is now,—a love, in brief, that is rooted and grounded in *reason,* and not in filial instinct merely—a love resting upon abiding foundations of *service,* recognizing you as in a certain real sense the author of all I have to be grateful for! I bless God for my noble, strong, and saintly Mother and for my incomparable father. Ask "Dode" if he does not subscribe and tell him that I love my brother passionately.[13]

From his lonely home the father informed his son that while dining with some other clergymen at a New York meeting, there was among the guests a freshman from a woman's college. When Dr. Wilson was introduced to her, she said enthusiastically: "I am so glad to meet you, Dr. Wilson, for I admire your son so much. I am following his career with great interest." Dr. Wilson replied: "I am beginning to be known as the father of my son." [14]

In addition to his university work, Wilson lectured off campus and continued his writing. In January, 1889, he delivered two lectures in Providence, before the Brown University History and Economic Association. The subject of his first lecture was "Sys-

[13]Wilson to his father, December 16, 1888, in Wilson Collection, Princeton.

[14]Only part of this letter remains. The date is shortly before Wilson's reply on January 13, 1889. Joseph R. Wilson to Wilson, n.d., in Wilson Papers, Library of Congress.

tems of Municipal Organizations." [15] After tracing the development of municipal organizations, Wilson concluded: "If I have made a single impression, I have meant it to be this, that there are other ways of reforming a city than by changing the disposition of power. The imperious demand is to get citizens to become stirred up and interested. In the greatest centers of corruption one single day of public indignation sweeps all away and leaves the atmosphere purified for months or years afterwards." [16]

To his father, Woodrow confided: "I was extremely well received and think that I can say that I made a decided hit." He was introduced by a Colonel Goddard, who was "one of the richest men in an extremely rich town, as well as a man of sense and of cultivated tastes." This gentleman, said Wilson, "took me to his house and entertained me most handsomely. He tried to make me believe, by almost every turn of his conversation, that I was quite a distinguished man. I came home so puffed up that I could hardly condescend to speak even to my own family! I lecture there again next Friday on 'The Government of Berlin'—a model government of its kind." [17] For the two lectures, the Wesleyan professor received $48, of which $28 was for railroad fare.[18]

Wilson took his annual leave from teaching to spend about six weeks at Johns Hopkins, where he was to deliver a series of twenty-five lectures to the graduate students on "Local Government." [19] He found the long absence from his family to be a dreary business, "but Ellie and the babies must be supported so therefore must the separation be." [20] Apparently, he had not found the time for careful preparation of the lectures before reaching Baltimore, and he felt that they were not being well received. "I have gotten the impression, somehow (perhaps through my imagination)," he wrote Ellen, "that my two lectures, so far delivered, have fallen rather flat, and I feel a whit discouraged: but the attention of the class must, shall, be conquered

[15] *Wesleyan Argus,* XXII (February 1, 1889), 88.

[16] Providence (R.I.) *Journal,* January 12, 1889.

[17] Wilson to his father, January 13, 1889, in Wilson Collection, Princeton.

[18] J. Franklin Jameson to Wilson, January 22, 1889, in Wilson Papers, Library of Congress.

[19] *Wesleyan Argus,* XXII (February 1, 1889), 89.

[20] Wilson to his father, January 13, 1889, in Wilson Collection, Princeton.

before I get through with them. It's my sensibilities, rather than my courage, that are wounded." [21]

While he was in Baltimore, Woodrow learned from his sister Marion that his father was not happy in Clarksville.[22] To his favorite son the father confessed: "How in my solitude have I longed for the presence of that dear son in whose large love I trust so implicitly and in the wealth of whose generously furnished mind I take such delight: him in whom my affections center as my child and my confidences as my friend. I can readily sympathize with you in the satisfaction you experience in getting back to Johns Hopkins once more, where intellectual life rolls its highest waves. . . . I feel very proud of you when I think of what you are doing and doing so well." [23]

When the Johns Hopkins lecture series was completed, Wilson returned to his family, to his professional routine at Wesleyan, and to his writing. One of his articles, "An Old Master," had been published in the *New Princeton Review* a few months earlier. It discussed the art of classroom lecturing. "Are not our college classrooms," asked Wilson, "in being robbed of the old time lecture, and getting instead a scientific brief of data and bibliography, being deprived also of that literary atmosphere which once pervaded them?" The way to instruct and inspire students, Wilson believed, was "to penetrate the secret of style." The only instrument of conquest was "the sword of penetrating speech." [24]

In April, soon after returning home with a check for $500 in payment for the series of lectures at Johns Hopkins, Wilson made what was apparently his first investment. Through Edward W. Sheldon, a Wall Street attorney who acted as broker, he bought $2,000 worth of Omaha and St. Louis Railroad bonds at $75 per $100 share.[25] At about the same time he received an invitation from Professor Albert B. Hart of Harvard to write the

[21]Wilson to his wife, February 13, 1889, in Axson–Wilson Letters, Princeton.

[22]Marion Kennedy to Wilson, March 22, 1889, in Wilson Papers, Library of Congress.

[23]Joseph R. Wilson to Woodrow Wilson, March 6, 1889, in *ibid.*

[24]*Princeton New Review* (September, 1888), 210–20.

[25]See Edward W. Sheldon to Wilson, April 20, 22, 24, 1889, in Wilson Papers, Library of Congress.

third volume of *Epochs of American History,* a three-volume textbook. He was promised sufficient time for completion of the manuscript and publication within a year by Longmans, Green and Company in both New York and London. There would be payment of $500 upon the appearance of the book.[26]

Wilson wished to accept but thought he could not possibly complete the manuscript in a year, and wrote Hart that he was still committed to write a textbook on government. The following winter, he said, there would also be twenty-five new lectures for him to prepare on administration for a graduate class in Baltimore. In addition, he was afraid of his nervous disposition if he suspended over himself "the whip of a contract" to do something barely possible if he retained the best of health. "My health would, I am afraid, inconveniently desert me at the critical moment." [27]

Although the publishers were anxious to have the third volume out as soon as possible, they granted Wilson the two years that he suggested. "One special reason, among many others," Hart wrote, "why I have been anxious to get your consent to this proposition is the feeling that the work ought to be done by a man who can impartially judge the South, and its degree of responsibility and its share in the restoration of the Union." [28]

Wilson accepted the task with pleasure: "I particularly appreciate your reference to judging the part played by the South during the period of which I am to write. Your confidence in my impartiality I greatly value—and shall hope to deserve. Though born in the South and bred in its sympathies, I am not of Southern-born parents. My father was born in Ohio, my mother in England. Ever since I have had independent judgment of my own, I have been a Federalist. It is this mixture of elements in me—full identification with the South, non-Southern blood, and Federalist principles—that make[s] me hope that a detachment of my affectionate, reminiscent sympathies from my historical judgments is not beyond hoping for." [29] The role of historian would be a new one for Wilson.

[26]Albert B. Hart to Wilson, April 23, 1889, in *ibid.*

[27]Wilson to Hart, May 13, 1889, in Albert Bushnell Hart Papers, Harvard University.

[28]Hart to Wilson, June 1, 1889, in *ibid.*

[29]Wilson to Hart, June 3, 1889, in *ibid.*

Upon learning that Woodrow had been invited to become the author of a volume in the Epoch series, his father wrote: "I am beginning to think that there is no limit either to your acquirements or to your ability to use them—I am certainly vastly proud of my noble boy, in every way." Then, more specifically about the essay: "Your style seems to me to be constantly improving. It has lost nearly altogether that gauze veil which sometimes either suspended or disguised the meaning." The minister, who during his son's youth had been so careful to train the boy to express himself correctly, wrote, "I altogether envy you your facility and your freshness of expression, and your ability to get down to the bottom of things."

Members of Wilson's family were appealing to him in the midst of his busy life for counsel in their intimate affairs. Marion's husband, Ross Kennedy, was ill with tuberculosis, and she realized that she must soon become the breadwinner for their children. She was studying to prepare herself again to teach music, and she was also renewing her interest in two modern languages as well as Greek. Future conditions, she wrote, looked too dreadful for her and the children. "Come, if possible," she pleaded with Woodrow.[30]

Joseph, the younger brother, was in love with Julia Lufton, but could not bind her in formal engagement without the prospect of a job. Should he tell the girl's parents that he was unemployed and had no prospect for immediate work? If Woodrow could put him in contact with a job, he wrote, that would solve his problem. If not, would not the older brother tell him what to do about this love affair with Julia? He promised to do as Wilson thought best.[31] These demands upon Woodrow for his counsel, and later for his financial assistance, were to continue from members of his immediate family throughout the rest of his active life. These requests in the summer of 1889 were merely the first.

During the Princeton commencement, a few of Wilson's classmates, led by Bobby Bridges, formulated a plan to have Presi-

[30]Marion W. Kennedy to Wilson, June 18 and July 17, 1889, in Wilson Papers, Library of Congress.

[31]Joseph Wilson to Woodrow Wilson, June 13, 1889, and Marion W. Kennedy to Wilson, June 18, 1889, in *ibid.*

dent Patton invite Wilson to join the faculty of his alma mater. The plan was not new. The preceding summer, before Wilson left Bryn Mawr, there had been talk of establishing a chair of political science at Princeton. John Wanamaker, the Philadelphia merchant, had indicated that he would be interested in endowing such a chair. Wilson confided to Bridges that he would certainly be a candidate,[32] and Bridges promised that when the time came all their friends would be behind the movement.[33] Now in the early summer of 1889, after conferring with Patton, Bridges informed Wilson that the three of them would have luncheon in New York on July 22—an invitation Woodrow readily accepted.[34] Immediately after lunch, his friend excused himself, leaving Wilson and the Princeton president together. The results were relayed to Bridges: "Our conversation after you left became immediately pertinent in the most natural possible manner by my telling him in answer to his questions, as to the nature of the textbook whose proofs were calling me home, just my views as to the field of that book, the field of my own special studies. We went on easily into talk about Princeton plans." Patton offered Wilson a job to teach political economy for one year, with the expectation that at the end of that year he would teach public law. This, said Woodrow, "I discouraged because (1) of my obligations to the people here who have been much too generous to me to be left in the lurch for next year, (2) of my engagement for a portion of next year at Johns Hopkins, and (3) of my disinclination to teach Political Economy." Wilson had every reason to believe that he was Patton's choice for the chair of Public Law, and felt that he would accept it.[35] Wilson's father supported his decision completely. "My pride in you," the father wrote, "is complete whatever may betide." [36]

Wilson had committed himself to Dr. Patton to remain in Middletown for another year. He could not recede from that

[32]Wilson to Bridges, August 26, 1888, in Meyer Collection, Princeton.

[33]Bridges to Wilson, August 28, 1888, in Wilson Papers, Library of Congress.

[34]Bridges to Wilson, July 15, 1889, in *ibid.*

[35]Wilson to Bridges, July 23, 1889, in Meyer Collection, Princeton.

[36]Joseph R. Wilson to Woodrow Wilson, July 25, 1889, in Wilson Papers, Library of Congress.

position without serious loss of dignity. Besides, the argument for remaining was a good deal stronger than he had made it seem either in the interview with Patton or in his letter to Bobby Bridges. Instruction in political economy at Princeton would of necessity be by lectures and require constant, originative work—so much as to make it impossible for him to push the work on the American epoch which he had promised to have ready by the spring of 1891. At Wesleyan, Woodrow would teach American history and concentrate his energies on the preparation of the epoch, to do added work with prospect of still more arduous duties the year following would be impossible.

That was the personal side of the matter, but there was another side, and this Wilson took note of in his letter to Bridges: "I am under no *contract* obligations to stay here any longer than I choose; but when I came here the department of which I have charge had, in incompetent hands, greatly run down at the time of my election. They wanted it built up; that I have been partially able to do: but, were I to leave it now it would collapse again, for a small college like this has by no means the same chances for obtaining a good or even a tolerable man on short notice that Princeton has." He respected and admired his colleagues very much. They were earnest and "capable teachers and liberal men." The college was getting "a new president of unknown tendencies" just as it had decisively undertaken "a new and liberal policy likely to make the college thoroughly first class of its kind." He believed another year's work would enable him not only to clear his own docket but also to "put a deep stamp on the department"; possibly to choose his own successor—certainly to do his full duty by the college—and he was inclined to "regard these considerations as conclusive." He knew that they would not have called him there had they not felt reasonably assured of keeping him at least two years—and they had treated him not only "honorably but generously." [37]

Having made the decision to remain at Wesleyan another year,

[37]Wilson to Bridges, August 8, 1889, in Meyer Collection, Princeton. "It's immensely gratifying to me that the longest letter I ever received from you concerned altogether my own affairs. By contrast, this long one from me concerns nothing but my own affairs," Wilson wrote.

Wilson sought someone to replace him the following year when he hoped to accept the call to Princeton. In thinking over strong possibilities, he fastened his mind upon Frederick Jackson Turner. Five years younger than Wilson, Turner was among the graduate students who had enrolled in his lecture series at Johns Hopkins in 1889.[38] During the more than six weeks in which Wilson lectured at that university, he and Turner had occupied rooms at the same boardinghouse. At mealtime they talked much and lingered afterward to continue their interesting conversations. Possessed of brilliant minds, both teacher and student were essentially original and independent thinkers. Both of these men, who soon became fast friends, were essentially philosophers. The older man was a political philosopher; Turner was more of a social philosopher. Not intrigued with current politics, he was a devotee of the cultural past.[39]

Both were conscious of the undue emphasis given to the role of New England in the development of American history, of the inability to see beyond the Hudson River. Wilson the southerner and Turner the westerner felt the great need to correct the perspective of northern and eastern writers by filling in their sectional omissions. When Wilson returned to Middletown, he wrote, asking Turner for help in locating materials for the writing of his volume, which he had decided to title *Division and Reunion, 1829–1889*. "I very much need your assistance in the work," declared the Wesleyan teacher. With regret, Turner informed Wilson that he would not be able to aid him very much in his research. In fact, Wilson's only chance of aid would be for Turner to direct a few graduate students as they selected materials from which Woodrow might gather his desired information. Turner added: "I know of no one whose good opinion I would sooner have than your own, and so I am glad indeed if you at all reciprocate the regard I formed for you as a scholar and

[38]Fulmer Mood, "Turner's Formative Period," in *Frederick Jackson Turner, Early Writing,* Louise P. Kellogg (ed.) (Madison, 1938), 3–39; Johns Hopkins University History Seminar Records, 1877–92, pp. 556–57, in Johns Hopkins University Library, Baltimore.

[39]George C. Osborn, "Woodrow Wilson and Frederick Jackson Turner," *Proceedings of the New Jersey Historical Society,* LXXIV (1956), 208–29.

friend at Baltimore. I count the weeks that you spent at Miss Achton's the best of my stay at Johns Hopkins."

In the late spring of 1889 Turner was appointed assistant professor of American history at the University of Wisconsin. Wilson congratulated his former pupil and confided that he was seriously considering moving the following year. "If I go elsewhere next year, would you want to come to Wesleyan?" he asked. "I do wish to feel at liberty to urge your name in case I think it best to accept a call elsewhere; for you will permit me to confess that during our acquaintance in Baltimore I conceived a very sincere admiration for you, and that I have ever since had a strong desire to serve your best interests." [40] Although not entirely surprised to learn that Wilson contemplated moving, "for it was only a question of time when you would go where you could do your work in politics," Turner wanted to know more about the Wesleyan matter before his name was used for any vacancy created by his former teacher's leaving.[41]

When Wilson learned that Turner hoped to become head of the history department at Wisconsin, he wrote, as suggested by Reuben G. Thwaites, who was then resigning as editor of the *Wisconsin State Journal* to become secretary and superintendent of the Wisconsin State Historical Society at Madison, to members of the Board of Regents in Turner's behalf.[42] He wrote to George H. Paul, president of the board, that in the interest of historical scholarship in America, he felt it his plain duty to inform him of Turner's ability.[43] To Thwaites, Wilson confessed: "I not only admire Mr. Turner: I learned, during the six weeks of my acquaintance with him last winter, to have a positive affection for him; and it is a matter of unalloyed pleasure to me to have so early an opportunity to be of some service to him." [44] Both Thwaites and Turner wrote to thank Wilson for his efforts

[40]Wilson to Frederick Jackson Turner, August 23, 1889, in Frederick Jackson Turner Papers, Harvard College Library.

[41]Frederick J. Turner to Wilson, August 31, 1889, in Wilson Papers. Library of Congress.

[42]Reuben G. Thwaites to Wilson, December 23, 1889, in *ibid.*

[43]Wilson to George H. Paul, quoted in Wilson to Thwaites, December 26, 1889, in Reuben G. Thwaites Papers, University of Wisconsin Library.

[44]Wilson to Thwaites, December 26, 1889, in *ibid.*

in Turner's behalf. "It would be a great pity, indeed, for the University [of Wisconsin] not to promptly recognize this sterling young worker in American history," concluded Thwaites.[45] Turner was eventually made head of the history department, and therefore was not interested in succeeding Wilson at Wesleyan.[46] Wilson, however, did not forget his resolution to have Turner as a colleague.

Sometime before Wilson left Bryn Mawr, he reached an agreement to write a textbook for D. C. Heath and Company. In January, 1889, when he went to Brown University to lecture, he took a section of the manuscript for Professor Jameson's critical reading. To his diary, Jameson confided: "Went through Wilson's chapter on the governments of Greece and Rome, which he left with me for that purpose. It disappoints me greatly by its insufficiency and want of perspective and entire grasp. Of course, it is clear and well presented." Again on the following day, Jameson worked on other portions of Wilson's manuscript—probably chapters on Roman dominion and law, and Teutonic policy and government during the Middle Ages. These chapters impressed the Brown University professor more favorably, though he thought them "still inadequate in respect to many points of detail." [47]

During the spring of 1889 Wilson spent much time working on the manuscript. Upon investigation, the publishers concluded that there would be many colleges, especially in the South and West, that would have no place in their curriculum for a course in which *The State: Elements of Historical and Practical Politics* would prove a feasible text. As a consequence, Wilson accepted a suggestion that he issue the longest chapter as a separate book—*The State and Federal Governments of the United States: A Brief Manual for Schools and Colleges.* Heath promised to promote the sales in southern and western colleges by letters, advertisements, and circulars noting the main points in which Wilson's book systematically differed from the usual government manuals. In a

[45]Thwaites to Wilson, December 30, 1889, in Wilson Papers, Library of Congress.

[46]Frederick J. Turner to Wilson, February 5, 1890, in *ibid.*

[47]John Franklin Jameson, *Diary* entries of Wednesday, January 16, 1889, and Thursday, January 17, 1889.

brief preface, the author said of his manual: "The prominence given by it to the state governments ought to recommend it, I should think, to those who are discovering, with the ablest of our critics, that the states are the vital and essential units of our great national system." [48]

The author's opinion of his text was partially revealed in a letter to Heath Dabney: "A fact book [such as *The State*] is always a plebian among books, and it is a fact book; but a great deal has gone out of me into it, none the less." [49] An author's opinion about his own book is significant, but hardly objective. More important are the opinions of others. The London *Daily Chronicle* lamented that the author had provided no rational basis for the state; he merely declared it to be derived from the social nature of man. "The treatment given to early governments was good," asserted the *Chronicle,* but that "of modern Europe incomplete." [50] The Boston *Daily Advertiser* was "divided between admiration and irritation." Each page seemed a battle between the desire for completeness and the need for brevity. Finally, there was a curious omission of any treatment of the governments of Italy, Russia, and Spain.[51] To the Chicago *Dial,* Wilson was "a shrewd and careful student" in the presentation of his views of the futures of the most important governments. The work of comparison was mainly left to the reader.[52] The Boston *Literary World* observed that though "intended as a textbook [its] size and scope would probably confine it largely to the private reader." [53]

At this point in his career, Woodrow's emotions were deeply stirred by a long message from his father. "I have no excuse for not writing except the singular one of too much love," began the old minister. He did not wish to bore his busy son with commonplaces. "I could," said the father, "think of you without disturb-

[48]See Woodrow Wilson, *The State and Federal Governments of the United States: A Brief Manual for Schools and Colleges* (Boston, 1889), prefatory note, dated August 22, 1889.

[49]Wilson to Dabney, October 31, 1889, in Dabney Papers, Virginia.

[50]London *Daily Chronicle,* August 21, 1889.

[51]Boston *Daily Advertiser,* n.d., clipping in Wilson Papers.

[52]Chicago *Dial,* March, 1890, n.d., in *ibid.*

[53]Boston *Literary World,* March 15, 1890.

ing anyone—and this I have done with plentifulness and a constancy worthy of the object of my affections. Ah, my son, this old heart—you fill it, and with a charm that is quite unspeakable so that I am made to feel that after all I can never be forgetting—and do always remember—the other children, who are very close to my sympathies." But with Woodrow it was different. "You were my companion more entirely than they," wrote the elder Wilson. Not only was Woodrow a son, attached by a tie of natural regard, "but my *friend* to whom community of thought binds by ligatures which are thicker than blood." The father was certain that they were the two who thoroughly—most thoroughly—comprehended each other. "You satisfy my intellect, as I believe I am able to contest yours. You gratify my pride also, and I feel assured that your corresponding emotion has its demands measurably met in me, to whom you have long been accustomed to look up with an eye that perceives in me more than there is, of goodness and largeness." The father hoped his son "would pardon an old man's fondness; which, when it enjoys the opportunity for a little airing can hardly find the place where it ought to stop." [54]

Soon after *The State* made its appearance, the *Atlantic Monthly* printed Wilson's article on "The Character of Democracy in the United States." The author declared that in America the "progress of popular education and the progress of democracy have been inseparable." In a very real sense Wilson was describing his own future political leadership when he declared that "our separation from our leaders is a greater peril because democratic government more than any other needs organization in order to escape disintegration." With the national leadership of that day in mind the Wesleyan professor wrote: "Never before was consistent leadership so necessary; never before was it necessary to concert measures over areas so vast, to adjust laws to so many institutions, to make a compact and intelligible unit out of so many factions, to maintain a central and dominant force where there are so many forces!" [55]

[54] Joseph R. Wilson to Woodrow Wilson, October 5, 1889, in Wilson Papers, Library of Congress.

[55] Woodrow Wilson, "The Character of Democracy in the United States," *Atlantic Monthly,* LXIV (November, 1889), 577–88.

With prompting from Ellen, Woodrow shelved his work for a few days in the fall of 1889 and made his first voyage, to Boston. To Bobby Bridges he wrote: "My sea-voyage to Boston was pretty rough and I lost interest in my meals to some extent. But I kept my grip very much better than I expected and was not positively seasick at all. My cold gradually wore off and before very long I was feeling bully." [56] After a conference with D. C. Heath in Boston, Wilson caught an early train to Middletown.

In October, Wilson was invited to deliver the first of a series of lectures at Brown University. Professor Jameson wanted someone to treat "in a scholarly fashion the opposing theories respecting the functions of government in such matters as factory legislation, prison reform, state charities and the relations of the state to education." [57] In this lecture on "The State and Social Reform," delivered on November 11, Wilson declared that America must devise a new philosophy to fit an age when every person seemed a rival of every other. In such circumstances, he admitted, many had turned to socialism which, if ever realized, would be "the golden age of civilization. Everyone who believed in the perfectibility of man must be "within lawful bounds a socialist." Since the attainment of socialism was not an immediate possibility, Wilson continued, "government must be recognized as a beneficent and indispensable organ of society" because "nowhere but government is society recognized as an element." Americans must look to government to guarantee equality of opportunity, more specifically, to control hours and wages of workers, the labor of women and children, the conditions under which people worked, and the natural monopolies. This was the first time that Wilson had spoken of an active, positive role of government in the national economy. Herein lay some of the ideas of the Wilsonian New Freedom and the Roosevelt New Deal.

Not knowing of Wilson's contemplated return to Princeton, Horace Scudder, a trustee of Williams College, wrote to ask if he would accept an endowed chair there as professor of American history, literature, and eloquence.[58] "You are, in a sense, my liter-

[56] Wilson to Bridges, November 6, 1889, in Meyer Collection, Princeton.

[57] J. Franklin Jameson to Wilson, October 1, 1889, in Wilson Papers, Library of Congress.

[58] Horace E. Scudder to Wilson, December 20, 1889, in *ibid.*

ary Godfather," Wilson began his tactful reply, "but, unhappily—for a chair of American History has a very strong claim upon my interests and desire—I am in the present case obliged to plead 'a previous engagement.' " Wilson told Scudder that his strongest interest lay in the institutional side of politics, in the history of political habit and of those legal relations and concepts which underlie Public Law. Princeton was creating such a professorship and he felt bound to accept it if it were offered to him. Moreover, Wesleyan, having recently received generous gifts of money, had offered to create such a chair as he wanted if he would stay, and if he did not go to Princeton, he would "feel bound on many grounds to accept this offer." [59]

The Princeton trustees held a meeting early in November, 1889. Immediately after, one of the group told Bobby Bridges "confidentially" the objections that were offered to Wilson. Forthwith, Bridges relayed to his boyhood friend "the lamentations of the Philistines": (1) "Wilson is a fine scholar but he comes from the South and we want to know more about his patriotism and his general views on national topics. (2) He is, we hear, a little heterodox. (3) He is too learned and drab to interest his students. (4) We are fearful of his strong affection for the English institutions." With personal reassurances, Bridges added: "These things are 'chaff' which intelligent men laugh at, but we know that there is an element at Princeton which is hardly reasonably intelligent." [60]

Now that Wilson knew why he had received no further encouragement from Patton since their long conference in July, he wished to talk with him again. He made the suggestion to Bridges, and a meeting with the Princeton president was arranged.[61] After the second interview with Patton in New York, Wilson lacked the confidence that followed the July meeting. Subsequently, he learned that the trustees had postponed the election of Professor

[59]Wilson to Scudder, December 23, 1889, in Horace E. Scudder Papers, Library of Congress.

[60]Bridges to Wilson, November 5, 1889, in Wilson Papers, Library of Congress.

[61]Wilson to Bridges, November 6, 1889, in Meyer Collection, Princeton; Bridges to Wilson, November 7, 1889, in Wilson Papers, Library of Congress. Wilson was to meet President Patton at Astor House in New York on November 9 at 8 P.M.

Johnston's successor until February, 1890, and he asked Bridges for the significance of the move as it regarded him. He was more than ever anxious to know the final attitude of the trustees toward him because of the Wesleyan offer. It was a "queer, strained situation, altogether," concluded Wilson.[62] Bridges talked with President Patton and several trustees of Princeton and informed Woodrow that in every instance he was assured that his election was a certainty.[63] "You are the most extraordinary proxy I have ever heard of," declared Woodrow. "You act and converse for me better than I can act and talk for myself."

In view of the way things were shaping up for the Wesleyan professor, Bridges feared his friend might decline a Princeton invitation when it came. Woodrow hastened to assure him: "You need not be uneasy on the score of your assurances that I would gladly accept an appointment at Princeton. That is still strictly true, notwithstanding the new opportunities here." Although Wesleyan was a delightful place to work, it was not a sufficiently stimulating place—"largely because the class of students here is very inferior in the point of preparatory culture. They come from a parentage for the most part of narrow circumstances and of correspondingly narrow thought." Moreover, said Wilson, "the New England men among them . . . have an added New England narrowness in political study." The only possible doubt about his going to Princeton, he wrote, was raised by the question of salary. He would have to buy new books in changing his field of work, besides providing for other expenses, and unless Princeton offered him a full professor's salary he would be "obliged to hesitate about moving just at the present." He took it for granted that he would be offered the full $3,500. [64]

A month later, while Wilson was in Baltimore delivering his annual series of lectures at Johns Hopkins, he received a telegram from trustee Moses Taylor Payne: "We elected you full professor today. Trust you will accept." [65] Not waiting until he had official notification from the clerk of the Board of Trustees as

[62]Wilson to Bridges, November 18, 1889, in Meyer Collection, Princeton.

[63]Bridges to Wilson, November 19, 20, 1889, in Wilson Papers, Library of Congress.

[64]Wilson to Bridges, January 27, 1890, in Meyer Collection, Princeton.

[65]Apparently the telegram was lost, but it is quoted in Wilson to Bridges, February 13, 1890, in Meyer Collection, Library of Congress.

to the terms of his election to the faculty, Wilson, within the hour of receiving Payne's telegram, wrote Bridges that he supposed his election meant a full professor's salary and that the only thing to be negotiated was the continuation of his "present arrangement with Johns Hopkins." The giving of twenty-five lectures annually at Johns Hopkins for which Wilson received $500 was, he said, of so great an advantage to him that he would be loath to give it up. He was certainly correct when he stated to Bridges that he felt his election was "due in large part, if not entirely, to you." [66]

The terms of his election to Princeton Wilson learned directly—he had been unanimously elected professor of jurisprudence and political economy at a salary of $3,000 per annum, wrote E. R. Cravens, clerk of the Board of Trustees.[67] President Patton, in Baltimore for a Princeton alumni dinner, explained that Wilson would receive the same salary his predecessor, Johnston, had received. According to Patton, Professors Theodore W. Hunt, Alexander T. Ormond, and Andrew F. West would be jealous of anyone's getting more salary. More importantly, the income from large blocks of Princeton investments was decreasing appreciably. Wilson would teach not more than four hours a week, with salary and class work about the same as he was receiving at Wesleyan. Patton would not promise Wilson permission to continue his lectures at Johns Hopkins.

Wilson was inclined to insist on either a salary of $3,500 or continuation of his Johns Hopkins lectures.[68] Bridges urged caution. He had written Patton urging a salary of $3,500, but Woodrow must not make an ultimatum; he must work out a compromise.[69] In the end, Patton assured Wilson that he could accept with the full confidence that the trustees would consent to his continuing his engagement at Johns Hopkins.[70] On his way back to

[66]Wilson to Bridges, February 13, 1890, in *ibid.*

[67]E. R. Cravens to Wilson, February 17, 1890, in Wilson Papers, Library of Congress.

[68]Wilson to Bridges, February 18, 1890, in Meyer Collection, Library of Congress.

[69]Bridges to Wilson, February 20, 1890, in Wilson Papers, Library of Congress.

[70]Wilson to Bridges, March 8, 1890, in Meyer Collection, Library of Congress.

Middletown the visiting lecturer stopped at Princeton for conferences with his friends and future colleagues.

Wilson's health failed him again during the last week or so of his lectures in Baltimore. He had grippe in a mild form, he informed his father, "but severely enough to make lecturing a torture and yet I was obliged to lecture, in order to get through in the time allotted me. . . . I was a very wretched individual; and when I reached home last Friday, a very much used up one." He was better now, and felt sure that it would not take long for home influences to make him well again. As nearly always when writing to his father, Wilson wrote with strong feeling: "It seems to me that the older I get the more I need you for the older I get the more I appreciate the debt I owe you and the more I long to increase it. It seems to me that my separation from you, instead of becoming a thing of wont, becomes more and more unendurable." Nor did Woodrow ever forget his younger brother. "I suppose dear 'Dode' [Joseph] will come north too this summer. I keep his picture on my desk all the time and all the time long to see him." [71]

Continuing a practice inaugurated at Bryn Mawr, Wilson invited Ellen's younger brother Stockton to live with them during their last year at Wesleyan. Stockton had been attending the University of Georgia as a student in journalism, but transferred to Wesleyan.[72] Within a few weeks after he became a member of the Wilson household, Ellen bore Woodrow a third daughter, Eleanor Randolph. "My big piece of news," Wilson wrote Bridges, "is that three weeks ago another daughter was born to us. Both mother and baby are doing and feeling splendidly. There is now 'the baby, the little baby, and the littlest baby of all.' " [73] Woodrow's disappointed father stated that somehow he had "hoped for a boy, but the Divine Father who has events in His own hands, moulds all these things for the best." [74]

It was about the time his third and last child was born that

[71] Wilson to his father, March 20, 1890, in Wilson Collection, Princeton.

[72] Stockton Axson to Wilson, May 10, 21, 1889, in Wilson Papers, Library of Congress.

[73] Wilson to Bridges, November 6, 1889, in Meyer Collection, Princeton.

[74] Joseph R. Wilson to Woodrow Wilson, October 20, 1889, in Wilson Papers, Library of Congress.

Wilson dispensed with his moustache. To mark the occasion, he had photographs made and sent them to relatives and friends. Marion, the older sister, wrote: "You have not improved yourself in my estimation, by discarding your moustache. What does Ellie think? You are good enough looking, anyway, but better looking with a moustache than without." [75]

During the Christmas vacation Wilson's cousin Mary Hoyt journeyed up from Bryn Mawr to be with the Wilsons and to see "little Ellie." "I was very keen to see the wonderful new baby," she wrote. "And I came in very close contact with her because, during those holidays, Ellen had a terrible accident." While in the kitchen instructing a new cook, Ellen Wilson had spilled a kettle full of boiling lard over her feet and was most painfully burned.[76] Every minute Woodrow could spare from his work had been devoted to helping her, he wrote Bobby Bridges. Now, at last, her burns were beginning to heal.[77] Ellen recovered slowly from the effects of her accident and months later was not completely well. [78]

Although Wilson was in Baltimore when he received notice of his official election to Princeton, he at once informed President B. O. Raymond of Wesleyan of the Princeton offer and of his probable acceptance. Raymond expressed regret at losing him: "I wish we could make it so attractive you would not leave. What about a successor? Will you not give us the names of some men in your field and your opinion of them?" [79] When Raymond learned that Wilson was having some trouble with President Patton over the terms of his going to Princeton, the Wesleyan official wrote: "Can we not emphasize the doubt of your leaving by dividing your work and giving you just the line of work you wish to carry." [80]

[75]Marion Kennedy to Wilson, October 12, 1889, in *ibid.*

[76]Baker, *Wilson Life and Letters,* I, 318.

[77]Wilson to Bridges, January 6, 1890, in Meyer Collection, Princeton.

[78]Wilson to Bridges, January 27, 1890, in *ibid.;* George Howe to Wilson, April 2, 1890, in Wilson Papers, Library of Congress.

[79]Apparently Wilson's letter to the Wesleyan president was lost but its receipt is acknowledged in B. P. Raymond to Wilson, February 25, 1890, in Wilson Papers, Library of Congress.

[80]Raymond to Wilson, March 3, 1890, in *ibid.*

A. W. Hazen, minister of the First Congregrational Church, joined Raymond in urging the professor to remain. "We here wish, with all our souls," the Reverend Mr. Hazen wrote, "that you might see your way open to decline the flattering proposal of your Alma Mater. Can we do anything to open it? Pres. Raymond assured me yesterday that the authorities here would grant you almost any request, if you could be induced to prolong your stay here for a time. And I must gratify myself," concluded the clergyman, "though I cannot hope to influence you, by saying that I should be a sincere mourner if you were to leave this city." [81]

The Wesleyan *Argus* noted that Wilson had "won the cordial esteem of the entire student body both by his work in the classroom and his active support of all the athletic interests of the college." His work, concluded the *Argus*, "has been an inspiration to the students who have sat under his instruction." [82]

As the Wilsons began to make definite plans for leaving Middletown, there were many expressions of regret. Woodrow's feelings were reflected in a letter he wrote to the Reverend Mr. Hazen: "I do not know, I am sure, how I have deserved the affectionate friendship you have offered me and I have so eagerly accepted, but I do know that friendship has itself done not a little towards rendering me worthy of it, so much have I been stirred and benefitted by it. Mrs. Wilson and I have regarded our relationship with you and Mrs. Hazen as one of the chief advantages and pleasures of our life in Middletown; and I sincerely wish that I might say that there was a prospect of our continuing to enjoy it. But I have virtually committed myself to the Princeton authorities, and must accept their call. . . . I shall leave Wesleyan," Wilson concluded, "with genuine and profound regret; but with many most valuable additions to the roll of my indulgent friends." [83]

Wilson's thirty-fourth year drew to a close as he left Wesleyan. The boyish feeling which he had so long was, he said, "giving place consciously to another feeling," the feeling that he no longer need hesitate to assert himself and his opinions "in the presence

[81]A. W. Hazen to Wilson, March 4, 1890, in *ibid.*

[82]Wesleyan *Argus,* XXIII (June 28, 1890), 173–74.

[83]Wilson to Hazen, March 8, 1890, in Baker Papers, Library of Congress.

of and against the selves and opinions of old men, 'my elders.' " [84] Wilson had matured slowly. Failures had beset him in early manhood. Rejected in his first love affair, he had succeeded in his second. His marriage to Ellen, their home life, were in every way ideal. A failure at law, Wilson had, within five years, triumphed as a teacher. Not only had he received two professional promotions, but he had received two degrees. He had been given honorary membership in Phi Beta Kappa and had been chosen president of Johns Hopkins University Alumni Association. He had published three books, all of which were well received. A number of his articles and essays were also in print by the end of his formative years. It was no wonder that, as he approached middle age, he at last thought "a distinct feeling of maturity" had come over him.

[84]Wilson to his wife, March 9, 1889, in Axson–Wilson Letters, Princeton.

CHAPTER X *Return to Princeton*

After concluding arrangements with President Patton and the Board of Trustees, Wilson began making plans to move his family to Princeton. "I find that everybody regards my election to Princeton as a sort of crowning success," he wrote his father. "Congratulations pour in from all sides; evidently I am 'writ down' in the category of 'Success Men.' "[1] The "Princeton gang" was especially happy that after twelve years Wilson was returning as a full-fledged faculty member to his alma mater.

Apparently, however, the newly elected professor of jurisprudence and political economy did not feel that he had arrived at the pinnacle of success. Indeed, he wrote: "I suppose that I ought to feel an immense accession of personal satisfaction of pride, but somehow I can't manage it." Here at last was an opportunity for

[1]Woodrow Wilson to his father, March 20, 1890, in Wilson Collection, Princeton.

Wilson to study, to teach, and to write as he wished and under conditions pleasing to him. As he told his father: "I feel grateful and full of courage at the prospect of having an opportunity to do just the studying and writing I want to do under the most favorable circumstances; but, so far as personal gratification is concerned, I would infinitely rather know that I was going to have a chance to be cured of the heartsickness from which I suffer because of my separation from you and 'Dode.' "

Wilson, supposedly aloof and cold, frequently wrote with warm feeling to members of his immediate family, especially to his father. "My *mind* can't give me gratification," he noted; "I know it too well and know it a poor thing. I have to rely on my *heart* as the sole source of contentment and happiness, and that craves, oh *so* fiercely, the companionship of those I love." [2]

While the Wilsons were making their plans for leaving Middletown, Woodrow was told by Professor Herbert Adams that he had been selected by the Board of Trustees to continue for a three-year period at $500 per annum his series of lectures at Johns Hopkins.[3] Besides Wilson, who would lecture on "Administration and Public Law," Professor Jameson would also speak, using "Constitutional and Political History of the Southern States" as his topic; Dr. Albert Shaw, soon to be editor of *Review of Reviews,* would comment on "Municipal and Social Problems"; James Schouler, author of *History of the United States under the Constitution,* would discuss "American Political History"; Carroll D. Wright, United States Commissioner of Labor, would talk on "Social Science"; and John A. Kasson, United States Minister to Austria and later to Germany, would lecture on "The History of Diplomacy." [4] Wilson, however, would deliver more lectures than any other member of the group.

In September, 1890, the Wilsons moved to Princeton. News of the professor's intellectual achievements and his well-earned professional prominence had preceded the family's arrival. At the

[2]*Ibid.*

[3]Herbert B. Adams to Wilson, June 4, 1890, in Wilson Collection, Princeton.

[4]See list of Johns Hopkins University History and Political Science Seminary Lectures during year 1890–91, in *ibid.*

little station at the foot of Blair Arch steps, a group of enthusiastic undergraduates assembled to cheer Wilson as he emerged from the small, dingy coach.[5] These boys, some of whom were to become his pupils, observed closely the man whose arrival they were applauding. He seemed taller than he was (five feet eleven inches) as he stood erect in well-fitting clothes. The face, with wide cheek bones, a firm chin, and a somewhat prominent nose, was dominated by brilliant blue eyes. Those eyes, said Withrop M. Daniels, a newly acquired friend, were "searching, significant, penetrating, unforgettable." [6] When the new Princeton professor doffed his well-worn hat as he alighted from the train, the cheering lads noted a high forehead and not overly thick, light brown hair which its wearer kept parted on the left side, combed across the top of his head and brushed back on both sides.

All smiles and cordiality, Wilson stepped from the train and turned to assist Ellen and their three daughters—Margaret, four; Jessie, three; and Eleanor, a little more than one. Crowded into the local dray, they were driven to 48 Steadman Street. There, in a very comfortable and roomy frame house, they were to live for approximately six years.

When the Wilsons came to Princeton, neither the town nor the College of New Jersey, as the school was called, had changed appreciably since Woodrow's graduation in 1879. Princeton, the village, and Princeton Junction, the railroad station, were still small, lazy, and indifferent to the stir of the outside world. The college was dominated by theological conservatism as it had been a decade earlier. No innovations in the fields of higher education were apparent. For example, no curriculum expansion had occurred to meet the demands of the industrial revolution for an increasingly large number of trained scientists and engineers. Indeed, the construction of a chemistry building was not announced until months after Wilson arrived, and did not open its doors to faculty and students until September, 1892. Plans for classrooms and laboratories for the several fields of engineering were only

[5]McMillen Lewis, *Woodrow Wilson of Princeton* (Narberth, Pa., 1952), 5–6.

[6]Winthrop M. Daniels, *Recollections of Woodrow Wilson* (New Haven, 1944), 9–10.

in the discussion stage in the fall of 1890, not to be added until the scholastic year 1892–93.

In 1888 Dr. James McCosh had retired as president of Princeton, but continued to teach classes in philosophy. Dr. Francis L. Patton, the new president and a Presbyterian clergyman, had formerly been professor of ethics. He was extremely conservative, and, unlike his predecessor, was a poor administrator. Scarcely recognizing the drift in American higher educational circles away from the classics and toward the newer fields of scientific studies, Patton was reluctant to accept the change. If he moved at all, he took the step very deliberately. Indeed, Wilson's return to his alma mater as specialist in political economy, as a teacher of public law, was in itself a recognition of change. Wilson at this time, however, was more Hamiltonian than Jeffersonian. In fact, he was a staunch Federalist. As biographer Baker says, he "would conciliate the new without really disturbing the old"; he was new blood, but safe.[7]

Among the excellent teachers with whom Wilson would serve were such scholars as Dr. Henry B. Fine, who as head professor of mathematics and later dean of the college was to become and remain a devoted and intimate friend of Wilson; Dr. Henry F. Osborn, professor of comparative anatomy, who would soon use his creative genius in developing the American Museum of Natural History; Dr. William F. Sloane, who, as professor of history and political science, had sought the presidency in 1888 when Dr. Patton was chosen, and who would soon accept a professorship at Columbia University; and Dr. Andrew F. West, professor of Latin, who years later, as dean of the graduate school, was to prove Wilson's equal in campus politics and thereby become one of Wilson's bitterest opponents.

According to the college catalogue, Wilson, a member of the Department of Philosophy and Jurisprudence and Politics, was to teach courses in American constitutional law, state and federal; international law; English common law; and general jurisprudence. Most of these were two-hour courses, that is, two lectures each week. Wilson was not to offer all of them at any one time and several of them were electives for juniors and seniors only.

[7]Baker, *Wilson Life and Letters,* II, 8.

The Wilsons had hardly settled in their house when Woodrow's father, sensing the enthusiasm which his son had for his new work and for the greater opportunity to achieve distinction, warned him to arrange his professional chores in such a way that overwork would not shake the very foundations of his health. He reminded his ambitious son that ill health had plagued him several times and that he must not fall victim to it again. The interested father was sure that his son's "thoughtful wisdom" would serve to provide for the present and the future both, so as to "ensure a success" which would not be "achieved at the cost of a too burdened mind and a broken body." [8]

Although the Wilsons attended religious services with some degree of regularity after moving to Princeton, it was not until the summer of 1897 that Woodrow yielded to Ellen's insistence and joined a church. While in New England they had left the Presbyterian Church for the Congregational Church. Now they hestitated to withdraw from the fellowship into which they had been so cordially received. As Wilson wrote to Dr. Hazen, the Congregational minister: "We *must* ask for a letter to the Second Presbyterian Church of Princeton. Indeed we have waited already too long, reluctant to break the last actual tie to Middletown!" In granting Wilson's request for dismissal, the minister replied affectionately: "You were *ideal* parishioners while here and your expressions ever since have been most friendly. I can never forget your reverent worship bearing in our services, nor your patient attention to my too barren needs." [9]

In the village of Princeton, hardly large enough, it would seem, for more than a single church of any one religious faith, the professor found two Presbyterian churches locked in keen rivalry. At first the Wilsons refused to unite with either of them. Ellen taught the girls the Calvinistic Shorter Catechism at home. Eventually, however, the family united with the Second Presbyterian Church where they were more needed and where Wood-

[8] Joseph R. Wilson to Woodrow Wilson, September 15, 1890, in Wilson Papers, Library of Congress.

[9] Wilson to Hazen, March 29, 1897, in Baker Papers, Library of Congress; Hazen to Wilson, April 1, 1897, in Wilson Papers, Library of Congress; Lewis, *Wilson of Princeton,* 10.

row subsequently was elected an elder. The Session minute books contain entries in Wilson's hand, and pew number 94, on the sixth row from the front on the minister's right, where Wilson sat is marked: "Woodrow Wilson; 1897–1905." [10]

The returning alumnus brought a fresh breeze into the academic circles of his alma mater. His colleagues accepted him cordially, delighted in his sense of humor, marveled at his charming manner, and paid little attention to his skirting of all social intimacies. In faculty meetings Wilson's uncanny ability in debate was quickly recognized. Professor Bliss Perry, who for seven years sat beside him at faculty meetings, wrote that "my seat for that day and for the next seven years was next to the chair of a long-jawed, homely, fascinatingly alert man who was addressed by the President as Professor Wilson. It was clear at once that he was a debator." [11]

Within a year after Wilson arrived on the Princeton campus, the faculty began to split into two factions. The younger men saw issues and questions from the same point of view and generally agreed on similar solutions for the perplexing problems that confronted the group. Although Wilson did not map out any strategy to split the faculty, he did emerge as the recognized leader of the younger members. He led them inevitably by his wit, his courage, and his prominence in faculty debates.[12] His Scotch-Irish temperament was quick to respond, and it was not always under perfect control. At times, his enthusiasm coupled with a well-trained eloquence prompted him to overstate his case.

Professor George M. Harper recalled that in one faculty meeting the newcomer made an unnecessarily long, tedious speech. When he concluded, Dr. Harper immediately rose and with animation declared: "We have had enough of this quibbling. Let us get on with the business." Whereupon Wilson bounced up "red in the face" and verbally attacked Harper, hurting him deeply. After the faculty meeting adjourned, Harper walked slowly home. Besides having his feelings wounded he was saddened over the thought of losing Wilson's friendship. But as he climbed the

[10]Bliss Perry, *And Gladly Teach* (Boston, 1935), 155.
[11]*Ibid.*
[12]Baker, *Wilson Life and Letters,* II, 16.

front steps of his home, he suddenly felt a hand pressed firmly on his shoulder and heard Wilson saying: "Don't let this little spat spoil our friendship." "We made up the quarrel then and there," remembered Harper, "and neither of us referred to it again." [13]

From the beginning of his teaching career at Bryn Mawr, Wilson had tried to impress his students with the cardinal virtue of honesty, demonstrating his faith in them by leaving them on their honor during examinations. This practice he had continued at Wesleyan. Hardly had be begun teaching at Princeton when Ellen learned of widespread cheating on tests and examinations and relayed the information to her husband. For some time Wilson discussed the matter with the southern students who frequented his home and for whom he and Ellen had a natural affinity. Students and teacher agreed that to practice dishonesty was to destroy the merit of learning. Wilson had observed that when the faculty endeavored to enforce honesty on examinations the students accepted the situation as a game of wits and frequently bested the instructor. In short, the faculty had the honor; the students had the system.

Woodrow assumed the leadership in the fight for the adoption of an honor system. At a faculty meeting the professor stated that the students should be treated like gentlemen, not supervised as if they were small children nor watched as if they were young criminals. A few of the students from the South assisted him in drawing up a pledge which would be required of each student at the conclusion of his test or examination: "I pledge, on my honor as a gentleman, that during this examination I have neither given nor received assistance."

In the faculty meeting at which the pledge was debated, President Patton called someone to the chair and took the floor in opposition. Patton began by attacking caustically that romantic conception of a gentleman's honor which, as he declared, "had once allowed a 'gentleman' to seduce a woman or kill a friend in a duel but would not allow him to cheat at cards." From an adjoining chair Professor Perry noted that, as Patton denounced

[13] William S. Myers (ed.), *Woodrow Wilson: Some Princeton Memories* (Princeton, 1946), 4.

with biting sarcasm the phrase "on my honor as a gentleman" in the proposed pledge, Wilson "grew white and very quiet," his facial features became tense, his muscles taut. Dr. Perry knew that under such conditions the professor "was most dangerous." Wilson, a product of the Southland, made a ringing reply. He knew the sentimentality that was attached to honor and to gentility. Moreover, he said, he was acquainted with the power of inspiring phrases for American undergraduates much better than any foreigner. (Patton was born in the Bermuda Islands, and had retained his English citizenship.) Wilson conveyed his points "with unmistakable clearness and with a passion that swept the faculty off their feet." With an overwhelming majority they voted to retain the phrase "on my honor as a gentleman" in the pledge.

Once established, the honor system was loyally supported by Wilson. "Our satisfaction with the system and its operation," Woodrow wrote Professor Gilbert Alleman, "is entire and enthusiastic. It has worked a sort of regeneration, and it has never since its establishment been for a moment discredited or in danger of missing success. But its establishment should not be 'by authority'. It ought to come from the students." [14]

The adoption of the honor system was a complete victory for the young faculty group. For Wilson it was a distinct personal triumph, not only for an ideal but because he had established his idealistic objective over the president's active opposition. Only professors who have taught under the deplorable detective and police system and under an efficiently administered honor system realize the vast difference the latter makes in the relations between teachers and pupils. Without the complete cooperation of all students any honor system is doomed to failure. By mutual watchfulness on the part of the Princeton students, the high standards set by their pledge of honor were maintained. The students themselves demanded the expulsion of any student caught "cribbing." [15]

By 1893 the young faculty members became a majority of the

[14]Perry, *And Gladly Teach,* 130–31; Wilson to Gilbert Alleman, June 8, 1898, in Wilson Collection, Princeton.

[15]For a long and laudatory discussion of Princeton's honor system see Philadelphia *Press,* June 4, 1895; H. B. Fine, "Student Honor in Examinations at Princeton," *Harper's Weekly,* XXXV (June 1, 1895), 509–10.

total staff at Princeton. For this situation Wilson was in part responsible. Soon after he came to Princeton he began trying to interest acquaintances whose lecturing, research, and writing evidenced intellectual growth in coming to Princeton. He would have a prospect write to him in some detail about his work with permission to send the letter to President Patton. Wilson, for example, tried to get Albert Shaw, whom he had known while a graduate student at Johns Hopkins. Although Shaw never applied for a professorship at Princeton, he warmed to the idea when his former schoolmate wrote several times about the matter. Somewhat abruptly Wilson informed his friend that, whether true or not, the powers that be at Princeton believed he held views and opinions that were not acceptable to the college. Shaw thanked Wilson for his frankness: "As for a professorship at Princeton, that would be very attractive on many accounts, yet my heart is not set on any place or position. I am not and have never been an applicant. . . . Princeton could hardly be a congenial place for me if I felt that I was a *suspect*." He would prefer a place "far more obscure," where he was "*wanted and trusted*."[16] In time, Shaw became editor of the *Review of Reviews*.

If Woodrow failed to bring Shaw to Princeton, he did succeed in making a colleague of his Wesleyan friend Professor Winthrop M. Daniels. "I, it seems, am to remain Professor of Jurisprudence and Political Economy," Wilson wrote Daniels in the spring of 1892, "and so be head of the Department of which you will be the other member: in short, I am to be, for the trial heat, your 'chief'. I am sure that I need not assure you that this arrangement will not involve any real curtailment of your liberty in your work. It will be pleasant to be thus consulting colleagues." Shortly thereafter Danials learned that his nomination was adopted "without the least objection." Moreover, added Wilson, "Dr. Patton said to the Committee very explicitly that this nomination looked towards the establishment of a full chair of Economics and a promotion."[17] Beginning the fall of 1892

[16]Albert Shaw to Wilson, November 6, 1890, July 1, 1891, in Wilson Papers, Library of Congress. Wilson to Shaw, November 15, 1890, June 20, 1891, in Baker Papers, Library of Congress.

[17]Wilson to Winthrop M. Daniels, May 16, 24, 30, 1892, in Winthrop M. Daniels Papers, Princeton University Library.

Daniels taught courses in political economy, enabling Wilson to devote himself entirely to jurisprudence and public law. Daniels ably supported his chief in his aggressive leadership of the young men on the faculty.

Not only did Wilson rapidly rise to a position of influence on the faculty but even more quickly he was recognized by the students as an able teacher. Within a fortnight after he started teaching at his alma mater, a Washington, D.C., attorney stated that he esteemed it "a good fortune . . . that my son should be enabled to benefit by your lectures in a course." [18] A minister wanted to know if the students in the Princeton Theological Seminary could attend Wilson's classes. So far as he knew, the professor replied, none of the boys from the seminary were attending but, "of course, students from the Seminary are welcome in any of my classrooms." [19]

Wilson had a sincere interest in his students. Many times he was their confidant and he thoroughly enjoyed their companionship. A good example was his relationship with John Bridges, nephew of Bobby Bridges, who came to Princeton in the fall of 1890. "Do instruct the Freshman to come to see me," suggested Woodrow to Bobby. "I find it hard to catch sight of him and to keep up with his status and prospects. I want to help him in every way he will let me." But John failed to measure up to Wilson's expectations. As the end of the semester approached, the freshman's test grades showed that he might fail his examinations. The boy's uncle was notified, whereupon the embarrassed Bridges wrote for more information about the affair and apologized for troubling his friend with it. Wilson replied at some length about the young man and concluded: "In the meantime, Bobby, a word with you. Don't ever again dare to speak of 'troubling' me about any affair which in any way concerns you. Even if I did not like John for his own sake, it would be enough for me that he is your nephew, and nothing I could do for him would be any 'trouble' at all, but only and wholly a pleasure. But I do like him, heartily —and have one complaint to make of him: that I have never been able to persuade him to make a confidential friend of me. I always

[18]T. A. Lambert to Wilson, October 20, 1890, in Wilson Papers, Library of Congress.

[19]Wilson to Reverend Dr. Charles A. Aiken, November 7, 1890, in *ibid.*

have to hunt him up and thrust questions and advice upon him." [20] Much to the professor's regret, John did not return to Princeton the next year.

At the end of Wilson's first academic year as a professor at Princeton, he summarized his feelings to an intimate friend: "The year here has done me good, I believe. I have the opportunity to do the work of as high an order as I am capable of doing. It has benefited me to have a try at the best things, hard as it has been to get through so much new work without overstraining myself. But I have been lonely, and that has been the worst feature of the year. There are many fine men here who command my entire admiration, and many of them are men of my own age; but I have not yet found the companion I want: and there is the mere need, as I selfishly reckon, that you should come to see me." [21]

As one of the recognized leaders of the young professors, Wilson was in the forefront of a movement to raise entrance requirements. The chief features of the revision were the modification of the minimum requirements and the introduction of maximum requirements to give those who showed great ability in one or more subjects advanced standing in those subjects at the very outset of their college course. All entering freshmen were urged to take the subjects constituting the minimum requirements, which consisted of Greek, Latin, and mathematics, with English and the elements of one modern language.[22]

Wilson's attitude towards his own students was "kindly and considerate." While many of them had a great enthusiasm for him as a professor, there was nothing of intimacy about it.[23] Students, with few exceptions, sat quietly and listened attentively for the full fifty minutes of his lectures. And the professor always lectured; he did not promote teacher-student discussions, nor did he engage in the Socratic question-answer method. Indeed, Wilson's forte was not teaching but lecturing.

[20]Wilson to Bridges, November 2, 1890, in Meyer Collection, Princeton; Bridges to Wilson, January 4, 1891, in Wilson Papers, Library of Congress; Wilson to Bridges, January 9, 1891, in Meyer Collection, Princeton.

[21]Wilson to J. Franklin Jameson, June 29, 1891, in J. Franklin Jameson Papers, Library of Congress.

[22]*Princeton College Bulletin,* V (April, 1893), 34–35.

[23]Julian B. Beaty to Baker, July 2, 1926, in Baker Papers, Library of Congress.

Few of the professor's students maintained that his mind was profound; even some undergraduates recognized the limitations of his intellectual horizons. Certainly, Wilson himself understood very well in what his genius consisted. Equally true, he learned how to work with those limitations and to develop his classroom talents to the fullest. So well did he succeed in the art of elocution, in the force of his delivery, that he held students in awe. If at times his language was "bafflingly evasive or floridly insipid his voice remained quiet, well-mannered and beautifully distinct." The Virginia-born professor had just enough of a southern accent, a charming grace, and a contagious ease of delivery to make his students oblivious of his somewhat homely face and his rigid body. The teacher completely dominated his classroom. He was as punctual in closing his lectures as in starting them; he insisted on prompt arrival of students. It was not unusual, in the least, for Wilson's lectures to end in hearty applause and stomping of feet, a favorite Princeton undergraduate method of saying "We enjoyed it immensely." [24]

Although the professor spent many hours working and reworking his lectures, and regularly devoted much time to conferring with his students, he continued his interest in athletics. His reputation as an amateur football coach at Wesleyan preceded him to Princeton. The boys knew of his enthusiasm for sports. Moreover they recognized Wilson's morale-building influence, the will to win with which he indoctrinated his athletes. In 1890 Princeton's football prospects were gloomy. The preceding year Wilson's alma mater had had a winning team, but all of the lettermen except three had graduated or had failed to return. Apparently, coaches at Princeton were as scarce as players. At any rate the new professor added coaching to his professional duties. Daily he strode up and down the gridiron with the boys, taking his place behind the team to watch them run plays of his conception.[25] If Princeton did not have a successful season that fall, it was not due to Wilson's lack of zeal.

After the first year Wilson did not actively participate in coaching, but he never lost his interest in the game. His love of

[24]Edmund Wilson, *Shores of Light,* 303–305; Baker, *Wilson Life and Letters,* II, 9–12; Lewis, *Wilson of Princeton,* 18–20.

[25]Parke H. Davis, *Princeton Alumni Weekly,* November 4, 1925.

sports was not confined to football; indeed, he liked baseball even more. He frequently attended practice, and always during home games he was in the bleachers encouraging the Princeton team. A visitor in the professor's home recalled her amazement when at a Yale–Princeton baseball game Wilson, usually so poised and in such perfect control of his emotional faculties, "sprang to his feet . . . and yelled like a madman!" "I beg your pardon, Cousin Mary," he said apologetically, "that was a Princeton play." [26] On another occasion, he dashed from the bleachers to join in a heated dispute with the umpire.[27] In the spring some of the younger faculty members organized two baseball teams. Although Wilson apparently never played in these intra-faculty games, he always served as umpire.[28]

Wilson was also a track fan. At Princeton, track was essentially an indoor sport. During a close race the professor's yells could frequently be heard, urging the Princeton contestant to victory. When he felt a need for exercise, Wilson occasionally went to the gymnasium and ran around the track a few times—*the wrong way,* according to the undergraduates. As a result of his enthusiastic interest in athletics, he was unanimously elected a member of the Graduate Advisory Committee of the University Athletic Association at the beginning of his second year.[29]

Wilson was constantly called upon to share in faculty academic routine, including serving on committees of graduate students. On June 7, 1893, he participated in the examination of John Grier Hibben, of the Princeton class of 1882, for the Doctor of Philosophy degree. Hibben's dissertation was on "The Relations of Ethics to Jurisprudence," a subject in which Wilson was particularly interested. Although Professor Ormond was Hibben's chief examiner, Wilson questioned the student in jurisprudence, one of the candidate's subsidiary subjects.[30] After receiving his doctorate, Hibben remained on the faculty of his alma mater and became a friend of Wilson's.

[26]Baker, *Wilson Life and Letters,* II, 15.
[27]Daniels, *Recollections of Wilson,* 56.
[28]*Ibid.*
[29]Lewis, *Wilson of Princeton,* 12; Jessie C. Williams to Wilson, September 25, 1891, in Wilson Papers, Library of Congress.
[30]*Princeton College Bulletin,* V (July, 1893), 53.

During the twelve years that Wilson was a professor at Princeton, he either coached or assisted the debating team. "Wilson, Daniels and I," wrote Professor Bliss Perry, "matched our wits [as coaches of intercollegiate debating teams] against teachers like Hadley of Yale and George B. Baker of Harvard." [31] Since Wilson was noted for his forensic ability, the undergraduate debaters naturally went to him for assistance and suggestions. He enjoyed a considerable reputation as a rising authority on questions of government, with which questions intercollegiate debaters habitually dealt. In the 1890's debating was taken with deadly seriousness. For a student to earn the privilege of representing his college or university on a debating team was adjudged by many a greater honor than to "make the varsity" in a major sport.

The debaters who sought Wilson's help found him a veritable storehouse of information, and he was always able to refer them to additional sources for their materials. One of the debaters remembered that the professor "was very insistent that we read, think, write and debate on both sides [of the question]. He did his best to keep us from writing out and committing to memory our speeches as early as we wanted to. His idea was to keep us working and developing as far up to the debate as possible, with the feeling that after a speech was written out, a man's ideas became fixed." [32] Wilson was largely interested in the subject matter of the students whom he assisted, leaving the coaching of delivery to Professor Perry of the English Department.[33]

During the years Wilson was away from Princeton he had not lost interest in the Whig Literary Society. As a former Whig, he was frequently called on after his return to act as a judge of debates or orations. "Almost as frequently as I asked him," recalled Hardin Craig, a Whig leader of the 1890's, "Wilson came to Whig Hall and made speeches to the boys about old times in Hall and what it meant in his education to come into mental clashes and encounter wits with his contemporaries." When others came to speak to the literary society, the professor would pen

[31]Perry, *And Gladly Teach,* 135.

[32]Dayton D. McKean, "Woodrow Wilson as a Debate Coach," *Quarterly Journal of Speech,* XVI (1930), 458–63.

[33]*Ibid.,* 461.

a note of appreciation, as when Bridges came down from New York on one occasion: "I hear golden opinions of your speech at the 'Literary' dinner from everybody who heard it. I hope that you will come as often as possible on such errands, with such messages." [34] From Wilson's early days on the faculty he was asked to sign the Hall diplomas for the Whig Literary Society members who were graduating.[35]

On one occasion at a Whig Hall smoker, the teacher regaled his audience with a story about a freshman track enthusiast who was invited to dine in Wilson's home. The young man, according to the professor, had a passion for records made in various track events. During the evening he and his host professor fell to discussing track records. When the student gave a wrong statistic, his host corrected him and stuck to his correction. Finally, after some minutes of arguing, the freshman with a disarming suddenness exclaimed: "By golly, you're absolutely right, sir! That just goes to show there isn't *anyone* you can't learn something from!" [36]

In addition to his contributions at Princeton, the professor lectured off campus. He began, for example, a series of lectures before the Connecticut Valley Economic Association on November 18, 1890, on the subject "How to Prevent Legislative Corruption." [37] In January, 1891, Wilson began to receive and to accept invitations to address the Princeton Alumni Association.[38] "I am truly glad, without being surprised," Woodrow's father wrote, "that you had such a successful time at Philadelphia at the Alumni meeting. How I would like to hear My Darling boy on such an occasion." [39] Another invitation was from Edmund J. James, editor of the *Annals of the American Academy of Political and So-*

[34]Hardin Craig to Baker, July 5, 1927, in Baker Papers, Library of Congress; Wilson to Bridges, May 23, 1893, in Meyer Collection, Library of Congress.

[35]Jacob N. Beam, *The American Whig Society of Princeton University* (Princeton, 1933), 193.

[36]Lewis, *Wilson of Princeton,* 13.

[37]J. B. Clark to Wilson, November 3, 1890, in Wilson Papers, Library of Congress.

[38]Philippus W. Miller to Wilson, January 17, 1891, in *ibid.* The address which Wilson accepted was to be in Philadelphia February 20, 1891.

[39]Joseph R. Wilson to Woodrow Wilson, February 26, 1891, in *ibid.*

cial Science, to read a paper at the February, 1891, meeting on the subject "Legal Education in the United States." [40]

When Horace E. Scudder of the *Atlantic Monthly* asked if he might send him Professor John W. Burgess' two volumes on *Political Science and Comparative Constitutional Law for* an essay review, Wilson accepted, but not without explaining his personal feelings. He did not know whether he should review the Burgess book or not. Although he would open the book "expecting to find a great deal in it to disagree with and criticize," he supposed that he could be impartial. He would try to admire what was admirable "even in a writer of an opposite school." [41]

Wilson began his review by saying that the Columbia professor's book commanded admiration but also provoked criticism: "It will be fortunate if the criticism does not overcrowd the praise." There were some things about the study that the reviewer liked: "There is the utmost clearness and adequacy of analysis . . . There is also . . . perfect consistency everywhere. . . . The reader enjoys the satisfaction, so rare in this day of easy writing, of being nowhere in doubt as to the author's meaning." Having summarized the merits of the book, Wilson devoted the rest of the essay to discussing its faults. He voiced the opinion that its greatest deficiencies consisted of "a mechanical and incorrect style, a dogmatic spirit, and a lack of insight into institutions as detailed expressions of life, nor readily consenting to be broadly and positively analyzed and classified."

Disagreeing with the author, the Princeton professor maintained that state and government were not identical except in mere point of organization. "It is the state which is sovereign; whatever person or body of persons constitutes the sole vital source of political power in a nation, that person or body of persons is the state, and is sovereign. . . . Only the state is superior to the laws; the government is subject to the laws. The state makes Constitutions; governments give effect to them." "We can no longer speak of a federal state," continued the reviewer, "but only of a federal government; neither does there exist any dual

[40]Edmund J. James to Wilson, January 10, 1891, in *ibid.*

[41]Scudder to Wilson, February 13, 1891, in *ibid.;* Wilson to Scudder, February 7, 1891, in Scudder Papers, Library of Congress.

state, though dual governments there may be and have been. Every state is single and indivisible, let governments have what duality and complexity they may."

Wilson quibbled with Burgess over disregard of public opinion as a political fact. The truth, he said, was that "political fact is made up largely of opinion," and this the author could not appreciate. According to Wilson, the national state was not born in 1774, as claimed by the Columbia professor, but came "slowly into existence, with the habit of cooperation and the growth of the national idea." The individual states were born in 1774, but the national state had evolved since then "by virtue of a revolution of ideas, by reason of national union and growth and achievement, through a process also of struggle and of civil war." [42]

The professional repercussions from this critical review must not have been to Wilson's liking. Thereafter, when editors asked him to review books he nearly always excused himself because of a lack of interest in the book or because of a rush of work which did not permit the time to do the review.

About the time the review of Burgess' book appeared, the Wilson family was recovering from a siege of illness. "Literally everybody in my little household, myself alone excepted," Wilson wrote Professor Hart, "was suffering with the grippe." [43] Worn out with anxiety and fatigue, he decided to forego his vacation in order that he might work on his voume in the Epoch series. With obvious regret, he announced that vacation had arrived, "or what is vacation with those happy mortals who do not have to write *Epochs*." [44]

The professor had learned the joy of prodigious labor. His work at Princeton was proving "very stimulating indeed." It was, he said, "like lecturing constantly to cultivated audiences, for my electives number about 160 men each." It stimulated him immensely "to have to interest so many minds in the more abstruse topics of jurisprudence." Wilson had been in charge of the

[42]Woodrow Wilson, "A Review of *Political Science and Constitutional Law,* by John W. Burgess," *Atlantic Monthly,* LXVII (May, 1891), 694–99.

[43]Wilson to Hart, May 19, 1891, in Hart Papers, Harvard.

[44]Wilson to Hart, May 22, 1891, in *ibid.*

courses in political economy, but he got rid of them when the college created a special chair of economics. When that departmental change was made, he wrote: "I shall be lecturing wholly within the special field of my choice, and shall expect to grow into some sort of power and success, especially if my dearest scheme, the establishment of a law school here on the Scotch and European plan of history and philosophy, as well as technical treatment should become a realized plan. And everything is ready for its realization, except the money!" [45]

During the summer Woodrow rediscovered an essay that had been on his desk for two or three years and sent it to the *Atlantic Monthly*.[46] One of his early literary essays, it was free from all political issues and opinions. The article, "The Author Himself," appeared in the September, 1891, issue of the magazine. "When once a book has become immortal, we think that we can see why it became so," he wrote. "It contained, we perceive, a casting of thought which could not but arrest and retain men's attention; it said some things once and all because it gave them their best expression." Wilson believed that "in every case of literary immortality originative personality is present," not merely creativity but that "origination which takes its stamp and character from the originator, which is his spirit given to the world, which is himself outspoken." He concluded: "The rule for every man is, not to depend on the education which other men prepare for him—not even to consent to it; but to strive to see things as they are, and to be himself, as he is. Defeat lies in self-surrender." [47]

Much favorable comment followed publication of the essay. A former colleague at Wesleyan wrote: "What a good English professor and critic was lost when you turned aside to history and political science! And yet not lost either, for you are not in a camp of Philistines, and a great deal of the best criticism and greatest literary work nowadays seems to me to come from

[45]Wilson to Dabney, July 1, 1891, in Dabney Papers, Virginia.

[46]Wilson to Bridges, September 22, 1891, in Meyer Collection, Princeton.

[47]Woodrow Wilson, "The Author Himself," *Atlantic Monthly,* LXVIII (September, 1891), 406–13.

men who are not in any narrow or technical sense literary men." [48] From Scribner's came the opinion: "You hit the weak point of the present school of writers exactly. It is an affectation of 'Sophistication' and it comes from New England. It does my heart good to hear you preach Southern individualism from the Yankee pulpit." [49]

One result of Wilson's successful lecturing, writing, and publishing was the increase in professional offers from other institutions. In the spring of 1892, for example, the professor was told that he would be recommended to the University of Illinois Board of Trustees for the office of president, at a salary of $6,000, provided he indicated he would accept.[50] Two of the trustees journeyed to Princeton to consult with him. To Ellen, who had gone South with the girls to visit friends and relatives, he wrote:

The Illinois University matter, about which I promised to tell you, is quite amusing. The two trustees waylaid me at my classroom door, told me immediately that they had come to look me over for their vacant presidency, and proceeded to do so! I was not embarrassed simply because I did not *care* what impression I made. They were in the East, it turned out, to look at several men to whom their attention had been directed! They did not make me any proposition; but, since they can offer as much as $6,000, I consented to wait to hear from them, and to 'consider' the matter! They were very intelligent men indeed, and made a most favourable impression upon me. Isn't the situation amusing? Would you like to move to Urbana, Illinois?" [51]

Ellen was interested but not excited. She raised several questions. Was the salary "*just* $6,000 or $6,000 *and* the usual president's prerequisites . . . a nice house and grounds; the grounds kept up by the college?" The most important consideration, however, she thought, was whether or not her husband would have time for original work. "I have always thought," she wrote, "that there must be something very *distracting* about the duties of a college president." [52]

But when Ellen learned that Woodrow had actually received

[48]C. J. Winchesture to Wilson, October 24, 1891, in Wilson Papers, Library of Congress.

[49]Bridges to Wilson, September 20, 1891, in *ibid.*

[50]F. M. McKay to Wilson, April 30, 1892, in *ibid.*

[51]Wilson to his wife, April 27, 1892, in Axson–Wilson Letters, Princeton.

[52]Ellen Wilson to her husband, April 30, 1892, in *ibid.*

the offer, contingent upon his decision to accept, she wished him to do so. For days he wrestled with the problem, seeking an answer, and then it came. At some length he explained to Ellen that he had heard President Angell of Michigan speak of the life of a president who had to extract grants from the state legislature and manage a political board of trustees. He added that Stockton Axson had told him that President Cranfield of the University of Nebraska once had great plans for original literary work, but that as a university president he had given up all idea of ever returning to books again. Wilson believed that the University of Illinois possessed potentialities for future greatness: "I even think that I could secure that future for it, by devoting all my energies (including those of the latent politician within me) to the task, in many ways a very inviting one." But in order to do this, he confided to Ellen, he would have to forego during the best years of his life his literary plans. After much reflection he concluded: "I am . . . deeply convinced upon these points. And I know that you will regard these considerations as conclusive." [53]

Wilson sought the counsel of President Daniel C. Gilman of Johns Hopkins. "Which," he asked Gilman, "is the more likely to have sufficient freedom of time and mind for effective literary work, a professor or a college president?" [54] Apparently, Gilman advised his protegé to remain a teacher.

"You certainly acted wisely in declining that Illinois venture," Wilson's father wrote him. "To dance attendance upon a legislature, to entreat for money to carry on one of its own institutions, would be intolerable to the fine nerve of my noble boy. Besides, you would be diverted from the specialty which you are so desirous to lift into conspicuity." [55] From Wesleyan, Ellen's brother Stockton wrote: "I am sure that time will witness the wisdom of this decision." [56]

[53]Wilson to his wife, May 9, 1892, in *ibid.* Shortly thereafter Wilson's salary at Princeton for the next year was fixed at $3,000, with an allowance of $500 for house rent. See E. R. Craven to Wilson, June 30, 1892, in Wilson Papers, Library of Congress.

[54]Wilson to Gilman, May 12, 1892, in Gilman Papers, Johns Hopkins.

[55]Joseph R. Wilson to Woodrow Wilson, May 25, 1892, in Wilson Papers, Library of Congress.

[56]Stockton Axson to Wilson, June 7, 1892, in *ibid.*

Wilson's program for his second summer at Princeton was like that of the preceding year. "I've carried out my programme for the 'vacation,' " wrote the Princeton professor in mid-August, "and am now nearing the end of that wretched little 'Epoch'—at least the first draft of it. I trust it will need very little revision to be the final draft. I've put into it already almost everything I knew and some things that I don't know but only believe." [57]

As Wilson began his third academic year at Princeton, he was well acquainted with his work. He had found his place in the quiet community; his classes were to his liking. He had secured an assistant in the department to teach those courses he liked least. He had pushed himself to the leadership of a group of young faculty members, and by determined effort had succeeded in having an honor system adopted for the students. In addition to these accomplishments he was reviewing a few books, writing articles, and working on the manuscript for a book. Off-campus lecturing was requiring more of his time. At home, Woodrow and Ellen were enjoying their three daughters. Years later Stockton Axson, who knew him intimately, stated that "Wilson's most tranquil years were his first five years as a Princeton professor." [58]

[57]Wilson to Bridges, August 18, 1892, in Meyer Collection, Princeton.

[58]Stockton Axson to Baker, June 4, 1927, in Baker Papers, Library of Congress.

CHAPTER XI *Teacher and Lecturer*

The years of Wilson's professorship at Princeton—before he entered upon the administrative duties of the presidency of his alma mater—were his finest years as a lecturer and teacher, as well as the time of his most prolific literary activity. From his youth Wilson had realized that there was strong persuasive power in a finely trained, highly cultivated voice. For years his ambition had been to achieve power over an audience through the lecture in the classroom or speech in the public forum. By the 1890's this ambition had been realized.

As a lecturer, Wilson spoke to several types of audiences. These included, first of all, his classes of students at Princeton, at Johns Hopkins, and elsewhere. He lectured with an easy preciseness, apparently never wanting for the right word and never hesitating for the correct combination of phrases to convey just the shade of thought that he desired to express. Occasionally, as best suited his lecture plan, he would pause and say: "Now, gentlemen, I recommend that you take this down."[1] Then he would slowly state one or two key sentences, making certain that each student could copy the statement in full in his notebook. In this way, the class was aware, as the lecture proceeded, of its outline. No student who paid attention was ever in doubt as to the structure of the professor's lecture.

Though he possessed neither a commanding presence nor a magnetic personality, and exhibited no great talent for showmanship, Wilson nevertheless made a distinct impression with his voice. His pupils heard easily every word of his lectures. Although his voice was not deep, it was not harsh or shrill. The professor lectured, as he spoke conversationally, in a resonant tenor voice. As the students listened, they were conscious of his almost complete dependence upon the matter of speech and upon the manner of delivery. Preciseness of word was coupled with expressiveness of language. The formality which marked Wilson's lectures might be modified upon occasion, but it was seldom lost completely.

Wilson always lectured on the premise that the ultimate purpose of delivery was communication, not a basic form of physical activity, and he spoke with a minimum expenditure of energy. The mere thought of vigorous physical or vocal effort wearied him. He seldom gestured. When a particular thought or idea demanded emphasis, he would raise his right arm to chest height and point his index finger at some person in the room. This professorial gesture was not invoked to chastise a student, nor hold him up for scorn. In fact, there was only a slight pause in the lecturer's delivery of his speech, not long enough to cause any focusing of attention upon a listener, but ample time to center attention on the lecturer.

Why did Wilson use few gestures in his lectures? This question was frequently asked by those interested in his popularity as an orator. At least three factors contributed to his rejection of gestures while speaking. First, he did not have a strong oratorical voice. Also, he was not very robust and would have quickly tired had he tried a vigorous physical delivery. As he once commented, "A lecture rather does me up; but the next morning I will be fit to enjoy myself again." In addition, Wilson believed

[1]Lewis, *Wilson of Princeton,* 18.

that only by the selective choice of words and by the superb control of his voice while speaking could he convey to his audience his own inner emotional responses. That he succeeded to such an unusual degree substantiates the accuracy of his conclusion.

In the classroom he was the instructor seeking to impart knowledge to his students. He tried to get them interested in reading the books that he listed in the course bibliography for their intellectual stimulation, as well as for their professional training. As a lecturer, the teacher was never a propagandist. Wilson was an avowed nationalist, as his students soon learned. Politically, he was a Democrat of the Virginia-born species. During his teaching tenure at Princeton he was a Cleveland Democrat, to the extent even of voting against William Jennings Bryan, the presidential nominee in 1896. Wilson the political conservative supported the Cleveland-controlled Gold Democratic ticket. "I sometimes think," he declared on one occasion, "I should have been a Tory had I lived at the time of the Revolution for I am a conservative." [2] These views were widely known, but in the classroom or on the lecture platform the speaker did not seek to indoctrinate his listeners with his political conservatism. Instead he sought to inform, he endeavored to instruct, and he determined to inspire.

Wilson's lectures were often made more stimulating by an apt illustration, or by a timely story, or by a suddenly injected bit of humor. An example of his class anecdotes is the tale he told of two frogs that accidentally fell into a large tub of milk. After unsuccessful efforts to climb out the frogs conferred briefly. Said one: "There's nothing to be done." Ceasing his efforts to stay afloat he sank and drowned. The other frog had a different philosophy. "You've got to keep doing something. You've got to keep doing something," he said, and continued to swim about in the milk. Hours later, he found himself sitting comfortably on a large lump of butter, amply rewarded for his determined efforts.[3]

No one has challenged the effectiveness of Wilson's lectures.

[2]Worcester (Mass.) *Spy,* January 30, 1902. Wilson made the statement in an address on "Patriotism" to the Women's Club in Associational Hall.

[3]Lewis, *Wilson of Princeton,* 21–22.

Numerous students who enrolled in his classes in constitutional government, in jurisprudence, in political economy, or in politics, have written that their teacher immediately gained rapt attention from his students. His power over his young listeners was such that, with a brilliant, forceful, well-turned phrase, he could bring from the students a vigorous round of applause. Wilson's unusual success as a classroom lecturer was in no small degree due to his persistent dissatisfaction with his lectures and to a constant revision of them. Such alterations were not made on the spur of the moment, but were effected only after intensive study. He was not only a gifted lecturer but, equally significant, a conscientious one as well. Seldom, if ever, did he repeat a lecture verbatim.

The professor spoke outside his Princeton classroom almost as often as he lectured to his students. By arranging lectures in states in which he had never traveled, he could visit new sections of the country and pay his expenses with the fees from his lectures. This accounted for his speech at the Columbian Exposition or World's Fair in Chicago in the summer of 1893. A year later he lectured in New England and again in the West.

In July, 1894, Wilson went by train to Colorado for a series of lectures in Denver. Another reason, perhaps a significant one, for this long westward journey was that his cousin Harriet Woodrow, now happily married to Edwin Welles, was living in that city. It had been years since Wilson had seen this cousin with whom he once fancied himself in love. And so, with Ellen's gladly given approval, he entrained for his first trip to the West.

For three nights Wilson spoke in Denver to small audiences, and for several days afterwards he relaxed and enjoyed the hospitality of his relatives. One morning, with the children at home and husband Edwin at work, Hattie and Woodrow took a long drive through the rocky "Garden of the Gods." As they jogged along serpentine roads that wound around extraordinary gorges amidst breath-taking scenery, of what did Wilson and his cousin Hattie speak? Did they relive their youthful romance? Did Hattie, who during the intervening years had continued to cultivate her musical talents, sing again for her audience of one? The answer to these questions will never be known. To Ellen, Woodrow was quite circumspect. Of the Garden of Gods he wrote only that it was appropriately named. "A more beautiful and extraordinary place I never saw."[4]

In the mid-1890's Wilson gave a series of lectures which he called "Great Leaders of Political Thought." Established under the auspices of the American Society for the Extension of University Teaching, these were listed as the University Extension Lectures. Included in the series were "Aristotle, the Father of Political Science"; "Machiavelli, the Politician of the Renaissance"; "Montesquieu, the French Political Seer"; "Burke, the Interpreter of English Liberty"; "De Tocqueville, the Student of Democracy"; and "Bagehot, the Literary Politician."[5] Although Wilson would give any one of these lectures as a single speech, he much preferred to contract for the entire series. The professor delivered these lectures both to academic groups and to the general public. Another lecture series that he occasionally gave consisted of "What is Constitutional Government?"; "Political Liberty: Its Nature and Exercise"; "Written Constitutions"; "Theory and Practice in Government Organization"; and "Organization and Powers of Congress." In the autumn of 1898, for example, Wilson delivered these lectures at Richmond, Virginia, to members of the bar, business people, physicians, teachers, and students.

Such lectures as those listed in Wilson's "Great Leaders of Political Thought" were of a historical nature, but he was frequently invited to address groups on topics of contemporary interest. Under these circumstances the Princeton professor assumed the role of critic of public affairs, discussing the significant trends in American cultural institutions. Wilson's address August 4, 1897, before the Virginia State Bar Association in Richmond illustrates this type of lecture.

Remembering the days of his youth during the Reconstruction period, Wilson declared that America, as no other nation in all history, had been transformed in a generation. Processes that rushed so fast were dangerous. The choices made in the midst of them, he said, were not deliberate but hasty and haphazard.

[4]Wilson to his wife, July 26, 1894, in Axson–Wilson Letters, Princeton.
[5]Copies of this pamphlet are in the Wilson Papers, Library of Congress, and in the Wilson Collection, Princeton.

In a democracy actions and choices were made by political parties and policy was made by mass opinion. The formation of mass opinion was "the whole art and mastery of politics." Wilson felt that with the national convention method of nominating candidates there came the dark horse—"some man hitherto little thought of; some one whom his friends have astutely known how to push in the secret conferences of separate delegations; some man whose personal tact of force has caught up of sudden the enthusiasm of the convention itself and of the crowds in its galleries; some man unheralded and untried." [6] With the emergence of the dark horse presidential candidate, a new figure appeared—the boss or manager behind the candidate—the one to whom the candidate, and possibly later the President, would be subservient. "Plainly the nominating convention has separated legislative and executive much more than the makers of the constitution intended; has brought utterly incalculable forces into play for the choice of our Presidents; and has cut us off once and for all from the old traditions of party leadership." [7]

After describing the lack of responsible leadership throughout the national government, the professor proposed a remedy. The heads of the executive departments should assist the representatives of the people to propose, defend, and explain administrative policy upon the floor of the Congress. Wilson was careful to state that he was not advocating cabinet or ministerial responsibility—the complete fusion as in England of the executive and legislative branches of the government—a move which would be "radical, indeed." He was not suggesting that initiative in legislation be confined to the administration; only that the department heads be given a free, though responsible, share in it. This, Wilson contended, would create a return to "models of statesmanship and political custom" of the founding fathers. He hoped that he was presenting to mature members of the bar "not a programme of reform, but a suggestion for thought." [8]

[6]Woodrow Wilson, *Leaderless Government* (Richmond, 1897). A copy of this pamphlet is in the Wilson Papers. Also see Baker and Dodd (eds.), *Wilson Public Papers: College and State,* I, 336–59.

[7]*Ibid.*

[8]*Ibid.*

Wilson frequented the banquet hall as well as the lecture platform. Although his first attempt at after-dinner speaking came out badly, he was undaunted by his initial failure. He persevered, profiting by his mistakes, until he was one of the most accomplished speakers of his generation. Perhaps Wilson's best known after-dinner speech was delivered before the New England Society of New York City on December 22, 1900. The speaker paused to note the "whimsical fortune" of a Scotch-Irishman's paying tribute to that particular audience. Since the Scotch-Irish came to America later than did the Puritans, he said, they had a better opportunity to observe Puritan characters and the cut of the latter's jibs. More recently, the lecturer stated amid laughter and applause, "we, like you, are beginning to form societies to annex the universe; we, like you, are beginning to elect memorialists who shall record how every line of strength in the history of the world is a line colored by Scotch-Irish blood." [9]

In characterizing the Puritan, the Princeton professor declared him to be "intensely human," one who apologized to God three times daily for the fact, and one whose creed included divesting himself of all pestiferous elements of the flesh. While the audience roared its approval, Wilson termed the Puritan's intolerance of disagreement "an eminently comfortable indulgence."

The Puritans of the 1890's, Wilson declared seriously, had preserved much from their fathers, retaining a great deal of the "old structural iron of character, the simple principle of discipline, of order, of polity." But the Scotch-Irish, as well as the Puritans, had contributed to the composite American picture with their spirit of daring, unrest, of mere adventure, "which made the level lines of the prairie seem finer and more inviting than the uplifted lines of the mountain; that made it seem as if the world were bigger on the plains, and as if the feet of young men were the feet of leaders." [10]

Wilson added that there was a way in which the national spirit contrasted with the New England spirit. In spite of the restraining discipline of the Puritans, it was the progressive spirit that

[9]New England Society of New York, *Proceedings 1900* (New York, 1901), 39–49. Also consult Baker and Dodd (eds.), *Wilson Public Papers,* I, 360–67.
[10]*Ibid.*

dominated the country's destiny. But many would-be reformers were really retro-reformers endeavoring to encase Americans in an old chrysalis which had once been broken, Wilson warned. They wanted the nation to go backward, not forward—to assume ancient outward forms when inner conditions were greatly altered. It was not so much the forms of American life but the principles that counted. Wilson delighted his audience with another story: "I can quote Scripture for this, though not Scripture which . . . would be regarded as exactly orthodox in Princeton. There was an old Negro preacher who said, 'The Lord said unto Moses, Come fo'th; and he came fifth and lost the race.' Now, I think we ought to come forth, and not come fifth and lose the race." [11]

Of all the dangers to democracy, the Princetonian thought the greatest was that mass disciplinary power should overwhelm the originative, creative individual instinct. Every man should speak his thoughts boldly. "I pray," said Wilson, "that the time may never come when we are not ready to do new things, when we are not ready to acknowledge that the age has changed."

This address showed Wilson at his best as an after-dinner speaker. Dwelling on the formidable contributions of the hardy Scotch-Irish, his own racial stock, he established a strong rapport with his audience as soon as he began speaking. With wholesome humor and penetrating wit, the speaker held his hearers' attention throughout the speech.

The reader is already familiar with Wilson's annual lecture series at Johns Hopkins University. Attended largely by upperclassmen and graduate students, the lectures were taken for course credit. In 1896, while Wilson was preparing his lectures on "Municipal Organization," Professor Herbert Adams informed him that a number of Baltimore townspeople would attend. The idea of outsiders in the audience startled Wilson a little at first, and he hoped it was understood that the lectures were not at all popular in theme or style.[12]

Public interest in the professor's course was enhanced by the scholarly condensations of the lectures which appeared in the

[11] *Ibid.*

[12] Wilson to Herbert B. Adams, January 13, 1896, in Herbert B. Adams Papers, Johns Hopkins Library.

Baltimore *News*. Prepared by Professor G. B. Lynnes, these summaries are significant because very little that Wilson said about municipal politics during this period has been preserved. Since these lectures presented a program of municipal reform, the accounts in the *News* are of inestimable value.

Wilson began his series on municipal organization by contrasting English town government with that in the American city, to the disparagement of the latter. The division of powers and the multiple elections of American cities, he labeled ridiculous. In short, the Princeton professor said, city government in the United States was characterized by a mayor who dominated all administrative machinery, a financial leader who spent the money, and a council checked within by a bicameral system and without by the mayor's veto. The city system of checks and balances was futile. The only effective check was public opinion. Wilson urged that municipal officials be made more directly responsible to the people.[13] He called bipartisan boards "an invention of the devil," created to confuse issues and to trade patronage. While recognizing and lamenting the disintegration of American city government, he rejected enlarging the powers of the mayor, objecting to the centralization of authority in one man.

Wilson offered his audience a seven-point program of municipal reform. His plan, not unlike the Commission Plan created in Galveston, Texas, in 1901, provided that: (1) The administrative and ordinance-making power should be concentrated in one body of which the mayor should be merely the chairman; (2) there should be a minimum of trained officials, chosen by competitive examination, on this governing board; (3) the elective majority of the board should be chosen by a city-wide ticket; (4) municipalities should own the utilities; (5) compulsory and free citizenship duties to the community should include the administration of charity, aid in tax assessment, and assistance in mercantile arbitration through a system of citizenship committees; (6) there should be a clear-cut separation of judicial and administrative functions in city government; and (7) there should

[13]Baltimore *News,* February 7–16, 1896.

be a certain amount of wise central control in the interests of administrative integration.[14]

Near the end of this lecture series, Wilson strongly urged municipal socialism to the extent of public ownership of gas works and street railways. He argued that "people are always interested in what they feel immediately concerns them. If, therefore, the convenience of the citizen is touched constantly by actions of the city administration, he will be much more apt to take care that the city be pure. Hence, I believe in municipal ownership of the gas system and of the street railways, both because the way in which they are managed affects the whole community, and because municipal ownership would lead citizens to take a greater interest in municipal affairs." [15]

In another lecture, "The City Budget," Wilson made his reform program more explicit. He attacked New York City's practice of electing its Board of Finance by the vote of those who owned taxable property in excess of $500. "The modern industrial city, with its wide social functions," Wilson declared, "must act in many things involving heaviest expenditures, not for property owners, but for workers and economically dependent classes." He did not believe that those who paid the largest taxes were the best judges of the needs of a city, and Princeton borough was cited as a case in point. Wilson said the influence and votes of the poorer minority groups there—Irish and Negroes—resulted in a better condition of municipal improvements than would have been the case had the wealthy classes been in control. These poorer districts threatened the health of the entire community; the improvement of drainage, garbage collection, sewage disposal, and of the streets in the poorer sections bettered health and sanitation throughout Princeton.[16]

In still another lecture Wilson urged a widening of municipal functions to include the operation of a rapid transit system. Lines should be provided to relieve the congested parts of the city whether those lines paid financially or not, he said. Charity also should be a municipal function, although not to the exclusion

[14] *Ibid.,* February 26–March 3, 1896.
[15] *Ibid.,* February 26, 1896.
[16] *Ibid.,* February 29–March 1, 1896.

of private charity. The valid arguments for public sanitation, the speaker thought, were equally logical for public charity—even more so, he added, because "public charity and public education are a sort of moral sanitation." [17]

In arguing for a separation of executive and judicial powers within the city, Wilson suggested that an exception be made of police courts passing upon offenses against city ordinances. He said that popular election of judges should be abolished but added that this accomplishment was in the far distance. "But everything comes to those who wait and know what they are waiting for," he concluded.

Unfortunately, the Baltimore *News* did not report Wilson's last lecture. Consequently, the degree of centralization that he thought desirable is vague. Certainly, he wanted vigorous local institutions capable of coping with the changing problems of an increasingly complex economic order.

On March 3, 1896, the day on which Wilson completed his series at Johns Hopkins, he gave what perhaps was his first actual political address. Baltimore was then in the midst of a political upheaval, with an open breach between Mayor Alcaeus Hooper and the councilmen and with graft and incompetence apparent in numerous city departments. The better elements of the city had organized a Reform League. The professor delivered his address in the Music Hall (Lyric Theater) before a mass meeting in support of Mayor Hooper. Others who spoke on the same occasion included, by a curious coincidence, Theodore Roosevelt, police commissioner of New York City. The crowd that jammed into the auditorium was estimated at between 3,600 and 4,000.[18]

A former citizen of Baltimore, Wilson declared that "no council for years has stirred up so much feeling and by offering themselves for reelection the councilmen can readily ascertain what that feeling is." The Princeton professor asked the members of the audience if their presence represented only a display of spas-

[17] *Ibid.,* March 3, 1896.

[18] Another speaker on this occasion was William Cabell Bruce, who had defeated Wilson twice in debate during their law school days at the University of Virginia. In 1896 Bruce, as a leader of the Maryland Senate, sponsored a bill which gave the Mayor of Baltimore absolute power of appointment. See Baltimore *News,* March 4, 1896.

modic strength or if they were putting shoulder to the wheel of good government. He told the voters that they had come to stay whereas the city council had not. Wilson noted that he was a believer in the processes of reform, adding hopefully, "Everything will come as you mean it if only you continue to mean it." [19]

The meeting failed in that the members of the council remained in control. The breach between the mayor and the council continued.[20] The initial adventure may have heartened the professor in the hope that if he could not realize his long-held ambition to become active in public service he might, like his intellectual idol Walter Bagehot, become a "literary politician." [21]

For years Wilson was, according to his wife, "forced to give by far too many lectures and addresses away from home." [22] Why did he set a pace for himself which, at times, resulted in illness? There are several reasons. For one thing, Wilson was in great need of a higher income during the 1890's. Three growing daughters made increasingly heavy financial demands on their father. In addition, the Wilsons built an expensive home during this period which had to be paid for. A memorandum in Wilson's diary for December 30, 1897, lists the following income anticipated from lectures during 1898.[23]

Wilmington Del. 3 lectures	$150.00
Pittsburgh University Extension Lectures	100.00
Pittsburgh Woman's Club	50.00
Schenectady Woman's Club	50.00
New York Local History Club	100.00
New York Law School (net)	250.00

[19]Baltimore *Sun,* March 4, 1896.

[20]Baltimore *Morning Herald,* March 4, 1896. "When Roosevelt talked his mouth took on that teeth-gnashing bulldog expression which is a true index to his determined character," it reported. "He talked . . . about affairs in New York City; how rotten they were before he took hold of things and how purified they have since become."

[21]Henry Wilkinson Bragdon, "Woodrow Wilson Addresses Citizens of Baltimore, 1896," *Maryland Historical Magazine,* XXXVII (1942), 150–70.

[22]Ellen Wilson to Anna Harris, January 31, 1899, in Axson–Harris Correspondence, Princeton.

[23]Wilson "Diary," December 30, 1897, in Wilson Papers, Library of Congress. Since some of the figures given were revised from earlier listed sums in the diary we may safely conclude that Wilson earned $1,700 from lecturing in 1898.

Brooklyn Institute lectures (net)	250.00
Oberlin College	100.00
Mount Holyoke College	100.00
Stanford (Conn.)	100.00
Johns Hopkins University (3 Donovan lectures)	300.00
Quill Club, New York City	50.00
Vanderbilt University	100.00
1898–Total anticipated from lectures	$1,700.00

In addition to earning money needed by his family, Wilson was able to see old friends again as he traveled about lecturing. When he lectured annually at Johns Hopkins he renewed his friendship with his teachers of his graduate school days. If he lectured at Brown University, there was his former teacher, Professor Jameson, who had moved to Providence and a new position at Brown. Equally as fascinating to the lecturer was the privilege of making new friends. From Plymouth, Massachusetts, July, 1894, Woodrow wrote his wife that he had "found some old acquaintances here and of course made a few new ones." [24] Of the latter, Mrs. Crawford H. Toy of Harvard became a lifelong friend. Through his lectures at Johns Hopkins, Wilson met and formed lasting friendships with Frederick Jackson Turner, James Schouler, Professor and Mrs. Henry F. Reid, and others.

Having determined to remain at Princeton, the professor realized the value of establishing friendly contacts with influential alumni. No matter where he lectured, Wilson never overlooked the opportunity of creating or renewing friendships with graduates of Princeton.[25] As a university professor his salary did not permit extensive travel; as a public speaker, he was able to pay for the tours out of the proceeds from lectures.[26] Years later when Wilson forsook the university campus for the political arena, the value of this practice became obvious.

Finally, one of the most powerful motives for Wilson's constant lecturing was his irrepressible ambition for building a repu-

[24]Wilson to his wife, July 14, 1894, in Axson–Wilson Letters, Princeton.

[25]See accounts of many examples of Wilson's contacts with Princeton alumni in the Wilson Papers, Library of Congress, and in the Wilson Collection, Princeton.

[26]Apparently, Wilson netted nothing from his series of lectures in Colorado, 1894. He paid for the trip out of the proceeds of his lectures. See Wilson to his wife, July 30, 1894, in Axson–Wilson Letters, Princeton.

tation and for playing a significant role in any group in which he found himself. He was always the reorganizer, the readjuster, always aspiring to the role of leader in the councils of the group. From his college days he realized the unusual power that could be exerted by public speech. Having made of himself one of the foremost lecturers of his generation, he practiced his finely developed art whenever and wherever he found the opportunity.

If the Princeton faculty member's unusual mental talents, his great breadth of vision, and his devotion to lofty ideals aided him in establishing a reputation as a lecturer, he also possessed traits that made a remarkable teacher. Foremost among the qualities that impressed the professor's students was his thorough knowledge of the subject matter of his courses. In addition, he organized his courses logically and presented the material forcefully. He was never satisfied merely to give information to his students; he endeavored to impart knowledge. Wilson was deeply concerned with the indifference of undergraduates towards the processes of learning. He was disappointed in their obvious apathy to their opportunities for equipping themselves for successful leadership. As a teacher, he molded himself into a classic example of what he thought his students should be. He combined a zest for teaching with a grim determination for study and with a passionate devotion to leadership in public service.

Apparently, Wilson was in complete control of his classes at all times. For example, if a student displayed a newspaper, there was a pause, a sudden dead silence broken by Wilson's stern reminder: "I think I said that there was no newspaper reading in this room." Once a bulky athlete immersed in the sports pages of a metropolitan daily failed to respond. The teacher waited for a moment; then, with eyes fixed intensely and with a firm tone, he threatened: "Mr. Smith, if you do not stop reading that newspaper, I will have to come down and make you." Wilson's stern rebuke brought a hearty round of applause from the class.[27]

The Princeton teacher did not permit students to talk among themselves during a recitation. The undergraduates were aware of this rule, and usually respected it. Occasionally, however, there were violators. A pair of whisperers would receive a withering

[27]Lewis, *Wilson of Princeton,* 19.

stare from the teacher, followed by a stern admonishment: "There are those who hunger after the very husks of knowledge, and yet men are sent here that care little for the opportunities offered by this institution." [28]

At Princeton during Wilson's professorship many students had dogs that frequently accompanied them to class. Once a bulldog entered the classroom, walked down the aisle to the front of the room, and climbed the steps to the platform where the lecturer stood. As he concluded a paragraph, the professor turned and smiled at the intruder. Bending over, he extended his right hand, and the dog wagged his tail vigorously as he lifted a paw to the proffered hand. By vigorous gestures the lecturer induced the animal to return to his master near the back of the room. Turning to his desk Wilson prefaced the return to his classroom instruction by the following: "I am a great admirer of character and good breeding. I also like obedience. But sometimes I find more of these three good qualities in the so-called brute than in the so-called master." [29]

Wilson's tests and examinations were demanding but never unfair. Once a student complained that the examination was unfair and the professor asked exactly what he meant. The boy pointed out a specific question: "Well, I don't think it's fair, sir. It makes a fellow think." [30] Apparently, Wilson strongly disliked the tedious chore of reading and grading examination papers. He read them carefully, however, and established the grades meticulously. At times he seemed to take the mistakes of his students as a personal hurt.

Wilson's social relations with his students were always cordial. In his home, he was a source of spontaneous gaiety, and regaled the boys with humorous stories. He was always thoughtful of his students, especially those who showed honesty in their assignments and serious motives in his classes. One of his students suffered a nervous breakdown in February of his senior year. Returning some weeks later for his trunk, the boy met his professor who stopped, inquired of his health, and of the prospect

[28] *Ibid.*
[29] *Ibid.*, 20.
[30] *Ibid.*, 27.

of his graduating. When the boy expressed keen disappointment at not being able to graduate with his class, the teacher declared: "You have done honest work in my classes." Wilson added: "I shall be willing to pass you in my course. Go see your other professors and tell them what I will do, and let me know how you get along." Returning later the student reported that all except one of his teachers had agreed to pass him, whereupon Wilson declared: "Let me handle him!" The boy graduated with his class.[31]

Wilson sometimes taught small groups in addition to his large classes. Before the latter he habitually stood on an elevated platform at the front of the room and lectured. In a small class he usually sat and confined himself to conversational discourse. A member of Wilson's department wrote that while in a small group of students the "arrangement of topics was excellent and clear; the sequence was logical, the analysis well sustained." There was nothing, however, of the remarkable quality which characterized his larger classes.[32] Wilson preferred the large class, disliked the intimacy of the smaller group.

A teacher in any institution of higher learning must be able to get along with other members of the faculty. Although not antisocial, Wilson seemingly did not achieve wide popularity among his colleagues at Princeton. Whether among students or with faculty members, he never saw his role as a university professor as a personality contest. Indeed, he realized all too well that a campaign for popularity too frequently entails breaches of professional ethics which he could not condone and which he habitually condemned.

Yet within a very short time after the teacher returned to his alma mater in the autumn of 1890, he was recognized as the leader of the younger members of the faculty. Beginning in 1894, for example, Wilson was named chairman of the Faculty Committee on Special and Delinquent Students. About the same time, he was made a member of the Committee on Library and, beginning in

[31] *Ibid.*, 32.

[32] Daniels, *Recollections of Wilson,* 4; O. W. Mosher, Jr., "Woodrow Wilson's Methods in the Classroom," *Current History,* XXXII (June, 1930), 502–505.

1899, served as chairman.[33] However, it was among the faculty when assembled as a group that Wilson displayed his talent for leadership. A past master in the art of debating, an expert parliamentarian, he won the esteem of many of his colleagues by sheer eloquence. As the professor's popularity, established by able leadership and not by social camaraderie, became more obvious, it was natural perhaps that he should gain the enmity of President Patton. Conservative and sound, the president lacked much in dynamic leadership. Wilson, as we have seen, defeated Patton on the honor system debate. On occasion thereafter when the latter took the floor to defend or to refute a proposal before the faculty, it was usually Wilson who took the opposite side of the measure and bested the president.

Several times misunderstandings developed between the president and the professor over the hiring of personnel. It is difficult to assess the blame in every case but certainly Wilson thought more than once that he had been misled by Patton into believing that a recommendation for the addition of a staff member had been received favorably, when apparently quite the reverse was true. As chairman of a department, Wilson found himself in the situation of having informed a prospective newcomer to the faculty that his name would be suggested by President Patton to the trustees. Later the chairman would have to retract the message and inform the applicant of his rejection.

On one occasion the professor informed Patton that he had treated him "something less than frankly, something less than courteously" in not telling him of the action of the Board of Trustees in regard to the chair of history which Wilson wished created.[34] Courteously, the president assured the professor that "nothing could have been further from my mind than the thought of doing anything discourteous or of failing to do everything that my warm friendship for you could deem to call for." [35] Apparently, the professor sensed that Patton's reserve, if not dislike, in

[33]See Princeton catalogues for the years 1890–1902 for Wilson's committee appointments. A memorandum of these faculty assignments is in the Baker Papers, Library of Congress.

[34]Wilson to Francis L. Patton, March 20, 1897, in Wilson Papers, Library of Congress.

[35]Patton to Wilson, March 29, 1897, in *ibid.*

dealing with him stemmed in part from Wilson's enlarging influence as a Democrat while the president, a British subject, leaned toward the Republicans.

As Wilson continued to lecture extensively, as his reputation as a teacher spread, as his writings found an ever widening audience, he received numerous offers to teach or to become an administrator elsewhere. When the Board of Regents and many alumni urged him to accept the presidency of the University of Virginia on his own terms, he was torn emotionally by his love for his two alma maters. For days he and Ellen discusssed the proposition. He confided his dilemma to Princeton trustee Cyrus McCormick, who immediately consulted another trustee, Cornelius Cuyler, in New York. Together they urged Wilson not to leave Princeton. McCormick regretted the unfortunate circumstances in regard to the history department but added that better days were coming. "No one of the younger professors holds a more conspicuous position than you do," he told Wilson, "and no one has a brighter outlook for the future." [36]

Those representing the University of Virginia were crushed by Wilson's decision to remain at Princeton. George W. Miles, a friend of the professor, wrote that he did not know how sorely he was needed and added: "Nothing would have refreshed our hopes and energies in the South, after our 33 years of poverty and struggle, more than to have seen such a man as yourself turn back Southward to take the leadership of its greatest institution of learning." [37]

When informed of the possibility of Wilson's departure from Princeton because of a higher salary offered him by the University of Virginia, several trustees—including McCormick, Cuyler, John L. Cadwalader, and Cleveland H. Dodge—agreed to contribute $2,500 annually to Wilson's salary for a period of five years, beginning with the academic year 1898–99, provided the professor agreed that he "would not sever his connection with Princeton University in order to accept a call to any other institution of learning; and that he would not during that time give

[36]Wilson to Cyrus H. McCormick, March 27, 1898, and McCormick to Wilson, April 2, 1898, in *ibid.*

[37]George W. Miles to Wilson, April 25, 1898, in *ibid.*

any course of lecture at any other institution of learning that would interrupt or interfere with his regular duties of instruction at Princeton University." [38] Before this agreement expired, Wilson had become president of Princeton.

[38]The agreement, dated April 30, 1898, was sent to Wilson for his files. Cornelius C. Cuyler to Wilson, May 16, 1898, in *ibid.* For the letter in which Wilson received his first check for $2,500 see Cuyler to Wilson, December 23, 1898, in *ibid.*

CHAPTER XII *The Educator*

In the course of his career as a university professor, Wilson evolved a philosophy of education. After some eight years of teaching in the college classroom, he could formulate his views with the assurance which only experience brings. These ideas he set forth in a significant formal address to the International Congress of Education on July 26, 1893. The congress, held in Chicago in connection with the World's Fair, was perhaps a more representative university gathering than any previously held in America. The prevailing spirit of the convention was temperate, but its convictions, as advanced by the speakers, were enthusiastically for a "disciplinary liberal culture, of organization and training, as opposed to lax standards or unregulated study." [1]

Wilson spoke on the topic "Should an Antecedent Liberal Education be Required of Students in Law, Medicine, and Theology?"

[1]*Princeton College Bulletin,* V (November, 1893), 71–72.

He noted that the question could be dismissed from two points of view: that of an individual seeking professional instruction as a means of gaining a livelihood and that of society itself, wishing to be well served by its professional classes. The community, contended the professor, would be prone to require more of its professional classes, while the individual, eager to enter his chosen profession, would curtail his liberal education in the interest of his professional training. Unfortunately, antecedent liberal education was not necessarily liberal. Indeed, Wilson said, it was often so illiberal in its survey of subjects "as to leave upon the mind no trace of the generalizing habit." One who was not fortunate enough to receive a liberal education could never secure a subsequent equivalent and would always remain shut in by a narrow intellectual horizon.

As an example, Wilson emphasized the necessity of a liberal education in the early training of a physician. It was impossible for the student of medicine to understand the physical life of man, he said, without understanding the physical life of the universe. The physical life of man was made distinctive, after all, by his singular mental life. The physician would lose trace of causes of great moment to his own art if he knew nothing of the laws of the mind, of not only physiological psychology, but of pure psychology too. According to Wilson, one could not get this range of knowledge in medical school; one must get it from an antecedent liberal education.

There were equally valid reasons why students of theology and law should have liberal educations prior to their professional training. The physician should not be content merely to be a "successful empiric, and learn useful practical lessons from his daily experiences." Nor should the minister rest on his laurels if he only "please his congregation by agreeable sermons and still more agreeable pastoral visits." And the lawyer should aspire to be "more than an expert in a technical business." Pessimistically, perhaps, Wilson said that as many of these professional men would go without a liberal education as the community would permit.

In the United States, said Wilson, there was great freedom in choice of occupations. It was the responsibility of the institutions of higher learning to create and to maintain the widest opportunity for every young person to train properly for his profession. Any reform, he affirmed, "must come piece-meal and by example: not all at once and by authority." Wilson's remedy for the educational conditions of 1893 was stated succinctly: "Let leading universities and colleges that have or can get money enough to make them free to act . . . first erect professional schools upon a new model of scholarship, and then close the doors of those schools to all who have not a first-rate college training. It would not take the country long to find out that the best practical lawyers and doctors and preachers came out from those schools—and the rest would be discredited."

No law school, or medical, or theological school, ought to be a separate educational institution; each ought to be organically and in situation a part of a university, Wilson said. Moreover, the university should permeate and dominate the professional college to the extent of creating an intellectual atmosphere in which it would thrive, in extending to it university methods and in exemplifying for it a liberal spirit of learning. Indeed, the separation of general and special training was to Woodrow Wilson "an acute symptom of the disease of specialization," by which educational institutions were then "so sorely afflicted."

The Princeton professor was firmly convinced that when the universities put students trained in chemistry, biology, and psychology into their own medical schools, when students drilled in economics, in history, and in "the natural history of society" were placed in law schools, when students knowledgeable in the various areas of contemporary thought and in the literature of all ages went into schools of theology, then Americans in all walks of life would benefit through contacts with real lawyers, capable physicians, and powerful preachers. The professor argued that these professions would then deserve the title of learned professions.

In conclusion, Wilson declared that knowledge was trustworthy only when it was balanced and complete. Areas of knowledge must be knit together by well-trained faculties dedicated to the task of making knowledge whole. In achieving this laudable objective, the liberal education provided for professional students must not only be antecedent to but concurrent with their technical training. As liberal an education as possible, the Princeton teacher thought, was needed "if only to open the eyes and accustom the faculties to a nice manipulation of thought." [2]

For this speech, probably Wilson's first devoted entirely to his philosophy of education, he was fortunate in his listeners. With an audience of professional educators, like himself, he was among sympathetic friends. As an initial expression of a promising professor's faith in a liberal education, the speech struck a responsive chord. Along with other able speeches delivered by leading educators, Wilson's address received wide comment in professional circles.

Thirteen months later, on August 23, 1894, Wilson addressed the American Bar Association at Saratoga Springs. His topic, "Legal Education of Undergraduates," [3] was one with which he had had some experience as a young man and about which he had subsequently formed some conclusions. The lawyer, he said, was everywhere sadly discredited, since the world was "searching for prophets, not barristers." It wanted change, not judgment. Because of the lawyer's exactness of phrase and certitude of provision, reformers were prone to ignore him and deem his counsel disheartening. For this situation, Wilson said, the legal profession was not without blame. There were striking examples of lawyers acting "as very stubborn and very stupid obstructionists," refusing to participate in necessary, even inevitable, changes in the law of the land. No man in the audience was so professionally blind as not to see that the law limped lamely at many points, that it had failed to keep pace with the swift and radical changes that had transformed industrial society beyond recognition almost within a single generation. While admitting that law of contract and association and taxation and tenure needed a general overhauling, Wilson deprecated the haste, the ignorance, and the intemperance of many who posed as reformers.

The professor believed that under such conditions the law might cease to be a liberal profession and lose its guiding place in society

[2]Woodrow Wilson, "Should an Antecedent Liberal Education Be Required of Students in Law, Medicine and Theology?" *International Congress of Education of the World's Columbian Exposition Proceedings* (New York, 1894), 112–17.

[3]*American Bar Association Report 1894* (Philadelphia, 1894), 439–51.

accordingly. The need was for the laymen who understood the necessity for law and of lawyers who realized the necessity for reform and visualized safe means of effecting it. Law, Wilson contended, was a branch of political science and should be studied as such. Lawyers with this background would drink more deeply at the fountains of the law than the mere technical barristers. Having explored the sources of the streams of law, these lawyers would stand in court as advisors as well as pleaders. In brief, the lawyer must be made "on the other side of the law school."

While admitting that every citizen should know the nature of law—how it came into existence, what relation its form bore to its substance, and how it gave to society its fiber and strength and poise of frame—Wilson declared that the lawyer should be well versed in the philosophy and in the history of law. However, time did not permit the law school to devote time to these subjects. The legal student must be given such courses prior to entering the law school. Wilson apparently had some doubt about the exact courses that the would-be lawyer should take. He was convinced, however, that the instructors in such courses should be political scientists and sociologists, for how could anyone possibly understand the law "without having a clear idea of how it was generated in society and adapted from age to age to its immediate needs and uses?"

Young men expecting to become lawyers should be instructed very carefully in the differences between private and public law. In addition, the prelaw student should be carefully grounded in the principles of general jurisprudence. After this historical survey of law, Wilson thought that "the method of instruction should at every step be both historical and comparative." Indeed, no other method could be called philosophical. Since it frequently stopped with one case in a series, the case method was inadequate. In like manner, the professor opposed the textbook method as neither philosophical nor really instructive unless the legal principles presented were "challenged, cross-examined and made to give a rational account of themselves."

In England, Wilson informed his audience, a distinction was drawn between attorneys and barristers, while in the United States such a distinction was unrecognized. American legal instruction was devoted entirely to the preparation of attorneys, who direct the *business* of the law and who must become technical experts. Few law students were trained in any systematic way to serve as barristers, who deal with the principles of the law in argument. As an inevitable result of this illogical type of legal training, the speaker declared, the need for judges had been forgotten; there were so many illiberal judgments from the courts because there were so many more attorneys on the bench. The barrister had a much higher function than the attorney and the judge had a higher function than either.[4]

Obviously, the solution lay in American colleges, Wilson concluded. They must invite undergraduates interested in law to become jurists and systematically train them for the legal bench. In this sense young men would be made to become lawyers before entering law schools. They would see the field of legal knowledge as a whole in its philosophy and historical relationship. Wilson was convinced that the purpose of discovering the whole significance of law and of imparting the discovery to others was the function not of the professional legal expert "but of the political scientist." [5]

Throughout the 1890's Wilson continued to formulate his philosophy of education. At times he expressed his thoughts in public addresses, and on occasion published his ideas in current periodicals. An example of the second avenue of expression was an article—"University Training and Citizenship"—which appeared in the *Forum,* September, 1894.[6] For years Wilson had been interested in the best program of university training for the ideal type of citizenship in a democracy. When Walter Hines Page, editor of the *Forum* and Wilson's friend of more than ten years, invited him to write a paper for publication in that magazine, he complied gladly.

Wilson began by discussing briefly European influences on American universities. The popularity of German higher educational practices, he said, was evidenced by the fact that more than half of the universities in the United States were experiment-

[4]*Ibid.*

[5]*Ibid.*

[6]Woodrow Wilson, "University Training and Citizenship," *Forum,* XVIII (1894), 107–16.

ing with German techniques. Some educators, including Wilson, were giving considerable thought to the advantages a young person received by reading widely and systematically with a tutor as the students did at Cambridge and Oxford. Frankly, Wilson wrote, he liked the "close contact between teacher and pupil, and the rather liberal and unscholastic way of handling many books," which such a method of instruction provided. The French system of higher education, with its liberal spirit and keen sense of form, also appealed to him. The Princeton professor did not believe that the needs of American students were met by European educational practices, however.

Wilson confessed that there was no American university ideal, and, because worthwhile learning was cosmopolitan, there should be none. Since truth knew no geographical boundaries, "no one could justly wish to observe a national bias in the determination of it." Scholarship to Wilson was, indeed, "an instrument and means of life." Persons individually and nations collectively should seek the truth and wisdom that would set them free. While admitting that a wise man, as a wise nation, must choose carefully what to learn, the writer pointed out that there was a "learning of purpose as well as a learning of science"; a truth of spirit as well as a truth of fact. He argued that in addition to the physical sciences, which were international, a university should have at the core of its curriculum a course in literature which contained the ideals of its race and all the proofs and subtle inspirations of the character, spirit, and thought of the nation which it served. The university must also offer classes in the history of those cultural institutions which had served the "nation's energies in the preservation of order and the maintenance of just standards of civil virtue and public purpose." These two basic types of courses should be required of all students, as the only means of schooling their spirits for their common life as American citizens. In advocating liberal, cultural courses for all university students, Wilson was two generations ahead of his time in anticipating the general educational programs that have become so popular in the middle twentieth century.

The Princeton professor was also beyond the contemporary thought of the 1890's in believing that the university's educational processes should emphasize and glorify nationalism. Certainly he, though Virginia born, was not proclaiming the doctrine of states' rights, nor was he voicing sentiments of southern sectionalism, when he wrote that each nation should use its universities to perfect the proper role of its advancing civilization. A university should serve as "an organ of memory for the State for the transmission of its best traditions," he contended. Moreover, every man going out from a university should be first a man of his nation, then a man of the world.

Privately, Wilson had established himself as a conservative educator in urging the teaching of the classics. Not only did he want Latin taught but he was quite emphatic in how it should be presented: "Boys, like generals, like fighting, like accounts of battles," he wrote understandingly; "if they could be given a just conception of the reality of this man Caesar . . . if they could be made to realize that these commentaries were written, in many parts probably, in the camp . . . when the deeds of which they tell were fresh in mind . . . if they could be given a fellow-feeling, an enthusiasm, or even a wonder for this versatile fellow-man of theirs, reading the *Commentaries* would be easy, would be fun, and their contents would never be forgotten." [7]

The teacher did not discount the dangers of socialism. Indeed, because of its scientific methods in a militantly scientific age, socialism was much more acceptable, and therefore more dangerous, than ever before. Especially was this true when two-thirds of the college graduates were not taught anything that would predispose them against accepting its logic or its purpose "to put all things into a laboratory of experiment and arbitrarily recombine the elements of society." People, Wilson declared, must remember that science was scarcely older than the nineteenth century and possessed of such youth it was apt to "despise old thought." Young men trained only as scientists were as pedantic in their narrowness as men trained exclusively in the classics, whose thought was all in the past. Any institution of higher education which developed men mentally, without very carefully establishing the connection of their thought with that of

[7]Wilson to Moses E. Slaughter, August 2, 1888, in Wilson Papers, Library of Congress.

the poet, was, according to Wilson, an "instrument of social destruction."

One serious problem was the lack of a sufficient number of instructors. In stating his solution to this perplexing question, Wilson, for the first time perhaps, outlined what came to be known a decade later as Princeton's preceptorial system. He suggested that teachers could be supplied by employing a considerable number of young tutors, serving their novitiate for full university appointments. Taking the students in groups of manageable numbers, suggesting the reading of each group, and checking by frequent interviews and quizzes, explaining and stimulating as best they could, they would not only get the required tasks performed, but would enrich the whole life of the university. This basic concept of Wilson's tutorial plan did not change; it only grew and developed. Fundamental courses in general education that would be required of all students and supervised by a group of able, young tutors would be made the meeting point of all degree candidates. It would become the field of knowledge where students of every sort might get a "liberalizing outlook upon the world of thought and affairs." Most important of all, Wilson added, these core subjects could be the means of indoctrinating the men, whom American universities sent forth as representatives of the power and worth of education, in nationalism.

The Princeton professor associated educational methods with the problems of advancing democracy. Neither in America nor elsewhere did all people attend classes in the schoolroom, but through the channels of commerce and the widespread influence of the press the entire world had become a school. According to Wilson, the very air was alive with the "multitudinous voices of information." Indeed, no idea could be kept exclusively at home in the land of its nativity; it was soon taken up by the explorer, the missionary, the reporter, the trader, the traveler, and given to the entire world in the memoir, the newspaper, the novel, the poem, and the treatise, until every community knew not only itself, but much of the world as well—all for the small price of learning to read and keeping its ears open. Thomas Carlyle, said Wison, unquestionably touched one of the obvious truths concerning modern democracy when he declared it to be the result of printing.

As powerful as these forces of information were, they in themselves were incapable of producing democracy. Only "trained capacity for self-government, practical aptitude for public affairs, habitual soberness and united action" could establish and maintain democracy. For, said the educator, "democratic institutions are never done; they are like living tissue, always a-making." America's success as a democracy depended upon training in her schools. The processes of the United States educational system must be attuned to the objective of promoting living democracy.

Wilson was aware that leadership could not belong to the multitude; masses of people could not possibly be self-directed. The sovereignty of the people was peculiar in that it was "judicial merely, not creative." The size of modern democracy necessitated, he thought, the exercise of persuasive power by dominant intellects in the shaping of popular judgments. However, there was no permanent place in the democratic leadership except for him who "hath clean hands and a pure heart." [8] The public school system might be geared to the welfare of the masses but higher educational institutions were for the training of leaders. If the function of the former was to encourage the masses in a developing democracy, the responsibility of the latter was to inform and inspire the leaders in creating a liberal progressive democracy.

Wilson believed two things absolutely essential in the education of the American leader. First, he should have a college or university period of four years, studying the great works and highest thoughts of the masters of language; then he should spend at least two years studying American cultural institutions. The young leader should comprehend and appreciate the government under which he lived and by which he was protected. He should understand and be filled with the thoughts and imagination of the literature of his country.[9]

Among the innovations of Wilson's generation destined to be

[8] Woodrow Wilson, "The Character of Democracy in the United States," 577–88.

[9] "The Work of a Southern Scholar," *Sewanee Review,* III (1895), 172–88.

greatly influential on the American higher educational scene was the admission of women students to institutions hitherto reserved for men. Wilson's conclusions about the movement of American young women into institutions of higher learning were given to a professor at Brown University. He noted that the first, experimental stage of college training for women had passed. The day was approaching for "a generation of young women who go to college of *course,* as young men have long done"; women who would come not because of special desire or earnestness or fitness or professional need to study, but "for the contacts, experiences, routine, enjoyment and incidental profit of college life." Wilson personally opposed the admission of women to coeducational institutions, but noted there was little past experience upon which to base a logical judgment for the future.[10]

Wilson had another opportunity to express some of his pertinent ideas in educational circles when the College of New Jersey celebrated its sesquicentennial. The professor's ideals were thrust into the national spotlight on the occasion of the transformation of Princeton College of New Jersey into Princeton University. Chosen by the trustees to deliver one of the orations, Wilson spoke on "Princeton in the Nation's Service." [11]

On that occasion he noted the oddity ("a thing against nature," he called it) of thinking that the man who was preoccupied with the world of thought was an unsafe man in world affairs. Certainly, the speaker said, no one should belittle culture by esteeming it merely an intellectual ornament, forgetting that it was a tool of power. The creation of a cultured mind was the highest objective to which a university could dedicate its facilities. In order to prevent any misunderstanding as to what he meant, the speaker defined a cultured mind as "a mind quit of its awkwardness, eased of all impediment and illusion, made quick and athletic in the acceptable exercise of power." It was a mind, continued Wilson, "at once informed and just, a mind habituated to choose its course with knowledge, and filled with full assur-

[10]Wilson to J. Franklin Jameson, February 21, 1892, in Jameson Papers, Library of Congress.

[11]Andrew F. West to Wilson, June 19, 1895, in Wilson Papers, Library of Congress.

ance, like one who knows the world and can live in it without either unreasonable hope or unwarranted fear."

Campus opinion, the Princeton professor noted, was changing. Formerly it was taken for granted that institutions of learning would be found always on the conservative side in political matters. More recently, Wilson explained, much had happened to disprove this long held presumption. The college or university around the turn of the century lay very near the affairs of the entire world. On the campus many of the latest experiments were being conducted; laboratories were filled with the latest discoveries; lecture rooms were alive with discussions of new theories of life and with novel programs of reforms. Indeed, revolutionary thoughts in the 1890's were as naturally harbored among the personnel of universities as they were once among the Encyclopedists, and, added Wilson, "there is no radical like your learned radical, bred in the schools."

If these conditions were true, what was the cause of the great shift of campus opinion from its conservative moorings of the past? The speaker said the scientific spirit of the age had wrought the change. While declaring that he stood with hat doffed and head bowed to the men who had made the age one of scientific knowledge, Wilson believed that, as a student of society, he would deem himself unworthy of comradeship with the great men of science were he not to speak the plain truth about what was so obvious. His laboratory was the world of books and men in which he lived. He was convinced that the scientific spirit of his generation had done humanity a great disservice in that it had bred in many "a spirit of experiment and a contempt for the past." It had caused many people to become "credulous of quick improvement, hopeful of discovering panaceas, confident of success in every new thing."

Wilson had no indictment against the many accomplishments of the scientists, but warned against the scientific atmosphere which had stolen from the laboratories into the lecture rooms of American universities. A child of the nineteenth century, science had transformed the world and owed little debt to any age of the past. The work of the scientists was so marvelous, so stupendous, that men of all other teaching subjects "have been set staring at their methods, imitating their ways of thought, ogling their results." It was the introduction of scientific influences and methodology into other areas of study that Wilson opposed. He strongly disliked the scientific attitude, prevalent throughout the university campus, of believing in the present and in the future more than in the past and of deeming the newest theory of society the likeliest. More specifically, the disservice of science, Wilson declared, was agnosticism in philosophy and anarchism in politics.

He pleaded for the ancient schooling in precedent and tradition for the keeping of an abiding faith with the past. All these, he felt, were an essential preparation for much needed leadership in the days of drastic social change that lay just ahead. Science was not given too great a place in our educational curriculum, but the professor was convinced that we had made a perilous mistake in extending scientific methods into every other field of study. The remedy for the mistake: "We must make the humanities human again . . . we must turn back once more to the region of practicable ideals." [12]

In the final analysis, Wilson contended, it was not a university's learning, not its scholarship—as important as these were in evaluating education—that established a place of recognition in the permanent annals of the nation, but its spirit of service. The proper environment, in which the spirit of service would thrive best, was one in which discussion of public affairs was promoted in all classrooms. Wilson explained that there world transactions should be evaluated, "the consciousness of the solidarity of the race, the sense of the duty of man towards man, of the presence of men in every problem, of the significance of truth for guidance as well as for knowledge, of the potency of ideas, of the promise and hope" that shone in the face of all knowledge.

Wilson concluded his speech with a jab at the Princeton administration. Affairs at the university were drifting. Not that President Patton did not have a firm grasp upon educational trends; he convinced an investigating committee on university affairs a few months later that he was well aware of the local

[12]Woodrow Wilson, "Princeton in the Nation's Service," *Forum,* XXII (December, 1896), 447–66.

situation. The obvious inefficiency, which Professor Thomas J. Wertenbaker has pointed out as campus-wide, resulted apparently from the president's inability to carry out administratively the policies that he conceived for the institution.[13] Knowing the local conditions, Wilson concluded his well-accepted speech with a superb peroration. After depicting the perfect place of learning as he pictured Princeton University of the future, he ended his address with the pertinent question: "Who shall show us the way to this place?"

The query was a two-edged sword. It revealed to the members of the Board of Trustees and influential alumni in the audience the fact that Wilson found President Patton unequal to the task of leadership. It also caused some to think of others, including the speaker, who might possess talents of leadership which, if given the opportunity, would show Princeton the way toward that excellent place of learning.

Wilson's speech on this occasion made a deep impression among educators nationally. A distinguished Philadelphia neurologist, Weir Mitchell, for example, did not remember ever having heard its equal. "It was strong and competent in argument—delightfully humorous—full of noble appeal and with here and there a starry glow of poetic statement." [14] Author John Davidson wrote of the "magnificent oration" and added: *"I was proud of you."* [15] For Wilson, however, it was another step along his professional highway towards greater success and wider recognition. To confidante Mary Hoyt, Ellen Wilson poured out her enthusiasm at the reaction to her husband's speech:

> We are just through with a great celebration . . . the greatest thing of the sort, every one says, that America has ever seen. It was a most brilliant,—*dazzling* success from first to last and such an ovation as Woodrow received! I never imagined anything like it, and think of *so* delighting such an audience, the most distinguished, every one says, that has ever been assembled in America—famous men from all parts of Europe. They declared there had been "nothing to equal it since Burke"; with scores of compliments equally great. . . . I was in the

[13]Thomas J. Wertenbaker, *Princeton 1746–1896* (New York, 1946), 383–85.

[14]Weir Mitchell to Wilson, October 21, 1896, in Wilson Papers, Library of Congress.

[15]John Davidson to Wilson, October 22, 1896, in *ibid.*

ladies gallery, and heard it all! As for the Princeton Men, some of them simply fell on his neck and wept for joy. They say that those who could not get at Woodrow were shaking each other's hands and congratulating each other in a perfect frenzy of delight that Princeton had so covered herself with glory before the visitors. And that is what makes it such a sweet triumph; it was not a selfish success, it all resounded to the Honour of Princeton before the academic world. How I wish you could have heard it; of course you can read it, but then he delivered it so superbly.[16]

During the twelve years of Wilson's professorship at Princeton, he frequently philosophized about the importance of education to the continuing development of American nationalism. On one occasion he addressed a large group of teachers on the topic "Spurious Versus Real Patriotism in Education." [17] While patriotism expressed itself in sentiment, Wilson began, it did not consist of sentiment. Quite the contrary, patriotism was a principle of devotion. Like unselfishness, it was grounded in a "certain energy of character, expressing itself outside the narrow circle of self-interest." No man could serve his country well, the speaker added, unless he knew the history of his country and what it stood for.

There were those, Wilson exclaimed, who branded as unpatriotic, even un-American, anyone who criticized public action or public officials. If to criticize was un-American, then a deep disgrace rested upon the origin of this nation. With subtle humor he continued: "We originated . . . in a kick and if it be unpatriotic to kick . . . the grown man is very unlike the child." The speaker admonished his fellow teachers not to forget the very principle of the country's founding, which was the right to object, to agitate, to resist. Americans, Wilson declared, "must know how to pull down and build up, even to the extent of revolutionary practices if it be necessary to readjust matters. I have forgotten my American history, if that be not true history," he added.[18]

Continuing the same idea of protest, the Princeton professor said that he loved more deeply than anything else the right of

[16]Ellen Wilson to Mary W. Hoyt, October 27, 1896, in Baker Papers, Library of Congress.

[17]Woodrow Wilson, "Spurious Versus Real Patriotism in Education," *School Review,* VII (December, 1899), 599–620.

[18]*Ibid.,* 602.

other men to hold views different from his own. In the university community where he lived he earnestly desired the "rigorous airs of differences of opinions." He was firmly convinced that a great weakness of the American character was that there were "so few grouchers and kickers among us."

Wilson urged his fellow instructors to present in the classroom a clearer conception of the central objects and characteristics of government. The essentials of American policy, he declared, were not only abstract but even worse, "*abstract and familiar*." He believed the three central abstractions that lay at the heart of U.S. government to be: "self-government, liberty, and equality." Self-government was the participation in the conduct of affairs of nonofficial persons who might be appointed because of their importance in the locality, i.e., justices of the peace. Self-government, Wilson felt, was the free expression of lay nonofficial opinion. Democracy furnished the soundest basis for self-government which in its essence was not necessarily democratic. The educator, however, wanted his listeners to realize that "there never has been and there never will be a government that is conducted by the majority. The majority may make all the noise they please, but a very small number of persons govern in affairs. That must always be the case." [19]

Wilson noted that liberty provided the "best adjustment between government and individual intuition." Liberty also involved restraint, however. Was not the sailing boat free because of her obedience to the wind? Was it not the ship's obedience to the great forces moving about her that put her own faculties at her disposal? Liberty was like the ingredients in food; excellent in the proper mixture but tasteless alone. In proportion as liberty was compounded it was an excellent thing. In order to have liberty men must learn to think of other men as they thought of themselves. This Golden Rule approach to liberty the professor insisted was easiest to follow "in a society of tolerable uniform economic conditions." This statement, however, should not be accepted as an expression of Wilson's faith in any kind of collectivistic economic democracy.

As to equality, the speaker reminded the audience that if

[19] *Ibid.*, 610.

people were born free and equal, as the Declaration of Independence stated, freedom and equality stopped at birth. One must not deceive himself by supposing that he could invent a machinery of government that would keep the slow runners up with the fast. Moreover, noted Wilson amidst great laughter, "we want to see a race." Americans must never forget that keen competition is the best training for the growth of the individual. They should not so dwarf themselves as to give every man a handicap that would make him equal with every other man. Criticism must be directed at the particular laws which created artificial advantages in competition for some, without others being able to share in them. It was the equality of opportunity, said Wilson, not the equality of result, that instructors must help their students to see.

What were Wilson's enduring contributions to American educational processes as revealed in his speeches and writings during the teaching years from 1885 to 1902? He strongly urged that students contemplating professional careers, in such areas as law, medicine, and theology, be required to take courses that would give them a liberal cultural background. He believed that those in training for a vocation in science should also be compelled to take some liberalizing basic courses to widen their intellectual horizons. Although doffing his hat to the marvelous scientific achievements of the Industrial Revolution, the teacher argued that science had done a disservice to the American educational system by proclaiming the success of everything new and the uselessness of everything old. The remedy lay, in part at least, in making the would-be scientists more familiar with the cultural past.

In urging a restoration of greater emphasis on the classics in the educational system, Wilson was fighting a losing battle. Courses in the fields of scientific study were to continue to compete successfully with the ancient classics for the attention of American youth. His campaign for widespread study of the classics and his opposition to coeducation indicate the influence of tradition upon the teacher in his role as an educator.

A group of liberalizing core courses required of every student, the Princeton faculty member thought, should be the heart of the curriculum of every American university. "I believe general training courses," Wilson said, "with no particular occupation in view, to be the very heart and essence of university training." [20] Indeed, he stated that in such a series of liberalizing courses universally required lay America's greatest opportunity to make a distinct contribution to world educational thought.

As a teacher of classes in jurisprudence and politics, Woodrow urged using the facilities of the universities for training in American citizenship. Nationalism should be promoted in educational institutions. Courses that emphasized literary heritage should be required of every student. The country's educational institutions should not become seed beds for spurious patriotism but should produce true, old-fashioned American patriotism.

In Wilson's own words, he saw the nation's colleges and universities as places of schooling "where passion may be cooled, prejudice enlightened, effort steadied, purpose given vision." He visualized educational institutions as communities where the chief product should not be "men of the closet but christened men of action; men schooled and fitted to carry forward the better tasks and to make prevalent the established lessons of the nation's life. Men who understand and lead and serve and interpret." [21] If the university functioned properly, the graduate upon leaving would soon realize that his formal educational training was not for "ornament or personal gratification, but to teach him how to use himself and to develop facilities worth using." [22]

After Wilson became president of Princeton, he was to prove the practical idealist in putting his philosophy of education into practice. His record of achievement was to establish him as one of the foremost educators in America.

[20]Robert Bridges, "President Woodrow Wilson and College Earnestness," *World's Work,* XV (January, 1908), 9792–97.

[21]Woodrow Wilson, "Our Last Frontier," *Berea College Quarterly,* IV (May, 1899), 5–6. Wilson gave this address at Berea College January, 1899.

[22]Woodrow Wilson, "When a Man Comes to Himself," *Century,* LXII (June, 1901), 268–73.

CHAPTER XIII *The Historian*

While Wilson's interest in history was subordinate to his interest in political science, he gave it considerable attention during his student and teaching careers. In his years as a professor at Princeton he often tried writing for historical periodicals. In July, 1893, Wilson received a letter from Frederick Jackson Turner concerning the latter's essay, "The Significance of the Frontier in American History," to be read before the American Historical Association meeting at the Chicago Columbian Exposition and World's Fair.[1] Of all papers presented before this professional organization for the next half century, Turner's essay would prove one of the most influential in American historiography. Wilson's former student commented briefly on his paper and promised his teacher an early copy of the work.

Wilson's interest in what came to be called the Turner thesis

[1]Frederick Jackson Turner to Wilson, July 16, 1893, in Wilson Papers, Library of Congress.

of American history is evidenced by his article, "Mr. Goldwin Smith's Views on our Political History," in the December, 1893, issue of *Forum.* The chief thread of United States history, wrote the Princeton professor, lay not in its European origins but in its American developments. Every element of the population and every cultural institution of the old life along the Atlantic seaboard that penetrated the continent was digested in the frontier atmosphere and became an element or an institution of new life. It was, said the author, that transformation that constituted the country's history. "That part of our history which is most truly national," concluded Wilson, "is the history of the West." [2]

Upon reading the article, Turner wrote that his former teacher's lucid and effective statement of the importance of the middle region and the West in the doctrine of American development, in contrast with the Germanic *genus,* was "quite gratifying." Wilson's efforts could not fail to contribute towards a more rational study of American history. "I am glad that you think," continued Turner, "I have helped you to some of these ideas, for I have many intellectual debts to repay to you." [3]

Wilson and Turner did not agree with the interpretation given American history by those who stressed the beginnings of American institutions and ideas in Europe, "notably in the German forests." [4] With a firm belief in social Darwinism, both men were convinced of the evolutionary development of American social institutions and historical processes. They were writing about the *development* of American cultural institutions rather than about their origins, and the regions where these institutions grew and developed were not in the old eastern seaboard but the young West and the New South.

At the suggestion of *Forum* editor Walter Hines Page, Wilson about this time wrote an article entitled "A Calendar of Great Americans." Such an essay, the author confessed, "would never have occurred to my home-keeping mind to write." It was sug-

[2]Woodrow Wilson, "Mr. Goldwin Smith's Views on Our Political History," *Forum,* XVI (1893–94), 489–99.

[3]Turner to Wilson, December 10, 1893, in Wilson Papers, Library of Congress.

[4]Thomas J. Pressly, *Americans Interpret Their Civil War* (Princeton, 1954), 167–68.

gested by the editor with "his theme-seeking mind."[5] In the Princeton professor's "calendar" not a single woman was mentioned. Outside of her role in the home as wife and mother no woman, thought the author, entered the spotlight of lasting historical acclaim. Wilson's world, so far as greatness was concerned, was a man's world.

In his selection of great Americans, the writer revealed his staunch conservatism. Evidence is his description of Alexander Hamilton, "certainly one of the greatest figures in our history." Hamilton's genius and steadfast spirit, Wilson thought, were absolutely indispensable to the American people. Only a great conservative genius like Hamilton could have succeeded against such stubborn obstacles. In contrast to Hamilton, Thomas Jefferson was "not a thorough American because of the strain of French Philosophy that permeated and weakened all his thought." As a philosopher, the sage of Monticello was "radical by nature as well as by acquirement." Although recognizing Jefferson's natural leadership, Wilson ascribed it to a "native shrewdness, tact and sagacity. The very aerated quality of Jefferson's principles gave them an air of insincerity."

John Marshall and Daniel Webster, said Wilson, expressed a new set of ideas which "all the world has received as American." These men, as constitutional lawyers, viewed the fundamental law as a "great organic product, a vehicle of life, as well as a charter of authority." The national importance and functions of these men, said Wilson, became more obvious when they were contrasted with men like John Adams and John C. Calhoun, "whose greatness was not national." As an eminent Puritan statesman, John Adams represented only one element of the national character; Calhoun was only a great provincial.

One of the first men to exhibit the American spirit "with an unmistakable touch of greatness and distinction" was Benjamin Franklin. If, as Wilson stated, Franklin was "versatile without lacking solidity," George Washington was "too colorless, too cold, too prudent." In Henry Clay there was a very authentic pattern of Americanism. Indeed, no one of Clay's generation represent-

[5]Wilson to Lyman P. Powell, February 8, 1894, in Lyman P. Powell Papers, Library of Congress.

ed the American more completely than he did. Entirely of the West, Andrew Jackson was a "new type of energy and self-confidence."

After describing Patrick Henry, Sam Houston, and Robert E. Lee as representing "only one cardinal principle of the national life," Wilson declared Abraham Lincoln to be "the supreme American" in whom all elements of American greatness were combined and harmonized. "The most singular thing about the wonderful career of the man is the way in which he steadily grew into a national stature."

In publishing his "calendar," Wilson pointed out the traits that great men of the future should possess. They should be of a "composite type of greatness, sound-hearted, hopeful, confident of the validity of liberty, tenacious of the deeper principles of American institutions." In an optimistic vein, the author concluded that some day Americans would be of "one mind, our ideals fixed, our purposes harmonized, our nationality complete and consentaneous; then will come our great literature and our greatest men." [6]

The essay was widely commented on by the press, prompting Wilson to declare that nothing he had ever written had attracted the attention of so large a number of people.[7] The author had cast a shadow over many men who used to be regarded as great, said the New York *Sun,* and "the sifting process was not always satisfactory." [8] The Duluth *Tribune* stated that "Wilson has an idea about our great men with which not everybody will agree," but admitted that "men of simple or local type have about disappeared from among the great leaders of the country, and the great men of our future will all be great Americans of a composite type of greatness." [9] The Philadelphia *Times* thought the Princetonian's efforts to fuse all the different characteristics of origin and locality into a single character that could be recognized as an American was incomplete. Moreover, several genera-

[6]Woodrow Wilson, "A Calendar of Great Americans," *Forum,* XVI (February, 1894), 715–27.

[7]Wilson to Walter Hines Page, December 5, 1894, in Baker Papers, Library of Congress.

[8]New York *Sun,* February 7, 1894.

[9]Duluth *Tribune,* February 11, 1894.

tions would be required before the country became homogeneous enough for the higher national ideal type to prevail.[10]

In April, 1895, shortly after Wilson's article appeared in *Forum,* professors of history from six universities met at the Reform Club in New York to name an executive committee to initiate a periodical for the recently organized American Historical Association. Wilson's close friend Professor Franklin Jameson of Brown University was selected managing editor of the new quarterly, the *American Historical Review.* Jameson asked Wilson to contribute to the periodical, but the latter enumerated the professional chores which made it impossible for him to comply.[11] "And so 'you see how it is'; and why I must still only look at the distinguished company who frequent the pages of the *American Historical Review,*" apologized the Princeton professor.[12]

Failing in his efforts to persuade Wilson to contribute an article to the young historical magazine, Jameson tempted him with a proffered book to review. Again, Wilson declined: "I beg that you will not deem me selfish or churlish when I decline this little scrap of work. The disabling of my right hand with writer's cramp and neuritis," he continued, "has made an enormous difference in my life, for I cannot afford a secretary. I can manage to do the big pieces of work by which I earn my living; but little jobs are just the very ones that are crowded absolutely out in the careful husbandry of minutes by which I manage to do the rest." As much as he wished to accommodate his friend, he dared not promise to do more.[13]

Although Woodrow turned a deaf ear during these years to the promptings of Jameson, he definitely was interested in the study of history. Moreover, he had some ideas on how American history should be written. In May, 1895, he delivered an address before the New Jersey Historical Society on "The Course of American History." As an example of Wilson's philosophy of history, this speech is significant.

[10]Philadelphia *Times,* February 5, 1894.

[11]Apparently this letter has been lost but Wilson's reply of November 11, 1895, mentions the letter.

[12]Wilson to J. Franklin Jameson, November 11, 1895, in Jameson Papers, Library of Congress.

[13]Wilson to J. Franklin Jameson, January 8, 1897, in *ibid.*

Speaking before a group that was especially interested in local history, the lecturer began by noting that the history of a nation was "only the history of its villages written large." [14] Wilson was frequently disappointed that local historians did not see more in the stories they sought to tell. True, national history had its own spreading patterns which could be seen only when the cloth was laid before the public in broad surfaces, but the individual threads of the fabric were found solely in local history. In the community, Wilson declared, was "all the intricate weaving, all the delicate shading, all the nice requirement of the pattern,—gold threads mixed with fustian, fine thread laid upon coarse, shade combined with shade." It was this that gave local history its importance.

From the neighborhood level, Wilson went to sectional interests. He told his audience that he regretted the neglect of the South and West and predicted that both areas would soon have interpreters of their contributions to the national life. American history written by New Englanders "smacked strongly of local flavor." The Princeton professor asserted that the local history of New York, New Jersey, and Pennsylvania—the middle section—was much more structurally a part of the characteristic life of the nation as a whole than was the history of the New England community or the local history of the southern region. Such ideas were contrary to accepted doctrine and by some would be branded as rank heresy, but Wilson contended that the ideas were true.

Although the frontier was practically gone in 1895, the speaker dwelt at length on its earlier influence. The frontier created among its inhabitants "that openness to every thought of enterprise or adventure, that nomadic habit which knows no fixed home and has plans ready to be carried any whither." [15]

When *Forum* editor Walter Hines Page urged Wilson to send an essay for publication, he revised his speech on "The Course of American History." In sending it to Page, Wilson wrote that this paper contained his creed as a historian.[16] With the title changed

[14]Woodrow Wilson, "The Course of American History," *Mere Literature and Other Essays* (Boston, 1900), 213–47.

[15]*Ibid.*

[16]Wilson to Walter H. Page, May 20, 1895, in Baker Papers, Library of Congress.

to "The Proper Perspective of American History," the essay appeared in the July, 1895, issue.[17]

The West was the great work in American history, said the author, and the westerner was the type and master of American life. However, the geographic frontier was lost, and the westerner would soon pass out of existence. Then a new epoch would open in which Americans would study the "delicate adjustments of an intricate society and ponder the niceties . . . of government." The new life of the West all the while reacted upon the old life of the East; yet the East molded the West. From the East the West drew aptitudes, strength, thought, and training, while the East's youth was renewed from the West's fountain of alert, fresh, vital origination. This great process, noted Wilson, was distinctively a national process. The interchange between these regions of ideas, purposes, and principles "constituted the moving force of our life as a nation." [18]

Wilson formulated his historical philosophy during the early era of the scientific school. As he expressed it in "The Truth of the Matter," the injunction to the historian was "give us the facts, and nothing but the facts." [19] This was an eminently reasonable requirement and one that the historian must adhere to or have himself placed in "a very undesirable class of persons." Because of the complexities of revealing the whole truth the historian was selecting that part of the truth most suitable to his taste and his talents and relating only that. Wilson described these historians as ones "full of the piquant details of personal biography, histories that blaze with the splendors of courts and histories that run upon the humbler but greater levels of the life of the people; colorless histories, so passionless and so lacking in distinctive mark or motive that they might have been set up out of a dictionary without the intervention of an author, and partisan histories, so warped and violent in every judgment that no reader not of the historian's own party can stomach them; histories of economic development, and histories that speak only of politics; those that tell nothing but

[17]Woodrow Wilson, "The Proper Perspective of American History," *Forum,* XIX (July, 1895), 544–59.

[18]*Ibid.*

[19]Woodrow Wilson, *Mere Literature and Other Essays,* 161–86.

what it is pleasant and interesting to know, and those that tell nothing at all that one cares to remember." [20]

According to Wilson, the historian must base his writing upon original research in authentic records; however, history could not be constructed by piecing together bits of original research any more than it could be written by the reprinting of state documents. By themselves, documents were "wholly out of perspective." Ordinarily, Wilson thought, the historian went about his task in the wrong way. With infinite care and admirable labor, he did meticulous research in documents. He then collected masses of details "for substance, verification, illustration." With notes piled high and with many pages of references he began his narrative, "thoroughly stuffed and sophisticated." Under such circumstances, it was impossible that he should begin naturally. The historian, Wilson thought, then became not "like one who tells a story so much as like one who dissects a cadaver." By having at his fingertips too much knowledge, he broke the spell for his imagination and marred his ability to "raise again the image of the days that are gone." The real drama of life could only be disclosed by revealing the whole picture "in authentic colors of nature." [21]

Some months later the Princeton professor published an article, "The Making of the Nation," in the *Atlantic Monthly*.[22] He wrote that two groups of American historians were in disagreement over the method of forming a united nation. One believed that the American people, through the "strong sentences of the law," were transformed immediately upon the ratification of the Constitution from a league of sovereign states into a people "single and inseparable." The second school saw the process of unionization as completed only with the emancipation of the slaves and the conclusion of the Civil War.

Wilson noted that throughout America's history the country had lain apart in sections. Each section marked a stage of developing nationalism as the people, by successive journeyings and en-

[20] *Ibid.*, 162–63.

[21] *Ibid.*, 170–85.

[22] Woodrow Wilson, "The Making of the Nation," *Atlantic Monthly*, LXXX (July, 1897), 1–14.

campments, migrated from East to West. The Constitution prohibited discrimination between sections or among the states. But Wilson observed that sectional differences were more marked and emphasized than ever before. The West by sheer growth had so altered its traits that it appeared to easterners as a region apart. He added, however, that there were currents of strong national life everywhere among the people. Although the country was of one mind in loyalty to the federal government and to the national idea, there was wide divergence of opinion as to what policies would best give strength and support to the national life.

Since the Civil War the South had joined with the West. In a similar stage of national development, they were like one region, "chiefly agricultural, without diversified industries, without a multifarious trade." Although there had never been a time in American history when there was no East or West, Wilson thought "the novel day when we shall be without them is now in sight." As the country grew older it would "inevitably grow homogenous."

In his writing, Wilson the devout Calvinist never strayed far from the Providential philosophy of historical interpretation: "Providence has presided over our affairs with a strange indulgence," he wrote. The making of the nation was not deliberately planned by the counsel of its leaders. However, as Wilson anticipated the needs of the country in the future, "the daily conduct and policy of a nation which has won its place of recognition in world affairs must be so planned." The great need, he wrote in conclusion, was to find a group of men, who represented the nation "in the origin and responsibility of their power." Such a group would bring the President, who directed foreign policies and who executed the laws, into a "cordial cooperation" with the Congress which sanctioned laws and policies.[23]

No one was more conscious than the Princeton professor that hitherto the nation had been devoted almost entirely to domestic development. At the close of the nineteenth century, finding that task roughly finished, she turned her attention outward towards

[23]*Ibid.*

the complex tasks of the world at large. As the United States found its place of power and position in the world a new age had dawned, "which no man may forecast." He firmly believed, however, that the key to the new age was the role America was destined to play—"the part of America lies at the center of modern history," he said.[24] By 1902 Wilson had become an internationalist.

In September, 1895, Wilson published an illuminating article, "On the Writing of History," in which he expressed some original ideas on the prerequisites for a successful writer of history.[25] "The unimpeachable first principle of right living," he wrote, was to tell the truth, and historians must always adhere to this principle. For the historian to relate the truth was not always an easy matter, because the truth was full of secret motives and shot through with transient passions and could never be reduced to statistics as newspaper items or officially recorded statements. The historian must have a keen eye for the truth, coupled with a vivid imagination. Even when the historian had seen the truth, the more difficult part was to so write the truth that others would see it as he had. Sometimes historians merely told the truth in part—the part most suitable to their taste and talents—and sought readers with similar tastes and talents.

Wilson believed that readers needed enlightenment as well as information; the historian should interpret as well as record. In addition to relating material facts, the function of the writer of history included relating moral facts. "Unquestionably every sentence of true history," the teacher contended, "must hold a judgment in solution."

Another of Wilson's criteria for the writing of history was that it be based upon original research and authentic record. The historian must know "good ore from bad; must distinguish fineness, quality, genuineness." A man of science as well as an artist, the writer of history must test carefully every bit of his material.

[24]Woodrow Wilson, "The Significance of American History," *Harper's Encyclopedia of United States History: From 458 A.D. to 1902* (New York, 1902), I.

[25]Woodrow Wilson, "On the Writing of History: With a Glance at the Methods of Macaulay, Gibbon, Carlyle and Green," *Century,* X (September, 1895), 787–93.

Once he had scrutinized it meticulously, he should "forget its origin and the dross from which it has been freed and think only and always of the great thing [he] would make of it."

Though Wilson was using most of his free hours to compile his thoughts on the matter of recording history, he did find time to deliver the commencement address at Oberlin College in the late spring of 1895. He chose the topic "Leaders of Men," revising a speech delivered originally at Knoxville for the University of Tennessee graduating class in 1890.[26] The oration was somewhat autobiographical. Now near the end of his first decade as a teacher, Wilson was experiencing an inner battle, seeking to find a way to reconcile his earliest ambitions with his profession. He wanted to be an active political leader, but was for the moment confined to gaining recognition through his teaching, lecturing, and writing.

In his speech Wilson noted that the perennial misunderstanding between the men who wrote and the men who acted had lain in the former's love of proportion and the other's neglect of proportion. The leader of action lacked certain sensibilities which the literary man had in an unusual degree. He was devoid of that "subtle power of sympathy which enabled the literary person to write fiction." The leader of men, Wilson felt, should have that sympathetic insight into the motives of men in mass. His main objective was to control, to dictate, to dominate. "Men are as clay," stated the speaker, "in the hands of the consummate leader."

If the leader of action would succeed, he must know the art of persuasion, a powerful force which could be exerted "by creeping into the confidence of those you would lead." Moreover, said Wilson, if one would lead he must lead his own generation, not the next. A man of words might be discovered by some later generation but not the man of action. Furthermore, if one would be "universally understood and numerously followed," he must emphasize the "unalloyed simplicity" of his principles. The popular idol, continued Wilson, must be satisfying to the eye as

[26] T. H. Vail Motter (ed.), *Leaders of Men by Woodrow Wilson* (Princeton, 1952).

well as to the ear. In addition to having a musical voice, he should be tall, sturdy, broad-shouldered, and clear-eyed. Daniel Webster, Henry Clay, John Bright, and Daniel O'Connell were men the professor described as having these physical traits.

Wilson believed that the question of leadership always received a practical test in a popularly elected legislative assembly. Revolutions throughout the modern world had brought forward a new type of leadership among legislators. The statesman must be adept at interpretation; he must know the common thought; he must calculate very carefully the preparation of the people for the next step forward in the pathway of progressive politics.

According to Wilson, political leadership consisted of the ability to discern and to strengthen the tendencies that make for national development. Practical leadership did not call to the slow masses of men from some dim pinnacle. It must feed daily on the bread of commonality; it must walk along the practical paths of simple understanding. "The forces of the public thought may be blind: he must lend them sight; they may blunder: he must set them right." The demagogue might see and seek self-interest, but not so the statesman. The demagogue thought only of the moment; the stateman was more obedient to the permanent minds of the public good. The former adjusted his sails to the breezes of the day, while the latter planned for the slow progress of the years. The one served himself and, possibly, a selfish interest group; the other ministered to his fellow man.

Wilson looked prophetically into his own future when he said that men who stood alone at the inception of a movement or cause and whose voices then seemed "the voices of men crying in the wilderness" were simply "the more sensitive organs of Society—the parts first awakened to consciousness of a situation." With the irritation of a rude and sudden summons from sleep, "Society resents the disturbance of its restful unconsciousness, and for a moment racks itself with hasty passion." But once completely aroused, concluded Wilson, Society would sanely meet the necessities of conduct revealed by the hour of its awakening.[27]

In addition to his essays and speaking engagements, Wilson

[27]*Ibid.*, 50.

worked on three books during the nineties. Although his historical works reveal no originality of interpretation, nor productive erudition, his writings have some significance. Perhaps undue importance has been attached to his historical works; but, since Wilson the maker of history cannot be divorced from Wilson the historian, his role as such deserves attention. The Princeton teacher's own definition of history is refreshing: "History is not a record of all the facts; that were impossible. It is order and combination with such colour and life as shall cause them, if possible, to make the same impression upon us as that they must have made on those who were actors in the midst of them." [28]

Wilson took up another writing task when he and Professor Reuben Thwaites of the University of Wisconsin were invited by Professor Albert B. Hart to contribute to a three-volume *Epochs of American History,* designed for the general reader as well as for the student. After three years of painstaking work, Wilson's volume in the series, *Division and Reunion: 1829–1889,* was completed and appeared in the spring of 1893. He was reviewed widely and generously. The New York *Sun* thought it the "most useful handbook in political history which has been published since the Civil War." Wilson, said the *Sun,* had demonstrated that the time had come to discuss American history without suppression of truth, and had done so "brilliantly and delightfully." [29] The New York *Tribune* saw "many delightful passages of real autobiography" in the book, though the "passages do not take that form of expression." The professor sometimes gave evidence of struggling for effect—and there was a fondness for weaving strange or obsolete words into the most ambitious sentences. The *Tribune* review added, "Wilson's preaching would be more effective after doing more practicing." [30] A South Carolina paper said the book contained an unusual amount of information, and a true insight into the southern character and mode of life.[31] The author successfully looked with the impartiality of an upright judge charging a jury, ventured another reviewer. The book con-

[28]Wilson to John F. Genung, May 30, 1900, in Wilson Collection, Princeton.

[29]New York *Sun,* March 12, 1893.

[30]New York *Tribune,* March 17, 1893.

[31]Aiken (S.C.) *Recorder,* May 26, 1893.

tained "admirable pen-portraits of the great personalities of the period," [32] but its greatest triumph was the "frankness and candor" with which it dealt with secession, the South, and slavery.[33]

Frederick Jackson Turner wrote that he was enthusiastic about *Division and Reunion.* "In style it is your most attractive work," the University of Wisconsin professor stated, "and in treatment judicial." Some of the chapters were "destined to live with the classics of our literature and history." With a promise to write more in detail later, Wilson's former pupil ventured one criticism. "You hold the doctrine of survival of state sovereignty in too absolute a form. The South did remain behind the procession of American advance, but she did not remain *preserved* by the ice of slavery like a Siberian mammoth. She changed greatly." Turner's final appraisal of *Division and Reunion* came some eighteen months later. After rereading the little book, he informed the author that it was at "once a contribution to knowledge and an example of the wedding of a good literary form to historical writing." [34]

Between Wilson's *Epoch* and his *History of the American People,* he wrote his only book-length biography. This volume, *George Washington,* first appeared serially in *Harper's.*[35] Having accepted a contract for the articles on Washington, the professor confided to Turner the circumstances: "It would not have occurred to my home-keeping mind to write a series for one of the vulgar-rich magazines, had it not been pressed upon me by the editor. It being proposed to me, however, 'on terms honorable to them and grateful to me', I could not be unmindful of the fact that I was building a house, which would certainly have to be paid for some time, and the sooner the better, and so I did." [36] In answering an inquiry, the Princeton professor made plain the nature of

[32]*University of North Carolina Magazine,* May, 1893, newspaper clipping in Wilson Papers, Library of Congress.

[33]Knoxville *Tribune,* August 21, 1893.

[34]Turner to Wilson, July 16, 1893, December 24, 1894, in Wilson Papers, Library of Congress.

[35]Henry M. Alden to Wilson, June 28, 1895, in *ibid.,* contains the terms of agreement.

[36]Wilson to Turner, November 11, 1895, in Turner Papers, Harvard.

these biographical articles—"to make Washington real and thoroughly human to the imagination." [37]

With only slight revision, the articles were published in book form late in 1896. Contemporaneously with Wilson's *George Washington,* Paul L. Ford's *The True George Washington* appeared. Reviewers compared and contrasted the two biographies with the laurels going to Ford. Ford's book was more scholarly, more objective, more factual. The Princeton professor's book was more an epic or historical novel, written from the literary artist's point of view.[38] The critics saw Ford as the realist and Wilson as the idealist.

Just when Wilson first conceived the idea of writing a history of the United States is not known. In the summer of 1893 when he wrote Turner of the proposed work, the latter replied: "Let

[37]Wilson to John D. Adams, December 20, 1895, in Baker Papers, Library of Congress.

[38]An interesting indication of Wilson's success as a writer can be found in the statements from his publishers:

Sales January 1, 1897 to June 30, 1897

D. C. Heath and Company				
413 copies of *The State*	@	10%	49.56	
151 copies of *State & Federal Govt.*	@	10%	6.04	55.60
Harper and Brothers				
3,175 copies *George Washington*	@	15%	1,428.75	1,428.75
Houghton Mifflin & Company				
135 *Congressional Government*	@	12½%	16.88	
274 *Mere Literature*	@	15%	41.10	57.98
				$1,542.33

(See D. C. Heath to Wilson, July 1, 1897; Harper and Brothers to Wilson, July 31, 1897; Houghton Mifflin & Company to Wilson, July 31, 1897; all in Wilson Papers, Library of Congress. Statements from Longmans, Green and Company for sales and royalties on Wilson's *Division and Reunion* and from Charles Scribners' Sons for *An Old Master* were not located. Royalties from his writings must have approximated $2,000 during the first half of 1897. During the last six months of the year sales were off slightly. Early in 1898, *The State* was revised and a total of 1,103 copies of the new edition were sold by June 30. Furthermore, revision plans were made for the *Epochs of American History Series.* Sales of that series would eventually exceed 100,000 copies.

(See D. C. Heath & Co. to Wilson, August 1, 1898; Albert B. Hart to Wilson, June 7, 1897; Longmans, Green & Company to Wilson, October 16, 1897, all in Wilson Papers, Library of Congress. Heath and Company sold 1,963 copies of *The State* from January to July, 1899. See D. C. Heath and Company to Wilson, August 1, 1899, in *ibid.*)

me say now simply that I am delighted to learn that you contemplate a history of the United States. I believe no one is so well qualified to do for us what Richard Green did for England and I shall be glad to be of any service." [39] "I devoutly pray that my history," Wilson informed his former student, "may be what you expect; and it heartens me greatly that you expect such grand things of it. But, oh, it goes hard!" If what made hard writing made easy reading, "it ought to go with a most excellent relish on the palates" of the public.[40]

Although the work was so near its beginning that Wilson did not want it mentioned widely, he did admit that he was writing a history of the United States similar to J. R. Green's *Short History of the English People.* Its composition would take several years and would be the professor's one absorbing occupation, for he would "not be content without examining most of the sources" himself.[41] When Walter Hines Page requested that the author submit the manuscript to Houghton Mifflin Company, Wilson replied that the completion of the work was several years away. Moreover, he wanted to indulge himself in "the luxury of writing quite without promises made to anybody about the work, as slowly, as fast, as voluminously, as briefly," as he pleased, as if there were no publishers, and he was writing the thing for himself alone.[42]

Wilson was urged to write his short history for publication in *Harper's Magazine* in 1901. It would appear in the magazine in twelve parts which *Harper's* would subsequently publish as a book. The author would receive $1,000 for each installment and 15 per cent royalty on retail price of all books sold.[43] Beginning in June, 1900, the Princeton professor dispatched his history, in

[39]Turner to Wilson, July 16, 1893, in *ibid.*

[40]Wilson to Turner, December 27, 1894, in Turner Papers, Harvard.

[41]Wilson to Walter Hines Page, May 20, 1895, in Baker Papers, Library of Congress.

[42]Page to Wilson, October 20, 1895, in Wilson Papers, Library of Congress; Wilson to Page, October 24, 1895, in Baker Papers, Library of Congress.

[43]Henry M. Alden to Wilson, January 9, 1900, in Wilson Papers, Library of Congress.

sections, to *Harper's*. Upon reading the first part, editor Henry Alden wrote that it was all that could be desired, and added that he hoped the publisher could do his part as well as the author had done his.[44]

In 1901 when the completed manuscript arrived at *Harper's*, the publishers were elated: "We are so impressed with the importance and charm of your work that, after careful consideration, we have concluded best to issue it first in four volumes with a subscription edition of Green's *History of England*." [45] When the publisher suggested several titles, the author rejected all of them and suggested *A History of the American People*.[46]

Wilson's history appeared in 1902. The author on at least two subsequent occasions explained why he wrote the book. "I was guilty myself of the indiscretion of writing a history," he confessed in 1909, "but I will tell you frankly . . . that I wrote it, not to instruct anybody else, but to instruct myself. I wrote the history of the United States in order to learn it." [47] After the author became President he reiterated this thought: "At one time I tried to write history. I did not know enough to write it, but I knew from experience how hard it was to find an historian out, and I trusted I would not be found out." [48]

From these two statements can be drawn a conclusion in evaluating Wilson's history. That the Princeton professor learned much about his own country in the writing of his book, no one doubts. That the writer could have been more familiar with the primary sources, the mainsprings of American history, is obvious to the fellow craftsman who carefully reads the *History of the American People*. Written in an intriguing style, it greatly enhanced the author's reputation as a popular writer, but in no

[44]Alden to Wilson, July 12, 1900, in *ibid.* The first of twelve checks for $1,000 was enclosed for Part I of the history.

[45]Harper and Brothers to Wilson, May 8, 1901, in *ibid.*

[46]Harper and Brothers to Wilson, December 5, 1901, and Wilson to Harper and Brothers, December 7, 1901, in *ibid.*

[47]Woodrow Wilson, *Robert E. Lee: An Interpretation* (Chapel Hill, 1924), 22–23. The speech was given on January 19, 1909.

[48]Woodrow Wilson, "Militant Christianity," in Baker and Dodd (eds.), *Public Papers of Woodrow Wilson: New Democracy* (New York, 1926), I, 199–209. The address was to a YMCA celebration in Pittsburgh, October 24, 1914.

sense did it measure up to its model—Green's *History of the English People.*[49]

Professor Turner thought his former teacher was "the first Southern scholar of adequate training and power to deal with American history as a whole in a continental spirit." [50] Although fortunate in adequate training and gifted in literary expressive power, Wilson dealt gently and generously with his native Southland. For example, more than five pages were devoted to the operations of the Ku Klux Klan—more text space than was given to Jay's Treaty of 1794, the conspiracy of Aaron Burr, the achievements of Decatur in the Mediterranean Sea, and the Missouri Compromise all combined.[51]

As busy as Wilson was with writing and lecturing, he never lost sight of his plan to have Turner as a colleague at Princeton. Because of his writings, especially his essay on "The Significance of the Frontier in American History," Turner reached national distinction almost overnight. In 1896, when Wilson endeavored to salvage enough money from the increased gifts to Princeton for a chair of American history, he recalled the pledge made to himself and wrote his former pupil. "I have told you before," said Wilson, "how much I desired you for a colleague and now I wish to give substantial proof of that purpose." [52]

The University of Wisconsin professor immediately answered at great length. Princeton was an institution with which any man would be proud to be connected, and to have Wilson as a colleague would give him the greatest personal satisfaction, Turner said. But he had made his field of study western history—especially the frontier—and as he grew older he thought he should become more influential. There were so few scholars doing research and writing in that field, he told Wilson, that to have them diminished by one would be regrettable. All his life he had lived in the West and loved it. Against such strong ties as these Turner made long

[49]Stockton Axson, "The Literary Historian," *Rice Institute Pamphlet,* XXII (1935), 262.

[50]Quoted in Michael Kraus, *A History of American History* (New York, 1937), 461.

[51]Marjorie L. David, "Woodrow Wilson—Historian," *Mississippi Valley Historical Review,* XXI (June, 1934–March, 1935), 361–74.

[52]Wilson to Turner, November 5, 1896, in Turner Papers, Harvard.

counterarguments, and he bombarded Woodrow with many questions about conditions at Princeton. Wilson confessed that the weakest link in Princeton's educational chain was the library. Until a new building could be constructed and amply shelved with books, Turner would have to follow him to the Lenox Library in New York for his research. With the creation of the chair in American history, there would be a special fund for purchasing needed books. Turner was assured that he could continue his study of the middle region and add thereto studies in the back country of the South. This region, said Wilson, was as rich in possibilities as any and was crying out for reconstructive writing.[53]

Turner was a bit uneasy about the acceptance of his religious faith at Princeton: "Of course I am no radical or propagandist, but my sympathies are in the Unitarian direction." [54] No religious test, Wilson replied, was ever applied at Princeton but all were anxious that every instructor should be earnestly religious.[55] When Wilson discussed with several professors the possibility of adding a scholar who was a Unitarian to the faculty he found unsuspected opposition from a stubborn source in Professor Andrew F. West. This fact he did not reveal to Turner.

Princeton society, the Wisconsin professor learned from Wilson's letter, was in no disagreeable sense exclusive. Newcomers need have no fear that they would be received otherwise than most cordially. "Schools for children: Ah! there's the rub!" confessed the Princeton professor. Adequate schools did not exist in the community, at least not for girls. The Wilsons were puzzled as to what to do with their bright daughters, so far as a school was concerned. Thus far, Ellen Wilson had taught them at home. Living costs were rather high.[56]

With Wilson's statement of rents and provisions before him, the University of Wisconsin professor concluded that there was no financial gain involved in his moving. Wilson then informed his friend at Madison that Princeton needed a man in European

[53]Wilson to Turner, November 15, 1896, in *ibid.*

[54]Turner to Wilson, November 8, 1896, in Wilson Papers, Library of Congress.

[55]Wilson to Turner, November 15, 1896, in Turner Papers, Harvard.

[56]*Ibid.*

history in addition to an American historian, and Turner's attitude changed at once. In the strongest terms possible he informed Wilson of Professor Charles Haskins' virtues as a scholar and a teacher. He would consider the fact that he and Haskins were to continue together as one of the most attractive elements in any proposal to go elsewhere.

With sadness, however, Wilson wrote Turner that the Board of Trustees had rejected his plans for the creation of a department of history. In fact, there was likely to be less money for expenses the next year than the current year. The department head was chagrined with the sudden timidity of the Princeton trustees. Would not Turner be patient, hold the matter under advisement until he could wring something out of the board? "Our President," confided Wilson, "does not bolster us by having a mistaken policy; he daunts us by having no will or policy at all." [57]

On December 29, 1896, Turner's paper, "The West as a Field for Historical Study," was read before the American Historical Association meeting in New York by Professor Haskins. At the conclusion of the paper, Wilson arose. Amid the applause of the audience, he spoke of Turner as one who gained "the affection of every student of history" because he was not afraid of the "horrid industry of his task." To those in the audience from educational institutions located along the Atlantic seaboard, Wilson pointedly stated that all must get used to the idea that they did not constitute the nation there on the eastern coast, unpleasant though the thought might be.[58]

Back at Princeton, the professor continued his fight in behalf of Turner's admission to the faculty, but eventually was forced to admit defeat. Turner consoled his former teacher over the outcome of their correspondence. He admitted that Princeton, as portrayed by his former teacher, seemed very attractive, and in addition the prospect of having Wilson for a colleague would have made a very difficult choice for him "for my library and our lakes are pretty strong grappling hooks here." Nor was Turner willing for Haskins to leave either—for Princeton or elsewhere. "Perhaps it was after all a ladylike act in the fates to

[57] Wilson to Turner, December 15, 1896, in *ibid.*

[58] *American Historical Association Report* (1896), I, 281–87, 292–96.

settle it for me first and I value the incident as a proof of your regard." [59]

In the battle for Turner's appointment Wilson fought alone. Because of Turner's Unitarian faith, Professor West vigorously opposed bringing him to Princeton. It is likely that West expressed his views to President Patton and possibly to some members of the Board of Trustees. If so, this was the first battle of the Wilson–West Princeton war. Definitely, West was the winner. Wilson and Turner were not destined ever to teach in the same university, but they continued to be fast friends.

In this study of Wilson's historical writings he does not emerge as an outstanding historian. In fairness to him it should be admitted that in no sense did he consider himself a professional historian. He simply used his facile pen to write popular books. Whether or not his histories would command the serious attention of modern historians if their author had not himself earned a place in history is a question which can never be answered.

[59] Turner to Wilson, April 3, 1897, in Wilson Papers, Library of Congress.

CHAPTER XIV The Author

Wilson did most of his writing during the years in which he was a full professor. Although his first article was published in the *International Review* as early as 1879 and his *Congressional Government* appeared in 1885, before he began teaching, most of his publications were confined to the seventeen years that he commanded the classroom; then he had more time for writing.[1] Anything that Woodrow Wilson did he did wholeheartedly, frequently pursuing the task at hand so enthusiastically that he overtaxed his strength. His role as a writer was no exception.

Since the fruits of Wilson's pen in the early years of his teaching have been discussed briefly, the narrative here will include only an account of the writing that appeared in the last decade of

[1]Wilson published two articles, "Prince Bismark" and "William Earl Chatham," while a student at Princeton. Both of these articles appeared in the *Nassau Literary Magazine* (November, 1877, and October, 1878), a campus student publication.

his professorship. Within this ten-year span Wilson continued to discuss political science and worked on presenting his ideas in literary essays. He was ambitious for distinction as a writer and dealt with his material, said an English critic, "with a vigorous and comprehensive mind, fine literary culture, high ideals, and a broad, sympathetic humanity." [2]

Within the field of political writing, the professor was greatly influenced by an early and continuing interest in the ideas of such men as Walter Bagehot, who had for Wilson "a great and enduring fascination," [3] Edmund Burke, and William Gladstone. When his political essays were slanted towards economic issues, as they sometimes were, the influences of John Bright and Richard Cobden, England's great nineteenth-century champions of laissez faire and free trade, were obvious. Nor can one omit mention of Adam Smith's views on the proper relations between the economy and the polity, as expressed in his *Wealth of Nations*. According to one of Wilson's students, the professor was quite interested in the ideas held by America's founding fathers, and in the principles which they set forth in their writings; especially was this true of the Virginia statesmen.[4]

Once Wilson had published *Congressional Government* and *The State* in the field of political science, his further works in this area were essays. "Wilson began as an essayist," noted Bliss Perry, a Princeton colleague, "and it is as an essayist that his most distinguished writing has been done." [5]

In April, 1893, near the beginning of Grover Cleveland's second term as President, Wilson published an essay in the *Review of Reviews* on the Chief Executive's cabinet.[6] He stated that there was "much to arrest attention" in the men that composed Cleve-

[2]William Archer, "President Wilson As a Man of Letters," *Fortnightly Review,* CIX (January–June, 1918), 250–75.

[3]Wilson to Charles F. Bead, March 3, 1891, in Wilson Collection, Princeton.

[4]Frederic C. Howe, *The Confessions of a Reformer* (New York, 1925), 6.

[5]Bliss Perry, *Praise of Folly and Other Papers* (Boston, 1923), 152–67; Perry, "Woodrow Wilson As a Man of Letters," *Century,* LXXV (March, 1913), 753–57.

[6]Woodrow Wilson, "Mr. Cleveland's Cabinet," *Review of Reviews,* VII (1893), 286–97.

land's official family, a judgment others were to make in the spring of 1913 of President Wilson's cabinet. Cleveland, a typical American in whom, to quote Wilson, "his countrymen believe without always knowing why," chose his cabinet upon the premise that at moments of lethargy the government needed an infusion of new blood.

In analyzing the group, the Princeton professor declared that, with the exception of Richard Olney, a scholar, all were practical men like the President, whose minds were formed by experience rather than by books. Moreover, all of them, except David S. Lamont, were trained lawyers. Two, John G. Carlisle and Hilary A. Herbert, had years of public service as members of Congress. As practical men, Wilson said, they would overcome difficulties, including ignorance of their duties in their respective departments. The politicians who were frequently surprised by Cleveland's acts were dumbfounded by his cabinet choices, but young men were eager to serve the President. "A Democratic party of young men is the most formidable danger the Republicans have to fear—the best hope that the Democrats have to cherish."

Wilson saw the appointment of Herbert as Secretary of the Navy in the same light as he had viewed the naming of L. Q. C. Lamar as Secretary of the Interior eight years earlier. Both men had been leaders in the Confederacy and their appointments to serve as cabinet members in the very government which they had sought earlier to destroy was an eloquent testimony to the "healing and amalgamating force of a fair fight and of the sovereign determinations of policy under free institutions!"

From the discussion of cabinet personnel the writer shifted to a philosophical analysis and asked what *was* the cabinet? The question could not be answered from the Constitution itself. The Princeton professor contended that the Constitution was a vehicle of life, its chief virtue being that it was not too rigidly conceived. The President, who was the real party leader, could dominate the cabinet; nevertheless, it was impossible for him to make all the decisions affecting the executive departments. Wilson contended that the Presidency was inevitably put into the hands of a sort of commission, with the President as the directing head. Wilson when President, however, did not retain this commission concept of the executive branch.

Again Wilson expressed himself in favor of the English system of fusion between the executive and the legislative branches of government. Presidents should be encouraged through the pressure of public opinion to appoint to the cabinet "representative party men who have accredited themselves for such positions by long and honorable careers in public service." The professor saw in Washington a complete separation between the executive and the legislative branches of the government with each extremely jealous of its prerogatives. This condition would have dire consequences, unless remedied by a "harmonious, consistent, responsible party government instead of a wide dispersion of function and responsibility." The only way to achieve the ideal result, Wilson said, was to connect the President as closely as possible with his congressional party leaders.[7]

Four years later, as Cleveland's second term drew to a close, Editor Page invited Wilson to prepare an article, "Mr. Cleveland as President," for the *Atlantic Monthly*.[8] The evaluation of the first post-Civil War Democratic President by the teacher who was destined to become the second Democrat to occupy the White House after 1865 is worthy of notice. In assessing merit and in pointing out Cleveland's limitations, Wilson made plain his own ideas concerning the Presidency. He wrote unknowingly, but prophetically, about himself.

According to the professor, Cleveland was the sort of President the framers of the Constitution had in mind in that he was more a servant of the people than a colleague of the Congress, more an independent magistrate than a partisan leader.[9] As Wilson was to do later, Cleveland had broken many of the ordinary rules of politics. Despite his previous experience as mayor of Buffalo and as governor of New York, the President came almost as a

[7]*Ibid.*

[8]Walter Hines Page to Wilson, December 3, 1896, in Baker Papers, Library of Congress. Wrote Page to Wilson: "Any price you name is reasonable and satisfactory."

[9]Woodrow Wilson, "Mr. Cleveland As President," *Atlantic Monthly*, LXXIX (1897), 289–300.

political novice upon the national scene. Although he was known as a party man, Cleveland could not stomach many of the processes of party management. He had not sought, nor would Wilson seek, public office as a lifetime career. Each knew that the Democratic party could best be served by courage and integrity. According to Wilson, Cleveland realized that the American people loved a bold man, one who faced the fight without too much thought of himself or of his party's fortune.

In Cleveland, the party bosses saw a man with whom they could win. In neither Cleveland's case nor Wilson's did the managers understand the latent elements in their choice's power. The President did not seem to regard politics as a distinct science, set apart from the ordinary business of life. In the three executive offices which Cleveland had held, he served as if he were president of a giant corporation, "with incidental social functions," in the interest of all of the people who, as stockholders in the business, were vitally interested in its welfare.

All Democratic elements united in electing Cleveland because they wished a business-like administration more than they wanted any upsetting of old policies. They chose him, as they were to take Wilson later, because he was a certain winner rather than because he was an acceptable master. In Cleveland, the Princeton teacher saw no foundation for the fear that as President he would "arrogate to himself the prerogatives of political leadership, or assume the role of guide or mentor in matters of policy."

The President, wrote Wilson, "possessed an enormous capacity for work, shirked no detail of his busy function, carried the government steadily upon his shoulders." When Cleveland was bitterly assailed he went serenely about his work; many marvelled at his steadfastness during the storm of criticism. For a season the President endeavored to play the role of simple executive. Watching his party cut to pieces by factional quarrels on the tariff question, however, he could not stand idly by and "let a great opportunity and a great duty go by default." Wilson felt that the President stood at the very center of legislation as well as of administration, and when the latter realized this, he placed the mantle of party leadership about his broad shoulders.

In the realm of foreign affairs, Cleveland proved himself to be a very strong man, although he was no diplomat. He satisfied neither the Democrats nor the Republicans, and showed himself to be a man without a party. Never was the President so much alone as in the campaign of 1896. Wilson's final appraisal judged Cleveland to be the greatest personality on the political scene since Lincoln. When the professor dispatched this essay to the *Atlantic Monthly,* he confided to his diary that the article was "much too hastily done to be either toned, judged, or written well: it is too distinctly hack work, and yet I am certain of my deliberate and veritable judgment of the man." [10]

Five articles from Wilson's pen appeared over the Charles Scribner's Sons imprint in 1893 under the title *An Old Master and Other Political Essays.*[11] The first two of these essays—"An Old Master" and "The Study of Politics"—had been published earlier in the *New Princeton Review,* a campus periodical that gave faculty and students an outlet for their literary manuscripts. The fourth and fifth chapters—"Character of Democracy in the United States" and "Government Under the Constitution"—had appeared in the *Atlantic Monthly.* Only the middle essay—"Political Sovereignty"—was making its initial appearance.

This book, said the Boston *Beacon,* showed how "agreeable the study of political topics may be under the guidance of an intelligent thinker and an accomplished writer"; it was "graceful, yet forceful in expression." [12] According to the *Nation,* Wilson wrote with a facile pen when some people, at least, thought that the subjects of these essays demanded "a cautious pen which would record only guarded utterances." [13]

By no means did all of the reviews praise *The Old Master,* however. Even close friends wrote to express independent opinion

[10]Woodrow Wilson "Diary," January 15, 1896, in Wilson Papers, Library of Congress; Wilson, "Mr. Cleveland As President," 289–300.

[11]In other articles and speeches during these years Wilson expressed himself in the general area of political science. Because the article contained much that was history, rather than political science, it was thought best to reveal Wilson's concepts of history in "The Making of the Nation." The address—"Leaderless Government"—was probably his greatest oration before a professional off-campus group during the years of his professional period at Princeton. See Wilson, "The Making of the Nation," 1–14, and *Leaderless Government.*

[12]Boston *Beacon,* October 21, 1893.

[13]*Nation,* LVIII (January 4, 1894), 18.

about some of Wilson's conclusions, among them Frederick Jackson Turner. While writing of his delight in reading the small volume, Turner stated: "I cannot so entirely agree with your essay on sovereignty; though you put your thesis deftly and I may reach your conclusions as an acquired taste." [14]

In "An Old Master," the essayist wrote of Adam Smith, who in the eighteenth century became a leader in that science which tells how "other people's affairs should be managed, how the world's affairs are managed." Wilson summarized the Glasgow teacher's talents: "With the true instinct of the orator and teacher, Adam Smith saw what every one must see . . . that clearness, force, and beauty of style are absolutely necessary to one who would draw men to his way of thinking." [15]

In "The Study of Politics" the author reasoned that the great treatises on government revealed an exhaustive knowledge of statutes, of judicial precedents, and of legal and constitutional history; yet they were tacitly ignorant of anything more than this "gaunt skeleton of institutions." Although the author did not contend that all practical politicians would make the best instructors, he did state that frequently the active statesman was an "incomparable teacher." With no thought of being didactic, the statesman had a heart full of the high purpose of leading his fellow countrymen to do those things which he felt to be right.[16]

Politics was the very life of the state, and nothing that illustrated that life came amiss in the study of politics. Moreover, regardless of the point of view from which man was studied, he was always a political animal. The successful student of politics, the professor contended, should supplement the study of books with travel and observation. In order really to know anything about government one must see it alive. The object of the political writer should be to make government live again upon his page.[17]

Wilson began the most controversial essay of his book by giving

[14]Frederick Jackson Turner to Wilson, December 20, 1893, in Wilson Papers, Library of Congress. In all probability, Turner would have expressed himself more independently had he not been writing to a former teacher and a staunch friend.

[15]Woodrow Wilson, *An Old Master and Other Political Essays* (New York, 1893), 21.

[16]*Ibid.,* 34–39.

[17]*Ibid.,* 43–57, *passim.*

a popular definition of political sovereignty: "a person or body of persons existing in an independent political society and accorded the habitual obedience of the bulk of the members of society, while itself subordinate to no political superior." Americans maintained that popular sovereignty rested with the people. The people, however, acted always in state groups. In this capacity they accepted or rejected constitutional amendments, selected lawmakers, judges, or executive officials. They never chose policies, nor did they frame constitutional provisions.

Some argued that sovereignty was in the supreme powers of governing rather than in the relations of the people to those powers. If considered in the first light, Wilson said, sovereignty was originative and directive; it planned and it executed. Regardless of how sovereignty might be considered, it was always dependent upon "the temper and disposition of the people." In a democracy the desires of the body politic as a whole were always the foundation, as they were also in many instances "the direct and immediate source of law."

The professor did not deny the power of the people. They conditioned the action of those who governed and it was well that they did. Sovereignty, he wrote, was "the highest political power in the state, lodged in active organs, for the purposes of governing." Sovereign power, a positive thing, belonged to government and was lodged in organs of initiative. On the other hand, control, a negative matter, was lodged with the voters. The executive, the professor contended, was not the organ but the agent of sovereignty.

According to Wilson, law seldom originated in command, but resulted from the heterogeneous activities of the community, including its struggles, class against class, interest against interest, pressure groups against pressure groups. It was the by-product of the communities' many compromises and adjustments of opinion. The sovereign organ of the state, the Princetonian thought, was very properly its law-*making* organ.[18]

Written constitutions, said Wilson in his last essay of the series, were simply more or less successful generalizations of political experience. Written law was not more valid nor more sacred than

[18]*Ibid.*, 64–96, *passim.*

unwritten law, only more explicit, more definite and secure. Laws, including constitutions, had no other life than that given them by administration and obedience. The Constitution proved beneficial not because it was written, but because it was in accord with principles of government tested and approved by the people for which the Constitution was intended.

The Constitution was definite, "preserved by very formidable difficulties of amendment against inconsiderable change." The great strength which preserved the constitutional system was the strength of self-restraint. Moreover, "the grace of self-restraint" of the federal government, through its courts, had preserved the integrity of the powers of the states. While admitting that the federal courts had generally held Congress back from aggression upon the states, Wilson declared there was no *balance* between the state and federal governments.[19]

In the 1880's—when Wilson penned his article—Congress held a central place in government. It possessed the whole energy of origination; it was the single affirmative voice in national policy; it determined everything that was done. Congress was restrained only by the Constitution and by public opinion. It was within the power of Congress, Wilson contended, to overwhelm the opposition of the Supreme Court upon any question by merely increasing the number of justices and confirming only those who promised to change the opinion of the court.[20]

The writer pointed out that Congress distributed its powers among groups of its members in the form of standing committees and in this way confused its plans and obscured its responsibility. Was democracy so delicate a form of government that it would break down if given "too great facility or efficacy of operation?" Wilson strongly condemned the congressional practice of framing and initiating legislation by secret deliberations of committees whose proposals were seldom debated.

In its composition, Congress was the country in miniature. Although it was watched closely, its clandestine actions and confusing methods made it the object of widespread distrust. And as long as Congress continued to be governed by committees it

[19]*Ibid.,* 141–47, *passim.*
[20]*Ibid.,* 148–69, *passim.*

would remain the object of public distrust. To remedy this undesirable situation, Wilson urged integration. First, the preparation and initiation of all legislation should be placed in a single committee of each house, composed of the leading men of the majority in that house. Second, a common meeting-ground of public consultation needed to be established between the Chief Executive and the Congress. Third, only by conferring upon members of the President's cabinet some degree of ministerial responsibility did Wilson believe such integration to be possible. If important amendments to the Constitution became necessary, such changes in the constitutional system would not be too great a price to pay for the advantages secured by such a government.[21]

In any evaluation of Wilson as a writer, his ideas on states' rights cannot be ignored. A native of the section most vocal on this confusing issue, his opinions are of concern and importance. The professor's thorough discussion of the states' relations with the federal government in his textbook—*The State*—has been noted. Published in 1889, this treatise was widely used in the classroom before Wilson came to Princeton. In at least two essays, one published in England and the other in America, he came to grips with the question of states' rights, showing the contrasting influence and power of states' rights as a political issue during the decade before the Civil War and during the period of Reconstruction. The first essay, entitled "State Rights 1850–1860," was written for the *Cambridge Modern History* and appeared in its volume on the United States.[22] The central theme of this article was slavery, which Wilson dealt with on a state basis as expressed through members of the various state congressional delegations.

Slavery made the southern states unlike other states; it created a leisure class of men dedicated to *noblesse oblige*. From the beginning of the Revolution to the Age of Jackson this class of southerners led the nation. No one could deny that the states which composed the South had played a part in the central gov-

[21]*Ibid.*, 170–81, *passim*.

[22]Woodrow Wilson, "States' Rights, 1850–1860," in A. W. Ward, G. W. Prothero, and Stanley Leathers (eds.), *Cambridge Modern History,* VII (1902–1924), 405–42.

ernment which was altogether out of proportion to her importance in wealth or population.

Soon, however, the southern states were standing still while the rest of the nation grew away from them. When the South failed to develop the type of labor demanded in factories, she could not compete with northern states in industrialization. The slave states could not rival the free states in opening up territories in the expanding West, if southerners were prohibited from carrying their slaves with them into the new territories. Wilson saw, as John C. Calhoun had seen earlier, that through the protective tariff the southern states were paying for the maintenance of manufactures in the North.

Calhoun, said Wilson, did not originate the doctrine of states' rights. Expression was given to states' rights in the nullification theory in both South Carolina and in the New England states before Calhoun spoke of it. Whereas others had used it as a means of protest, the South Carolinian used it as a statesman's fundamental tenet and a premise for legal demonstration. According to Calhoun the federal union was composed of states; the people had identity with the union only through the states. The people had no citizenship except that of the state in which they resided, and they acted in the union not as a composite nation but separately in their respective community states as co-equal and associated commonwealths. Moreover, Calhoun deemed the Supreme Court of the United States unsuited to determine matters of states' rights because it was an agency of the very government whose powers were in dispute. Although the South Carolinian, the greatest exponent of states' rights the country produced, was accused of presenting "new and dangerous" doctrines, they were not novel. Only the logic of his reasoning was new.

According to Wilson, both the North and South approached the 1860 presidential election with great fear in their hearts. Both sections dreaded disunion. The southern states resented the jeopardy of their rights in excluding slaves from the national territories. The northern states feared the general ascendance of the slaveowning aristocracy. The issue was slavery; but, Wilson added, it need never have come to that had Stephen A. Douglas "kept his hand from the law."

To the South it was in finality a question of self-government. There were many men in the slave states who hated slavery but had a passion for self-government. The South fought for the principle of states' rights, the North for the preservation of the Union. "The principle for which the South fought meant standstill in the midst of change," Wilson wrote; "it was conservative, not creative; it was against drift and destiny; it protected an impossible institution and a belated order of society; it withstood a creative and imperial idea, the idea of a united people and a single law of freedom." [23]

In another essay, "The Reconstruction of the Southern States," which became the lead article in the January, 1901, issue of the *Atlantic Monthly*,[24] Wilson stated that laws which clothed cultural institutions must be loosely knit, allowing room for normal growth and healthful expansion. Reconstruction revealed a great rift which broke the continuity and thoroughness of constitutional development. Indeed, he wrote, the revolutionary forces of the post-Civil War period were much more formidable than those of the war itself. The effects of the war were temporary; the effects of the Reconstruction permanent.

The professor lauded Lincoln's statesmanship. The latter "never recognized any man who spoke or acted for the southern people in the matter of secession as the representative of any government whatever. It was not the southern states which had taken up arms against the Union, but merely the people dwelling within them," stated Wilson. Lincoln wanted to bring the southern people to submission and to restore allegiance, "to put them back defeated but not conquered or degraded, into the old-time hierarchy of the Union."

Lacking Lincoln's "insight, skill, or sweetness of temper," Johnson endeavored to lead by egotistically proclaimed power and vain self-assertions, Wilson wrote. Almost immediately he had Congress against him. The chief bone of contention was the lack of protection for the Negroes in their new rights as freemen. Johnson successfully pushed his program of reconstruction

[23] *Ibid.*

[24] Woodrow Wilson, "The Reconstruction of the Southern States," *Atlantic Monthly,* LXXXVII (1901), 1–15.

throughout 1865. The ratification of the Thirteenth Amendment was formally proclaimed in December with twenty-seven states assenting, of which eight had belonged to the Confederacy. Johnson made no demands upon the states about suffrage, stating they had rightfully exercised their free and independent choice "from the origin of the government to the present day."

The southern states were in a perilous condition, the author continued, created by the emancipation of the Negroes, who were a "laboring, lordless, homeless class . . . unpracticed in liberty, unschooled in self-control; never sobered by the discipline of self-support, never established in any habit of prudence; excited by a freedom they did not understand, exalted by false hopes; bewildered and without leaders, and yet insolent and aggressive; sick of work, covetous of pleasure—a host of dusky children untimely put out of school." It was not unnatural, Wilson thought, for the southern states to refuse these Negroes the right to vote.

Congress, accordingly, decided to take control of Reconstruction. Fortified by Republican and northern majorities in both houses and with southern representatives excluded, it began overriding Johnson's vetoes. For a decade thereafter the Congress, supported by an army of occupation, invaded the sphere of authority which, since the formation of the Union, had been known as the bastion of states' rights. The law of the Constitution had reigned supreme until that time. In that document were the rules by which the states were to live in "concert and union." There was not a word touching times of discord, disruption, or rebellion. The document was written for lawyers, not soldiers. The Civil War occurred when sentiment met sentiment, conviction met conviction, all of which were set deep in the emotions of the people where constitutions could neither originate nor limit, wrote Wilson. These conditions inevitably, perhaps, brought a "bitterness of death" to the defeated and a "dangerous intoxication" to the victors. The sentiment of nationalism, never before aroused to the full consciousness of its aspirations and power, was a new thing, aggressive and aware of its strength. The real revolution, Wilson warned, was not so much in the form as in the spirit of affairs—the spirit of a union of associated states had given way to the spirit of nationalism and of a new age. A government that had been federal became suddenly national in temper and point of view.

These great changes were as obvious on the federal level as on the state level. As long as the war lasted the President was master but subsequently Congress became the center of authority. The Thirteenth, Fourteenth, and Fifteenth Amendments bound the states equally. The states not drastically affected by them voluntarily ratified them, whereas the states revolutionized by them were under military rule and accepted them involuntarily.

True, the federal courts held that southern states were never out of the Union and justified congressional actions upon the grounds that the Constitution guaranteed to each state a republican form of government. Wilson argued that Congress went much further; it prescribed the suffrage for the reconstructed states. It demanded of the southern states that they should give Negroes the right to vote and the right to hold office, and that they should accord "all citizens equal school privileges, and never afterward abridge them."

The author noted that the imperial expansion around the turn of the century placed the country in "the very presence of the forces which make the politics of the twentieth century radically unlike the politics of the nineteenth." Looking well into the future, he declared: "the whole world has already become a single vicinage; each part has become the neighbor to all the rest." Isolationism and continentalism were of the nineteenth century, not the twentieth. With an abiding faith in destiny he concluded that if Americans but kept their ideas clear, their principles steadfast, they need not fear the change from continentalism to internationalism.[25] Certainly Woodrow Wilson, one of America's earliest converts to internationalism, was one of its most loyal devotees.

Wilson varied his political writing with essays of a purely literary nature. "The fact of the matter is," he wrote Horace Scudder, "that I am afraid to keep constantly intent upon my special topics of study. It is my creed that literary training and

[25]Woodrow Wilson, "Democracy and Efficiency," *Atlantic Monthly,* LXXXVII (1901), 289–99.

method are as essential to the production of good political science as to the production of good poetry or valid criticism. It is my practice, consequently, to try my hand, whenever I can, at various sorts of writing as unlike my professional tasks as possible." [26]

At times he endeavored to write poetry. All of his life he was to compose limericks and to quote them on occasion. He even tried to pen short stories during the early years of his adult life. By the middle 1890's he took an inventory of himself and confessed to Ellen:

> I am no poet, unless the mere fact of being an idealist of itself constitutes me one,—and these lines written the other day are no poem. The night I wrote them I thought they were. A hot fire was in my brain . . . and, while I wrote I thought I was writing poetry—for I thought I was writing down what was in my head. But reading the lines now I can see no reason for their measure (their occasional rhymes were purely accidental) : they are mere metrical prose. That I am an idealist, with the heart of a poet, I do not hesitate to avow; but that fact is not reassuring. On the contrary, it is tragical. . . . If I could only write prose that was delicate, imaginative, full at once of grace, force, and distinction, that would be something: my thoughts would at least go clad like aristocrats. But alas! I shall but wear my soul out trying.[27]

Apparently, at times, the professor regarded his literary writing chores more lightly. "Since I cannot work directly upon my *magnum opus*," he informed a friend, "I am half inclined to write, as bits of leisure may allow, on lighter, more literary themes, in order to loosen the joints of my style and vary the paces of my mind. Although I have spoken hitherto only on political subjects, knowing that in that direction, if in any, my special aptitudes lay, my taste for all sorts of themes that afford outlooks over men's life and thoughts has often tempted me to try my hand at other topics; and I have been deterred only by a strong sense of the importance of concentration." He wondered how much concentration was compatible with breadth, and how far limitation of topic entailed poverty of style. "The style being the personality

[26]Wilson to Horace E. Scudder, May 19, 1891, in Scudder Papers, Library of Congress.

[27]Wilson to his wife, February 19, 1895, in Axson–Wilson Letters, Princeton.

of the work, must not the style speak many interests and wide and various aptitudes if the work is to gain admission to patrician society in literature." [28]

In Wilson's endeavors to publish his literary essays, he frequently met with rejection. On one such instance he wrote Bobby Bridges that he did not blame the editor in the least for returning his manuscript: "I expected to see it come back." Wilson had made the writing "as light and as attractive" as he knew how, cleared it of all technicalities to make it as popular as he could; but the subject was such that a magazine editor would shy away from it.[29] A decade later, after publishing many literary essays, Wilson confided to his diary that if a man of letters would make the diary a place for the memoranda of his work it would be a "truer record of his life than if its entries were matter of fact." [30]

In 1896 Wilson published his only book of literary essays, *Mere Literature and Other Essays.* Seven of the eight had been published previously. Printed earlier in either the *Atlantic Monthly,* the *Century,* or the *Forum,* these essays had been read widely before they were brought together in the book form. Only "The Interpreter of English Liberty" appeared for the first time. In each essay the author breathed an intense and sincere love of literature, as in the following passage from "The Author Himself": "Culture broadens and sweetens literature, but native sentiment and unmarred individuality create it. Not all of mental power lies in the process of thinking. There is power also in passion, in personality, in simple, native, uncritical conviction, in unschooled feeling. The power of science, of system, is executive, not stimulative." [31]

A professor for nearly two decades, Wilson was vitally interested in scholarship. In the essay "Mere Literature," he stated candidly his opinion of the relation that scholarship bore to literature. Although scholarship could not exist without literature, literature could live without scholarship, though it might improverish

[28]Wilson to Scudder, January 1, 1887, in Scudder Papers, Library of Congress.

[29]Wilson to Bridges, March 3, 1887, in Meyer Collection, Library of Congress.

[30]Woodrow Wilson, "Diary," January 17, 1897.

[31]Wilson, *Mere Literature,* 35–36.

itself thereby. Exact scholarship valued things in proportion as they were verifiable; but with literature, wrote Wilson, it was a "thing of convictions, of insights, of what is felt and seen and heard and hoped for." Moreover, the personality of the writer was found in every sentence of real literature,[32] and in every example of literary immortality originative personality was present.[33]

Wilson himself was fully aware of the imperfections of his literary efforts. "I must straightway prove my right to call myself a critic," he wrote, "by pointing out . . . two defects in what I write. There is, first, a serious structural defect, noticeable most of all in the literary essays. . . . The transitions are managed *too* smoothly; the several stages of the argument are not distinct enough; you bring away no definite outline, but only a recollection of certain passages and general impression of the whole meaning. The treatment plays in circles; it does not move with directness along a clear course." There was fault of style, he noted, and here again the literary essays were the best field of observation. The phrasing was too elaborate and had not the "easy pace of simplicity." The sentences did not sound as if they had come spontaneously, but "as if they had been waited for,—perhaps waited for anxiously." But, Wilson wrote, this was untrue, they came "fast and hot enough usually" and seemed natural molds for his thought. He was speaking of the impression they made when read.[34]

Only to carefully selected friends did the professor reveal himself in this manner. One gains the impression that the essayist was endeavoring to be over-critical so as to draw forth helpful criticism, or perhaps praise. As he stated in one of his essays, in selecting those to whom he decried his own literary productions he was picking not as one who "chooses a costume, but like one who chooses a character." [35]

Wilson continued to write essays of a purely literary nature,

[32]*Ibid.,* 18–19.
[33]*Ibid.,* 31.
[34]Woodrow Wilson to Mrs. Edith Gittings Reid, June 18, 1897, in the Edith G. Reid–Woodrow Wilson Correspondence, Library of Congress.
[35]Wilson, *Mere Literature,* 58.

and in September, 1897, "On Being Human" appeared in the *Atlantic Monthly.* "The art of being human begins with practice of being genuine, and following standards of conduct which the world has tested," Wilson wrote.[36]

Two other essays from Wilson's pen found their way into print the following year.[37] The *Century Magazine* published in 1901 "When a Man Comes to Himself" [38] and "Edmund Burke and the French Revolution." [39] A man comes to himself, wrote the professor, "only when he has the best that is in him, and has satisfied his heart with the highest achievement he is fit for." Every man was forever seeking satisfaction, said the essayist. Christianity gave humanity, in the fullness of time, the perfect image of right living, the secret of social and individual well-being; "for the two are not separable, and the man who receives and verifies that secret in his own living has discovered the only way to serve the world, but also the one happy way to satisfy himself. Then, indeed, has he come to himself." [40]

What honorarium did Wilson receive for these essays? When Walter Hines Page was editor of *Forum,* he asked his friend to set his own price. As a rule Wilson had received $100 per essay, but when given the privilege of setting his own price, he upped his charge to $150.[41] Frequently when Wilson sent manuscripts to the *Atlantic Monthly* or *Century* he stated something like the following: "Please do not think it indelicate in me to say something about remuneration. I have of late received always at least one hundred and fifty dollars for an essay, and I should not like

[36]Woodrow Wilson, "On Being Human," *Atlantic Monthly,* LXXX (September, 1897), 320–29.

[37]Woodrow Wilson, "Lawyer With a Style," *Atlantic Monthly,* LXXXII (September, 1898), 363–75. The lawyer with the style was the English writer on constitutional history, Sir Henry Maine. Wilson, "A Wit and a Seer," *Atlantic Monthly,* LXXXII (October, 1898), 527–40. The wit and seer was Wilson's intellectual hero Walter Bagehot.

[38]Wilson, "When a Man Comes to Himself," 268–73.

[39]Woodrow Wilson, "Edmund Burke and the French Revolution," *Century,* LXII (September, 1901), 784–92.

[40]Wilson, "When a Man Comes to Himself," 268–73. These essays have never appeared in a volume.

[41]W. H. Page to Wilson, August 1, 1893, in Wilson Papers, Library of Congress; Wilson to Page, December 5, 1894, in Baker Papers, Library of Congress.

to fall *below par.*" [42] Sometimes he was above par. For example, Bliss Perry, writing for the *Atlantic Monthly* regarding Wilson's article on "The Reconstruction of the Southern States," asked if $300 would be satisfactory, and added: "This is two times the usual rate but we will be four times as glad to get it as an ordinary article. If you think the honorarium should be further increased . . . say so frankly and I will . . . make my assault on the powers that be." [43]

Wilson's literary essays were written for stylistic improvement, for the needed income, and for the sheer joy of creative accomplishment. The political writings show that he continued to believe in the English fusion system of government just as he had during his student days. His conversion to internationalism was among the earliest and a dedicated internationalist he would remain. Wilson sensed that great domestic change was in the political air in the 1890's, and he was slowly shifting his intellectual base from Federalism to progressivism, although public pronouncement of this would come later, at the end of the first decade of the twentieth century.

[42] Wilson to Richard W. Gilder, March 15, 1898, in Baker Papers, Library of Congress.

[43] Bliss Perry to Wilson, March 19, 1900, in Wilson Papers, Library of Congress.

CHAPTER XV *At Home and Abroad*

When Wilson moved to Princeton he purchased several choice lots, and, with an increase in real estate value, in 1895 he began to sell some of them. He was anxious to dispose of the property in order to get his plans for a new home on foot as soon as possible. Woodrow and Ellen planned for a house that would cost $7,000, "not including heating and mantels";[1] when the plans were delivered by the architect, the cost was $8,423 without plumbing and heating.[2] Ellen collaborated with the architect in working out details, but not all of her ideas survived. She did work out the plans for Woodrow's study, a room that would be inaccessible to chance visitors and afford him the utmost quiet. After the architect's agreement was signed, the Wilsons made a number of requests for minor changes. These were largely in the

[1]Wilson to E. L. Child, January 19, 1895, in Wilson Collection, Princeton.
[2]Consult "Articles of Agreement," June 10, 1895, in *ibid.*

nature of extras that Ellen and Woodrow decided they wanted, and those granted by the architect cost an additional $711.

The big problem for Wilson was the cost of the new home. This he met in several ways: by selling $1,000 worth of stock in the Charlotte, Columbia, and Augusta Railroad at $104.75 per $100 share;[3] by dividing and selling his choice Princeton lots; and by securing a $7,000 mortgage loan from Mutual Life Insurance Company of New York.[4] The professor was determined to pay for the house as soon as possible. He put himself at the disposal of the University Extension Society in Philadelphia as a lecturer, and soon was loaded with speaking engagements.[5]

When Wilson's father learned of the plans for the new home and the schedule of work which his son had set for himself to pay off the mortgage, he sent a check but said grudgingly: "Appropriate this $300 if you need it for your extravagant mansion." [6]

The Wilsons moved into the new house in the spring of 1896. It stood among large trees back some distance from the street on peaceful Library Place. Built on the popular English Norman country style, it was half-timbered with stucco. A frequent visitor to the Wilson home described the professor's sacred spot: "Wilson's study was, in most respects, the typical workshop of the scholarly college professor. Its location and arrangement (it had high windows) afforded a maximum of privacy; and while his working day was not one of long hours, it was one of intense application." [7] The study was a long, pleasant room lined with book shelves. Around the walls hung four or five crayon enlargements of photographs of men he most admired, including Webster, Gladstone, Walter Bagehot, Edmund Burke, and Dr. Joseph Ruggles Wilson. "These were the *dei penates* in whose spiritual company he steadily wrought during the early years of his Princeton professorship. . . . There was a notable orderliness

[3]Cuyler, Morgan and Company to Wilson, June 22, 1894, in Wilson Papers, Library of Congress.

[4]See bills of sales for lots and the cancelled mortgage loan, in *ibid.*

[5]Wilson to J. Franklin Jameson, November 11, 1895, in Jameson Papers, Library of Congress.

[6]Joseph R. Wilson to Woodrow Wilson, April 16, 1896, in Wilson Papers, Library of Congress.

[7]Daniels, *Recollections of Wilson,* 30.

about his desk and study. No letters or papers lay around unsorted or in temporary confusion." [8] When not in use his books were promptly replaced in their assigned location on the shelves.

The professor's library, declared one well acquainted with its contents, housed some four or five thousand books, most of them carefully selected by Wilson. Some of the more significant works included: *The American State Trials Series, The American Commonwealth Series, The American Nation Series, The American Statesman Series, The Cambridge Modern History, The English Men of Letters Series, Early Western Travels Series, History of North America Series, Journals of the House of Burgesses,* the *Works of Edgar Allan Poe,* and the writings of such early Americans as Benjamin Franklin, Thomas Jefferson, Alexander Hamilton, James Madison, James Monroe, and George Washington. Moreover, Wilson was collecting the writings of such contemporary historians as John Fiske, James Ford Rhodes, and James Schouler. Ellen Wilson proudly told Bliss Perry's wife that they were spending each year more money for books than they were for clothes.[9]

There came regularly to Wilson's study such periodicals as the *Century Magazine, Forum,* the *Atlantic Monthly,* and *Harper's Magazine.* Nor did the Princeton professor deny himself access to the professional journals, among them the *American Historical Review,* the *American Political Science Review,* the *Journal of the American Bar Association,* the *Journal of International Law,* and the *American Economic Review.* [10]

Although Wilson must have read most of the books and periodicals in his study, he never gave the appearance of being a bookworm. It could not have been said of him, as he said of Macaulay, that he was never seen without a book in his hand.[11]

[8] *Ibid.*

[9] Axson, "The Literary Historian," 195–207; Perry, *And Gladly Teach,* 134.

[10] See Woodrow Wilson Library in the Library of Congress and the list of its contents in the Wilson Papers. Many of Wilson's books and periodicals have the date they were purchased, or time they were received, written in them.

[11] Memo of interview between Stockton Axson and Ray Stannard Baker, February 11, 1925, in Baker Papers, Library of Congress.

It was not until later in life that Wilson began to read detective stories and novels. Throughout the years of his preparation and the period of his teaching he confined himself almost entirely to factual books and articles.

Wilson did not give the impression of being a particularly hard worker until the mid-1890's. He accomplished an immense amount of work, but the apparent effort belied the achievement. Outwardly calm and with almost complete self-control, the professor drove himself intensely. He functioned as a well-oiled machine, hitting on all cylinders, maintaining maximum results for his efforts. He was a most systematic man. And yet, at times he did have a certain amount of indecision in his makeup. Stockton Axson, who for years lived in the Wilsons' home, stated that his brother-in-law "seemed always torn between a desire to live a studious and scholarly life, doing creative work, and a life of action." [12] Although destined finally for a life of action, Wilson actually spent a much longer period in pursuit of the Muses. He did not make himself miserable, nor those about him unhappy, by habitually complaining about his routine of inaction—his life of talking, he sometimes called it. He did frankly confide his restless ambition to his family, however. To George Howe, a nephew who lived in his uncle's home several years while attending Princeton, Wilson once exclaimed: "George, if only I could be a man who didn't want something." [13]

Much of Wilson's time was spent in his study. When he entered this room and closed the door behind him, all knew that he was not to be disturbed. He did not demand perfect quiet throughout the house, only that he not be bothered. The maid and the governess helped Ellen keep all would-be intruders away. At infrequent intervals a fortunate visitor to the Wilson home might be taken into the book-lined study and offered a cigar. The professor, unlike his father, seldom smoked—not even cigarettes, which in the 1890's were just beginning to appear on American campuses.

[12]Memo of interview between Baker and Stockton Axson, March 12, 1925, in *ibid.*

[13]Memo of interview between Baker and Stockton Axson, February 11, 1925, in *ibid.*

Frequently the host proffered a glass of vintage wine—though in the 1890's Wilson's physician was forbidding him both alcohol and tobacco.[14]

The Princeton teacher was completely absorbed in his reading and writing, observed a fellow faculty member. In discussing his power of concentration with Bliss Perry, Wilson stated: "When you find yourself at a loss for the right word, don't you light your pipe and walk across the room and perhaps look out of the window? You lose your concentration. Now I *force* myself to sit with my fingers on the keys and *make* the right word come." Moreover, Perry added, his colleague was always sure that the word that came was right.[15] Wilson, when the occasion presented the opportunity, delighted in quoting the saying that "While a Yankee always thinks he is right, a Scotch-Irishman *knows* that he is right."

Although the professor seemed to possess a superlative amount of self-confidence, he was uncomfortable in the company of strangers. Many noticed the obvious difficulty that he had in meeting people. To some who knew Wilson well he appeared "lonely, repressed and uneasy." [16] He was excessively shy but, encouraged by his attentive wife, he persisted in his efforts to overcome this facet of his personality. Once the ice of strangeness was broken, Wilson proved an accomplished conversationalist. That he welcomed an illuminating comment, a penetrating remark, or a sagacious criticism should not be taken as meaning that he denied himself the spotlight.[17] For him the art of effective conversation required no great exertion; he found it an antidote for his usual tenseness. Knowing how much her husband enjoyed conversing with people—once he felt at ease—and how he relaxed as he displayed his intellectual brilliance before willing listeners, Ellen Wilson kept a constant stream of visitors coming into the Library Place home. Leading men in public service, prominent educators, eminent clergymen, and successful alumni, when visiting Princeton during Wilson's tenure as a

[14]Eleanor Wilson McAdoo, *The Woodrow Wilsons* (New York, 1937), 23; Perry, *And Gladly Teach,* 154.

[15]Perry, *And Gladly Teach,* 157.

[16]Edmund Wilson, *Shores of Light,* 307.

[17]Daniels, *Recollections of Wilson,* 42.

teacher, could always count on a cordial invitation to the Wilson home.

On Sunday afternoons during the 1890's the Wilsons would walk several blocks away to the home of a dear friend, Henrietta Rickitts, where they met the John Grier Hibbenses and the Bliss Perrys for tea. These faculty colleagues rarely mentioned politics or public affairs. "What we debated over the tea cups," Perry later recalled, "was books and general theories of life." In spite of the fact that Miss Rickitts was more widely read in European literature than any of her guests, it was Wilson who "usually outshone that little intimate company in sheer inventiveness and pungency of phrase." Perry felt that he "concentrated too much upon his own conversational game," and added that it was "often more delightful to listen to Wilson than to challenge the soundness of his opinions." [18] After tea, Woodrow and Ellen would take a walk of a mile or more before returning home just at nightfall.

As much as the Wilsons enjoyed the friendly teas at Miss Rickitts', as delighted as they were to entertain colleagues or friends from elsewhere, the professor scheduled his work so tightly that these social amenities were sandwiched in between extended sessions of work. Not for long did he permit a guest in his home, a local visitor, or a mid-afternoon tea to come between him and his labors. Upon returning home, he retreated into his sanctum to work.

Woodrow often turned to Ellen as his reader, and he could not have been more fortunate in having such a talented companion for the thankless task. Seldom did he seek beyond his own roof for a writing critic. On one occasion, however, he sought Frederick Jackson Turner's services as a reader: "Have you not known for a great while what was coming: that I was going to ask you to read my *ms.* and deal most faithfully with me in the criticism of it?" [19] The Wisconsin professor was doing research and writing in the same period, which created a difficulty. As Turner explained it, he was likely to publish at least monographs in the same field

[18]Perry, *And Gladly Teach,* 155.

[19]Wilson to Frederick J. Turner, December 10, 1894, in Turner Papers, Harvard.

before Wilson's book appeared and he feared that he might absorb into his own work some of Wilson's ideas. It was with real regret that he decided not to accept his former teacher's invitation to be a reader.[20] Wilson replied that his friend acted correctly in declining, and confessed that he was a bit ashamed of himself for having asked the favor.[21]

Although Wilson endeavored to presume upon his friendship for Turner to have his manuscripts read critically, he did not dedicate any of his books to his brilliant friend. *An Old Master and Other Political Essays* the author dedicated to the dearest friend of his Princeton student days: "To Robert Bridges with Hearty Acknowledgement of long and tried Friendship." Bridges was pleasantly surprised at Wilson's token of esteem, and wrote the author in appreciation at being remembered in such a way.[22] From his study in Library Place, the professor replied that he thought it "not improper between old friends" to let Bridges discover for himself the dedication, and he added: "I love and honor you, Bobby, with a depth of feeling which I like to acknowledge. The dedication was made to please myself, by associating my name with yours." [23]

Three years later, in 1896, when *Mere Literature and Other Essays* appeared, it too was dedicated to a man whom Wilson had known since the early 1880's: "To Stockton Axson, by every gift of mind a critic and lover of matters; by every gift of heart a friend: this little volume is affectionately dedicated." Again, it was a complete surprise to the recipient of the recognition. When Wilson's brother-in-law saw the dedication in the copy that the author sent him, he exulted: "How can I tell you of the mixed emotions of surprise, love and gratitude which surge upon me as I opened the volume *Mere Literature* which I have just received and find that you have done me the honor to dedicate it to me." [24]

[20]Turner to Wilson, December 24, 1895, in Wilson Papers, Library of Congress.

[21]Wilson to Turner, December 27, 1894, in Turner Papers, Harvard.

[22]Bridges to Wilson, October 10, 1893, in Wilson Papers, Library of Congress.

[23]Wilson to Bridges, October 12, 1893, in Meyer Collection, Princeton.

[24]Stockton Axson to Wilson, November 10, 1896, in Wilson Papers, Library of Congress.

Wilson dedicated the last two books that he wrote during the years that he occupied his study in the new home to his wife. In his *George Washington* he wrote: "To E.A.W. in Loving Acknowledgment of Gentle Benefits which can neither be Measured nor Repaid."

Ellen and Woodrow determined to give their children the sort of home in which the girls would develop a serenity of soul. To the three youngsters their father was all tenderness, gaiety, and play. "His hands seemed to his children to have life of their own. He could make his fingers cry like animals on the arm of his chair, or slapping his knees he could do the galloping horse—slappety-slap, slappety-slap, growing louder and then fading gradually as if in the distance." [25] Much of the professor's delight in the society of his family fireside was due to his own naivete and his childlike directness of feeling.

Very early the fortunate Wilson girls were taught to read. Children's books could be found everywhere about the house. A glimpse into the reading habits of the girls is found in a letter that little Jessie wrote to an adult friend: "Nellie has the green fairy book and I have the tales from Shakespeare and stories from Livy [?] and the blue fairy book and Margaret has the red fairy book and the Greek Heroes and our Children's Songs and Nellie has Poetry for Children and the Childrens Garland from the best Poets and all have a Bible." [26]

Although both parents aided in the schooling process, the mother shouldered most of the responsibility. As Ellen Wilson confided to a friend, "the 'School' which takes the morning until twelve, has gone on finely. I feel quite proud of my youngest pupil. She took her first lesson last October on the day after her fifth birthday, and in four months she could read fluently *anything* she could *understand*. She has now read through a number of books of fairy stories, Bible stories, poems, myths, etc." [27]

On Sunday nights after an early evening meal, Woodrow was met in the parlor by the youngsters, each waving a book of Bible

[25]Walter Walworth, *Woodrow Wilson* (New York, 1958), I, 75.

[26]Jessie Wilson to George M. Harper in Myers (ed.), *Princeton Memories,* 2.

[27]Ellen Wilson to Anna Harris, June 1, 1891; October 23, 1894; in Ellen Wilson–Anna Harris Correspondence, Princeton University Library.

stories or a copy of the Presbyterian Catechism for children. As their father sank into a roomy chair, each shouted for first attention. After reading from their books, their father might relate to them an Uncle Remus story about Br'er Rabbit and Mr. Fox, or sing to them in his clear tenor voice a children's hymn, or an Irish or Scottish folksong, or a southern Negro spiritual. Then, as little mouths began to yawn and as eyelids grew heavy, there would be the "Now I lay me down to sleep." After giving their father a good-night kiss and a tight hug, they would, with their mother's help, climb the stairs to their waiting beds.

In the autumn of 1898 the Wilson girls were all at school for the first time. Until the preceding year, their mother had taught them at home. Then the Wilsons imported a governess from Germany, Fraulein Clara Boehm, who was very successful with the children. With understandable pride Ellen wrote: "The children now speak German as fluently as English and write it very correctly, too." Glowing reports from their children's resident teacher delighted Woodrow and Ellen. Although the mother knew the girls were "very intelligent," she confessed that she was "honestly amazed to learn that they were 'well trained,' for I have always taught them with so little regard for method." [28]

Wilson was strict with his children, wrote a Princeton neighbor, "particularly in regard to their habits of speech." They were forbidden to use slang of any kind. Occasionally, one of the girls repeated her father's language without comprehending the meaning, as when one of them asked a playmate, "What is a dilettante?" "I don't know," confessed the youthful chum, "do you?" "No, but that is what my father said your father is," affirmed the Wilson child.[29]

Woodrow could never bring himself to punish one of his children, but Ellen spanked them whenever she felt they deserved it. In administering the punishment, the mother's face "always got quite pink and she invariably cried." She never told her husband how emotionally upset it made her to mete out the punishment.[30]

[28]Ellen Wilson to Anna Harris, January 1, 1899, in *ibid.*
[29]Daniels, *Recollections of Wilson,* 31; Perry, *And Gladly Teach,* 153.
[30]McAdoo, *The Woodrow Wilsons,* 9.

When the Wilson girls reached their early teens, they stayed up later, completing the family circle in the living room. Their professor father taught them the Irish jig. Sometimes he and one of the girls would do a swaying waltz while another played the "Blue Danube" or the "Missouri Waltz" on the family organ. Ellen never participated in the dancing or jigging, but she stood by smiling. If the fun grew too furious she would cry out: "Woodrow, what *is* the matter with you?"

Wilson occasionally exercised his gift of mimicry, much to the merriment of his household. "Dressing up for a charade, he would put on a lady's hat and a feather boa, wrap himself in a long velvet curtain, hold one hand high for a 'social' handshake and gush in high falsetto in burlesque of a grand dame." [31]

During most of Woodrow and Ellen's family life together they had at least one relative living with them. Usually there were two or three. These sojourners were brothers, sisters, nieces, nephews, or cousins who were attending the college or university where the professor was teaching. Wilson had no sons, but if this disappointed him, he seems never to have mentioned it. Instead he developed great fondness for his young brothers-in-law—Stockton and Edward Axson—and his sister Anne's son, George Howe. All three of these young men lived for years in the Wilson home; not all of them at the same time but at least one of them most of the years Woodrow taught.

A strong attachment sprang up between Wilson and each of these younger men. When Stockton completed his formal education, Wilson aided him in securing a job as a teacher of English literature. Within a few years Stockton was on the faculty at Princeton, where he remained until Wilson's departure from the campus in 1910. And when Stockton began writing short stories, which Ellen read critically, Wilson wrote his friends on the editorial staffs of popular magazines in behalf of his brother-in-law's literary manuscripts. When George Howe left Princeton after graduation, he accompanied a wealthy family on a year's European tour, acting as tutor for the children. Upon his return, Wilson worked through Bobby Bridges to secure his nephew a position in New York and aided in his promotion

[31] Walworth, *Wilson,* I, 77.

several times.[32] In 1904 Wilson was greatly shocked at the tragic death of Edward Axson, Ellen's favorite brother. Axson, his wife, and baby were drowned when runaway horses swept their carriage into a swollen river at Rome, Georgia.[33]

No narrative of Wilson's career as a teacher at Princeton would be complete without a discussion of his relations with his father during these twelve years. When the Wilsons came to Princeton in the fall of 1890, Dr. Wilson was in his sixty-ninth year and was beginning to think of retiring. He visited his son during that Christmas vacation, and together they discussed his retirement.[34] During the visit it was decided that the father should continue his teaching at Southwestern Seminary in Tennessee for a few years more, although he seemed quite anxious to become a member of the household of his favorite child. Apparently, the son did not wish to assume the additional financial responsibility of having his father live with him. A few months later, when Dr. Wilson learned his son's decision to buy some land near the college, he expressed surprise and sent a check for $1,500 to help in making the purchase. With a promise to send another check later, the father warned the son to see that the title to the land was cleared.[35]

When the Princeton professor, busy with his teaching, lecturing, and writing, failed to pen a note of love to his father, there came a long letter to "My Precious Son and Dearest Friend." Although Woodrow had numerous friends and deserved many admirers, said his father, he had only "one parent, the truest-of-all

[32]George Howe to Wilson, August 29, 1897, in Wilson Papers, Library of Congress; Wilson to Bridges, August 18, 1892, August 30, September 2, 1897, in Meyer Collection, Library of Congress; Annie W. Howe to Wilson, October 3, 1898, and George Howe to Wilson, October 4, 1899, in Wilson Papers Library of Congress; Wilson to Lyman P. Powell, February 8, 1894, in Powell Papers, Library of Congress.

[33]McAdoo (ed.), *The Priceless Gift,* 240.

[34]Joseph R. Wilson to Woodrow Wilson, December 13, 1890, in Wilson Papers, Library of Congress.

[35]See Wilson to his father, May 2, 1891, in Baker Papers, and Joseph R. Wilson to Woodrow Wilson, May 6, 1891, in Wilson Papers, Library of Congress. In 1893, when Wilson repaid the loan, the father wrote: "You well know that what is mine is also yours to the fullest extent possible." Joseph R. Wilson to Woodrow Wilson, September 25, 1893, in Wilson Papers, Library of Congress.

your friends, the intensest of all your admirers." Would the busy son not cultivate his friendship by a long letter? [36] Wilson soon found time to write his father an affectionate note.[37]

After a protracted illness in 1892, the old minister resigned his position, visited his children and returned to see the people whom he had served as pastor.[38] Everywhere he went he was joyously welcomed. He received more invitations to fill vacant pulpits than his ebbing strength permitted him to accept. As he traveled over the South his letters, regularly received by the professor at Princeton, revealed an abiding interest in his son's work. Repeatedly, the father mentioned articles which Woodrow had written. Wilson's *George Washington* held his father's enthusiasm, but not after he had read the book. "I am glad you permitted George to do his own dying," he wrote his son acidly.[39]

About the time Wilson's *Washington* was published, the author suffered a complete breakdown because of overwork. During his illness and an extended trip to regain his health, he largely ignored his father. Finally, after many months of waiting, the partially incapacitated son dictated a letter to his father, who was greatly feeling the pain of neglect.[40] Immediately, Dr. Wilson replied with trembling hand and stirred emotions: "I know you had not forgotten me nor had ceased to remember me affectionately. . . . I am always glad to get near you even if it be only through the medium of written words that are not altogether perfunctory." [41]

An obvious coolness clouded the feeling of close comradeship between these two men for more than two years. During this time the father was not invited to visit in Wilson's new home on Library Place, although the house had been built on land paid for

[36]Joseph R. Wilson to Woodrow Wilson, October 13, 1891, in Wilson Papers, Library of Congress.

[37]Wilson to his father, October 25, 1891, in Baker Papers, Library of Congress.

[38]Joseph R. Wilson to Woodrow Wilson, January 28, March 16, 31, May 25, 1892, in Wilson Papers, Library of Congress.

[39]Joseph R. Wilson to Woodrow Wilson, December 15, 1896, in *ibid.*

[40]Wilson to his father, December 13, 1896, in Baker Papers, Library of Congress.

[41]Joseph R. Wilson to Woodrow Wilson, December 15, 1896, in Wilson Papers, Library of Congress.

in part by the father. Seemingly, the loan of $300 sent by the aging minister as a contribution to the building of the house was accepted by the son. Only a few stilted and reserved letters passed between the two during this period. From a boardinghouse in Columbia, where Dr. Wilson had lived for months, he wrote feelingly to his son that "Josie and Kate [his younger son and daughter-in-law] usually *seem* to *want* me with them; at any rate I am glad to believe that this is the case. Old men as well as young like to be welcome." [42]

As early as 1890 the elderly minister had wanted to retire and live with Woodrow and Ellen. The son knew the father's overbearing traits, his teasing, jesting habits. He was also aware of Dr. Wilson's failing health. The old man suffered from high blood pressure, hardening of the arteries, and angina. At this time, Woodrow himself was not in good health, and he was far too busy to care for his father.

In the early spring of 1898, however, the son softened and wrote his father, as in former times, a long affectionate letter. The old man, who was in Wilmington, preaching again temporarily in his old church, was elated at the restored relationship. "It is like cool water to a parched tongue," he wrote, "to read again one of your dear love letters. It is no exaggeration to say that you are never out of my thoughts for the obvious reason that you are always in my heart." Everywhere he went, everyone he met mentioned the son's name "with loving praise," which was gratifying to paternal pride. In fact, the father declared: "I am thankful for you with a gratitude wordless." [43] Although their relationship was to remain warm and intimate as in the old days, Wilson permitted his father to remain in Wilmington until 1901—ill and under a physician's care much of the time—before bringing him to Princeton to live.

There were many visitors to the Wilson household and all were met with teasing, banter, humorous anecdotes, and sincere warm friendliness. Biographers have written that Wilson was the center of his household and that everything revolved around him. Ellen

[42]Joseph R. Wilson to Woodrow Wilson, November 5, 1897, in *ibid.*
[43]Joseph R. Wilson to Woodrow Wilson, March 16, 1898, in *ibid.*

idolized Woodrow, as did his three daughters. In spite of this, however, Wilson knew, as the youngest daughter wrote, that Ellen was "the center of it all." [44] Ellen was small, eager, and intensely alive, and Woodrow recognized in her the real ruler of the Wilson family. A splendid cook, a skillful gardener, a lover of poetry, an accomplished painter, a talented literary critic, a faithful proofreader, an expert seamstress, a sage counselor, an extremely versatile woman, Ellen Wilson was indeed the mistress of her home. If her husband uttered an impetuous or unkind opinion of another person, Ellen would interrupt: "Woodrow, you know you don't think that!" With a smile the professor would counter "Madam, I was venturing to think that I thought that until I was corrected." [45]

Because Wilson was often ill while in Baltimore giving his annual series of lectures at Johns Hopkins, Ellen conceived a scheme to keep him nearer home. To Professor John B. Clark of Columbia University she wrote: "A man or woman of the world would think us a pair of silly children to make a tragedy of a five weeks separation. But his temperament—his way of putting his *whole self* into every lecture, or written page, really makes it rather important for his physical and mental well being that I should be constantly on hand to 'rest him' as he says." Ellen hoped Professor Clark would say to the president of Columbia University: "By the way, Wilson of Princeton, who really is an enormously good lecturer, has a yearly furlough of five weeks in which he gives a course at Johns Hopkins. Wouldn't it be a good scheme if we tried to capture him for ourselves for those five weeks?" Ellen selected the course which Wilson should give at Columbia and gave her reasons for the choice: "I should like for him to give at Columbia some such course as his 'Public Law'—because it is really to some extent a course on good citizenship and I have seen what a stimulating and bracing effect it has on many of our fellows. They are all most enthusiastic over it. In that subject . . . his strong, high character 'tells,' no less than his capacity for clear thinking and forcible, vivid expressions. I should

[44]McAdoo, *The Woodrow Wilsons,* 13.

[45]Axson, "The Private Life of Woodrow Wilson."

like to see him a 'power for good' provided he did not have to *live* in it!" [46]

Professor Clark did as Ellen requested, but when President Seth Low referred the matter to Professor John W. Burgess of the political science department Ellen's scheme was doomed. As she expressed it, Burgess and Wilson did "not exactly constitute a mutual admiration society!" [47]

Another way in which Ellen helped her husband was by maintaining her pleasant optimism at all times. As she wrote to a dear friend, Woodrow was "terribly dependent" on her to "keep up his spirits and to 'rest' him as he says. So I dare not have 'the blues.' If I am just a little sky blue he immediately becomes blue black!" [48] Indeed Ellen devoted all her time promoting the advancement of her adored husband. Wilson's marriage to Ellen Axson was possibly his greatest achievement; without her as his balance wheel and his inspiration he might never have risen to world acclaim and lasting fame as he did.

Ellen encouraged Woodrow to keep his old friends, whom he sincerely missed. "I feel very lonely sometimes to think of you away off so many, many miles from me," he wrote to Heath Dabney, "and of all the stimulation and comfort I might get, if I could but renew our old comradeship. Distance and prolonged separation do not cool friendship; at least not friendships that struck deep as ours did, but they do sadly curtail opportunities for the sort of growth which is to be had only by intercourse with those whose minds and whose hearts alike you can repose perfect confidence in."

To Bobby Bridges, Wilson also wrote letters of warm friendship. When Bridges, on his thirty-third birthday, felt gloomy over his lack of literary achievement, Wilson dispatched a message of assurance and confidence: "You are prepared for anything you choose to undertake, and if you can escape becoming too critical

[46] Ellen Wilson to John B. Clark, June 3, 1897, in John B. Clark Papers, Library of Congress.

[47] John B. Clark to Ellen Wilson, June 6, 1897, *ibid.* Seemingly this letter has been lost but Ellen discusses in her letter to Clark of June 8, 1897, in *ibid.*

[48] Ellen Wilson to Anna Harris, January 31, 1899, in Wilson–Harris Correspondence, Princeton.

of your own work, I have every confidence in the result. To one who knows you as well as I do, it seems almost absurd that a birthday should bring you any dissatisfaction with what has so far been accomplished." [49]

Wilson always looked forward to seeing his old classmates at commencement. Each May there went letters from Wilson's study to members of the Witherspoon Gang: "You understand that you and the rest of the usual gang," read one of the messages written shortly before the twentieth graduation anniversary, "are to stay with me at the Reunion. We are counting on your coming, and welcome awaits you as big, as cordial and as inevitable as you can imagine. We couldn't enjoy the Reunion ourselves if we did not have you all here under our own roof." Wilson never overcame his enthusiasm for reunions of the class of '79. After he entered the White House and could not go to Princeton for the get-together, he had his classmates come to the White House, just as he and Ellen had invited them to their Library Place home years earlier.

When Walter Hines Page, whose friendship Wilson had cherished since they met in Atlanta years earlier, resigned as editor of the *Forum,* Wilson was "very much startled" and knew that he would "not be alone in deploring" Page's loss from the editorial chair.[50] Almost immediately he began "pulling strings" in an effort to help Page find a new job. Within a few weeks Wilson wrote: "I am sincerely glad to know that you are with the *Atlantic Monthly* and gratified to believe that I had some sort of part in the choice. I don't wonder that you enjoy the change; and I wish with all my heart that the truly *literary* and non-journalistic magazines might by some means gain a greater prominence and power." [51]

Another friend of Wilson's brief period as a lawyer in Atlanta was his law partner, Edward I. Renick. Until the latter's death

[49] Bridges to Wilson, September 15, 1891, in Wilson Papers, Library of Congress. Wilson to Bridges, September 22, 1891, in Meyer Collection, Princeton.

[50] Walter Hines Page to Wilson, July 2, 1899, in Wilson Papers, Library of Congress; Wilson to Page, July 4, 1895, in Baker Papers, Library of Congress.

[51] Wilson to Page, October 24, 1895, in Baker Papers, Library of Congress.

of typhoid fever in Paris near the end of Wilson's tenure as a professor, the two exchanged an occasional letter. "You and I sat nearly twenty years ago," wrote Renick to Wilson on Woodrow's forty-third birthday, "reading together the *Aeneid* and today we are as fresh and warm in our regard and affection—each for the other—as in those days of enthusiasm and romance. This I count among my dearest possessions—your genuine and abiding friendship." [52]

Quite naturally Wilson made friends among those associated with writing and publishing, such as Professor Albert B. Hart of Harvard and Horace E. Scudder. When Hart was casting about for able historians to write for the *American Nation Series* he wished to include Wilson, but was refused. "I have just now reached a point," Wilson answered, "at which I know the next ten or twelve years of my life must be devoted to an entirely different task, for which I have all along been in training, and for which now, if ever, I am ready. I should not be content to write only a single volume of the series you are planning; the measure of space would be too cramping; a fellow could not show the real pattern of his thought in it; and yet even a single volume would rob me of at least a year . . . and that I simply cannot spare." [53]

Horace Scudder was for years connected with the *Century Magazine* as well as with a publishing firm. He and Wilson became fast friends. In addition to professional conferences, social visits were exchanged between them over a period of years. Not many people could display the grace, the tact, and the command of literary talent that Wilson showed in rejecting an invitation to visit in the Scudder home:

> The invitation so cordially and generously extended to me by Mrs. Scudder and yourself in your last letter has gratified me more than I can say, and warmed me most delightfully in the region of the heart. It now appears, alas! as if I were not to be able to get away from home after all, so greatly do my tasks multiply as I seek to wade to the other side of them; and I am afraid that I must, however keen

[52] Edward I. Renick to Wilson, December 27, 1899, in Wilson Papers, Library of Congress.

[53] Wilson to Albert B. Hart, January 12, 1902, in Hart Papers, Harvard.

the disappointment, decline the invitation. That it would be delightful, and wholly delightful, to come to you I have not a moment's doubt. The companionship, the quiet, and the recreation you offer me are all equally seductive to my taste. It requires real courage, and fortitude in labour, to decline. But, since it must be done, I can only thank you, and hope for some other chance to see you and to make Mrs. Scudder's acquaintance. *Some* day, I trust, I may become more of a circulating medium.[54]

Feeling that she was not by nature "gamesome," Ellen Wilson welcomed and shared her husband's friendships with brilliant ladies.[55] Woodrow delighted in the charm and conversation of intelligent women, and he took great pleasure in displaying his literary skills before them. On one of Wilson's annual visits to Johns Hopkins he met Edith Reid, whose husband was on the university staff. Soon Woodrow was writing Mrs. Reid long, friendly letters. He made sure that Ellen knew all about the correspondence; in fact, she encouraged it. The letters between Edith Reid and Woodrow are interesting, but only platonic friendship is revealed in them. Not only did Edith Reid contribute to Wilson's happiness by writing him dozens of affectionate letters but she wrote a worthwhile book—*Woodrow Wilson: The Caricature, The Myth, and The Man.*

A few excerpts from their letters will show the tone of them all. The Princeton professor asked his friend for a critical opinion of his book *Mere Literature*: "I am sure you know to what straits a man is put to get frank criticism of such as will really help him to be somebody in the world. It is not my profession to write essays; but essays test a writer's quality, perhaps, as no other form of prose writing can,—show his touch, his notion of form, his turn of phrase, his range of wear, his mental and artistic make-up; and it is for that reason that I crave your judgment upon them." [56] After reading Wilson's book, Edith Reid replied: "My dear friend, you must be content to have me should you need one, your advocate not your judge. It is the very fact

[54]Wilson to Horace E. Scudder, August 24, 1892, in Scudder Papers, Library of Congress.

[55]Walworth, *Wilson,* I, 71.

[56]Wilson to Edith G. Reid, May 30, 1897, in Mrs. Edith G. Reid Papers, Library of Woodrow Wilson Foundation, New York City.

that I never assume the critical attitude with you that your presence is always a pleasure and restful." She knew the difficulty of forming a perfectly objective opinion of a friend's literary productions, but wrote Wilson: "You *are* a very great deal today, and, I believe, most absolutely, that when the end comes you will be with the very great in an incomparably higher atmosphere than the clever, literary, Caster-mangus of the day."

In a very warm way, Wilson replied: "Your generous appreciation stimulates me as much as your critical analysis of what I have *not* done interested me. Knowing you, I know how much it means that you should take, not the critical, but the sympathetic attitude when I write or talk for you. It must mean that you find me at any rate genuine; and it heartens me, as it should, that you so believe in me. A man who wishes to make himself by utterance a force in the world must—with as little love as possible, apply critical tests to himself; and the best critical tests, surely, are standards of those he can trust to see and utter the truth about the art he practices." [57]

Edith extended an invitation for the Wilsons to visit her at her summer cottage, but they were unable to accept at that time. Wilson stated that it warmed his and Ellen's hearts that she urged them so cordially to come: "It would have made us feel richer and younger, could we have gone," he wrote. "Mrs. Wilson already feels you her personal friend, having taken her knowledge of you from me; and I feel my life fuller by reason of your friendship so generously and cordially given." It was Wilson's desire that Edith and Ellen know each other "without an intermediary. Indeed, it must be arranged, some day, some way." [58]

In February, 1898, Ellen accompanied Woodrow to Baltimore, where they were guests in the home of Edith and Henry Reid for a few days while Wilson delivered some lectures on the Johns Hopkins campus.[59] Apparently, Ellen visited much with Mrs. Carey Gittings, Edith's mother. After the Wilsons left, Mrs.

[57]Edith Reid to Wilson, June 14, August 24, 1897, in Wilson Papers, Library of Congress; Wilson to Edith Reid, June 18, 1897, in Reid Papers, Wilson Foundation Library.

[58]Wilson to Edith Reid, October 3, 1897, in Reid Papers, Wilson Foundation Library.

[59]Wilson to Henry F. Reid, January 25, 1898, in *ibid.*

Gittings reported: "I have just had one of the great treats of my life in meeting Mrs. Woodrow Wilson. To find a person who isn't busying herself to write books . . . and yet knows so much and appreciates so much, is so much more a person of high education than so many of the people that I meet who pass as intellectuals." [60]

There were other visits and letters by the dozens between Woodrow and Edith. In January, 1901, Wilson wrote:

> I saw your handwriting again with a real delight. Since some perversity of fortune seems to deprive me even of such occasional glimpses of you as I might reasonably hope for, I wish my conscience could forget how selfish and essentially *un*reasonable it would be for me to propose a scheme of regular correspondence so that my pleasures might seem less haphazard and I might have always the zest of expectation to go before them! A conscience is a great nuisance! To know what you want and not be able to get your own consent to ask for it! To know that your friends have something very much better and more important to do than to attend to your pleasure! These are the things which strengthen character, no doubt; but they are also the things which make life look a sort of bluish grey. I *could* wage an unusual argument for indulging me in this case.[61]

This friendship between Woodrow and Edith lasted until near the end of Wilson's life. The Princeton professor wrote Mrs. Reid that when she consented to be his friend it made his life "once for all different and more delightful."

Although the number of Wilson's acquaintances was ever increasing, he possessed few real friends. The professor himself knew the reason for this and stated it accurately. "Sometimes I am a bit ashamed of myself, when I think of how few friends I have amidst a host of acquaintances," he wrote. Many people had offered their friendship to the Princeton professor but, "partly because I am reserved and shy, and partly because I am fastidious and have a narrow, uncatholic taste in friends, I reject the offer in almost every case; and then am dismayed to look about and see how few persons in the world stand near me and know me as I am,—in such wise that they can give me sympathy

[60]Memo of interview between Ray Stannard Baker and Stockton Axson, September 5, 1931 in Baker Papers, Library of Congress.

[61]Wilson to Edith Reid, January 27, 1901, in Reid Papers, Wilson Foundation Library.

and close support at heart." "Perhaps," he continued, "it is because when I give at all I want to give my whole heart, and I feel that so few want it at all, or would return measure for measure. Am I wrong, do you think, in that policy? And can one as deeply covetous of friendship and close affection as I am afford to act upon such a feeling?" [62]

As early as the middle 1880's, when Wilson began his teaching career, and more especially when he began planning to write *The State,* he realized the need for spending some time in Europe. He confided to Bobby Bridges that all of his plans for literary and professional work turned upon "an intimate acquaintance" with the actual constitutions of the European states, not only as they were in books but as they were in practice. "I must know not only comparative constitutional law but comparative constitutional *life,* and this last I cannot know without seeing foreign systems and foreign peoples as far as may be with my own eyes,—without coming into contact with living organisms of their governments." [63]

He hoped to go to Europe and live in the homes of the people he wanted to learn about. He planned to go abroad in the summer of 1887, staying overseas at least two years, but he was not able to carry out his plans. By that summer there were two babies in the family; in another year there would be three.

In the fall of 1895 the professor, overworked and badly in need of rest, fell ill. The illness proved more serious than at first thought. Although far from well, Wilson was soon up and driving himself furiously again. A few months later, in the spring of 1896, he developed in his right hand what was thought to be writer's cramp but which turned out to be neuritis. In the midst of finishing his series of articles on Washington, he obtained a pen with a large handle so as to place less strain on the right hand. Soon his iron determination had to give way, at least temporarily. Accepting the advice of the family physician for a complete rest, the Wilsons decided that Woodrow should have his long-delayed trip to Europe. Ellen was greatly disturbed by her

[62]Wilson to Edith Reid, February 16, 1902, in *ibid.*

[63]Wilson to Bridges, November 28, 1886, in Meyer Collection, Library of Congress.

husband's illness. He was put on a strict diet and forbidden to accept any more engagements for lectures or speeches.[64] Indeed, the Princeton professor had so much work planned already that any more delays would prohibit his leaving as planned.

Soon, however, he sailed on the *Ethiopia* for Glasgow. He made some new acquaintances on the way over and traveled some with them in England. Wilson had taken his bicycle with him and rode it hundreds of miles during the next few weeks both in Scotland and England. He visited the tomb of Adam Smith, about whom he had written an essay years earlier, and sent Ellen a blade of grass that he plucked from Smith's grave.[65] The professor was keenly disappointed in the town of Carlisle, because he could not find the church where his grandfather was pastor, nor the residence where he had lived.[66]

Wilson felt his wife's absence most keenly in Grassmere, the Wordsworth country. He described for Ellen the poet's cottage at Rydal Mount and sent home a fragrant small flower that he pinched from a nearby wall.[67] Throughout the summer, as he visited places sacred to England's literary traditions, he told Ellen how much more she belonged there than did he. "Oh, why was I ever so selfish as to come without you?" he wrote.[68] When he visited the National Art Gallery he was convinced that Ellen should be there. He was completely well and would be perfectly happy if only she were with him.

The highlight of Wilson's first trip to the land of his ancestors was his visit to Oxford. A mere glance at the place, Woodrow informed Ellen, was "enough to take one's heart by storm." If only there were a place for him at Oxford University, "America would see me again only to sell the house and fetch you and the children." [69] Undoubtedly, some of the professor's ideas in education, that he later sought to introduce at Princeton, came from this initial visit to Oxford: alteration of the curriculum so that

[64]Wilson to Howard Pyle, March 24, 1896, in Wilson Collection, Library of Congress.

[65]Wilson to his wife, June 14, 1896, in Axson–Wilson Letters, Princeton.

[66]Wilson to his wife, June 28, 1896, in *ibid.*

[67]Wilson to his wife, June 29, 1896, in *ibid.*

[68]Wilson to his wife, June 14, 1896, in *ibid.*

[69]Wilson to his wife, July 9, 1896, in *ibid.*

there would be coherence in the courses of study; employment of a body of able young men who would perform somewhat the same service as did the Oxford tutors; and reorganization of the extra-curricular life of the university to abolish the social clubs which prohibited the freshmen from associating with the older students, who could have more influence on them than the professor behind the desk.[70]

In Europe, Wilson's health improved daily; he rode a bicycle over thirty miles; his appetite and sleeping were superb. The neuritic right hand, however, did not improve. Throughout that summer Ellen received many letters, all of which were written in the peculiar script of Woodrow's left hand.

Upon returning home in September, he plunged into his lectures, the preparation of his oration for the sesquicentennial, and his writing. Slowly the right hand mended. Wilson began using it again sparingly during the autumn but when his right hand grew tired he switched to his left. Ellen could always tell at a glance with which hand Woodrow had written, but he learned to sign his name so well with his left hand that others could not tell which he had used. More than a year elapsed before the neuritis disappeared. Several times the teacher expressed pride in his ambidexterity: "For almost a year now I have been suffering with neuritis in my right hand. For months I was forbidden to use the pen at all and laboriously practiced the use of my left hand." [71]

In spite of Wilson's handicap, those closely associated with him noted that he drove himself unmercifully after returning from Europe. Gone was the habit of lingering after a meal, either at the table or in the library, to indulge in relaxing conversation. Gone was the custom of retiring for the night at ten or eleven o'clock. Now he went directly from the dinner table to the study and to work. Members of the household soon realized that he was working very late. It was in this period that Wilson, though greatly handicapped with neuritis, wrote the essay "When a Man Comes to Himself," which was so definitely autobiographical.[72]

[70]Memorandum of interview between Baker and Stockton Axson, March 15, 1927, in Baker Papers, Library of Congress.

[71]Wilson to A. W. Hazen, March 27, 1897, in *ibid.*

[72]Memo of interview between Baker and Stockton Axson, February 11, 1925, in Baker Papers, Library of Congress.

Although Wilson was working long hours, he sometimes relaxed a little. In his diary of January 17, 1897, he recorded: "I did not go to church this A.M.; partly because of the disinclination of leaving Ellen—partly because of laziness." [73] Upon the advice of those close to him, Wilson began learning to play golf. He played under the limitations of defective eyesight that would have discouraged many from playing the game at all, but "he played it with a patience, self-control and sense of enjoyment that made him a good companion; though it was inevitable that he should not play it particularly well." [74] On the golf course Wilson again showed himself to be a bit of a poor sport; he "hated to be beaten either in little or great things." When the professor lost his ball he searched endlessly for it, but when his opponent had the same misfortune Wilson soon fretted and exclaimed that they came to "play golf rather than to hunt lost balls." [75]

Wilson began playing billiards again, a game he had learned from his father.[76] He even answered an advertisement and enclosed a check for $20 for a course of exercises suitable for a middle-aged man.[77] These he began taking at night before he retired and reported that sleeping came easier afterwards.

In July, 1899, Wilson, accompanied by Stockton Axson, went on his second pilgrimage to Britain. The two traveled on bicycles along the same route from Glasgow to Edinburgh that Wilson had followed three years earlier. They lingered in the "Burns Country" and in the Wordsworth lake region. In Durham they witnessed a murder trial. In Dublin, Wilson rode his bicycle about the city. He was fascinated by the castle, the old Parliament houses, "but most particularly by the Trinity College." [78] When the travelers returned to Princeton, Ellen teased Woodrow about retracing the same journey. According to Stockton, Wilson answered: "Haven't you learned that I love to do the same things

[73]Wilson, "Diary," January 17, 1897, in *ibid.*

[74]Edward M. Chapman to Baker, December 23, 1925, in Baker Papers, Library of Congress.

[75]*Ibid.*

[76]Memo of interview between Baker and Stockton Axson, February 11, 1925, in Baker Papers, Library of Congress.

[77]See the exercise instructions in Wilson Papers, Library of Congress. In October, 1901, Wilson began the course.

[78]Wilson to his wife, August 20, 1899, in Axson–Wilson Letters, Princeton.

every day, that I love the English beautiful lake country better than any other spot!" [79]

The Wilson family spent their vacation in the summer of 1900 at Judd Haven, Ontario.[80] Ellen confided to a friend: "We are all in excellent health, thanks to our delightful summer outing. We spent six weeks in Muskoka district of Northern Ontario, an ideal summer country. There are three great, shining lakes dotted all over with islands, great and small—and such forests of beech and pine, and such an air, even I could row eight or ten miles without fatigue—of course, everyone lives on the water. We are so charmed with it and it proved such a tonic for Woodrow that we are thinking a little of keeping an island and building a summer cottage there." [81]

In October of that year Wilson requested a leave of absence from his teaching at Princeton. He wished to spend a year abroad in travel and study to prepare himself for a series of studies in political organization and development. The trustees complied at once, granting the year of absence with full salary.[82] Even though the request was made in sincerity and the grant was generously given, Wilson was not to spend the year in Europe. As Ellen stated, "So many things might happen to prevent that I do not count on it yet." [83]

In January, 1901, Wilson's father, still visiting among friends in Wilmington, suffered a severe illness. For some days the attending physician feared for the old minister's life. From friends Woodrow learned of his father's illness,[84] and went southward to be at his bedside. Upon Wilson's return to Princeton, he and Ellen abandoned their plans to go to Europe. Woodrow felt that

[79]Memo of interview between Baker and Stockton Axson, February 10, 1925, in Baker Papers, Library of Congress.

[80]Wilson to James C. Young, August 3, 1900, and H. M. Alden to Wilson, August 7, 1900, in Wilson Papers, Library of Congress.

[81]Ellen Wilson to Anna Harris, January 3, 1901, in Wilson–Harris Correspondence, Princeton.

[82]Wilson to Princeton University Trustees, October, 1900, in Wilson Papers, Library of Congress.

[83]Ellen Wilson to Anna Harris, January 3, 1901, in Wilson–Harris Correspondence, Princeton.

[84]A. C. Robinson to Wilson, January 11, 1901, and James Spruitt to Wilson, January 12, 1901, in Wilson Papers, Library of Congress.

he dared not put the Atlantic between himself and his father now. The hardy father mended some and was taken to his son's home at Princeton, but the trip caused a relapse. For a few days the family was uneasy about him.

Dr. Wilson's health greatly improved and he decided to spend the summer at the Danville Sanatorium. Woodrow concluded plans for buying an island in a Canadian lake and building a cottage there in which the Wilson family could spend their summer vacations. This news surprised the stricken father. He wrote of his eagerness to share financially in the Canadian venture, but of his inability to do so, and of his unbounded joy if he could only "look forward to a summer to be spent with you all on your island home." [85] This happiness was never to be realized.

Ellen, Woodrow, and the girls spent a few weeks in the Northern Ontario region in the late summer of 1901, but never again were they able to venture into that picturesque island country. In a practical mood Wilson sold his property there, added his income from his writings, the royalties from his books, the honorariums from his lectures, and his salary beyond the family and household living expenses, and in January, 1902, invested a total of $13,080 in stocks and bonds.[86]

Much has been written by biographers of the Wilson family's great surprise at Woodrow's being named president of Princeton at commencement in June, 1902. There is some circumstantial evidence to support the idea that the whole thing was a well-laid scheme shrewdly manipulated into full fruition. One can only list those things that possibly, even probably, brought Wilson to the presidency of his alma mater.

First, Wilson was a graduate of the university and so were all, or practically all, of the trustees. Second, Wilson was the best lecturer and public speaker on the campus, and customarily someone from the campus was selected for the presidency. Although oratory was not essential to the office, it was certainly an asset. Third, Wilson was a generation younger than President Patton, thereby fitting into the plan for naming a younger man to the presidency. Fourth, Wilson may not have been the best writer

[85]Joseph R. Wilson to Woodrow Wilson, February 13, 1901, in *ibid.*
[86]Cuyler, Morgan and Company to Wilson, January 9, 1902, in *ibid.*

on the Princeton faculty, but he was among the best and certainly was among the most prolific. Fifth, at forty-five years of age Wilson realized that he had to begin immediately the work that he would do best. As he explained to Frederick Jackson Turner:

> I was forty-five three weeks ago and between forty-five and fifty-five . . . is when a man ought to do the work into which he expects to put most of himself— I love history, and think that there are few things so directly rewarding and worthwhile for their own sakes as to scan the history of one's own country with a careful eye, and write of it with the all absorbing desire to get its cream and spirit out. But, after all, I was born a politician, and must be at the task for which, by means of my historical writing, I have all through the years been in training. If I finish at fifty-five, shall I not have fifteen richly contemplative years left, if the Lord be good to me! But, then, the Lord may prefer to be good to the world! [87]

As the recognized leader of the younger faculty members, who by 1902 had been in the majority for several years, Wilson had a majority of the staff behind him in his leadership several years before the change was actually made. Moreover, this fact was apparently raised abroad: "Wilson, is not unlikely," stated the Waterbury *American,* "to be chosen as successor of Dr. Patton as a representative of the younger Princeton [faculty members]." [88]

For years before 1902 Wilson had spoken across the country to many more Princeton alumni clubs than had Patton. Moreover, he was a much more accomplished after-dinner speaker than was the president. In writing to trusted friends among the alumni, especially active members of the class of '79, Wilson did not hesitate to make derogatory comments about Patton's policies. Note, for example, the following: "We [the Wilsons] go home from our vacation tomorrow, and an immense pile of work awaits me. But I shall attack it with zest and finish it, I have little doubt, without distress. *The only distress I suffer will come from the conditions under which the college is administered.*" [89]

Not only was Wilson opposed to Patton's policies, but he for years had strongly disliked him personally. When a graduate stu-

[87] Wilson to Turner, January 21, 1902, in Turner Papers, Harvard.

[88] Issue of December 14, 1899.

[89] Wilson to Bridges, September 2, 1897, in Meyer Collection, Princeton. Italics are the author's.

dent at Johns Hopkins, Wilson heard Dr. Patton speak and wrote his impression to Ellen Axson: "As soon as I saw him I was disappointed: a tall, lean, spare-visaged man, with narrow knit brow and a mouth set to the taste of vinegar. As soon as I heard him I was grieved: the angular wrists and darting forefingers developed in his delivery made me nervous, his didactic manner made me antagonistic and his rasping voice, together with his niggardly treatment of the vowels of the language, made me indignant and amused by turns." [90]

Another point in Wilson's favor was his friendship with several of the most influential members of the Princeton Board of Trustees. They were among his correspondents. He visited them at their places of business in New York, in Chicago, and elsewhere. He was entertained in their homes. Some of them received gift copies of his books. Several of them in 1898 began paying Wilson $2,500 annually in excess of his salary to prevent the professor from accepting the presidency of the University of Virginia.

Out of this intimate friendly association between the professor and several trustees came a scheme of Wilson's in March, 1902, for the creation of a committee to consist of two members of the Board of Trustees and three faculty members to be appointed by the board. Although he was author of the idea, Wilson was happy to have two trustees, David B. Jones and Cyrus H. McCormick, accept it as theirs and to have them present it to President Patton for his acceptance. This committee was "to formulate and recommend" to the faculty and to the board in four wide areas of university policy-forming and decision-making, thereby actually relieving the president of the customary control of the university. When members of the board arrived on the campus several days before an official meeting of the trustees and began to pressure Patton to accept their (really Wilson's) plan, the president was very upset. This committee plan was kept secret, although Wilson was fully aware of it.[91] On June 9, 1902, Patton resigned as presi-

[90]Wilson to Ellen Axson, January 6, 1884, in Wilson–Axson Letters, Princeton.

[91]See Wilson Papers, Library of Congress, for numerous letters and memos between Wilson and David B. Jones and Cyrus H. McCormick in March, April, and May, 1902.

dent and asked to retain his professorship of ethics and philosophy of religion. To those who saw him soon afterwards, he seemed as "happy as a school boy when vacation time swings around the corner." "You may say to the associated press that I resigned as president today and within an hour saw named and elected as my successor one of Princeton's most brilliant sons, Woodrow Wilson," he said.[92]

After the announcement, when Dr. Patton returned to Prospect, the seniors appeared and sent up a yell. Patton came to the steps, calling them close to him: "You and I will graduate at the same time. I have taken this action on my own accord. These fourteen years when I have looked ahead, it did not seem long, but now when I look back over the past it seems a long while and I am tired. You will be, I know, and I want you to be, loyal, every one of you, to the new administration and to Woodrow Wilson. And yet I want you to keep a place—just a little place—in your hearts for me." [93]

Cheer after cheer rent the air as the seniors, joined by many others, made their way to the Wilson home on Library Place. When they called for the president-elect, Wilson walked from his living room onto the porch and stated briefly: "A Princeton man always has the interest of the University as his own. It is too early to say more." [94] Later he confided to Ellen that his election to the presidency had "settled the future" for him and given him "a sense of *position* and of definite, tangible tasks." [95]

With his election to the presidency of Princeton an important chapter of Wilson's life drew to a close. Now the long years of preparation were over; the years of action, of leadership, were about to begin.

[92]H. L. Bowlby, "Woodrow Wilson—Birthday Reminiscences," Newark *Evening News,* December 20, 1932.

[93]See Philadelphia *Press,* June 10, 1902, and New York *Times,* June 10, 1902.

[94]*Ibid.*

[95]Wilson to his wife, August 10, 1902, in Axson–Wilson Letters, Princeton.

Bibliography

MANUSCRIPT COLLECTIONS

Herbert Baxter Adams Papers, Johns Hopkins University Library.

James B. Angell Papers, Library of Congress.

Ellen Axson–Anna Harris Correspondence, Firestone Library, Princeton University.

Ellen Axson–Woodrow Wilson Letters, Firestone Library, Princeton University.

Ray Stannard Baker Papers, Library of Congress.

John B. Clark Papers, Library of Congress.

Robert Heath Dabney Papers, Alderman Library, University of Virginia.

Winthrop M. Daniels Papers, Princeton University Library.

Richard T. Ely Papers, Wisconsin State Historical Society Archives.

Daniel Coit Gilman Papers, Library of Johns Hopkins University.

Albert Bushnell Hart Papers, Widener Library, Harvard University.

John Franklin Jameson Papers, Library of Congress.

Karl A. Meyer Collection of Correspondence of Woodrow Wilson and Robert Bridges, Library of Congress.

Karl A. Meyer Collection of Correspondence of Woodrow Wilson and Robert Bridges, Firestone Library, Princeton University.

Lyman P. Powell Papers, Library of Congress.

Edith G. Reid–Woodrow Wilson Correspondence, Library of Congress.

Edith G. Reid Papers, Library of Woodrow Wilson Foundation.

Horace E. Scudder Papers, Library of Congress.

Edwin R. A. Seligman Papers, Library of Congress.

Reuben G. Thwaites Papers, University of Wisconsin Library.

Frederick Jackson Turner Papers, Houghton Library, Harvard University.

Ellen Wilson–Anna Harris Correspondence, Firestone Library, Princeton University.

Woodrow Wilson Collection, Boston Public Library.
Woodrow Wilson Collection, Firestone Library, Princeton University.
Woodrow Wilson Papers, Library of Congress.
Woodrow Wilson Papers, New Jersey State Library, Trenton.

UNPUBLISHED DOCUMENTS

Bursar's Record Book, University of Virginia Library.

Francis G. Garmony's Autograph Book, Firestone Library, Princeton University.

John Franklin Jameson Diary, Library of Congress.

Jefferson Literary Society Roll Book, 1856–86, Alderman Library, University of Virginia.

Jefferson Literary Society Minutes, Alderman Library, University of Virginia.

Minutes of First Presbyterian Church, Columbia, South Carolina, South Carolina Department of Archives and History, Columbia.

Minutes of History and Political Science Seminary, 1884–85, History Department, Johns Hopkins University.

Records of Bryn Mawr College, 1885—88, Bryn Mawr College Library.

Records of Eumenean Literary Society, 1873, Davidson College Library.

Records of Registrar's Office, Davidson College Library.

Whig Literary Society, Minutes, Firestone Library, Princeton University.

Whig Literary Society, Records, Firestone Library, Princeton University.

Woodrow Wilson Diary, Library of Congress.

PUBLISHED DOCUMENTS

American Historical Association *Report,* 1893.

American Historical Association *Report,* 1896.

Directory for the City of Augusta and Business Advertisers for 1859 (Augusta, 1859).

Princeton College Alumni, 1890.

Princeton College Bulletin, 1893.

Princeton College Catalogue, 1890–91; 1901–1902.

United States Congressional Record, 64th Congress, 1st Session (1913).

United States House of Representatives, Miscellaneous Documents, 47th Congress, 2nd Session, 1882–83, vol. III.

Wesleyan University Alumnus 1888–90.
Wesleyan University Catalogue, 1888–89.

ARTICLES

Archer, William. "President Wilson As a Man of Letters," *Fortnightly Review,* CIX (1918), 250–75.

Axson, Stockton. "The Literary Historian," *Rice Institute Pamphlet,* XII (1935), 195–207.

——— "The Private Life of Woodrow Wilson," *New York Times Magazine* (October 8, 1906).

Beckley, Zoe H. "At the Old Home," *World Magazine* (January 19, 1913).

Bowlby, H. L. "Woodrow Wilson—Birthday Reminiscences," *Newark Evening News* (December 20, 1932).

Bradford, Gamaliel. "Shall the Cabinet Have Seats in Congress?," *Nation,* XVI (April 13, 1873), 223–34.

——— "The Way Congress Does Business," *Nation,* XVI (February 27, 1873), 145–46.

Bragdon, Henry W. "Woodrow Wilson Addresses Citizens of Baltimore, 1896," *Maryland Historical Magazine,* XXXIII (1942), 150–70.

Bridges, Robert. "President Woodrow Wilson and College Earnestness," *World's Work,* XV (January, 1908), 9792–97.

"Collegiana," *University of Virginia Magazine,* XIX (December, 1879), 193.

David, Marjorie L. "Woodrow Wilson—Historian," *Mississippi Valley Historical Review,* XXI (1934), 361–74.

Davis, Edward P. "Woodrow Wilson's Early Years," *Saturday Review of Literature,* IV (November 19, 1927), 319–20.

Dudden, Arthur P. "Woodrow Wilson at Bryn Mawr College," *Bryn Mawr Alumni Bulletin,* XXVI (1955), 6–7, 32–33.

Edmunds, Charles K. "New Light on Woodrow Wilson's Formative Years," Newspaper Clipping in Hilah Kirby's Scrapbook, Norfolk, Va.

Kent, Charles W. "Woodrow Wilson's Undergraduate Days at the Virginia Alpha," in Harry S. Gorgas and James D. Campbell (eds.), *Centennial History of the Phi Kappa Psi, 1852–1952.* Binghamton, N.Y., 1952.

McKean, Dayton D. "Woodrow Wilson as a Debate Coach," *Quarterly Journal of Speech,* XVI (1930), 458–63.

Michlejohn, Alexander. "Woodrow Wilson, Teacher," *Saturday Review of Literature,* I (May 30, 1925), 785–86.

Mosher, O. W. Jr. "Woodrow Wilson's Methods in the Classroom," *Current History,* XXXIII (June, 1930), 502–505.

Osborn, George C. "The Influence of Joseph Ruggles Wilson on His Son, Woodrow Wilson," *North Carolina Historical Review,* XXXII (1953), 519–43.

——— "Woodrow Wilson and Frederick Jackson Turner," *Proceedings of the New Jersey Historical Society,* LXXIV (1956), 208–29.

——— "Woodrow Wilson as a Speaker," *Southern Speech Journal* XXII (1956), 61–72.

Perry, Bliss. "Woodrow Wilson as a Man of Letters," *Century,* LXXV (March, 1913), 753–57.

Sears, Louis M. "Woodrow Wilson," in William T. Hutchinson (ed.), The Marcus W. Jernegan Essays in American Historiography (Chicago, 1937), 102–21.

Thackwell, Helen W. "Woodrow Wilson and My Mother," *Princeton University Library Chronicle,* XII (1950), 6–18.

Weisenburger, Francis P. "The Middle Western Antecedents of Woodrow Wilson," *Mississippi Valley Historical Review,* XXIII (1936), 375–90.

Williams, C. L. "Woodrow Wilson as an Undergraduate," *Current History,* XXXI (January, 1930), 698–702.

——— "When He Was Just Tommy," *Ladies Home Journal* (November, 1918), 138.

——— "Woodrow Wilson's Student Days at the University of Virginia," *University of Virginia Magazine,* LXXIII (1913).

"X"–"The Work of a Southern Scholar," *Sewanee Review,* III (1895), 172–88.

ARTICLES, BOOKS, AND SPEECHES OF WOODROW WILSON

Articles

"The Author Himself," *Atlantic Monthly,* LXVIII (September, 1891), 401–13.

"A Calendar of Great Americans," *Forum,* XVI (February, 1894), 715–27.

"Cabinet Government in the United States," *International Review,* VI (1879), 146–63.

"The Character of Democracy in the United States," *Atlantic Monthly,* LXIV (1889), 477–88.

"Committee or Cabinet Government," *Overland Monthly,* series 2, III, 17–33.

"Culture and Education at the South," n.p., in Wilson Papers, Library of Congress.

"Democracy and Efficiency," *Atlantic Monthly,* LXXVII, 289–99.

"Discussion of James Bryce, The American Commonwealth," *Political Science Quarterly,* IV (1880), 153–69.

"Edmund Burke and the French Revolution," *Century,* LXII (1901), 784–92.

"Lawyer With a Style," *Atlantic Monthly,* LXXXII (1898), 363–75.

"The Making of the Nation," *Atlantic Monthly,* LXXX (July, 1897), 1–14.

"Mr. Cleveland's Cabinet," *Review of Reviews,* VII (1893), 286–97.

"Mr. Cleveland as President," *Atlantic Monthly,* LXXIX (1897), 289–300.

"Mr. Goldwin Smith's Views on Our Political History," *Forum,* XVI (1893), 489–99.

"Of the Study of Politics," *New Princeton Review,* III (1887), 188–99.

"An Old Master," *New Princeton Review,* IV (1888), 210–20.

"On Being Human, *Atlantic Monthly,* LXXX (1897), 320–29.

"On the Writing of History: With a Glance at the Methods of Macaulay, Gibbon, Carlyle and Green," *Century,* X (September, 1895), 787–93.

"Our Last Frontier," *Berea College Quarterly,* IV (May, 1899), 5–6.

"Prince Bismark," *Nassau Literary Magazine,* XXXIII (1878), 99–105.

"The Proper Perspective of American History, *Forum,* XIX (July, 1895), 544–59.

"Reconstruction of the Southern States," *Atlantic Monthly,* LXXXIII (1901), 1–15.

"Responsibile Government Under the Constitution," *Atlantic Monthly,* LVIII (1886), 542–53.

"A Review of *Political Science and Constitutional Law,* by John W. Burgess," *Atlantic Monthly,* LXII (May, 1891), 694–99.

"The Significance of American History," *Harper's Encyclopedia of the United States History,* 10 vols. (New York, 1902), I, xxvii–xxxii.

"Spurious Versus Real Patriotism in Education," *School Review,* VII (December, 1899), 599–620.

"States Rights, 1850–1860," *Cambridge Modern History,* 13 vols. Cambridge, 1902–24), VII, 405–42.

"The Study of Administration," *Political Science Quarterly,* II (1887), 197–222.

"University Training and Citizenship," *Forum,* XVIII (1894).

"When a Man Comes to Himself," *Century,* LXII (1901), 268–73.

"William Earl Chatham," *Nassau Literary Magazine,* XXXIV (1878), 99–105.

"A Wit and a Seer," *Atlantic Monthly,* LXXXII (1898), 527–40.

Books

Congressional Government (Boston, 1885).

Division and Reunion, 1829–1889 (New York, 1893).

George Washington (New York, 1897).

History of the American People, 5 vols. (New York, 1902).

Leaders of Men, T. H. Vail Natter, ed. (Princeton, 1952).

Mere Literature and Other Essays (Boston, 1896).

An Old Master and Other Political Essays (New York, 1893).

The State: Elements of Historical and Practical Politics (Boston, 1889).

The State and Federal Government of the United States: A Brief Manual for Schools and Colleges (Boston, 1889).

Speeches

"Abraham Lincoln: A Man of the People", February 12, 1909, at Chicago.

"Address," April 30, 1889, at the North Congregational Church, Middletown, Connecticut.

"Baccalaureate Address," June 10, 1910, at Princeton University.

"The Bible and Progress," May 17, 1911, at Denver, commemorating the Tercentenary Celebration of the Translation of the Bible into English.

"Leaderless Government," August 4, 1897, at Richmond, Virginia, before the Virginia Bar Association.

"Legal Education of Undergraduates," August 23, 1894, at Saratoga Springs before the American Bar Association.

"Princeton in the Nation's Service," October 21, 1896, at Princeton University Sesquicentennial Celebration.

"Robert E. Lee: An Interpretation," January 19, 1909, at University of North Carolina, Chapel Hill.

"Should an Antecedent Liberal Education be Required of Students in Law, Medicine and Theology," July 26, 1893, at Chicago, before the International Congress of Education of the World's Columbian Exposition.

"The Young People and the Church," October 13, 1904, at Pittsburgh, before the annual convention of the Pennsylvania State Sabbath School Association.

BOOKS

Baker, Ray Stannard (ed.). *Woodrow Wilson, Life and Letters,* 8 vols. New York, 1927–39.

———and William E. Dodd (eds). *Public Papers of Woodrow Wilson,* 6 vols. New York, 1925–27.

Barrett, John G. *Sherman's March Through the Carolinas.* Chapel Hill, 1956.

Beam, Jacob N. *American Whig Society of Princeton University,* Princeton, 1933.

Black, Harold G. *The True Woodrow Wilson: Crusader for Democracy.* New York, 1946.

Bridges, Robert. *Woodrow Wilson: A Personal Tribute.* n.p., n.d.

Craig, Hardin. *Woodrow Wilson at Princeton.* Norman, Okla., 1960.

Cranston, Ruth. *Story of Woodrow Wilson: Twenty-eighth President of the United States, Pioneer of World Democracy.* New York, 1945.

Culbreth, David. *University of Virginia.* New York, 1908.

Cummings, Mary G. Smith. *Two Centuries of Augusta: A Sketch.* Augusta, 1926.

Curtis, W. G. *Reminiscences.* Southport, N.C., 1921.

Daniels, Josephus. *Life of Woodrow Wilson: 1856–1924.* Philadelphia, 1924.

Daniels, Winthrop M. *Recollections of Woodrow Wilson.* New Haven, 1944.

Donnan, Elizabeth and Leo F. Stock (eds.). *An Historian's World: Selections from the Correspondence of John Franklin Jameson.* Philadelphia, 1950.

Federal Writers Project, *Augusta.* Augusta, Ga., 1938.

Finch, Edith. *Carey Thomas of Bryn Mawr.* New York, 1947.

Galbraith, Robert C. Jr. *History of the Chillicothe Presbytery.* Chillicothe, 1889.

Godwin, H. *A History of the Class of 1879: Princeton College.* Privately printed, 1879.

Henning, Helen Kahn (ed.). *Columbia, Capital City of South Carolina, 1786–1936.* Columbia, 1936.

Howe, Frederic C. *Confessions of a Reformer.* New York, 1925.

Jones, Charles C. and Salem Dutcher. *Memorial History of Augusta, Georgia.* Syracuse, 1890.

Kellogg, Louise P. *Frederick Jackson Turner, Early Writings.*

Kraus, Michael. *A History of American History.* New York, 1937.

Lawrence, David. *True Story of Woodrow Wilson.* New York, 1924.

Lewis, McMillen. *Woodrow Wilson of Princeton.* Narbeth, Pa., 1952.

Link, Arthur (ed.). *The Papers of Woodrow Wilson,* 3 vols. Princeton, N.J., 1966–67.

——— *Wilson: The Road to the White House.* Princeton, 1947.

McAdoo, Eleanor W. (ed.). *The Priceless Gift: The Love Letters of Woodrow Wilson and Ellen Axson.* New York, 1962.

———. *The Woodrow Wilsons.* New York, 1937.

McIlwaine, Richard. *Memories of Three Score Years and Ten.* New York, 1908.

Myers, William S. (ed.). *Woodrow Wilson: Some Princeton Memories.* Princeton, 1946.

Patterson, A. W. *Personal Recollections of Woodrow Wilson.* Richmond, 1929.

Perry, Bliss. *And Gladly Teach.* Boston, 1935.

———. *Praise of Folly and Other Papers.* Boston, 1923.

Pressly, Thomas J. *Americans Interpret Their Civil War.* Princeton, 1954.

Reid, Edith G. *Woodrow Wilson: The Caricature, the Myth and the Man.* New York, 1934.

Reilly, J. S. *Wilmington, Past, Present and Future.* Wilmington, 1885.

Sprunt, James. *Chronicles of the Cape Fear River, 1660–1916.* 2nd ed. Raleigh, N.C., 1916.

Strickler, G. B. *Memorial of the Centennial Anniversary of the First Presbyterian Church of Augusta, Georgia.* Augusta, 1904.

Trowbridge, John T. *The Desolate South 1865–1866, A Picture of the Battlefields and of the Devastated Confederacy.* Gordon Carroll, ed. New York, 1956.

Vander Velde, Lewis G. *Presbyterian Churches and the Federal Union.* Harvard Historical Studies. Cambridge, 1932.

Vessey, John H. *Mr. Vessey of England, Being the Incident and Reminiscences Travel in a Twelve Weeks Tour through the United States and Canada in the Year, 1859.* Brien Waters, ed. New York, 1956.

Waddell, John N. *Memorials of Academic Life.* Richmond, 1891.

Walworth, Arthur. *Woodrow Wilson,* 2 vols. New York, 1958.

Wertenbaker, Thomas J. *A History of Princeton College, 1746–1846.* New York, 1946.

White, William Allen. *Woodrow Wilson: The Man, His Times and His Task.* Boston, 1924.

Williams, James F. *Old and New Columbia.* Columbia, 1939.

Wilson, Edmund. *Shores of Light: A Literary Chronicle of the 1920's and 1930's.* New York, 1952.

NEWSPAPERS

Aiken (S.C.) *Recorder,* 1893.

Atlanta *Constitution,* 1882, 1956.

Augusta (Ga.) *Chronicle and Sentinel,* 1860.

Augusta *Daily Chronicle and Sentinel,* 1861–69.

Augusta *Daily Constitutionist,* 1859.

Baltimore *Morning Herald,* 1896.

Baltimore *News,* 1896, 1897, 1902.

Baltimore *Sun,* 1896.

Boston *Beacon,* 1885.

Boston *Christian Register,* 1897.

Boston *Commercial Bulletin,* 1885–86.

Boston *Daily Advertiser,* 1889–94.

Boston *Literary World,* 1890.

Bowdoin *Oriest,* 1890.

Charlotte *Observer,* 1894.

Chicago *Daily Tribune,* 1885.

Chicago *Dial,* 1885–1890.

Columbia (S.C.) *Daily Union,* 1872–73.

Columbia *Daily Phoenix,* 1872–74.

Columbia *Phoenix,* 1870–72.

Duluth *Tribune,* 1894.

Knoxville *Tribune,* 1893.

Lancaster (Va.) *New Era,* 1895.

Lebanon (Pa.) *Lutheran Church Review,* 1897.

London *Daily Chronicle,* 1889, 1893.

Louisville *Courier-Journal,* 1885–86.

Milwaukee *Journal,* 1897.

Minneapolis *Tribune,* 1885.

Newark *Evening News,* 1932.

New Orleans *Times Democrat,* 1897.

New York *American Hebrew,* 1889.

New York *Critic,* 1897.
New York *Herald,* 1880.
New York *Independent,* 1897.
New York *Nation,* 1885, 1893.
New York *Post,* 1893.
New York *Sun,* 1893–94.
New York *Times,* 1893, 1931.
New York *Tribune,* 1893.
New York *World,* 1882.
Omaha *World Herald,* 1894.
Princeton *Alumni Weekly,* 1925.
Princetonian Daily
Princeton New Review, 1887–88.
Philadelphia *Press,* 1877.
Philadelphia *Times,* 1894.
Providence *Journal,* 1889.
Raleigh *News and Observer,* 1955.
Richmond *Daily Dispatch,* 1880.
Religious Herald, 1898.
Rochester *Post Express,* 1897.
San Francisco *Daily Evening Bulletin,* 1885–86, 1893.
San Francisco *Southern Presbyterian and Presbyterian Index,* 1871.
Trenton *Evening Times,* 1912, 1924.
Waterbury (Conn.) *American,* 1889.
Wilmington (N.C.) *Morning Star,* 1876–85.
Wilmington *Messenger,* 1901.
Wilmington *Star,* 1885.
Wesleyan *Argus,* 1889.
Worcester *Spy,* 1902.

Index

Adams, Anne (grandmother of Woodrow W.), 3–4
Adams, Herbert B.: as head of the Johns Hopkins History and Political Science Department, 103; as pioneer in monographic method, 113; helps Wilson get doctorate, 155; mentioned, 104, 147.
Alden, Henry, 276
Alleman, Gilbert, 209
Angell, James B., 171
Armstrong, Andrew C., 178
Atlanta: as business center, 85, 88–89; Wilson disappointed in, 100–101
Augusta Female Seminary, 70
Axson, Edward (brother-in-law of Woodrow W.): at Wilson's wedding, 144; as resident in Wilson home, 167; Wilson's fondness for, 309; death of, 310
Axson, Edward (father-in-law of Woodrow W.): as pastor of First Presbyterian Church, Rome, Ga., 128; attitude toward Wilson, 130; mental illness of, 137; death of, 138
Axson, Ellen (Wilson's first wife): meets Wilson, 128–29; Wilson's courtship of, 129–34; broadens Wilson's literary and artistic horizons, 130, 135; as heir to father's estate, 139; studies art in New York, 139; marriage of to Wilson, 143–44; at Bryn Mawr, 151–52; as mother, 152–53, 162, 169, 198, 206, 307; as manager of household, 162–63, 168, 300–301; at Wesleyan, 178–79; at Princeton, 203, 255–56; as Wilson's helpmate, 304, 305, 313–14; Wilson dedicates book to, 307; visits Mrs. Edith Reid, 318–19; vacations in Ontario, 324; mentioned, 103, 112–13, 136, 138, 155, 169, 181, 199.
Axson, I. S. K., 144
Axson, Stockton (brother-in-law of Woodrow W.): as resident in Wilson home, 198; suggests Wilson continue at Princeton, 221; Wilson dedicates book to, 306; gets job at Princeton, 309; tours Europe with Wilson, 323–24; mentioned, 158–59, 222, 303

Bagehot, Walter: as author of *English Constitution,* 117; as influence on Wilson, 168, 234, 282, 301
Baker, Felies, 8
Baker, Ray Stannard: as author of *Life and Letters of Woodrow Wilson,* 6, 149
Baldwin, James H., 25
Barnwell, Charles H., 24–25
Bayard, James A., 171
Bellamy, John D., 33
Bemis, Edward W., 107
Boggs, W. E., 23
Bones, James W. (uncle of Woodrow W.): sends books to Wilson, 56–57; as attorney-at-law for Janet Wilson, 127; moves to Rome, Ga., 128; mentioned, 18, 70–72

Bones, Jessie Woodrow: as Wilson's playmate, 18; as student at Augusta Female Seminary, 71–72, 80; marriage of, 128; mentioned, 28, 74
Boylston, Mrs. J. Reid, 89, 98–99
Brackett, George R., 29
Bradford, Gamaliel, 116, 154
Bridges, Robert: as member of "Witherspoon gang," 42; friendship with Wilson, 49, 63; death of father, 177–78; seeks Wilson's return to Princeton, 186–87; Wilson dedicates book to, 306; mentioned, 82–83, 103, 131, 143, 148, 161–62
Brown University, 182
Bruce, William Cabell: as law student, 53; as rival of Wilson, 61–62, 64
Bryan, William Jennings, 67
Bryn Mawr College: founding of, 125; Wilson on faculty of, 143, 145; Wilson's departure from, 154, 172, 175–76, 178
Burgess, John W., 217–18, 314
Byrd, Richard E., 53

Cadwalader, John L.: as Princeton trustee, 240; contributes to Wilson's salary, 240–41
Calhoun, John C., 291
Carlisle, John G., 283
Clark, John B., 313–14
Clarksville (Tenn.): as home of Wilson's father, 141, 173–74; Wilsons visit in, 159
Cleveland, Grover, 283–85; discussed by Wilson, 284–86
Columbia (S.C.), 22–30, 32, 173, 312
Columbia Theological Seminary, 26–27
Congressional Government, 116–22, 281–82
Craig, Hardin, 215
Cravens, E. R., 197
Crawford, Morris B., 178
Cuyler, Cornelius: as Princeton trustee, 240; urges Wilson to remain at Princeton, 240; contributes to Wilson's salary, 240–41

Dabney, Robert Heath: as classmate of Wilson, 53; receives doctorate, 151–52; teaches at Indiana University, 161; mentioned, 64, 173–74
Daniels, Winthrop M., 204; goes to Princeton, 210; assists Wilson, 210–11
Davidson College, 25, 30–31
Depew, Chauncey, 154
Derry, Joseph T., 20–21
Dewey, Davis R., 107
Dewey, John, 107
Division and Reunion: 1829–1889, 184–85, 189, 272–73
Dixon, Thomas, Jr., 169
Dodge, Cleveland H.: as Princeton trustee, 240; contributes to Wilson's salary, 240–41

Echols, William, Jr., 53
Ely, Richard E.: as professor at Johns Hopkins, 104; asks Wilson to collaborate on book, 124
Erwin, Lizzie Adams, 169
Eumenean Literary Society, 31

Felton, William H., 97
Fine, Henry B., 205
Fort Lewis (Va.), 67, 73, 74
Fraser, A. M., 31
Freeman, Edward A., 107

Gainesville (Ga.): as birthplace of Wilson children, 152, 169; Wilson visits, 158
Garmany, Francis C., 45
Gibson, Thomas R., 21
Gilman, Daniel Coit, 102; consulted by Wilson about presidency of University of Illinois, 221
Glass, Frank P., 34
Glenn, Robert, 31
Gould, E. R. L., 107
Grady, Henry W., 88
Grant, Sarah Frances, 98

Harper, George M., 207–208
Hart, Albert B.: as professor at Harvard, 184; invites Wilson to write *Epoch* book, 184–85; asks Wilson

to write for *American Nation Series,* 316; mentioned, 218
Hazen, A. W.: as minister of Congregation Church, 179, 206; urges Wilson to remain at Wesleyan, 200
Heath, D. C. & Company: as publisher of Wilson's *The State,* 153, 191
Hedding, William W., 178
Henderson, Robert R., 42
Herbert, Hilary A., 283
Hibben, John Grier, 214, 305
Hillyer, Judge George, 90
History of the American People, A, 273–77
Hopkins, Edward W., 146
Houghton-Mifflin: as publisher of Wilson's *Congressional Government,* 116, 119
Howe, George, 23, 27
Howe, George, Jr.: marries Anne Wilson, 23
Howe, George, III, 303, 309–310
Hoyt, Mary W.: as resident in Wilson home, 167; attends Bryn Mawr, 167; spends Christmas with Wilsons, 199
Hunt, Theodore W., 197

Interstate Commerce Commission Act, 166

James, Edmund J., 216
Jameson, J. Franklin: as professor at Johns Hopkins, 104, 165; reads Wilson's manuscript, 191; lectures at Johns Hopkins, 203; assists in forming the American Historical Association, 264; as editor of *American Historical Review,* 264
Jefferson Literary Society: receives Wilson, 57; elects Wilson president, 67; Wilson writes new constitution for, 67–68
Johns Hopkins Literary Society. *See* Matriculate Debating Society
Johns Hopkins University: denies Wilson fellowship, 100; status of, 103, 106; grants Wilson fellowship, 119; Wilson's graduate career at, 126; alters Ph.D. requirements for Wilson, 155–56; Wilson lectures at, 164–65, 173, 183–84, 196, 203–33; Wilson president of Alumni Association, 201; mentioned, 327
Jones, David B., 327

Kasson, John A., 203
Keiser, Edward H., 146
Kenner, William, 21

Lamar, Joseph R., 21
Lamar, L. Q. C., 283
Lamont, David S., 283
Leckie, John W., 30
Lee, William B., 42
Levermore, Charles H., 107
Lodge, Henry Cabot, 49, 51

McCormick, Cyrus: as Princeton trustee, 240; urges Wilson to stay at Princeton, 240; contributes to Wilson's salary, 240–41
McCosh, James: as president of Princeton, 34; teaches philosophy, 205
McKay, Douglas, 27
Mahone, General William, 97
Mallett, J. W., 61
Mary Baldwin Academy, 7
Matriculate Debating Society: Wilson joins, 112; becomes Hopkins Literary Society, 112; becomes Hopkins House of Commons, 112; Wilson writes new bylaws for, 112
May, Robert H., 14–15
Mayrant, Katie, 98
Mere Literature and Other Essays, 296–98
Middletown (Conn.): as home of Wilsons, 178, 200
Minor, John Barbee, 52
Mitchell, Charles W., 42
Moore, John Bassett, 53

Negroes: in Dr. Wilson's church, Augusta, 16–17; in Dr. Wilson's church, Columbia, 24; in Atlanta, 89

Nichelson, Frank W., 180

Old Master and Other Political Essays, An, 286–90
Olney, Richard, 283
Ormond, Alexander T., 197
Osborn, Henry F., 205

Page, Walter Hines: as lawyer in Atlanta, 89; as reporter for New York *World,* 91–93; invites Wilson to send article to *Forum,* 247, 261; urges Wilson to send book manuscript to Houghton-Mifflin, 275; helped by Wilson to find job, 315
Patton, Francis: as president of Princeton, 186–87, 327–28; offers Wilson job, 187; confers with Wilson, 195–196; as a conservative, 205; envious of Wilson, 239; policies of criticized, 326–27; mentioned, 255
Paul, George H., 190
Pelot, Henry, 21
Perry, Bliss: as colleague of Wilson, 207; as debate coach, 215; mentioned, 305
Phi Beta Kappa, 200
Phi Kappa Psi: accepts Wilson, 55; represented by Wilson at National Convention, 56; elects Wilson Grand Page, 68; Wilson's attitude toward, 69
Philadelphia Society, 40
Presbyterian Church of Confederate States: organized, 13
Price, Carl F., 179
Princeton College (University, 1896) : awards degree to Joseph R. Wilson, 4; attended by Woodrow Wilson, 34, 36–43, 46; compared with University of Virginia, 54–55; Wilson's nostalgia for, 62–63; Wilson's return to, 187, 195–96, 203–204; becomes Princeton University, 252; mentioned, 163, 218–19, 240–41, 277

Raymond, B. O., 199–200
Reid, Mrs. Edith G.: as friend of Wilsons, 165, 318–19; mentioned 235, 317
Renick, Edward: as lawyer in Atlanta, 89; in partnership with Wilson, 89 ff, 101; employed in Treasury Department, 153; tries to get Wilson a job in State Department, 171; death of, 316
Renick, Harriet, 7
Rhoads, James E.: as trustee of Bryn Mawr, 125; as president of Bryn Mawr, 146; stand on Wilson's departure, 174–75
Rice, William N., 178
Ricketts, Henrietta, 305
Rome (Ga.) : Wilson visits, 127–28, 130, 137; funeral of Dr. Axson at, 138
Roosevelt, Theodore: speaks from platform with Wilson, 233

Salmon, Lucy, 151
Savannah (Ga.) : as site of Wilson's marriage, 143
Schouler, James, 203
Scott, Charlotte A., 146
Scudder, Horace: as editor of *Atlantic Monthly,* 158–60; as trustee of Williams College, 194; asks Wilson to review Burgess book, 217; invites Wilson to home, 316
Shaw, Albert: as graduate student at Johns Hopkins, 107, 114; reviews Wilson's *Congressional Government,* 122; edits *The National Revenues,* 173; lectures at Johns Hopkins, 203; considers Princeton professorship, 210
Shorey, Paul, 146
Simonton, Samuel H., 27
Sloane, William F., 205
Smith, Francis, H., 62
Southhall, Stephen O., 52
Southwestern Seminary (Tenn.), 141
State, The, 153, 191–92, 282, 290
Staunton (Va.) : 7–8, 70
Stephens, Alexander H., 97–98
Stovall, Pleasant, 21

Talcott, Charles A.: as member of "Witherspoon gang," 42; friendship of with Wilson, 45, 47, 124, 142–43
Tariff Commission, 91–93
Thomas, Carey: as dean of Bryn Mawr, 125; receives Ph.D., 146; Wilson's attitude toward, 147–49; urges Wilson to get Ph.D., 155; stand on Wilson's departure, 174–75
Thwaites, Reuben G., 190
Toy, Mrs. Crawford H., 235
Turner, Frederick Jackson: as graduate student under Wilson, 189; refuses Wilson's offer at Wesleyan, 189–91; accepts chair at University of Wisconsin, 190; on "The Significance of the Frontier in American History," 260; on "The West as a Field for Historical Study," 279; mentioned, 165, 190–91, 235, 277–79, 305
Turpin, Mrs. James S., 89

Virginia, University of, 51–52; contrasted with Princeton, 54–55; literary society debates 60–61; reprimands Wilson for excessive absences, 73; Wilson withdraws from, 69; mentioned, 82

Wade, Louisa: birth of Wilson's daughter at home of, 152; visited by Wilson, 158–59
Wake Forest College, 169
Webster, J. Edwin, 42–43
Welles, Edward Freeman, 81
Wertenbaker, Thomas J., 255
Wesleyan University: employs Wilson, 175; Wilson's attitude toward, 181, 187–88; Wilson's departure from, 200–201
West, Andrew F.: as professor at Princeton, 197; as dean of graduate school, 205; as Wilson's rival, 205, 278–80
Whig Literary Society, 37, 215
Williams, C. L., 43
Williamson, Marion (grandmother of Woodrow W.), 5
Wilmington (N.C.), 32–33, 51, 68–69, 76–77, 80, 130–31, 137, 141, 313
Wilson, Anne (sister of Woodrow W.): early life, 10; marriage of, 23; mentioned, 44, 143
Wilson, Eleanor Randolph (daughter of Woodrow W.): birth of, 198; arrives in Princeton, 204; mentioned, 307–309
Wilson, Ellen Axson. *See* Axson, Ellen
Wilson, James (grandfather of Woodrow W.), 3–4
Wilson, Jessie Woodrow (daughter of Woodrow W.): birth of, 169; arrives in Princeton, 204; mentioned, 307–309
Wilson, Joseph Ruggles (father of Woodrow W.): early life, 4; marriage of, 4; moves to Augusta, 8; physical description of, 9; family devotions, 10; attitude toward correct English, 11; sermons of reported in press, 12; as clerk of Presbyterian Church Assembly, 13; as minister at Augusta, 14–17; at Columbia Theological Seminary, 22, 25–26, 29–30; as minister in Wilmington, N.C., 32–33, 141; advises Wilson, 37–38, 99, 101, 124, 137, 148, 165, 182, 192–93, 206, 221; accepts teaching position, 141; assists at Wilson's marriage, 144; attitude toward grandchildren, 169, 198; at wife's death, 173–74; helps Wilson pay for house, 301; aids Wilson in buying land, 310; visits at Princeton, 310; retires from teaching, 311–12; ill health of, 312, 324–25; goes to live with Wilson, 325
Wilson, Joseph Ruggles, Jr. (brother of Woodrow W.): birth of, 18–19; as Latin pupil, 78; urges Wilson to write, 181–82; seeks Wilson's counsel, 186
Wilson, Margaret (daughter of Woodrow W.): birth of, 152, first seen

by Wilson, 158–59; begins walking, 167; arrives in Princeton, 204; mentioned, 307–309

Wilson, Marion (sister of Woodrow W.): early life, 10; as student at Mary Baldwin Academy, 22; writes Wilson of father's unhappiness, 184; seeks Wilson's counsel, 186

Wilson, Woodrow: ancestry, 3–7; birth of, 7–8; as father's companion, 9–10, 11; attitude toward mother, 9–10, 173–74; and religion, 12–13, 27–28, 114–15; and Civil War, 13–16, 17; joins Lightfoot Club, 18–19; disinterest of in education, 20–22; at Houghton Institute, 21; at Barnwell's school, 25; attends father's class, 26; influence of Francis Brooke on, 27; learns shorthand, 28, 32; at Davidson, 30–31; enters Princeton, 33–34; diary of, 35–36; class rank, 36; as member of Whig Literary Society, 37, 39; as president of Princeton Baseball Association, 40; as editor of *Princetonian,* 40; on Bismarck, 41; on William Earl Chatham, 41–42; organizes "Witherspoon Gang," 42–43; at Alligator Club, 43; attitude of toward Confederate Memorial Day, 44; graduates from Princeton, 46; friendship of with Bobby Bridges, 49; in University of Virginia law school, 51–52, 68–69; contrasts University of Virginia with Princeton, 54–55; as member of Phi Kappa Psi, 55–56, 68; in University of Virginia Glee Club, 56; as member of Jefferson Literary Society, 57, 60–62, 67–68; friendship of with Heath Dabney, 64; rivalry of with William Cabell Bruce, 64; opposes national party nominating conventions, 65–66; and courtship of Hattie Woodrow, 71–74, 80–83; Atlanta law practice of, 84–85, 89–90, 99–101; deletes Thomas from name, 86–88; appears before Tariff Commission, 91–93; on "Convict Labor in Georgia," 95–96; on culture and education, 96; on Alexander Stephens, 97; at Johns Hopkins, 100, 102, 106; in history and political science seminary, 107–108; writes *Congressional Government,* 118–22; matures emotionally, 127; settles mother's estate, 127; and courtship of Ellen Axson, 128–29, 132–35, 137, 140–44; at Bryn Mawr, 145–76; as after-dinner speaker, 154, 229–30; and his children, 153, 158–59, 169, 307–309; receives doctorate, 155–56; visits Europe, 160–62, 320–24; as Hopkins lecturer, 164–65; receives honorary degree from Wake Forest, 169; attitude toward co-education, 170, 252; at Wesleyan, 175–201; as member of "Conversational Club," 178; as member of Congressional Church, 179; and athletics, 180–81, 213–14; as lecturer at Brown University, 182–83, 194; writes volume for *Epochs of American History,* 185, 189, 272–73; writes *The State,* 191–92; sails to Boston, 194; refuses offer to teach at Williams College, 195; as professor at Princeton, 196, 202–22; as member of Phi Beta Kappa, 201; as president of Johns Hopkins Alumni Association, 201; as member of Second Presbyterian Church, 206–207; as faculty leader, 207, 209; introduces honor system, 208; and President Patton, 209, 239; helps raise entrance requirements, 212; attitude toward students, 212; speaks before Princeton Alumni, 216; reviews Burgess' book, 217–18; rejects offer of presidency of University of Illinois, 220–21; traits of as a teacher, 223 ff, 236–38; votes Gold Democratic ticket, 225; lectures in West, 226–27; addresses Virginia Bar Association, 227–28; on "Municipal Organization," 230–33; delivers first political speech, 233; as chairman of Faculty Committee on Special and Delinquent Students, 238; offered presidency of University of Virginia, 240; trustees add to salary of, 240; addresses International Congress of Education, 242 ff; on liberal education as essential for law, medicine, and theology, 242–45; addresses American Bar Association, 245–47; on education and nationalism, 249; urges teaching of classics, 249; on "Princeton in the Nation's Service," 252–55; makes enduring contributions to education, 258–59; and Frederick Jackson Turner's frontier thesis, 260–61; and his calendar of great Americans, 261–63; addresses New Jersey Historical Society, 264; on Providential philosophy of history, 268; addresses Oberlin College, 270–71; writes biography of George Washington, 273–74; writes *History of the American People,* 274–77; tries to hire Frederick Jackson Turner for Princeton faculty, 277–80; writes *An Old Master and Other Political Essays,* 286–90; on states' rights, 290–92; advocates internationalism, 294; attempts to write poetry, 295; as author of literary essays, 296–99; builds house, 300–301; library of, 302; election of to Princeton presidency, 325–28

Winchester, Caleb T., 178

Woodrow, Harriet Augusta (Hattie): as student at Augusta Female Seminary, 71; studies music in Cincinnati, 78–79; attitude toward Sabbath, 79; Wilson's proposal to, 80–82; influence of on Wilson, 88; Wilson visits, 226

Woodrow, James (uncle of Woodrow W.), 8; as seminary teacher, 27; German education of, 115; tried for teaching evolution, 115–16

Woodrow, Janet (mother of Woodrow W.): early life, 4; marriage of, 4; personality of, 9; inherits estate, 24; plans new home, 24; attitude toward Wilson's marriage, 133, 137; death of, 173; mentioned, 73, 127, 131–32, 152

Woodrow, Jessie. *See* Woodrow, Janet

Woodrow, Marion (aunt of Woodrow W.), 18, 71

Woodrow, Thomas (grandfather of Woodrow W.), 4–5; emigration of from England, 5; as minister, 5–6; visits in Augusta, 17–18

Woodrow, Thomas (uncle of Woodrow W.), 71, 73, 81

Woodrow, William (uncle of Woodrow W.), 24

Woodrow, Wilson, 81–82

Woods, Hiram: as member of "Witherspoon Gang," 42–43; at Phi Kappa Psi convention, 56; Wilson visits home of, 113; practices medicine, 113

Wright, Carroll D., 203

Wright, Mrs. Josiah, 34

Yager, Arthur, 107

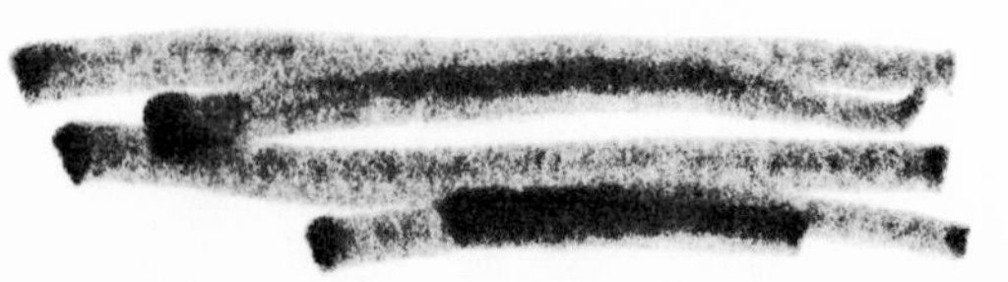